SAMURAI DEEPER KYO

キョウ

VOLUME TEN

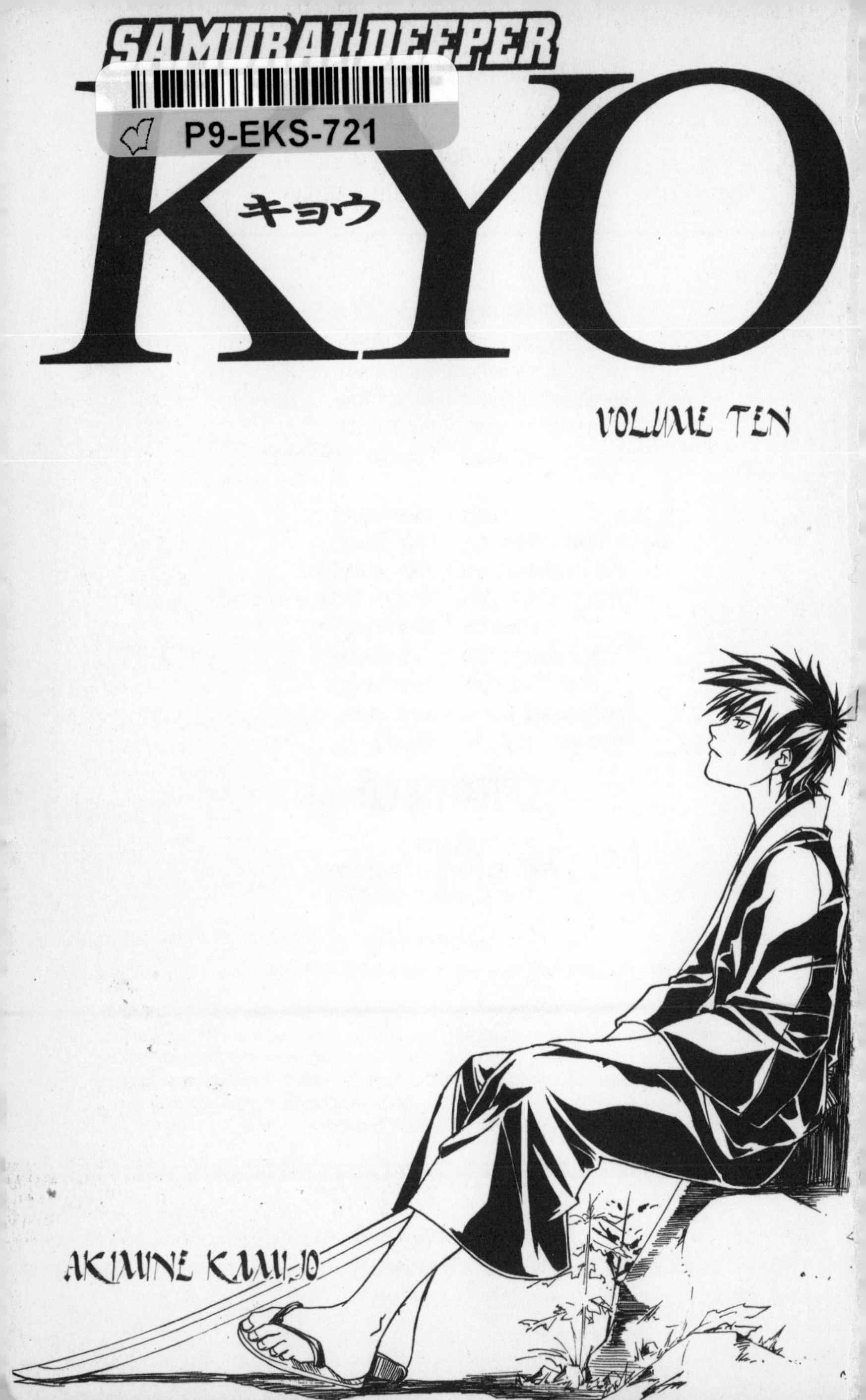

AKIMINE KAMIJO

Samurai Deeper Kyo Vol. 10
Created by Akimine Kamijyo

Translation - Alexander O. Smith
Script Editor - Rich Amtower
Copy Editor - Peter Ahlstrom
Retouch and Lettering - Patrick Tran
Production Artists - Eric Pineda
Cover Design - Raymond Makowski

Editor - Jake Forbes
Digital Imaging Manager - Chris Buford
Pre-Press Manager - Antonio DePietro
Production Managers - Jennifer Miller and Mutsumi Miyazaki
Art Director - Matt Alford
Managing Editor - Jill Freshney
VP of Production - Ron Klamert
President and C.O.O. - John Parker
Publisher and C.E.O. - Stuart Levy

A  Manga

TOKYOPOP Inc.
5900 Wilshire Blvd. Suite 2000
Los Angeles, CA 90036

E-mail: info@TOKYOPOP.com
Come visit us online at www.TOKYOPOP.com

ISBN: 1-59532-450-X

First TOKYOPOP printing: December 2004
10 9 8 7 6 5 4 3 2 1
Printed in the USA

SAMURAI DEEPER Kyo

Vol. 10
by Akimine Kamijyo

HAMBURG // LONDON // LOS ANGELES // TOKYO

DRAMATIS PERSONAE

...According to Tora.

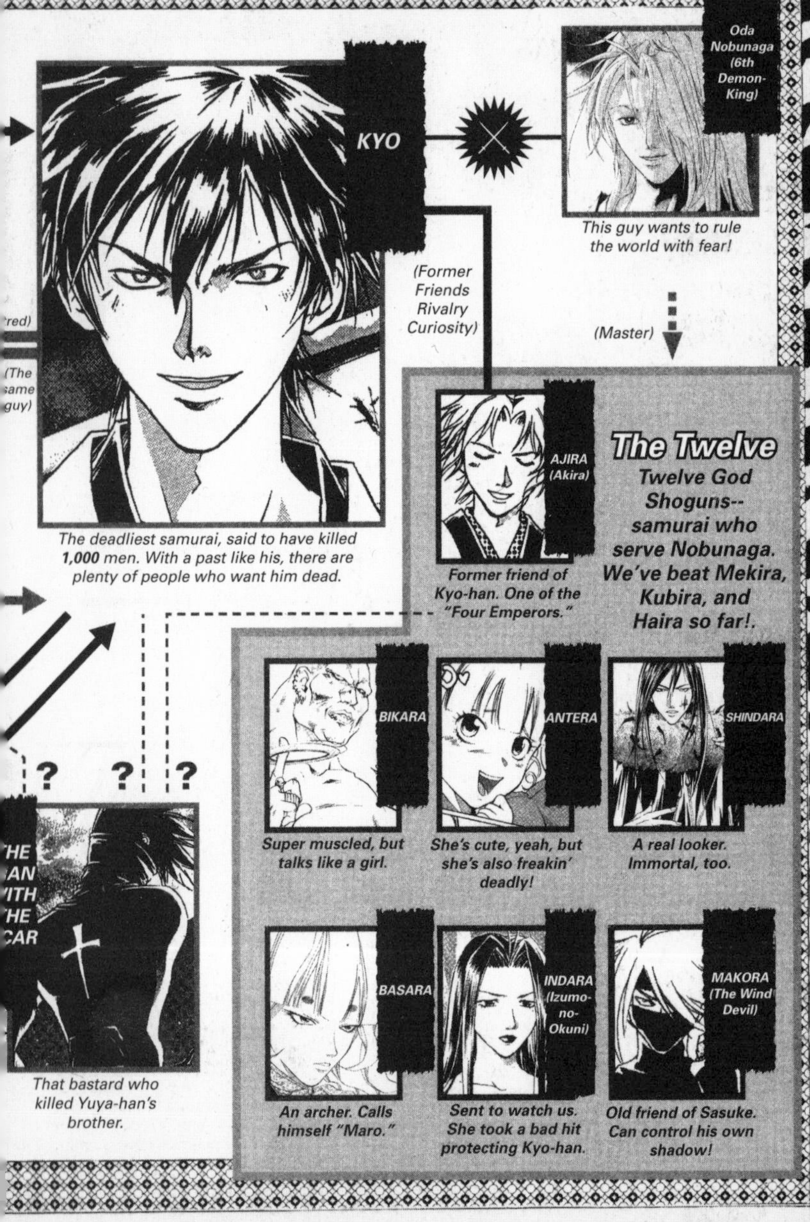

Oda Nobunaga (6th Demon-King)
This guy wants to rule the world with fear!
KYO
The deadliest samurai, said to have killed 1,000 men. With a past like his, there are plenty of people who want him dead.
(Former Friends Rivalry Curiosity)
(Master)
The Twelve
Twelve God Shoguns--samurai who serve Nobunaga. We've beat Mekira, Kubira, and Haira so far!.
AJIRA (Akira)
Former friend of Kyo-han. One of the "Four Emperors."
SHINDARA
A real looker. Immortal, too.
ANTERA
She's cute, yeah, but she's also freakin' deadly!
BIKARA
Super muscled, but talks like a girl.
MAKORA (The Wind Devil)
Old friend of Sasuke. Can control his own shadow!
INDARA (Izumo-no-Okuni)
Sent to watch us. She took a bad hit protecting Kyo-han.
BASARA
An archer. Calls himself "Maro."
? ? ?
That bastard who killed Yuya-han's brother.

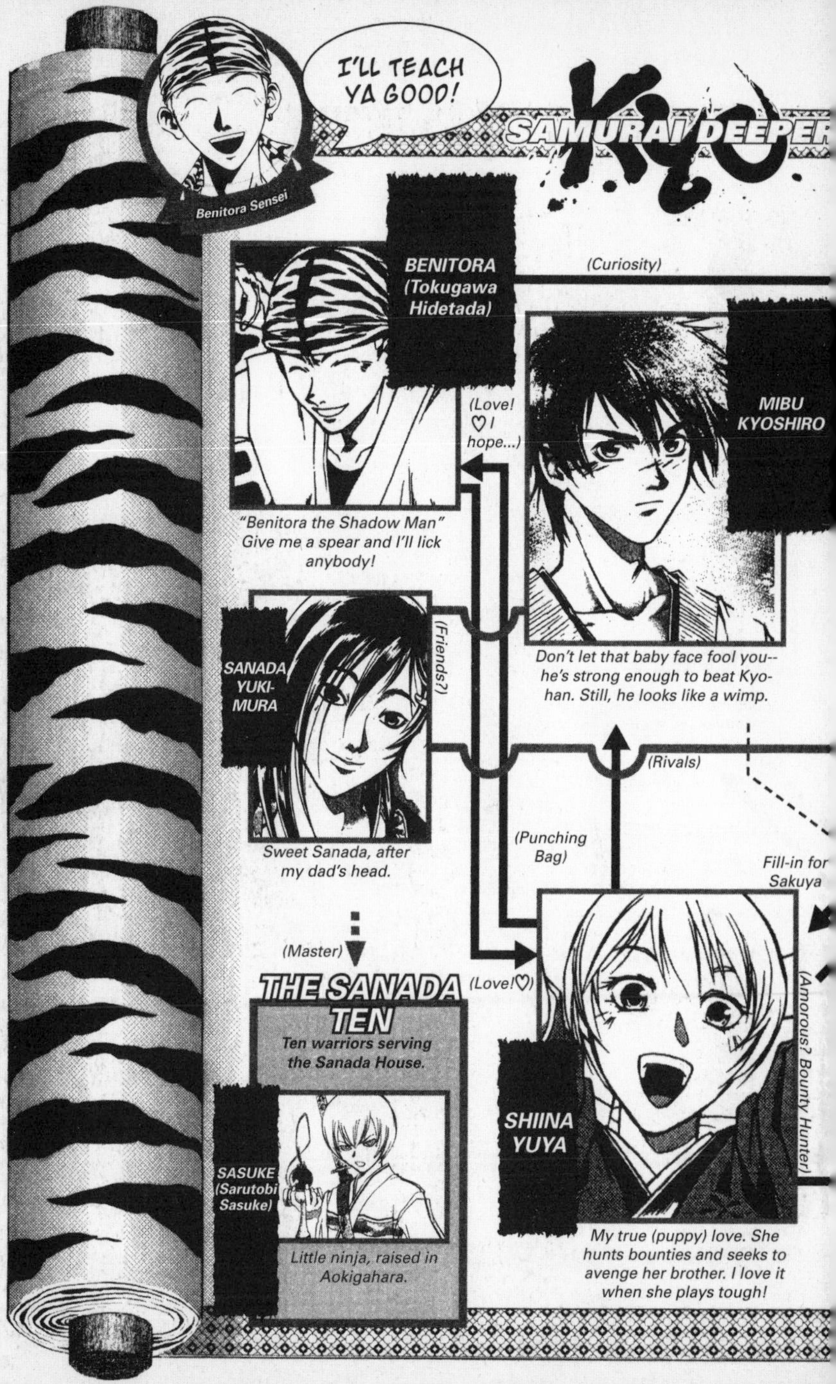

I'LL TEACH YA GOOD!
Benitora Sensei
SAMURAI DEEPER KYO
BENITORA (Tokugawa Hidetada)
"Benitora the Shadow Man" Give me a spear and I'll lick anybody!
(Curiosity)
MIBU KYOSHIRO
(Love! ♡I hope...)
Don't let that baby face fool you-- he's strong enough to beat Kyo-han. Still, he looks like a wimp.
SANADA YUKI-MURA
(Friends?)
Sweet Sanada, after my dad's head.
(Rivals)
(Punching Bag)
Fill-in for Sakuya
(Master)
THE SANADA TEN
Ten warriors serving the Sanada House.
(Love!♡)
(Amorous? Bounty Hunter)
SASUKE (Sarutobi Sasuke)
Little ninja, raised in Aokigahara.
SHIINA YUYA
My true (puppy) love. She hunts bounties and seeks to avenge her brother. I love it when she plays tough!

Kyo and his companions came to ***Aokigahara Forest*** to search for Demon Eyes' ***true body.***

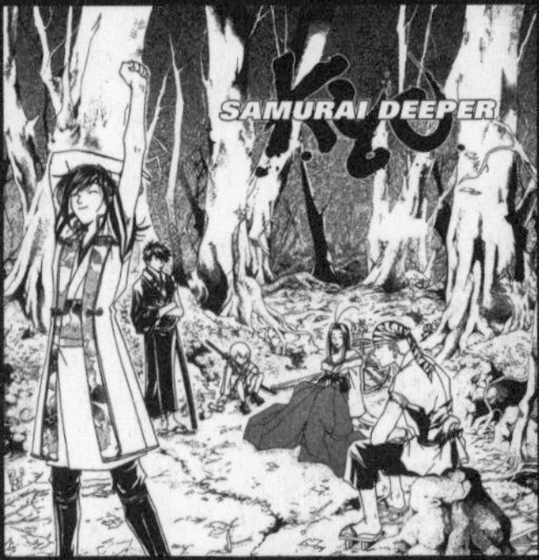
SAMURAI DEEPER
KYO

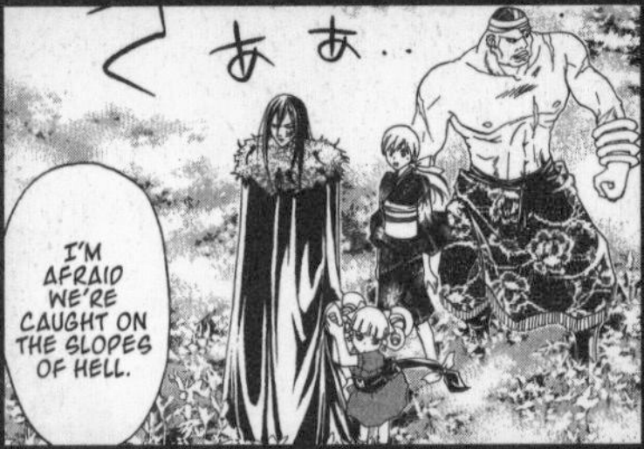
くああ..
I'M AFRAID WE'RE CAUGHT ON THE SLOPES OF HELL.

Soon after entering, Yuya was taken hostage by Bikara, Antera and Shindara, three members of ***The Twelve.*** Together with the mysterious Ajira (formerly Akira) they travel the ***Slopes of Hell*** to get to Kyo's body.

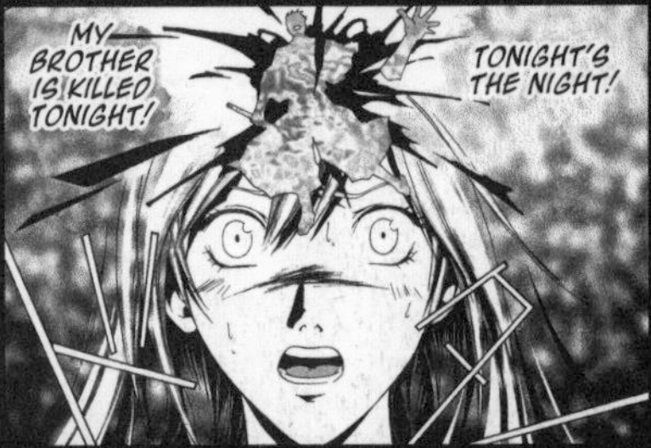
TONIGHT'S THE NIGHT!
MY BROTHER IS KILLED TONIGHT!

On the flowery slopes Yuya experiences a troubling vision from her past in which she sees that ***Kyoshiro killed her brother***!

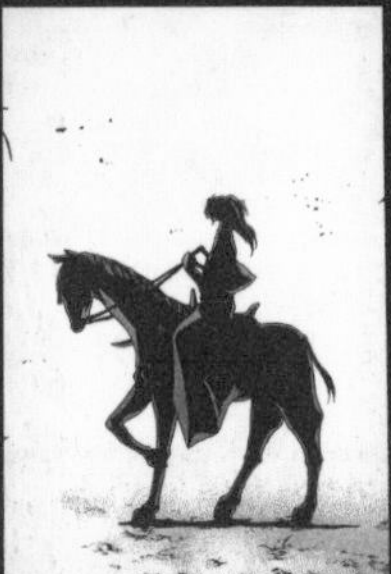

Meanwile, Kyo and his companions make it to the ***Gates of Hell*** where they meet the one who leads The Twelve...***The Master***...

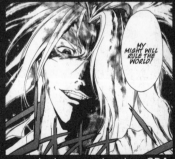

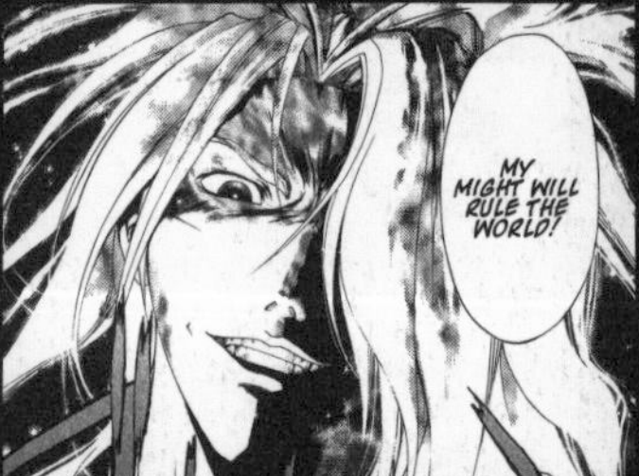
MY MIGHT WILL RULE THE WORLD!

...who is none other than ***ODA NOBUNAGA!***

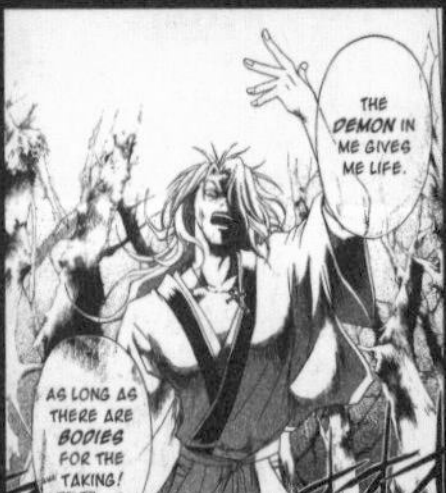
THE DEMON IN ME GIVES ME LIFE.
AS LONG AS THERE ARE BODIES FOR THE TAKING!

Nobunaga, assumed dead, has been resurrected in a new body.

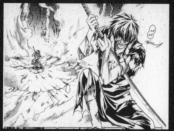

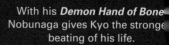

With his ***Demon Hand of Bone*** Nobunaga gives Kyo the stronge beating of his life.

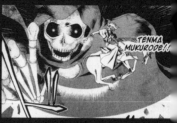

TENMA MUKURODE!!

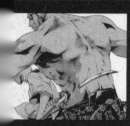

Near death, Kyo drops to his knees, giving Nobunaga an opening for a finishing blow.

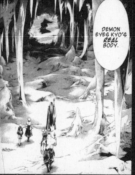

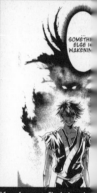

...SOMETHI ELSE I WAKENIN

But Kyo's not finished he recovers with an al ***supernatural strengt***

DEMON EYES KYO'S REAL BODY.

...but his ***10 minute limit*** runs out before he can defeat Nobunaga...

allowing ***Kyoshiro*** to regain control!

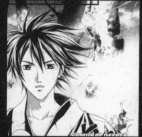

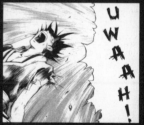

UWAAH!

At that time, at the heart of the forest, Yuya's captors reach the cav where ***Kyo's body*** is frozen...

...but ***Akira*** proves a ***traitor*** and turns on the fellow members of The Twelve!

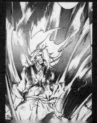

Before Kyo deals with his back-stabbing friend, can he defeat his greatest enemy—a ***Demon King*** who cannot be killed?!

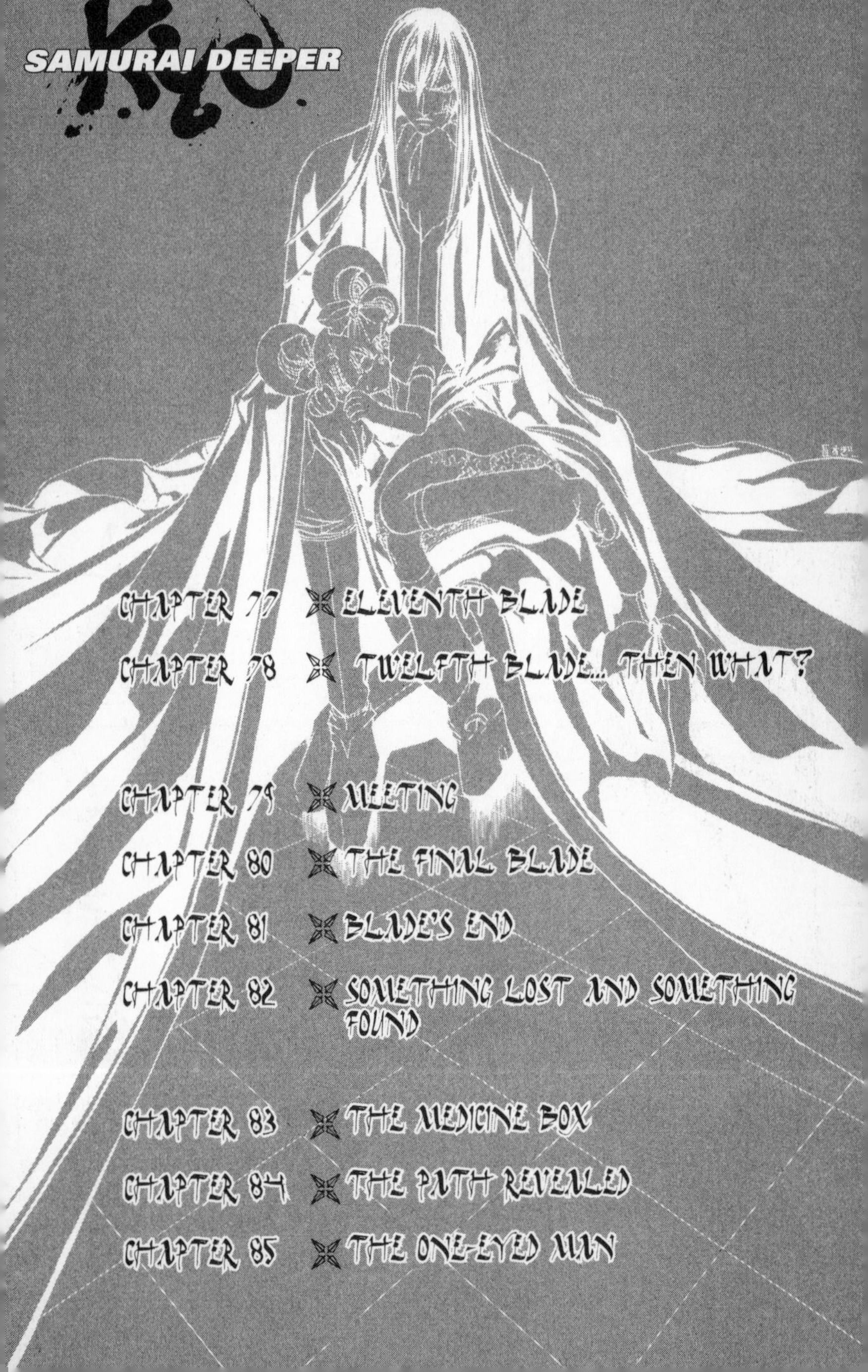

SAMURAI DEEPER KYO

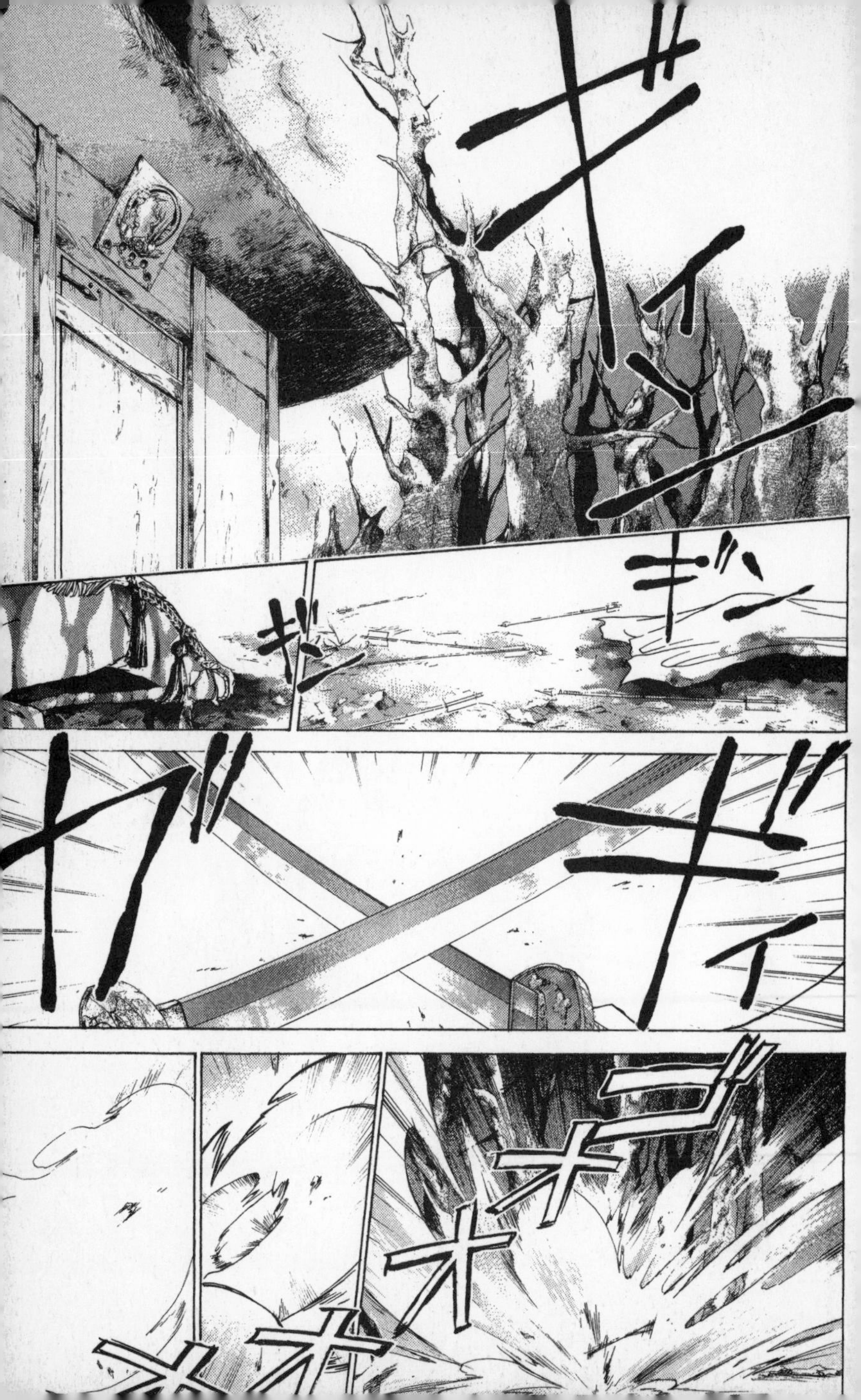
ギィンー
ギン
ギン
ギィ
ガ
ゴォォォ

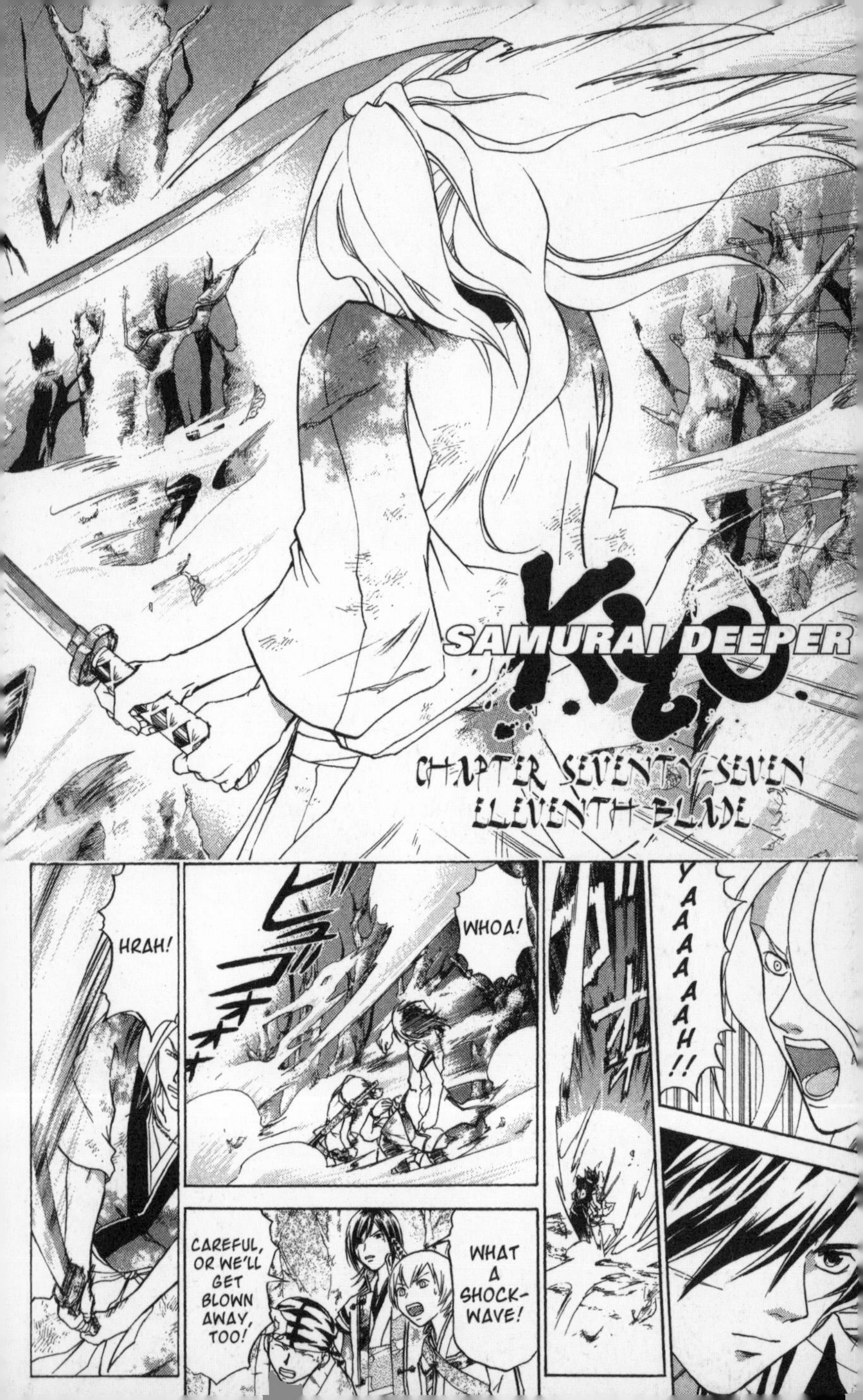
SAMURAI DEEPER KYO
CHAPTER SEVENTY-SEVEN
ELEVENTH BLADE
YAAAAAAAH!!
WHOA!
WHAT A SHOCK-WAVE!
CAREFUL, OR WE'LL GET BLOWN AWAY, TOO!
HRAH!

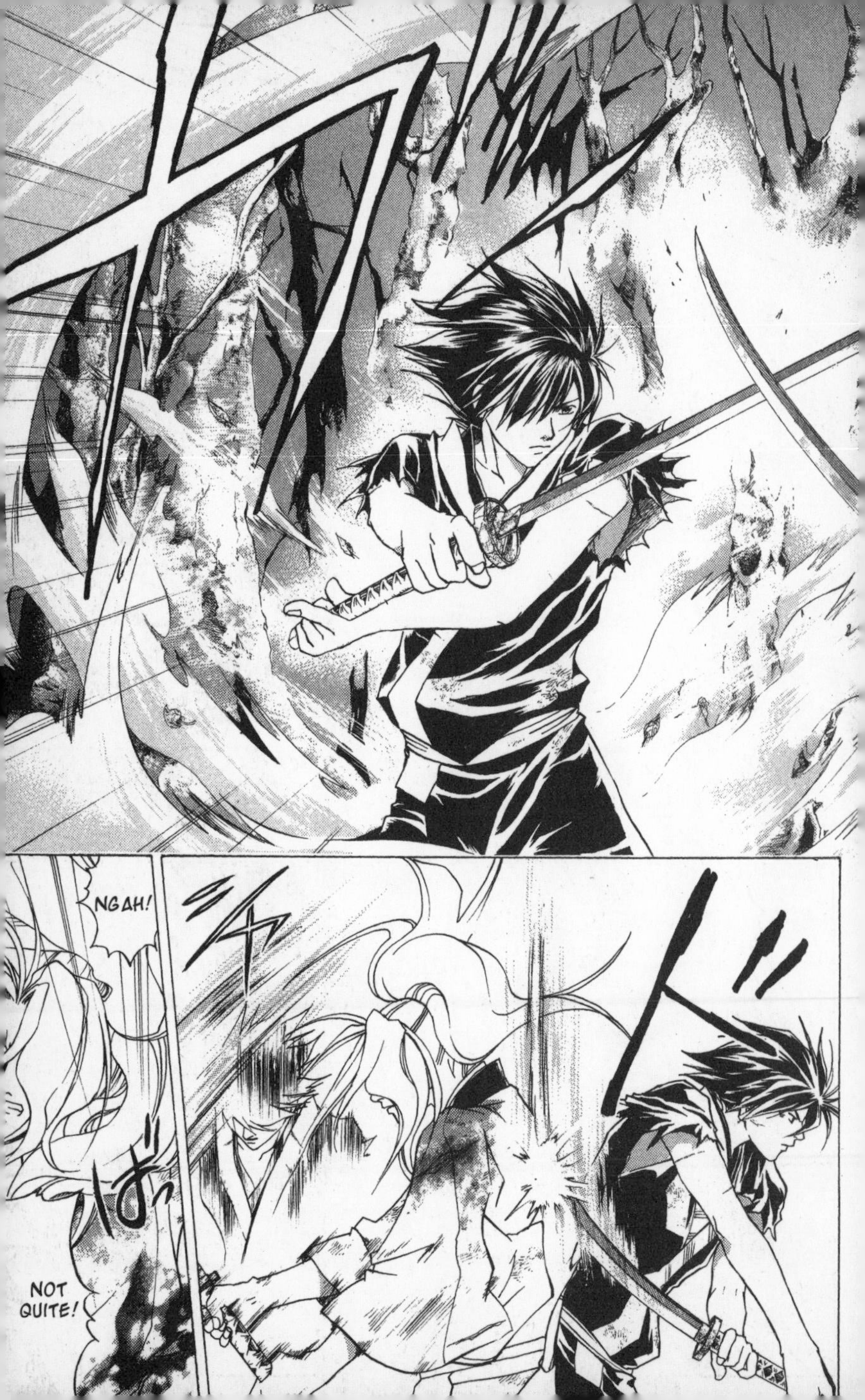
NGAH!
NOT QUITE!

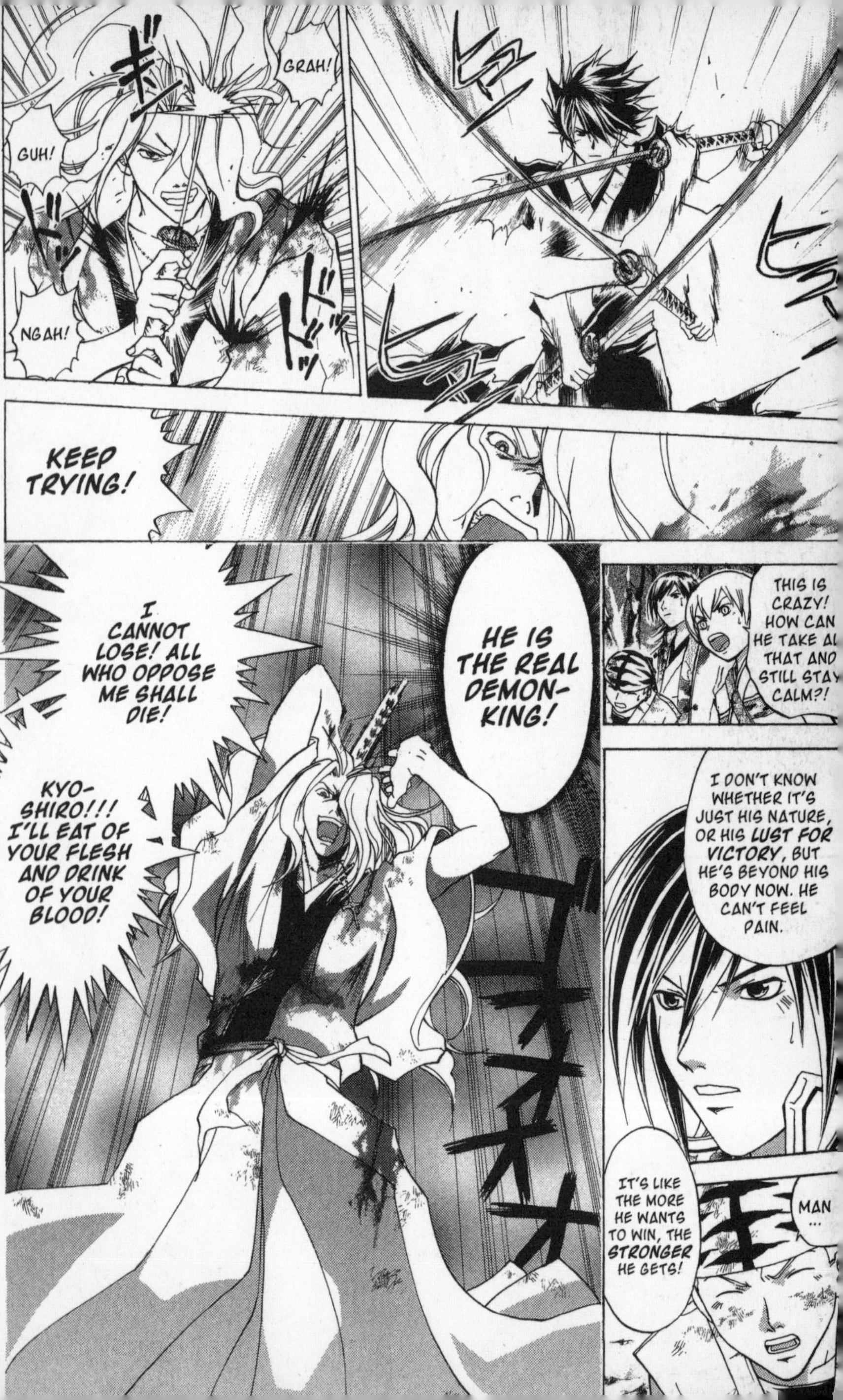

GRAH!
GUH!
NGAH!
KEEP TRYING!
THIS IS CRAZY! HOW CAN HE TAKE AL THAT AND STILL STAY CALM?!
I DON'T KNOW WHETHER IT'S JUST HIS NATURE, OR HIS LUST FOR VICTORY, BUT HE'S BEYOND HIS BODY NOW. HE CAN'T FEEL PAIN.
MAN ...
IT'S LIKE THE MORE HE WANTS TO WIN, THE STRONGER HE GETS!
HE IS THE REAL DEMON-KING!
I CANNOT LOSE! ALL WHO OPPOSE ME SHALL DIE!
KYO-SHIRO!!! I'LL EAT OF YOUR FLESH AND DRINK OF YOUR BLOOD!

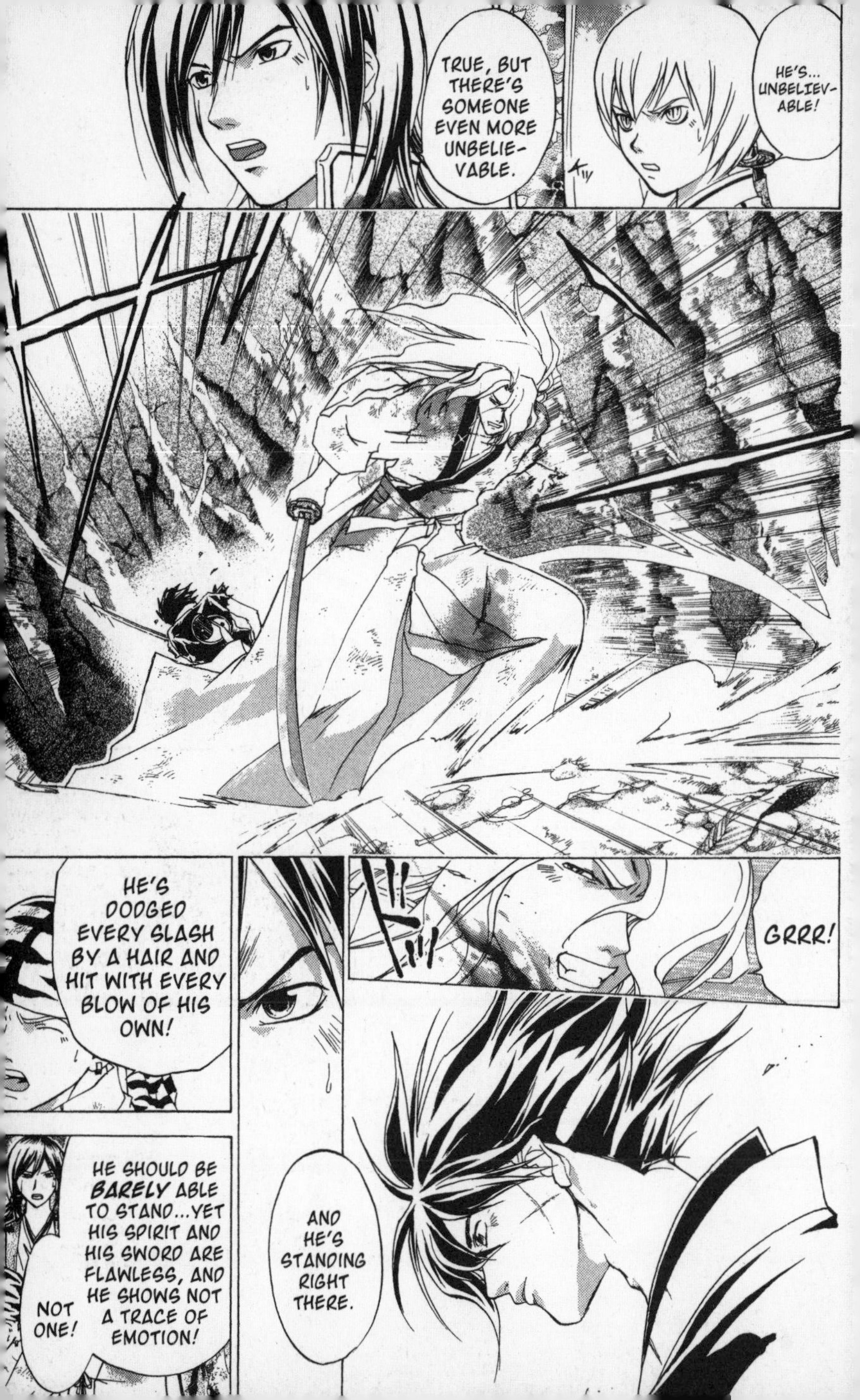

HE'S... UNBELIEVABLE!
TRUE, BUT THERE'S SOMEONE EVEN MORE UNBELIEVABLE.
GRRR!
HE'S DODGED EVERY SLASH BY A HAIR AND HIT WITH EVERY BLOW OF HIS OWN!
HE SHOULD BE **BARELY** ABLE TO STAND...YET HIS SPIRIT AND HIS SWORD ARE FLAWLESS, AND HE SHOWS NOT A TRACE OF EMOTION!
NOT ONE!
AND HE'S STANDING RIGHT THERE.

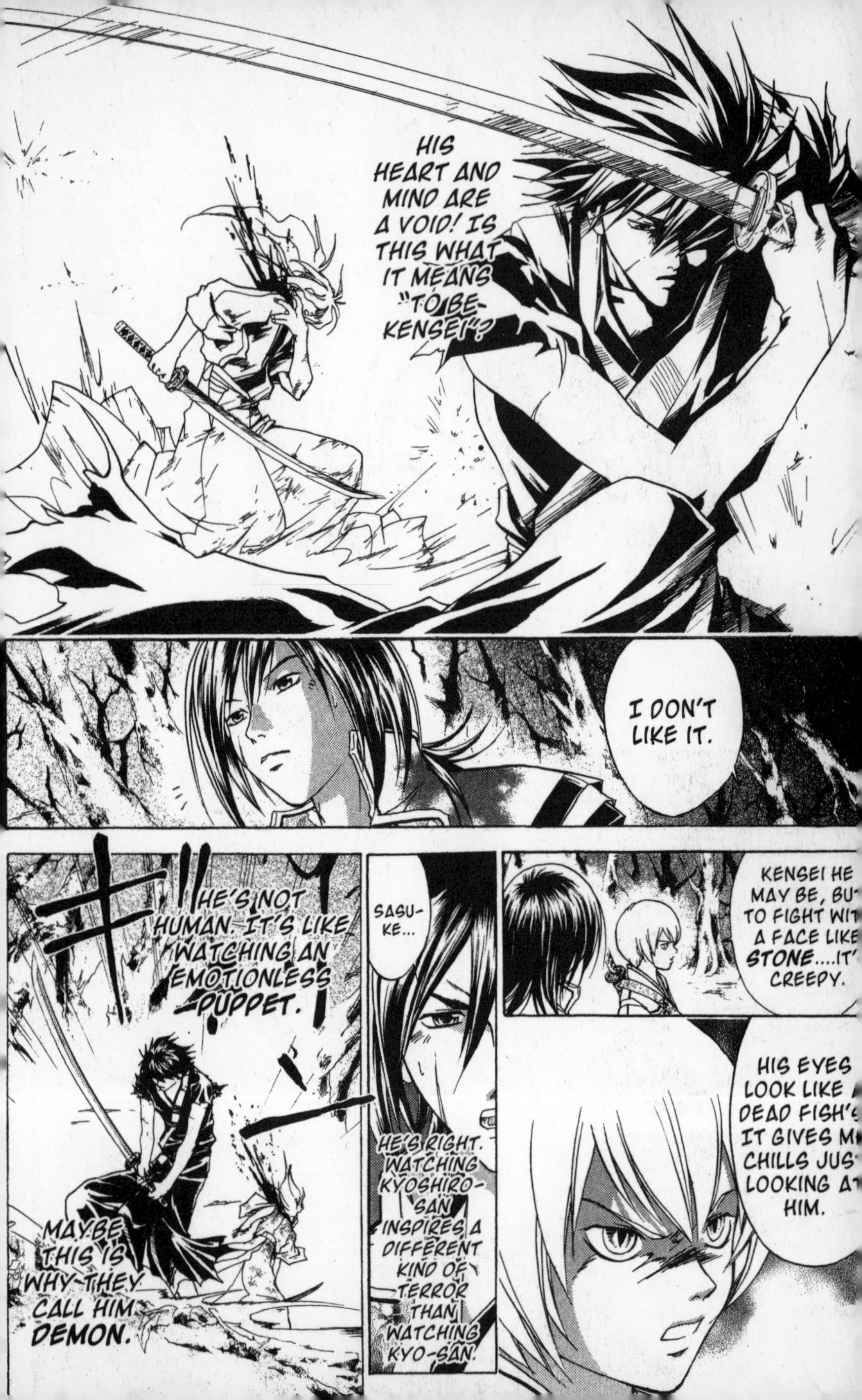
HIS HEART AND MIND ARE A VOID! IS THIS WHAT IT MEANS "TO BE KENSEI"?
I DON'T LIKE IT.
KENSEI HE MAY BE, BU- TO FIGHT WIT A FACE LIKE STONE....IT' CREEPY.
HIS EYES LOOK LIKE DEAD FISH' IT GIVES M CHILLS JUS LOOKING A HIM.
SASUKE...
HE'S RIGHT. WATCHING KYOSHIRO-SAN INSPIRES A DIFFERENT KIND OF TERROR THAN WATCHING KYO-SAN.
HE'S NOT HUMAN. IT'S LIKE WATCHING AN EMOTIONLESS PUPPET.
MAYBE THIS IS WHY THEY CALL HIM DEMON.

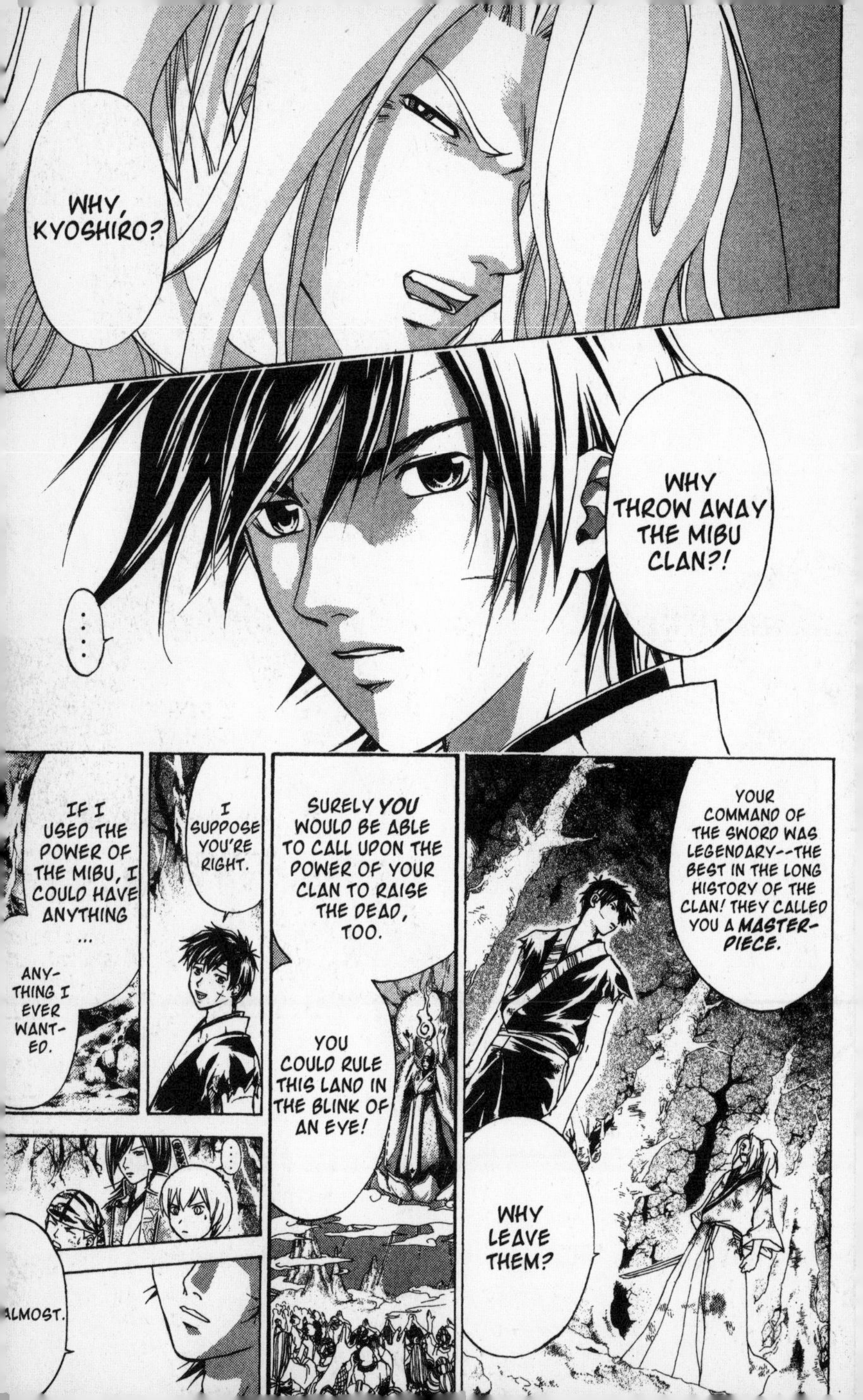
WHY, KYOSHIRO?
WHY THROW AWAY THE MIBU CLAN?!
....
YOUR COMMAND OF THE SWORD WAS LEGENDARY--THE BEST IN THE LONG HISTORY OF THE CLAN! THEY CALLED YOU A *MASTERPIECE.*
WHY LEAVE THEM?
SURELY *YOU* WOULD BE ABLE TO CALL UPON THE POWER OF YOUR CLAN TO RAISE THE DEAD, TOO.
YOU COULD RULE THIS LAND IN THE BLINK OF AN EYE!
I SUPPOSE YOU'RE RIGHT.
IF I USED THE POWER OF THE MIBU, I COULD HAVE ANYTHING ...
ANYTHING I EVER WANTED.
...
ALMOST.

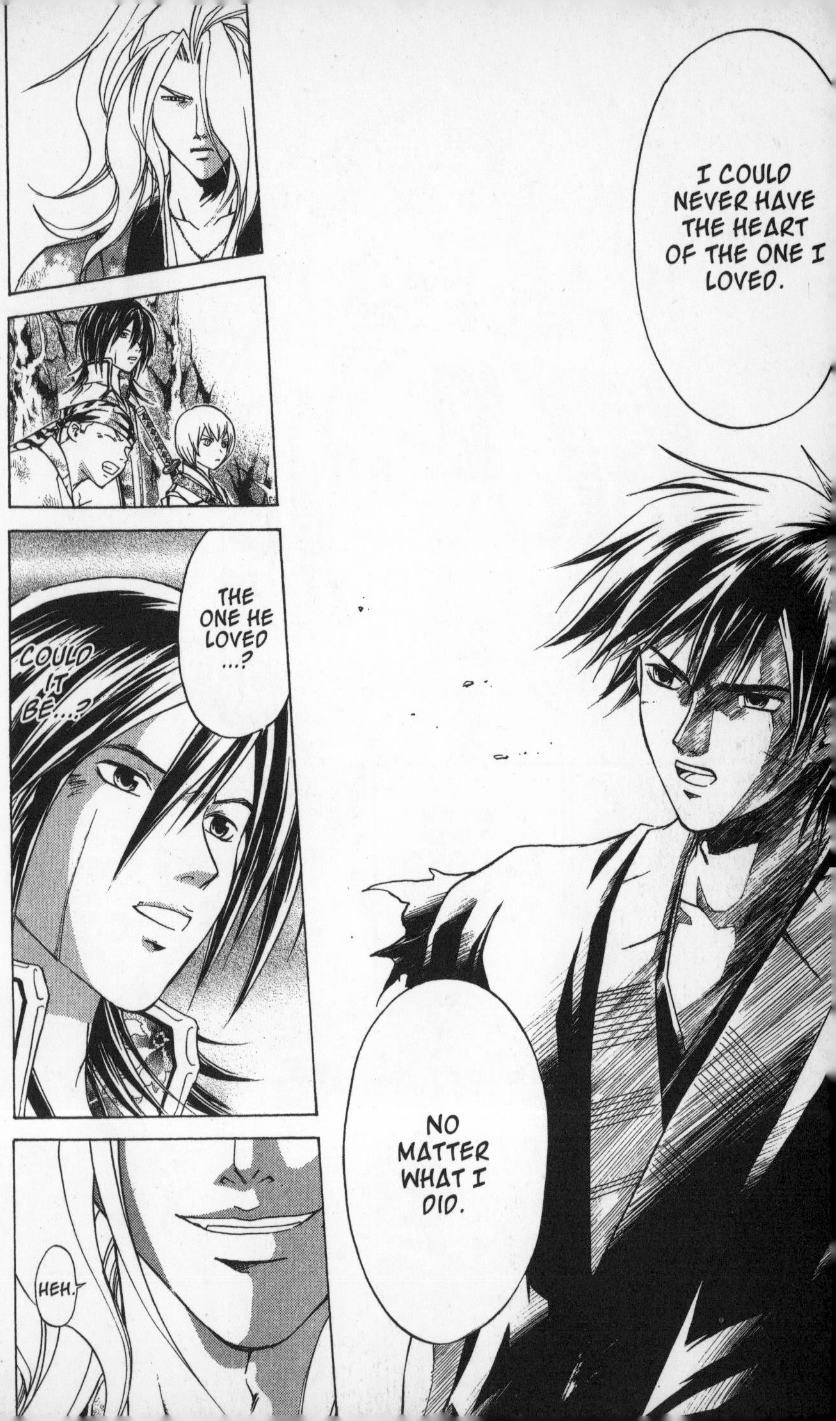
I COULD NEVER HAVE THE HEART OF THE ONE I LOVED.
NO MATTER WHAT I DID.
THE ONE HE LOVED ...?
COULD IT BE...?
HEH.

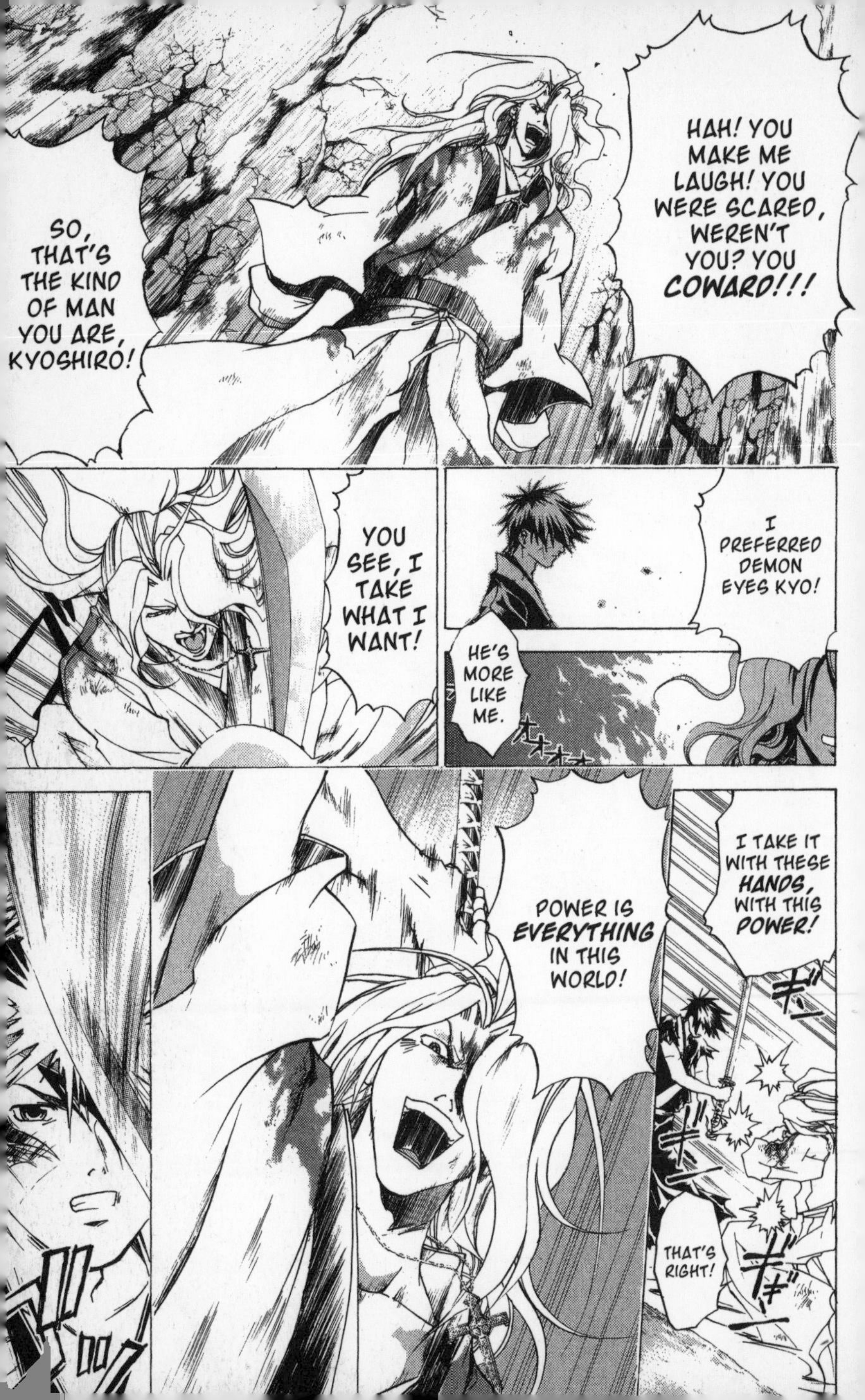
HAH! YOU MAKE ME LAUGH! YOU WERE SCARED, WEREN'T YOU? YOU COWARD!!!
SO, THAT'S THE KIND OF MAN YOU ARE, KYOSHIRO!
I PREFERRED DEMON EYES KYO!
HE'S MORE LIKE ME.
YOU SEE, I TAKE WHAT I WANT!
I TAKE IT WITH THESE HANDS, WITH THIS POWER!
THAT'S RIGHT!
POWER IS EVERYTHING IN THIS WORLD!

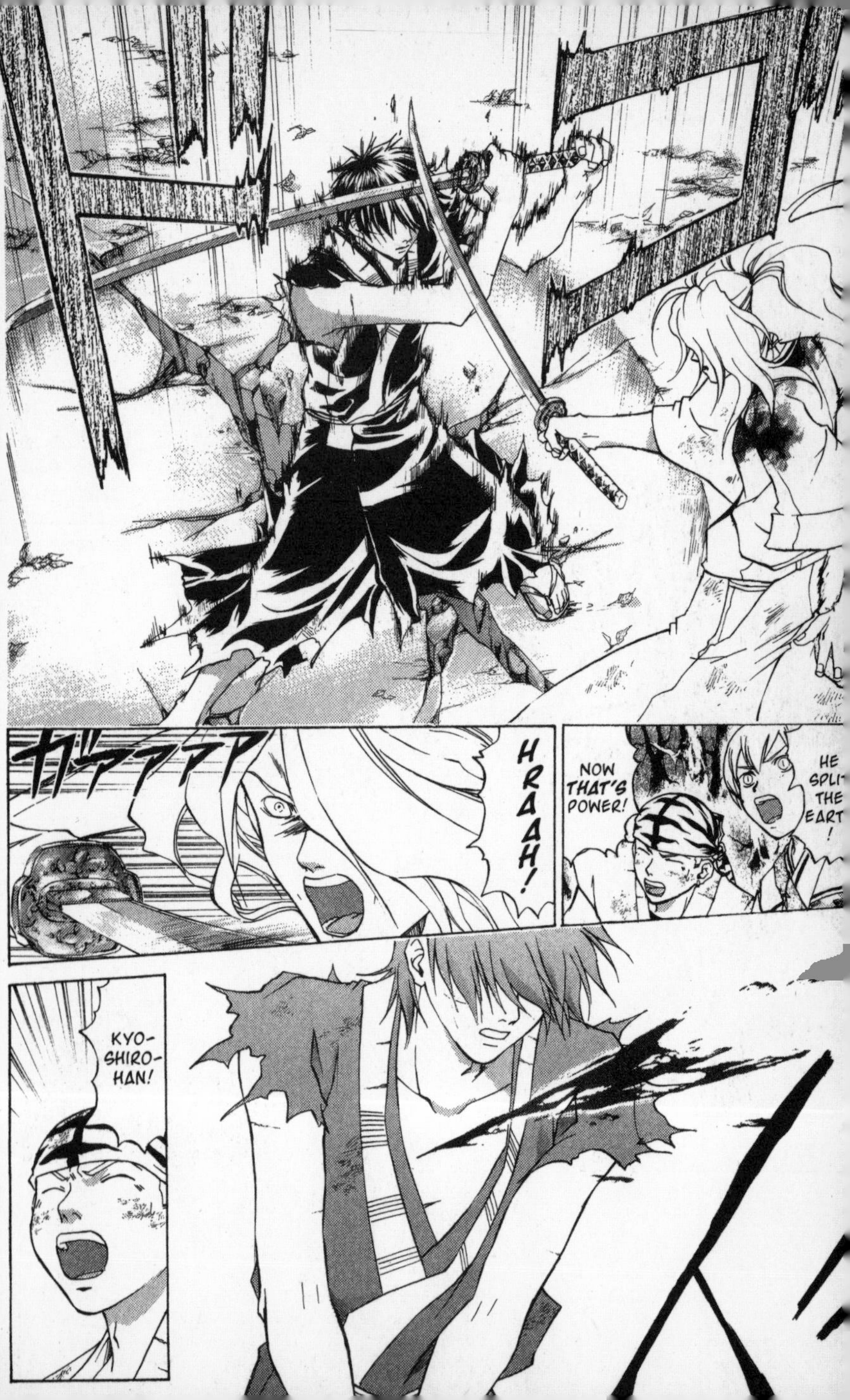
HE SPLI THE EART!
NOW THAT'S POWER!
HRAAAH!
ガァァァァ
KYO-SHIRO-HAN!

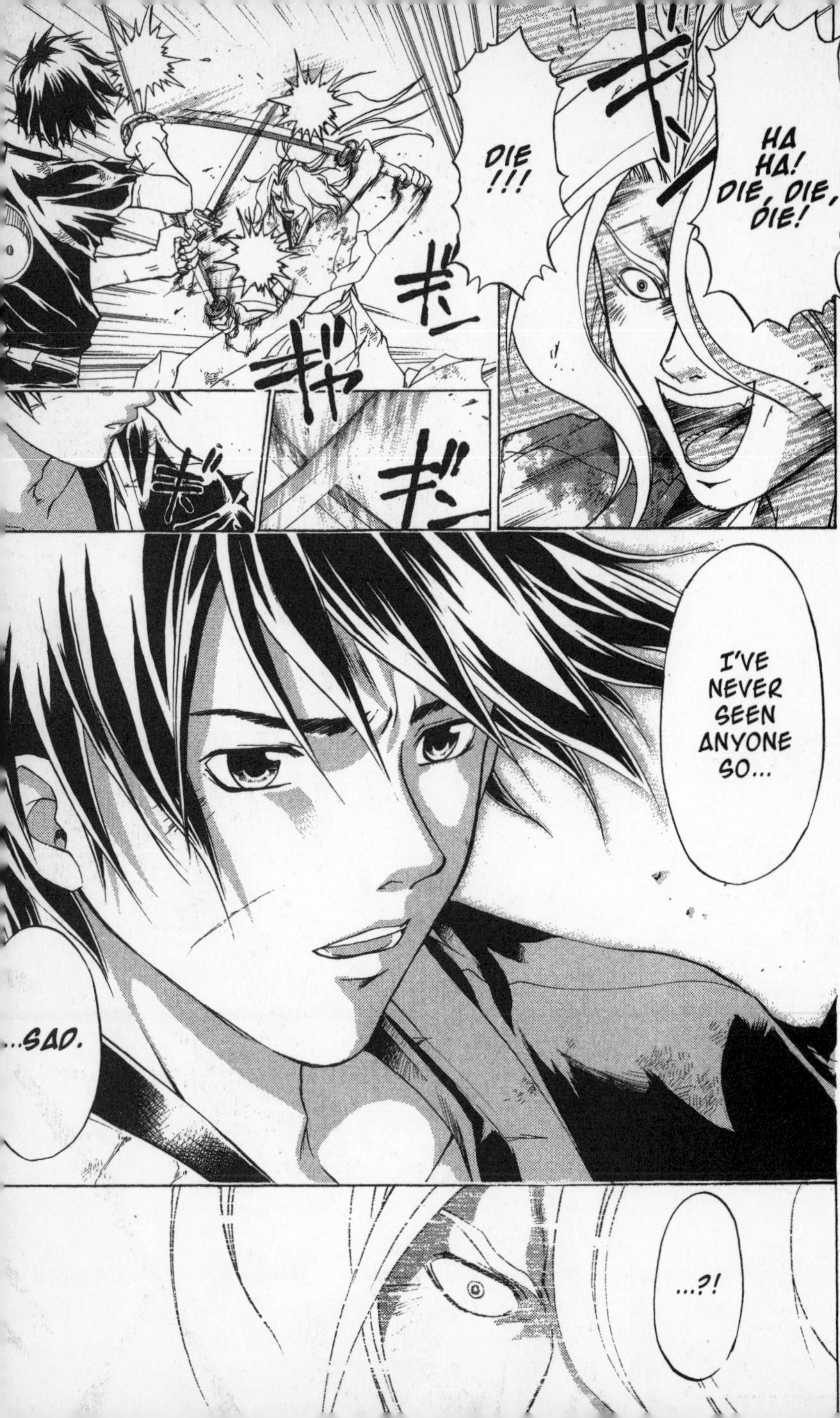
HA HA! DIE, DIE, DIE!
DIE!!!
I'VE NEVER SEEN ANYONE SO...
...SAD.
...?!

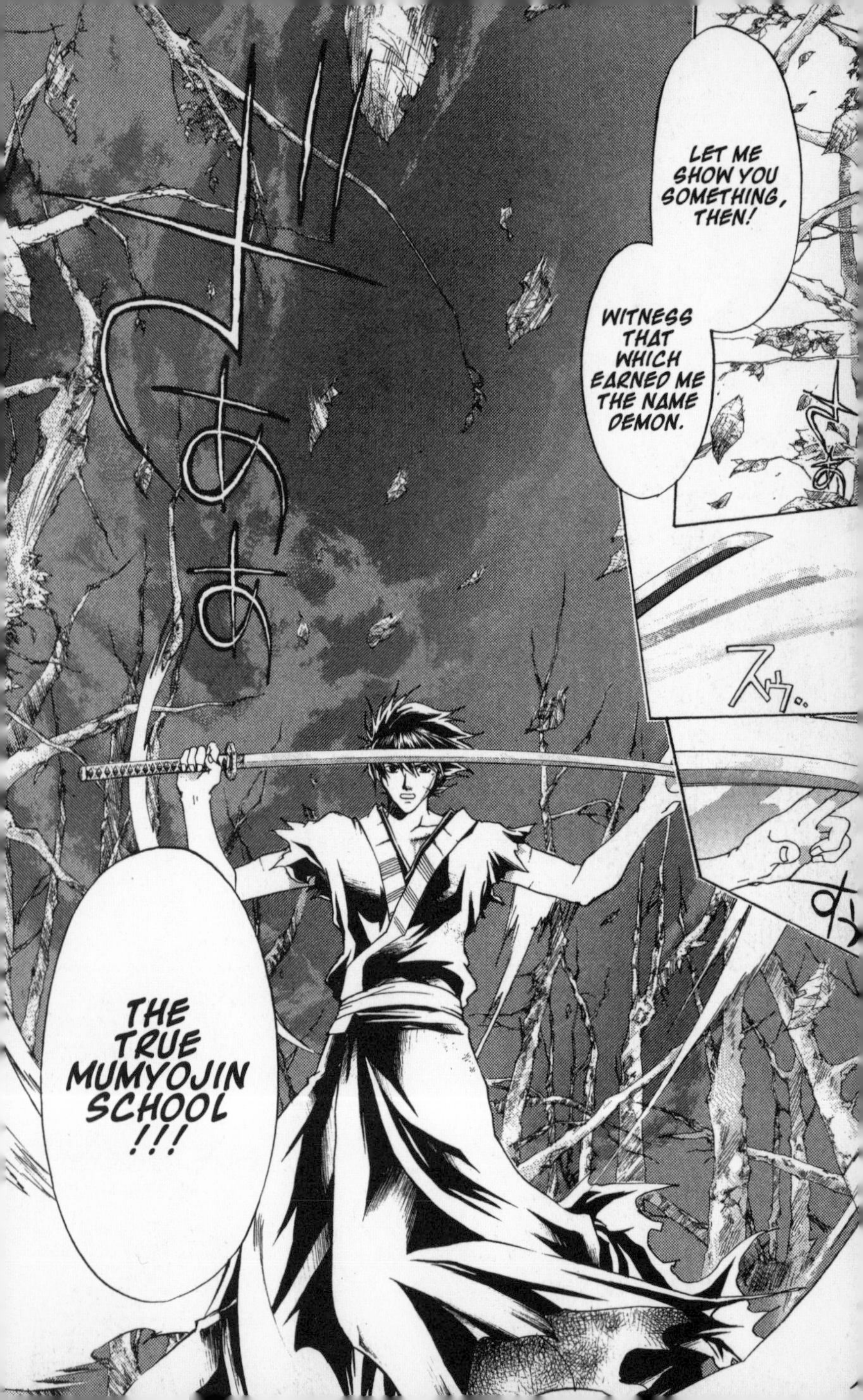
LET ME SHOW YOU SOMETHING, THEN!
WITNESS THAT WHICH EARNED ME THE NAME DEMON.
THE TRUE MUMYOJIN SCHOOL!!!

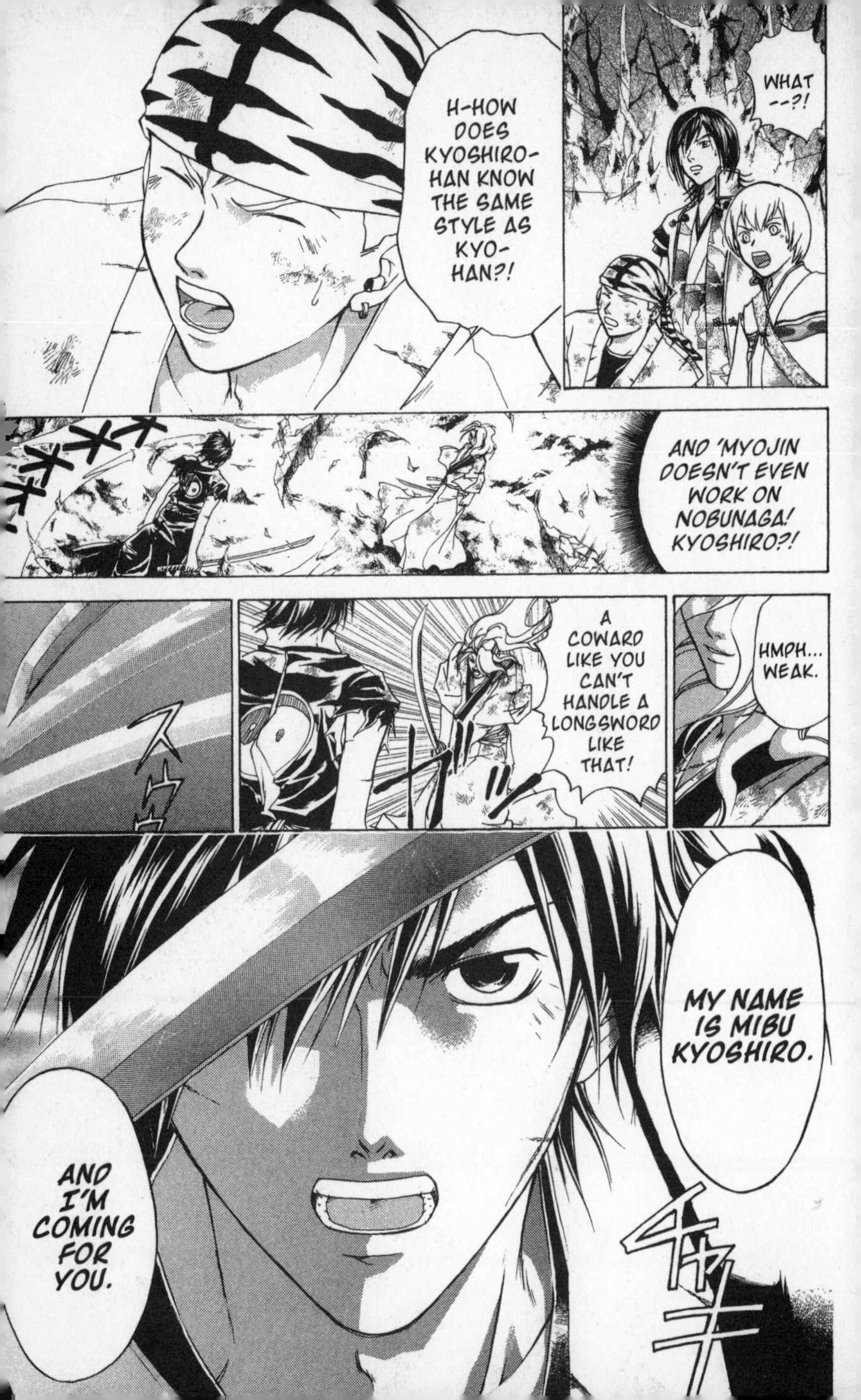
WHAT--?!
H-HOW DOES KYOSHIRO-HAN KNOW THE SAME STYLE AS KYO-HAN?!
AND 'MYOJIN DOESN'T EVEN WORK ON NOBUNAGA! KYOSHIRO?!
HMPH... WEAK.
A COWARD LIKE YOU CAN'T HANDLE A LONGSWORD LIKE THAT!
MY NAME IS MIBU KYOSHIRO.
AND I'M COMING FOR YOU.

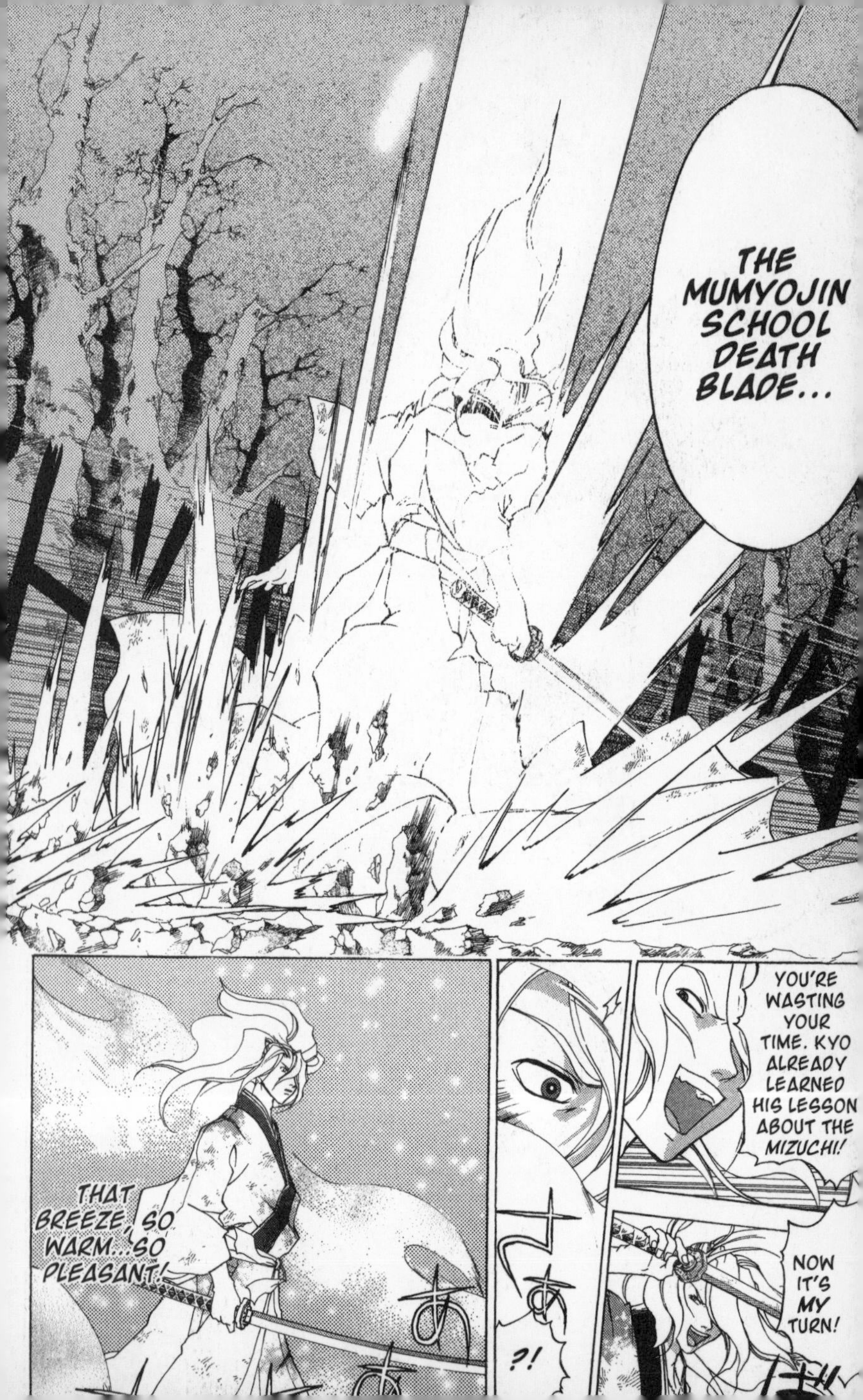
THE MUMYOJIN SCHOOL DEATH BLADE...
YOU'RE WASTING YOUR TIME. KYO ALREADY LEARNED HIS LESSON ABOUT THE MIZUCHI!
NOW IT'S MY TURN!
?!
THAT BREEZE, SO WARM... SO PLEASANT!

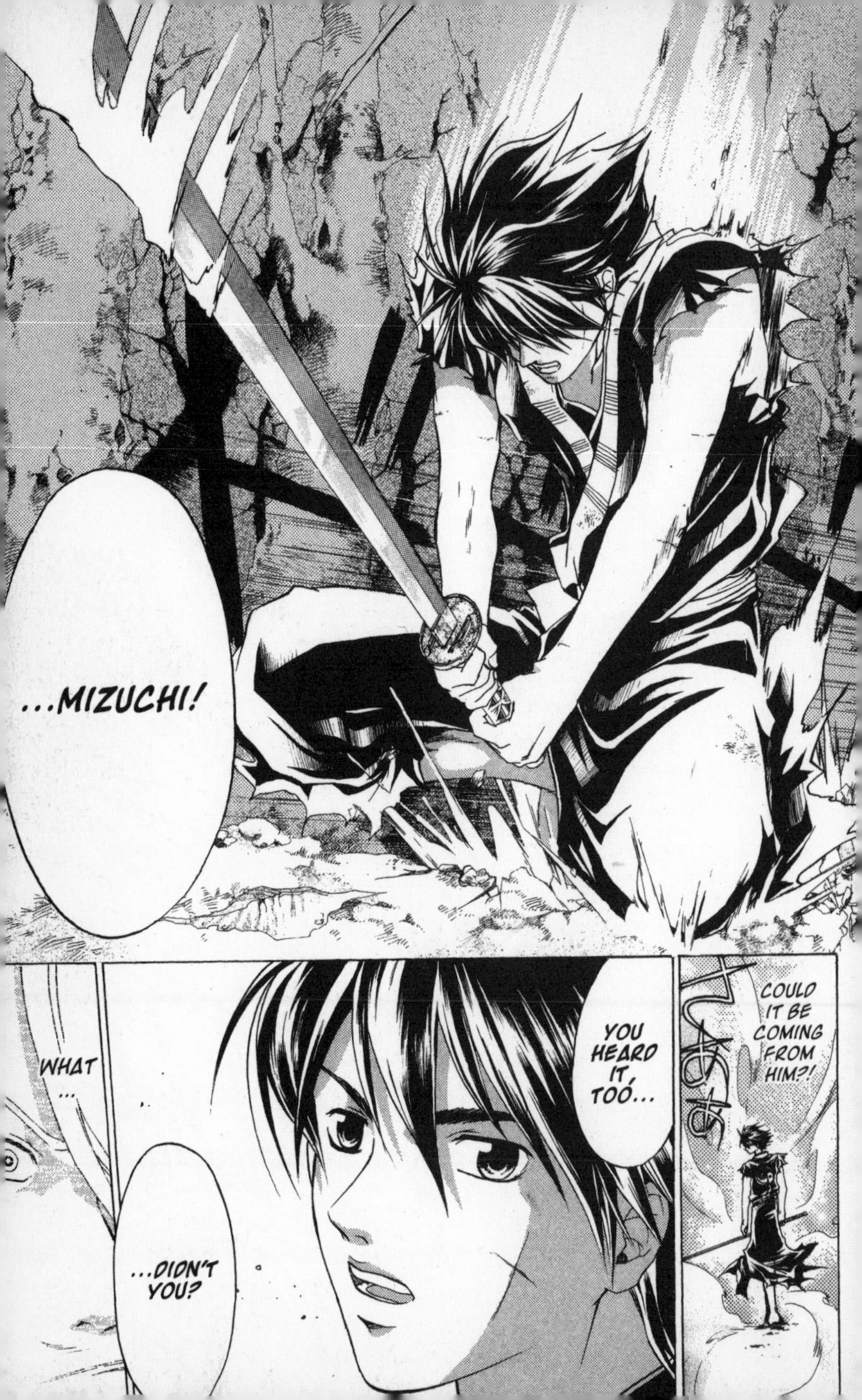
...MIZUCHI!
COULD IT BE COMING FROM HIM?!
YOU HEARD IT, TOO...
...DIDN'T YOU?
WHAT ...

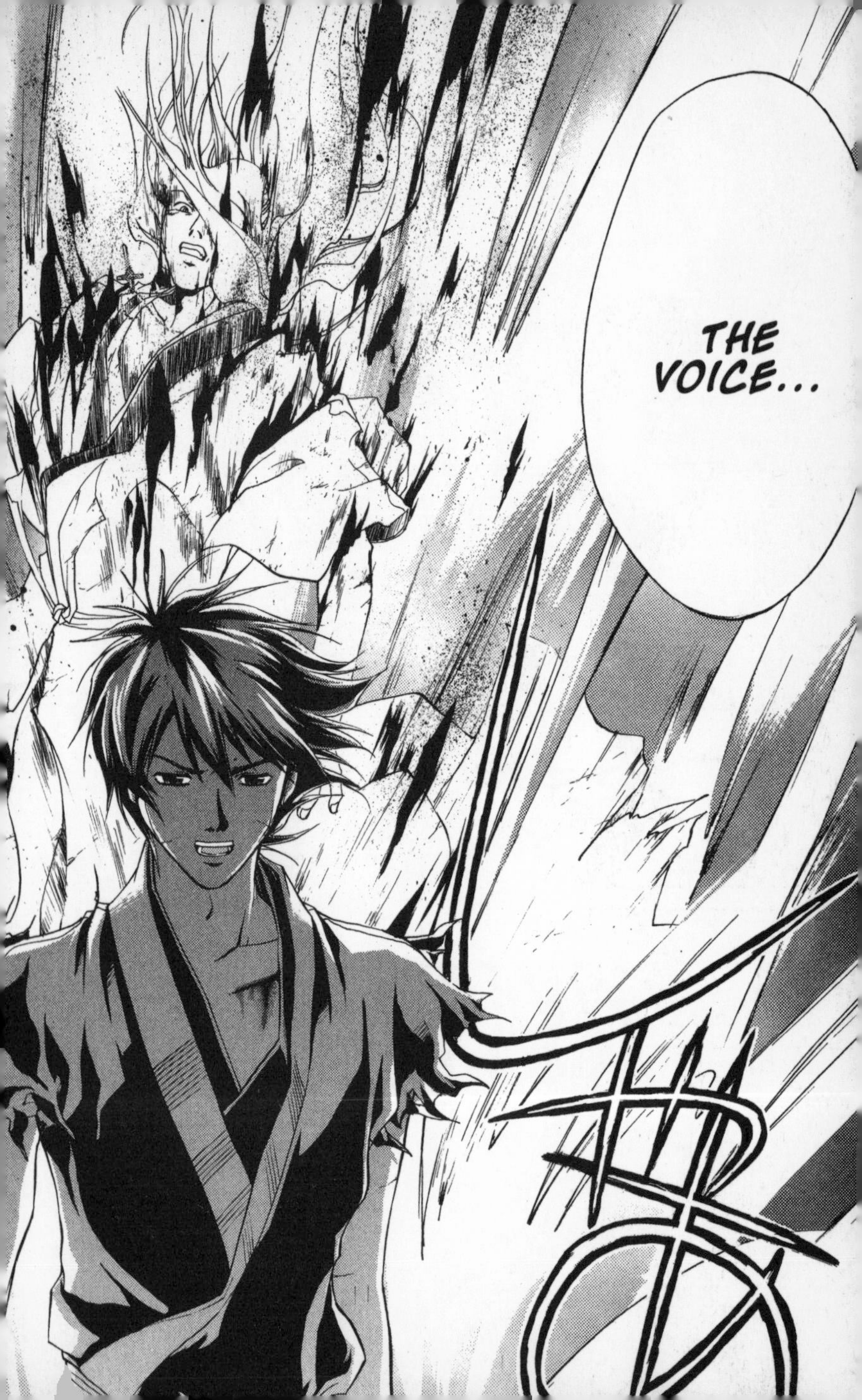
THE VOICE...

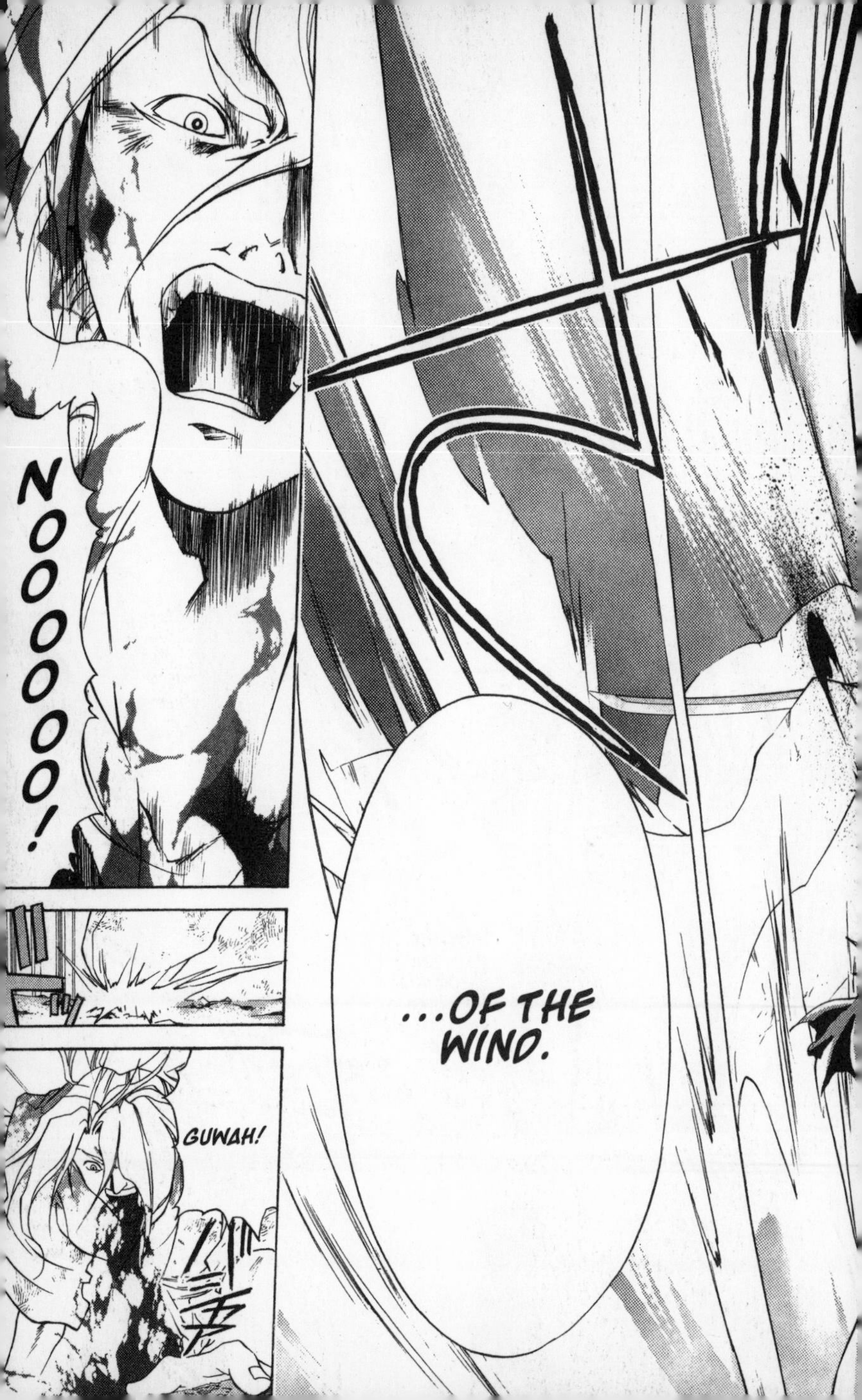
...OF THE WIND.
NOOOOOO!
GUWAH!

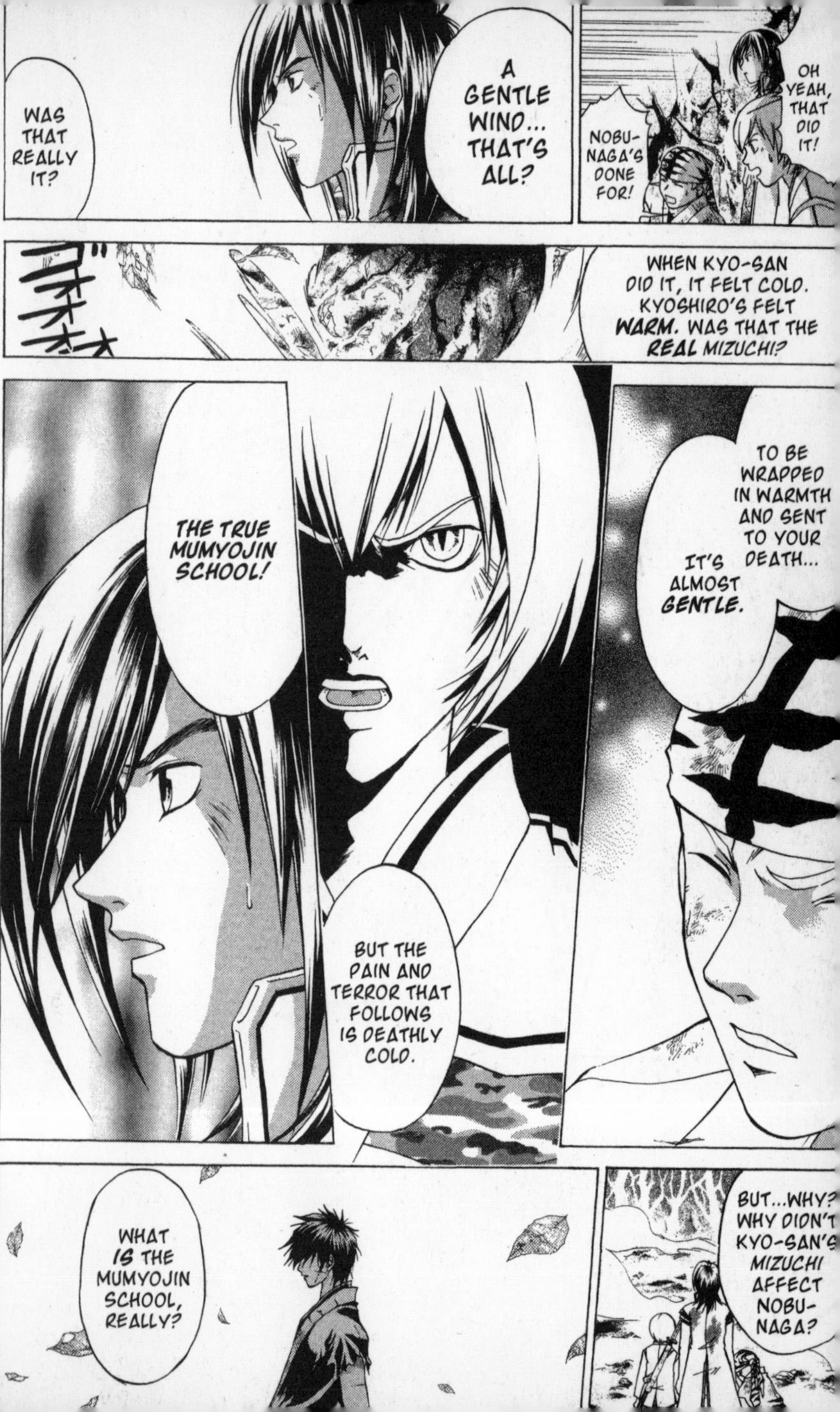
OH YEAH, THAT DID IT!
NOBU-NAGA'S DONE FOR!
A GENTLE WIND... THAT'S ALL?
WAS THAT REALLY IT?
WHEN KYO-SAN DID IT, IT FELT COLD. KYOSHIRO'S FELT **WARM**. WAS THAT THE ***REAL*** MIZUCHI?
TO BE WRAPPED IN WARMTH AND SENT TO YOUR DEATH...
IT'S ALMOST **GENTLE**.
THE TRUE MUMYOJIN SCHOOL!
BUT THE PAIN AND TERROR THAT FOLLOWS IS DEATHLY COLD.
BUT...WHY? WHY DIDN'T KYO-SAN'S MIZUCHI AFFECT NOBU-NAGA?
WHAT ***IS*** THE MUMYOJIN SCHOOL, REALLY?

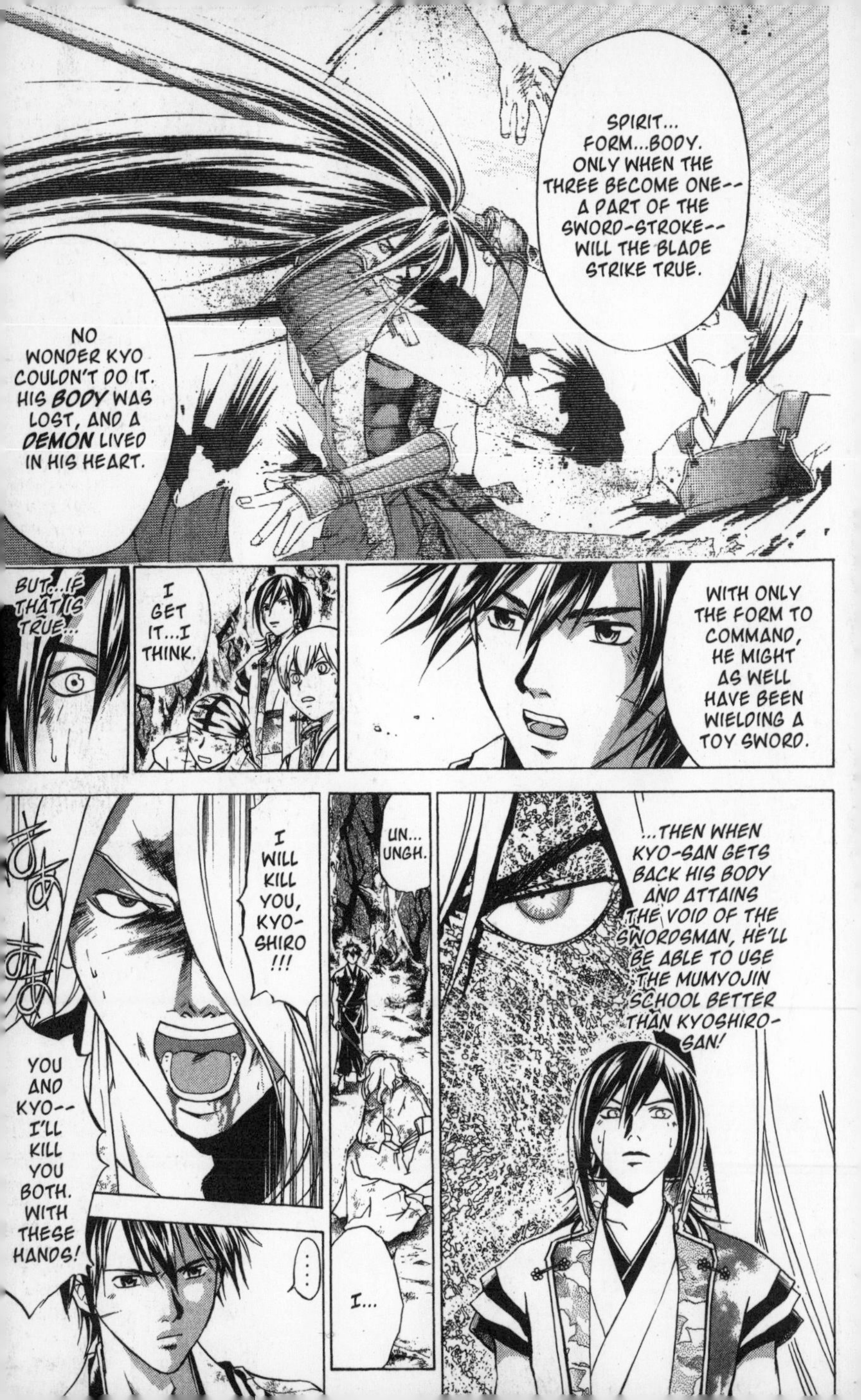
SPIRIT... FORM...BODY. ONLY WHEN THE THREE BECOME ONE-- A PART OF THE SWORD-STROKE-- WILL THE BLADE STRIKE TRUE.
NO WONDER KYO COULDN'T DO IT. HIS *BODY* WAS LOST, AND A *DEMON* LIVED IN HIS HEART.
WITH ONLY THE FORM TO COMMAND, HE MIGHT AS WELL HAVE BEEN WIELDING A TOY SWORD.
I GET IT...I THINK.
BUT...IF THAT IS TRUE...
...THEN WHEN KYO-SAN GETS BACK HIS BODY AND ATTAINS THE VOID OF THE SWORDSMAN, HE'LL BE ABLE TO USE THE MUMYOJIN SCHOOL BETTER THAN KYOSHIRO-SAN!
UN... UNGH.
I...
I WILL KILL YOU, KYO-SHIRO!!!
YOU AND KYO-- I'LL KILL YOU BOTH. WITH THESE HANDS!
...

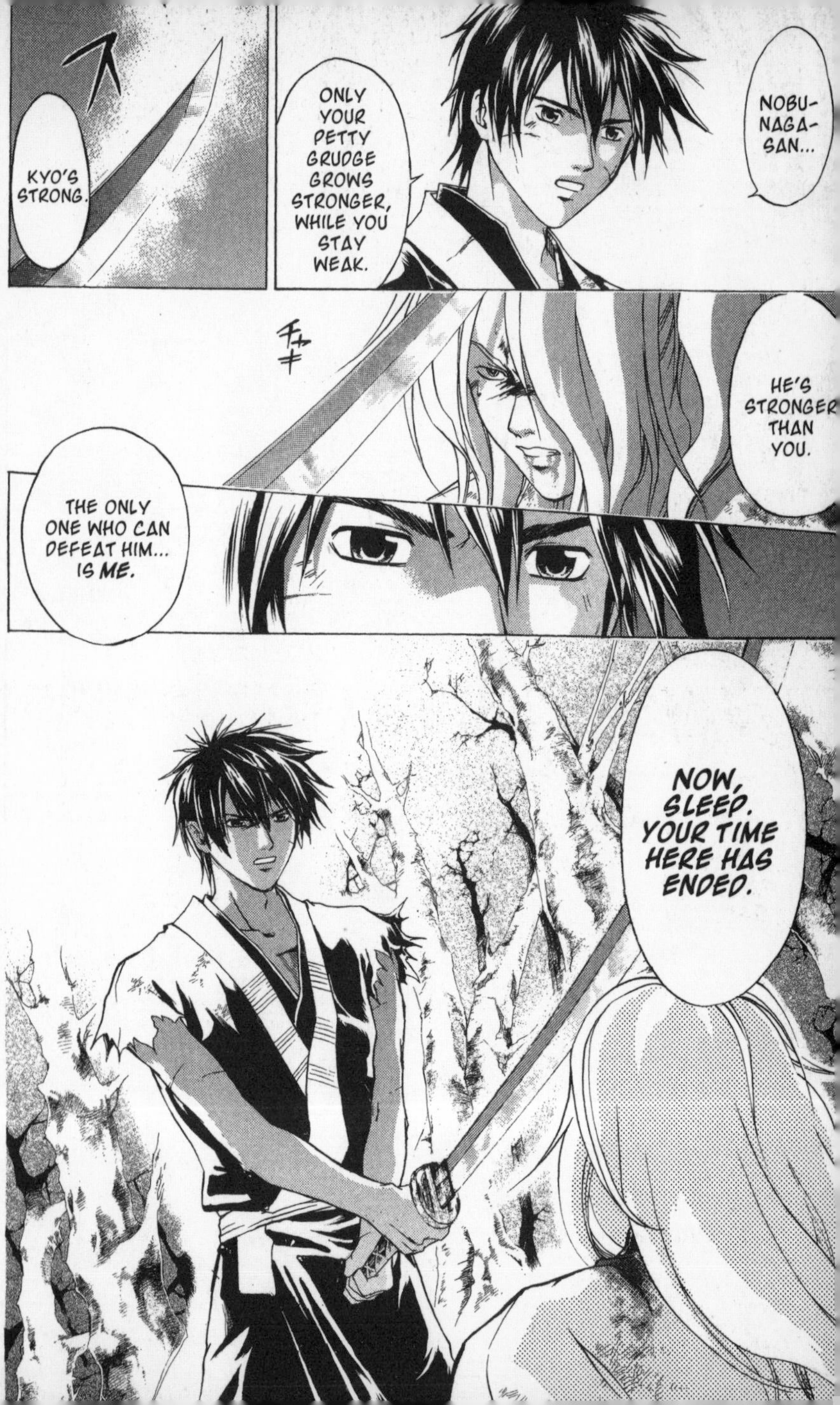
NOBUNAGA-SAN...
ONLY YOUR PETTY GRUDGE GROWS STRONGER, WHILE YOU STAY WEAK.
KYO'S STRONG.
HE'S STRONGER THAN YOU.
チャキ
THE ONLY ONE WHO CAN DEFEAT HIM... IS **ME.**
NOW, SLEEP. YOUR TIME HERE HAS ENDED.

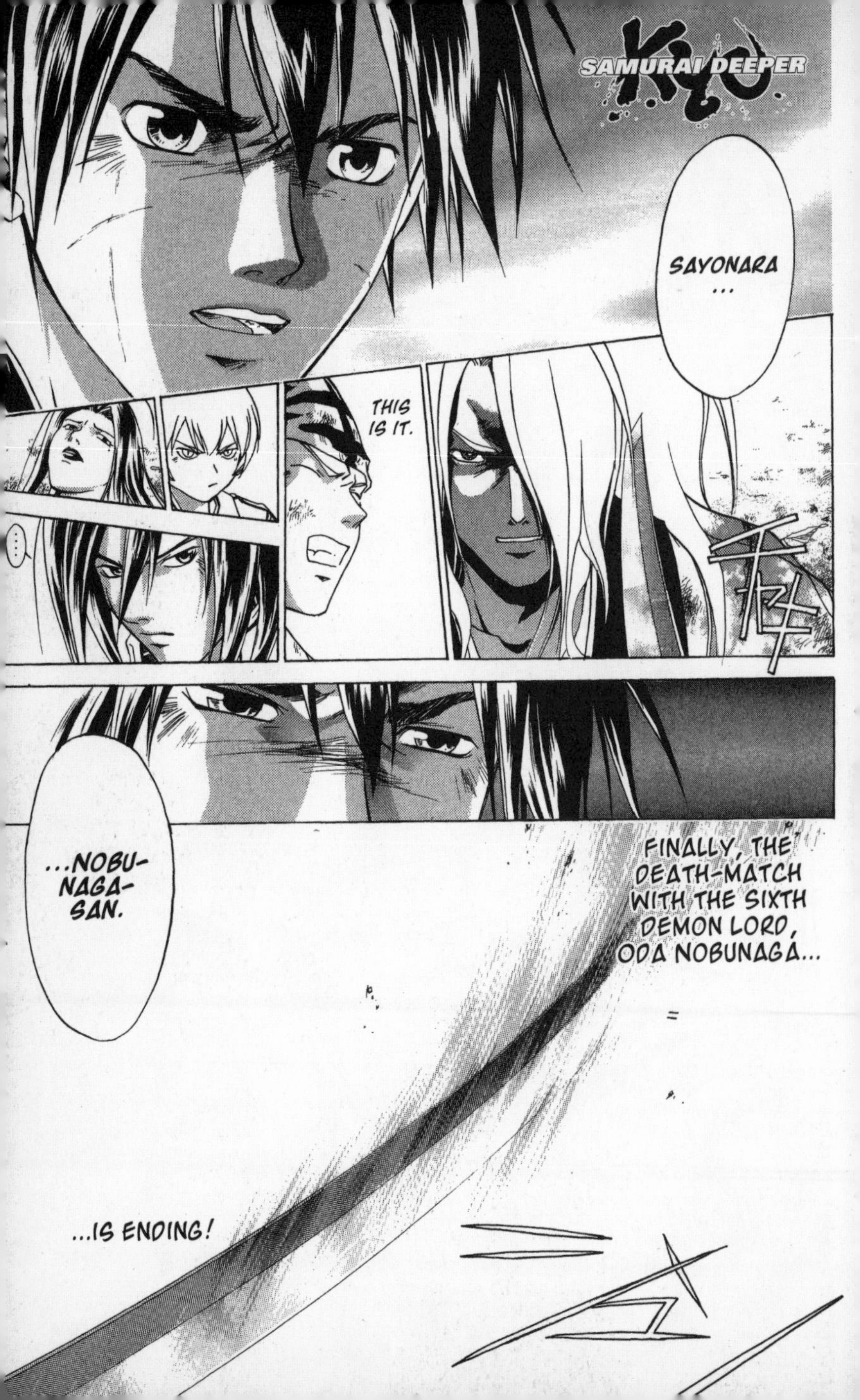
SAMURAI DEEPER KYO
SAYONARA ...
THIS IS IT.
...
...NOBUNAGA-SAN.
FINALLY, THE DEATH-MATCH WITH THE SIXTH DEMON LORD, ODA NOBUNAGA...
...IS ENDING!

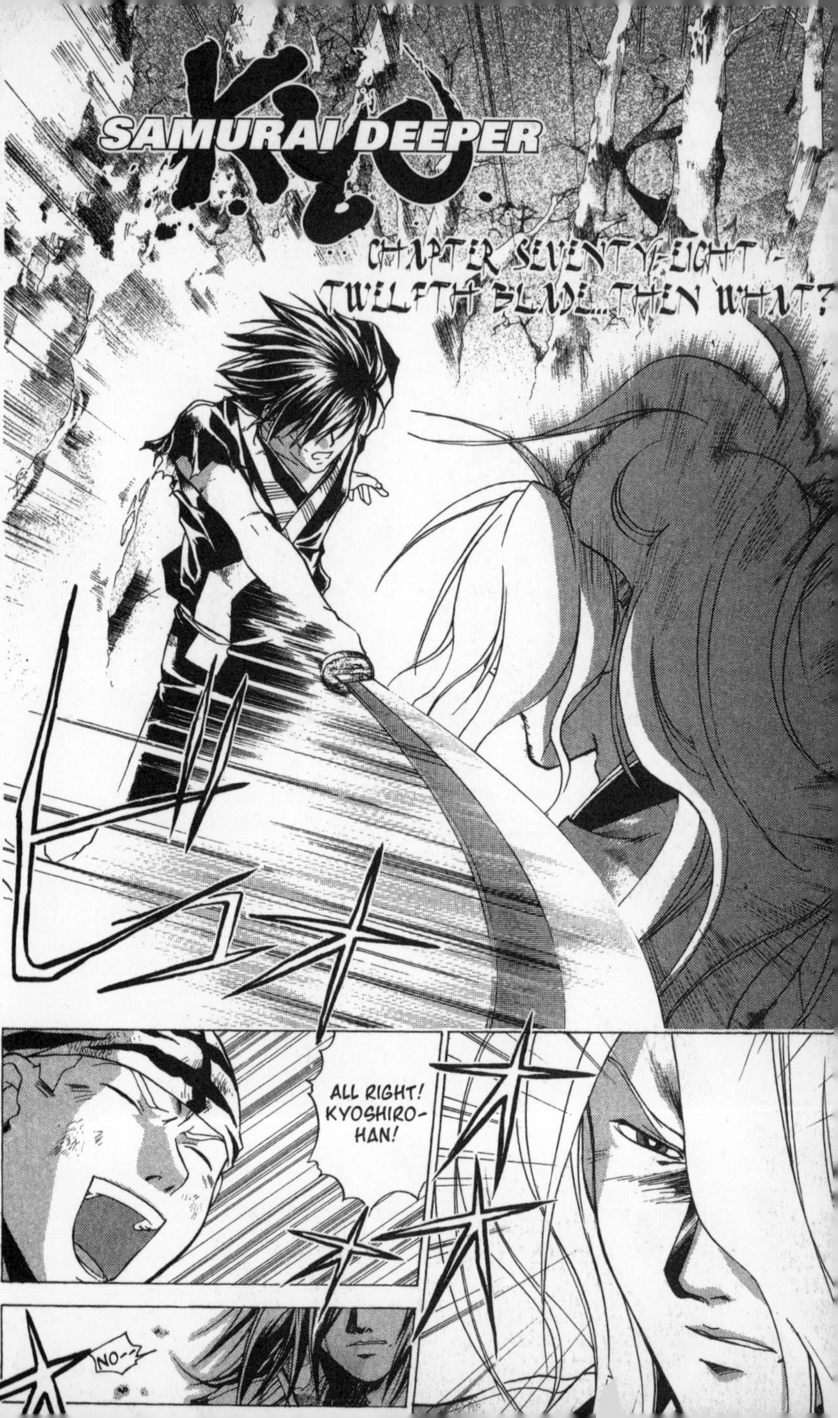
SAMURAI DEEPER KYO
CHAPTER SEVENTY-EIGHT - TWELFTH BLADE...THEN WHAT?
ALL RIGHT! KYOSHIRO-HAN!
NO--!

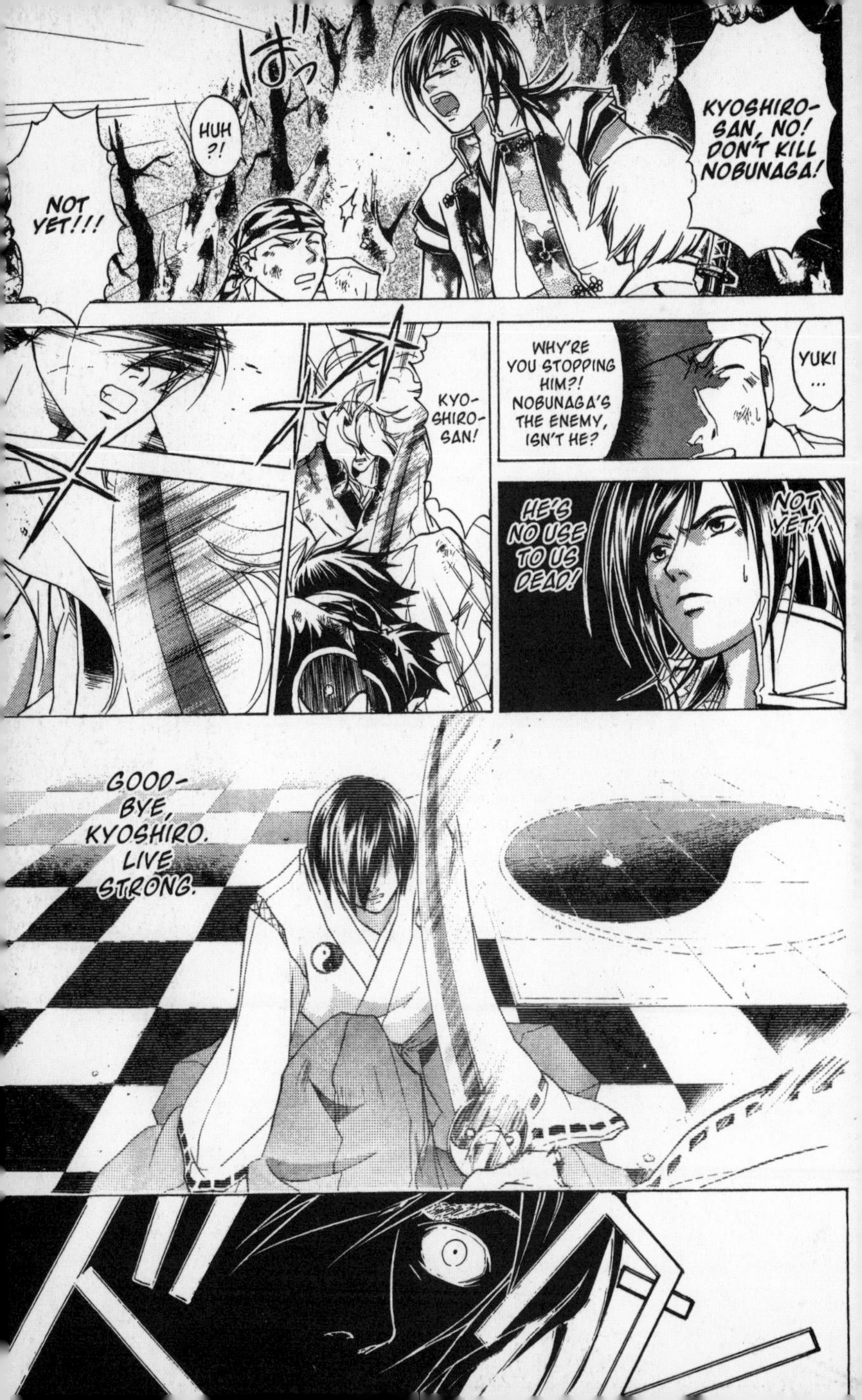
KYOSHIRO-SAN, NO! DON'T KILL NOBUNAGA!
ばっ
HUH ?!
NOT YET!!!
YUKI ...
WHY'RE YOU STOPPING HIM?! NOBUNAGA'S THE ENEMY, ISN'T HE?
NOT YET!
HE'S NO USE TO US DEAD!
KYO-SHIRO-SAN!
GOOD-BYE, KYOSHIRO. LIVE STRONG.

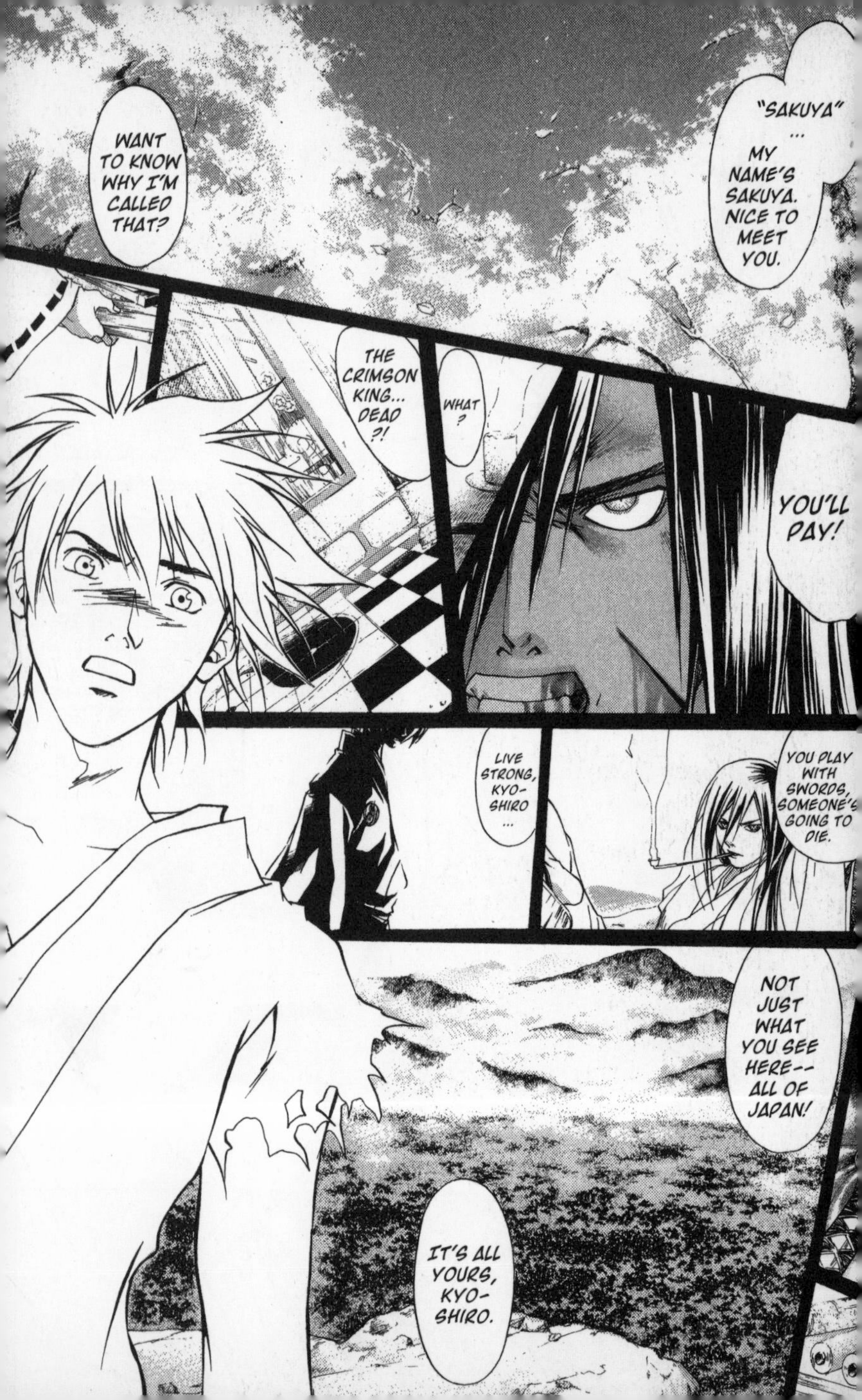
"SAKUYA"... MY NAME'S SAKUYA. NICE TO MEET YOU.
WANT TO KNOW WHY I'M CALLED THAT?
WHAT?
YOU'LL PAY!
THE CRIMSON KING... DEAD?!
YOU PLAY WITH SWORDS, SOMEONE'S GOING TO DIE.
LIVE STRONG, KYO-SHIRO...
NOT JUST WHAT YOU SEE HERE--ALL OF JAPAN!
IT'S ALL YOURS, KYO-SHIRO.

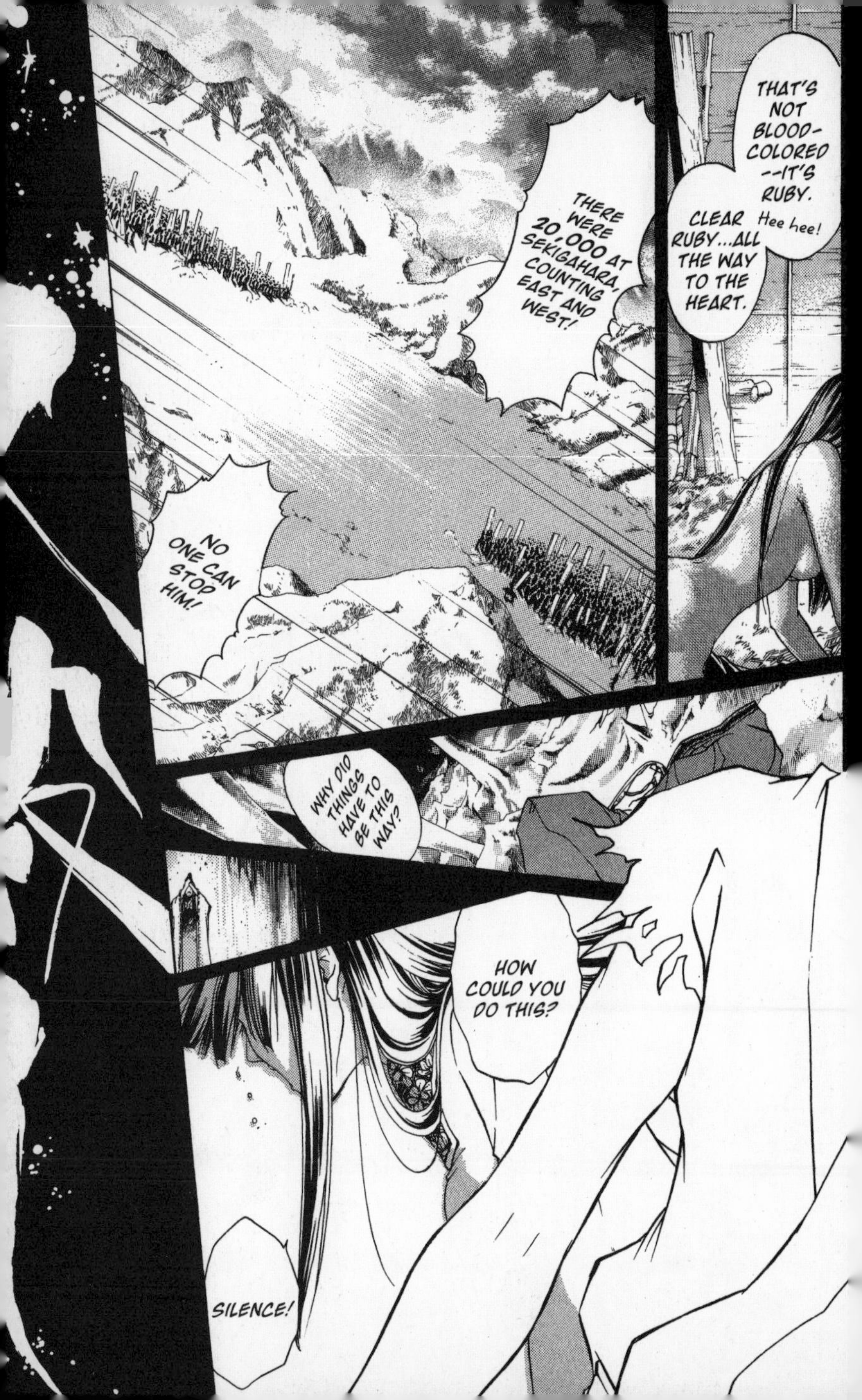
THAT'S NOT BLOOD-COLORED --IT'S RUBY.
Hee hee!
CLEAR RUBY...ALL THE WAY TO THE HEART.
THERE WERE 20,000 AT SEKIGAHARA, COUNTING EAST AND WEST!
NO ONE CAN STOP HIM!
WHY DID THINGS HAVE TO BE THIS WAY?
HOW COULD YOU DO THIS?
SILENCE!

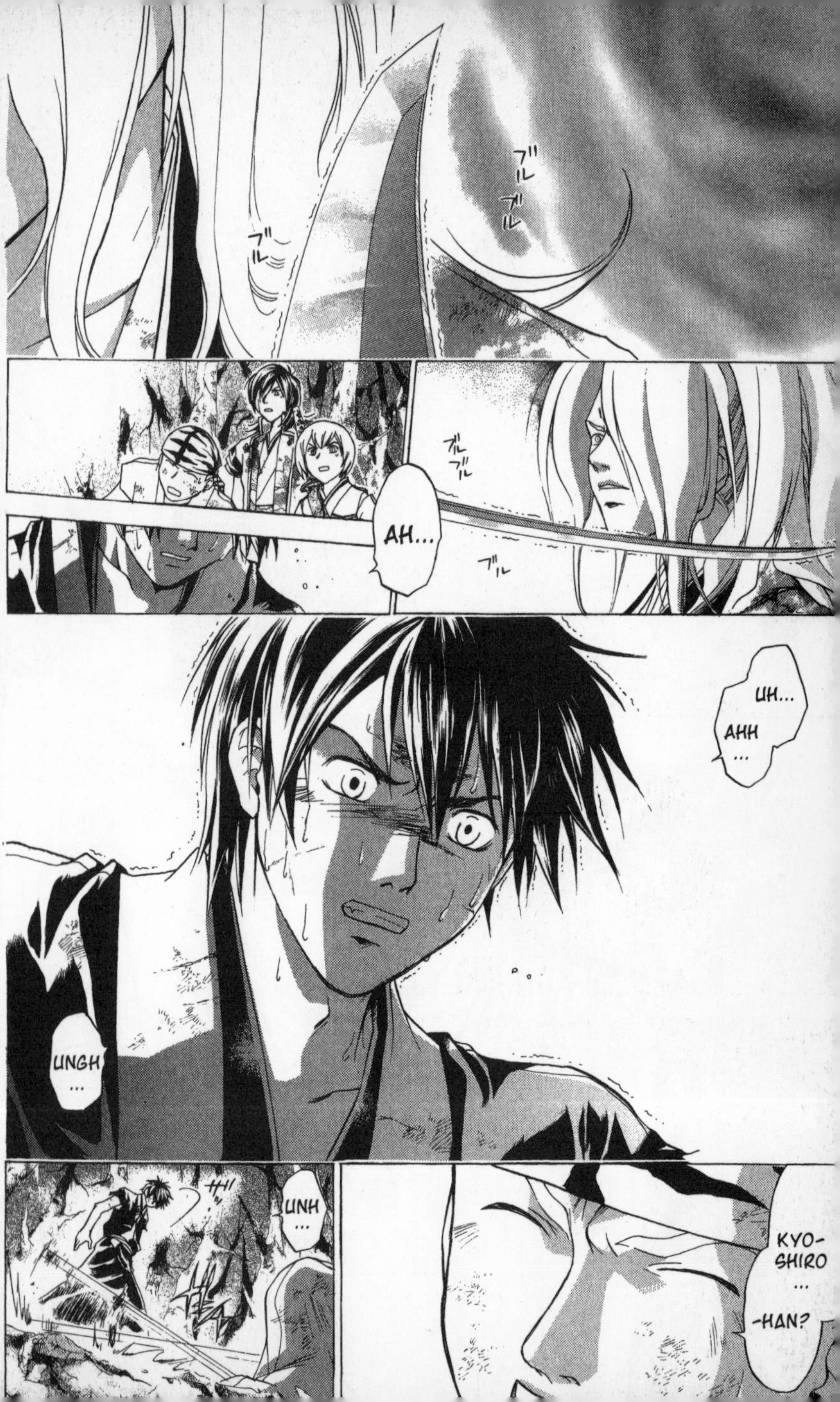
ブル
ブル
ブル
ブルブル
AH...
ブル
UH... AHH ...
UNGH ...
KYO-SHIRO ... -HAN?
UNH ...

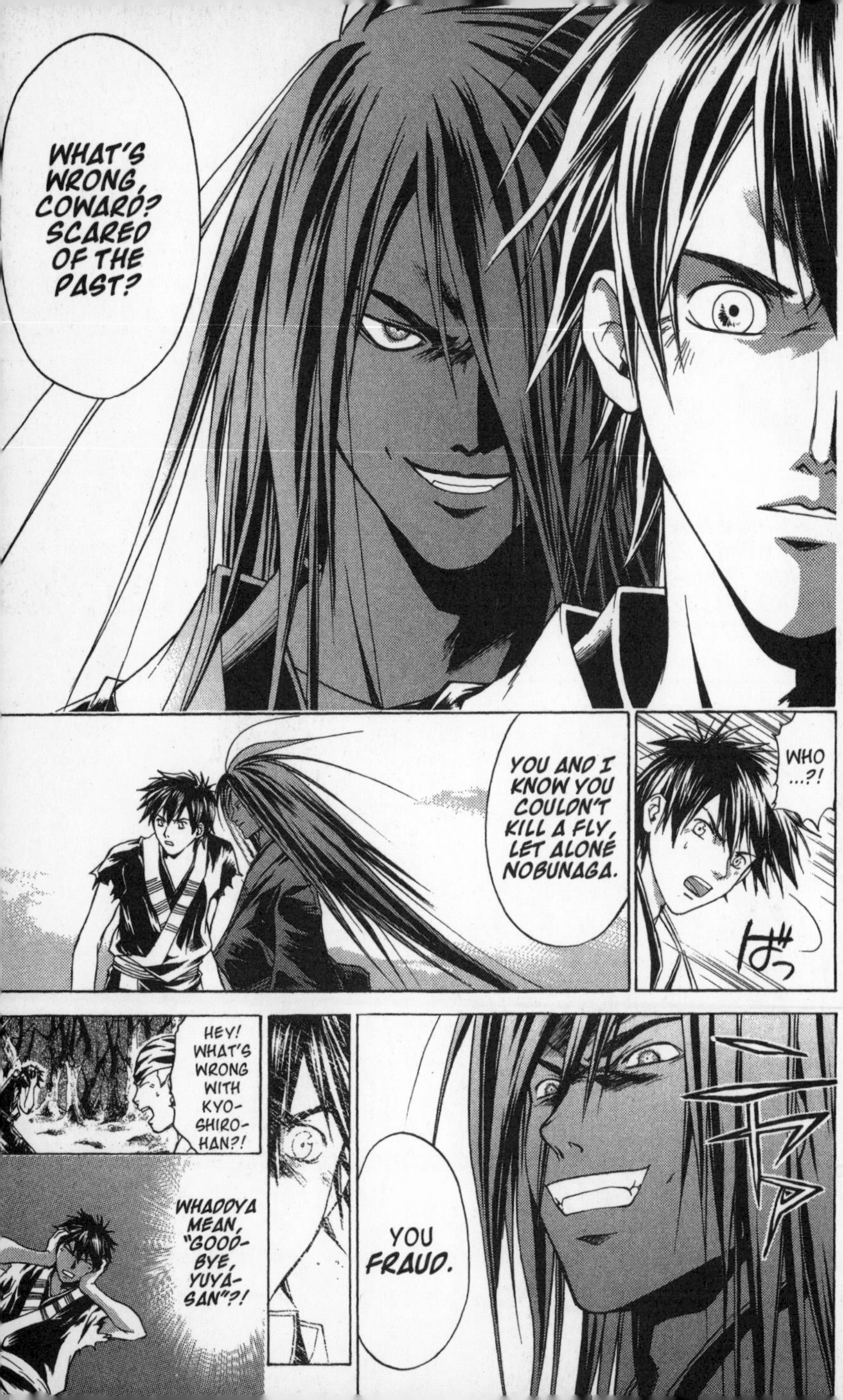
WHAT'S WRONG, COWARD? SCARED OF THE PAST?
WHO ...?!
ばっ
YOU AND I KNOW YOU COULDN'T KILL A FLY, LET ALONE NOBUNAGA.
YOU FRAUD.
HEY! WHAT'S WRONG WITH KYO-SHIRO-HAN?!
WHADDYA MEAN, "GOOD-BYE, YUYA-SAN"?!

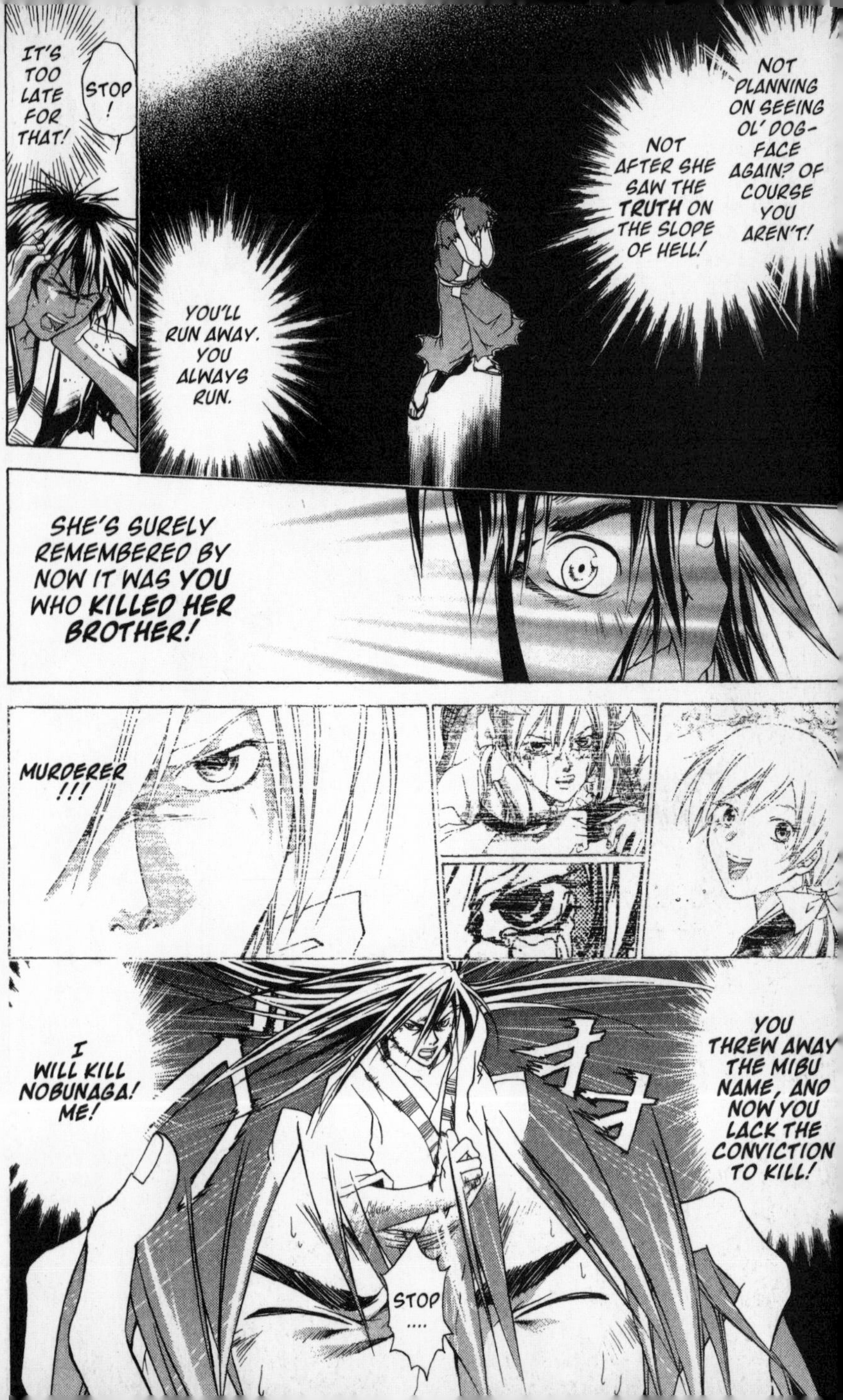
NOT PLANNING ON SEEING OL' DOG-FACE AGAIN? OF COURSE YOU AREN'T!
NOT AFTER SHE SAW THE TRUTH ON THE SLOPE OF HELL!
YOU'LL RUN AWAY. YOU ALWAYS RUN.
STOP!
IT'S TOO LATE FOR THAT!
SHE'S SURELY REMEMBERED BY NOW IT WAS YOU WHO KILLED HER BROTHER!
MURDERER!!!
YOU THREW AWAY THE MIBU NAME, AND NOW YOU LACK THE CONVICTION TO KILL!
I WILL KILL NOBUNAGA! ME!
STOP....

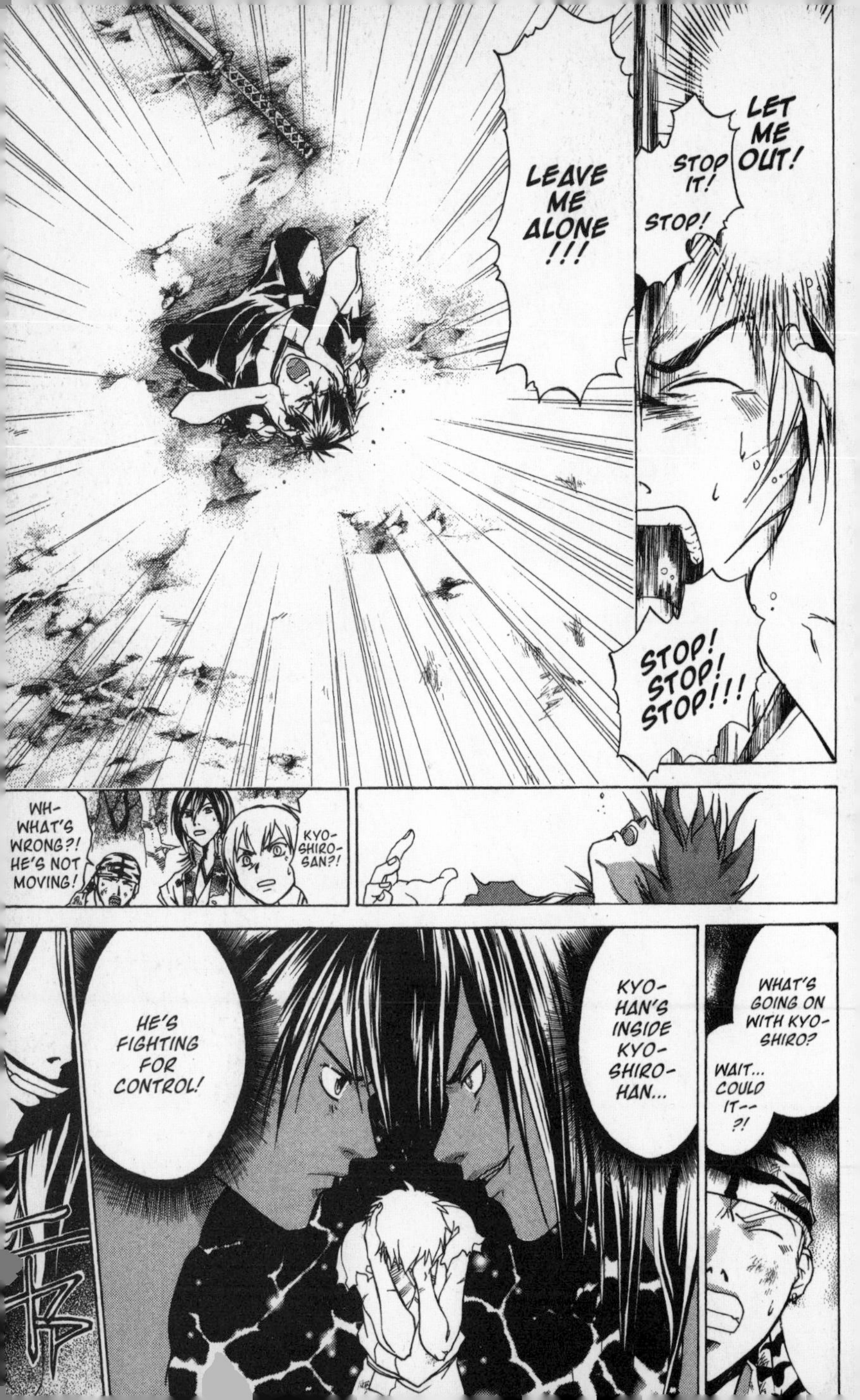
LET ME OUT!
STOP IT!
STOP!
STOP! STOP! STOP!!!
LEAVE ME ALONE!!!
KYO-SHIRO-SAN?!
WH-WHAT'S WRONG?! HE'S NOT MOVING!
WHAT'S GOING ON WITH KYO-SHIRO?
WAIT... COULD IT--?!
KYO-HAN'S INSIDE KYO-SHIRO-HAN...
HE'S FIGHTING FOR CONTROL!

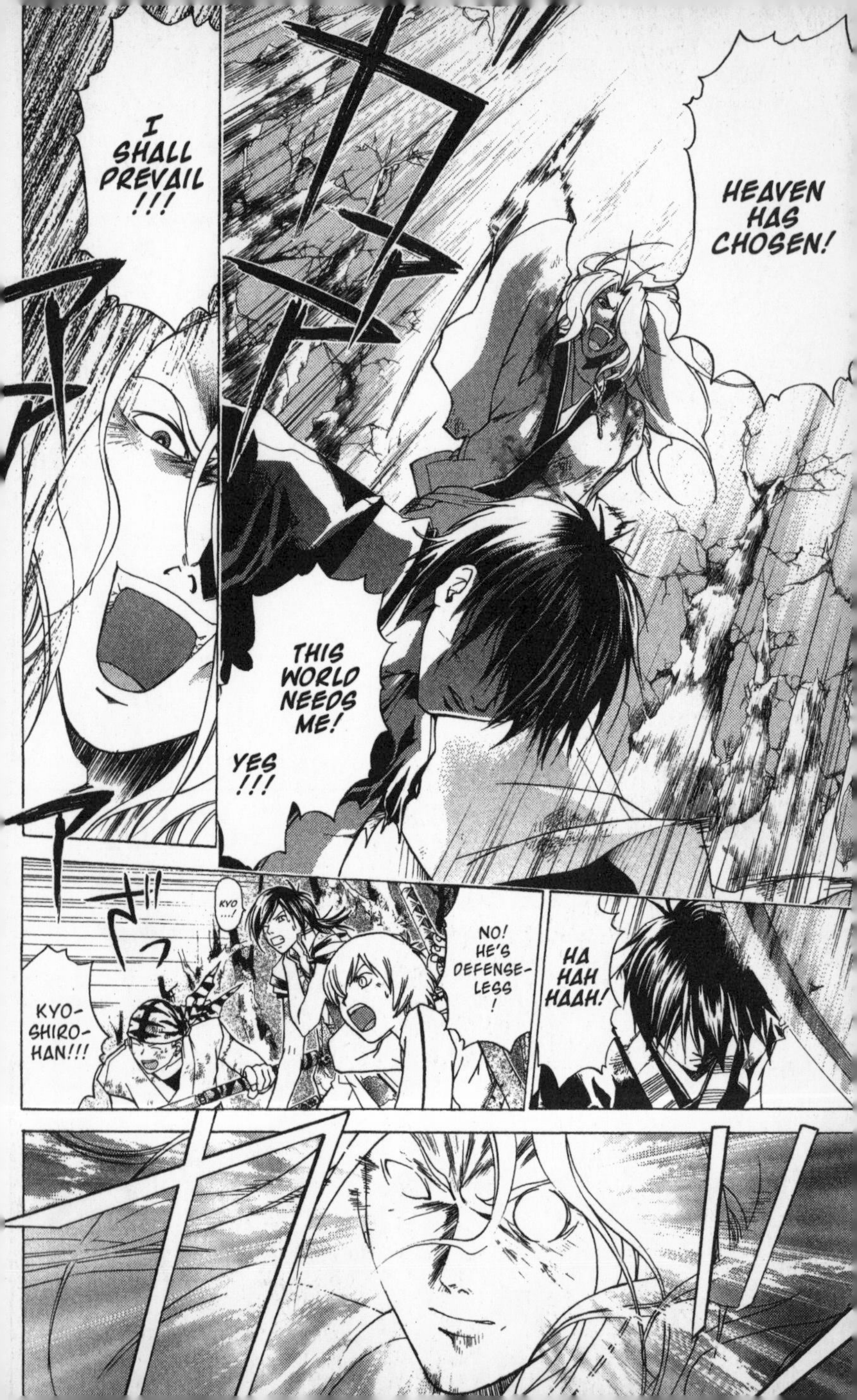
HEAVEN HAS CHOSEN!
THIS WORLD NEEDS ME!
YES!!!
I SHALL PREVAIL!!!
HA HAH HAAH!
NO! HE'S DEFENSE-LESS!
KYO...!
KYO-SHIRO-HAN!!!

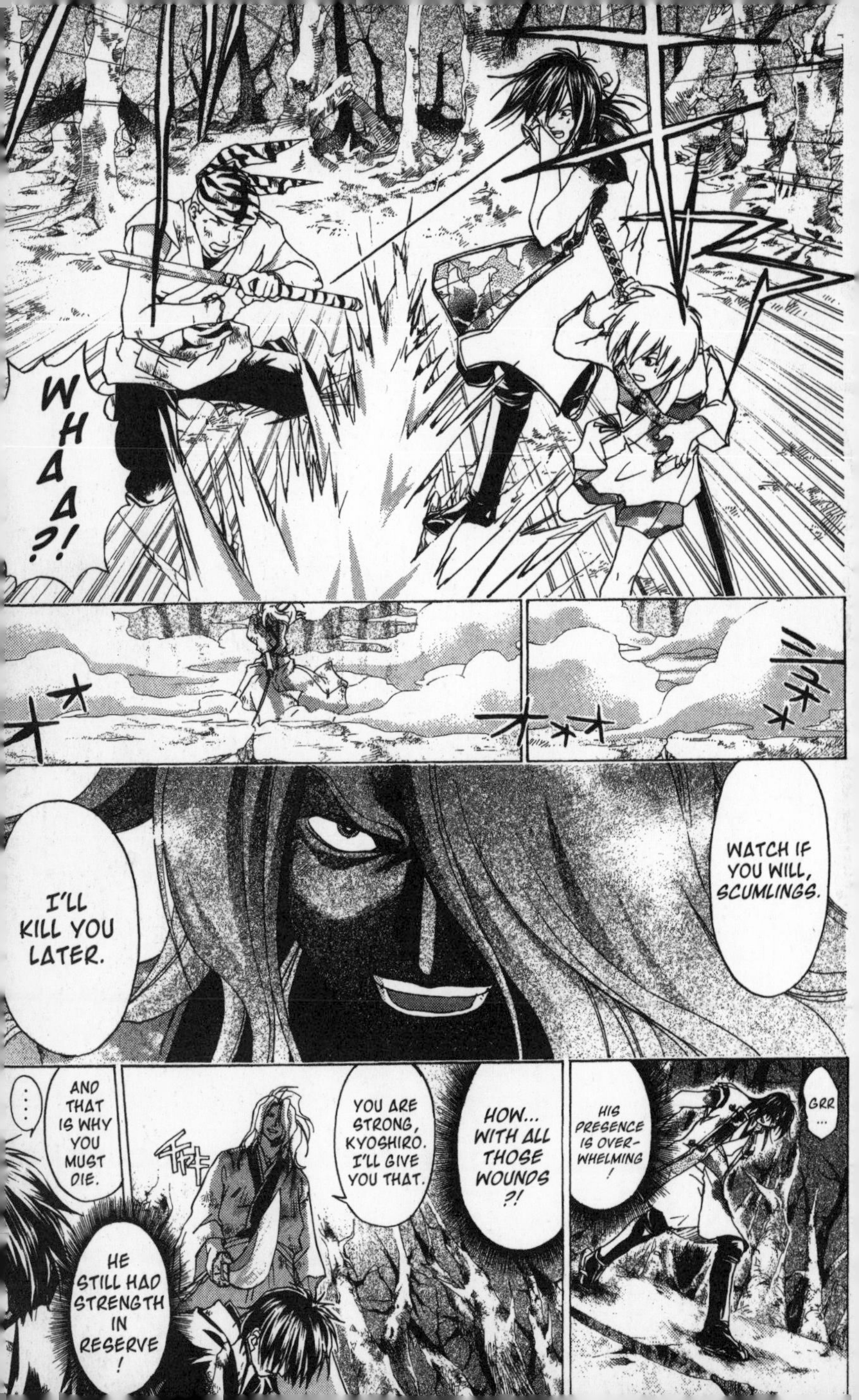
WHAAA?!
WATCH IF YOU WILL, SCUMLINGS.
I'LL KILL YOU LATER.
GRR...
HIS PRESENCE IS OVER-WHELMING!
HOW... WITH ALL THOSE WOUNDS?!
YOU ARE STRONG, KYOSHIRO. I'LL GIVE YOU THAT.
AND THAT IS WHY YOU MUST DIE.
.....
HE STILL HAD STRENGTH IN RESERVE!

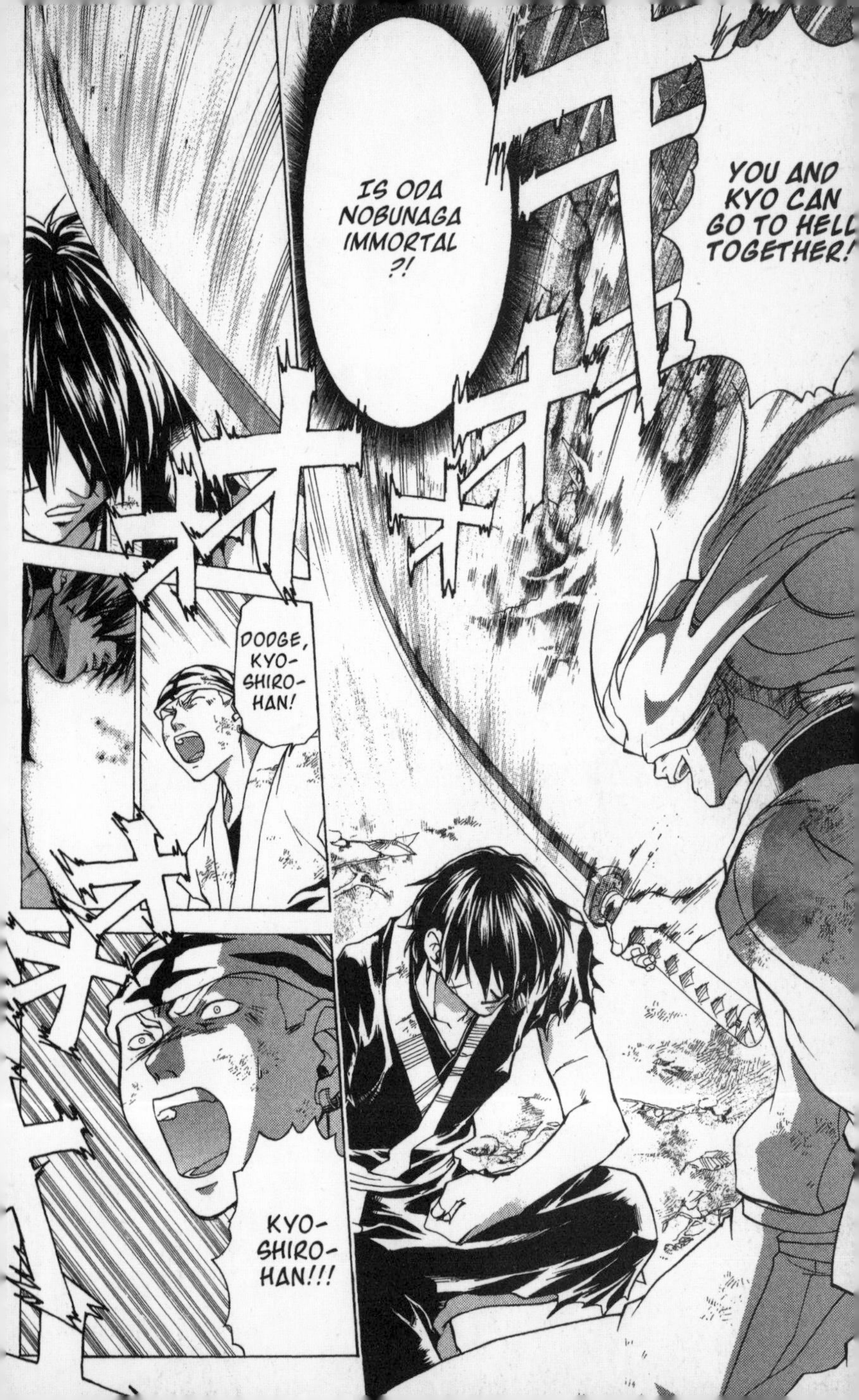
YOU AND KYO CAN GO TO HELL TOGETHER!
IS ODA NOBUNAGA IMMORTAL ?!
DODGE, KYO-SHIRO-HAN!
KYO-SHIRO-HAN!!!

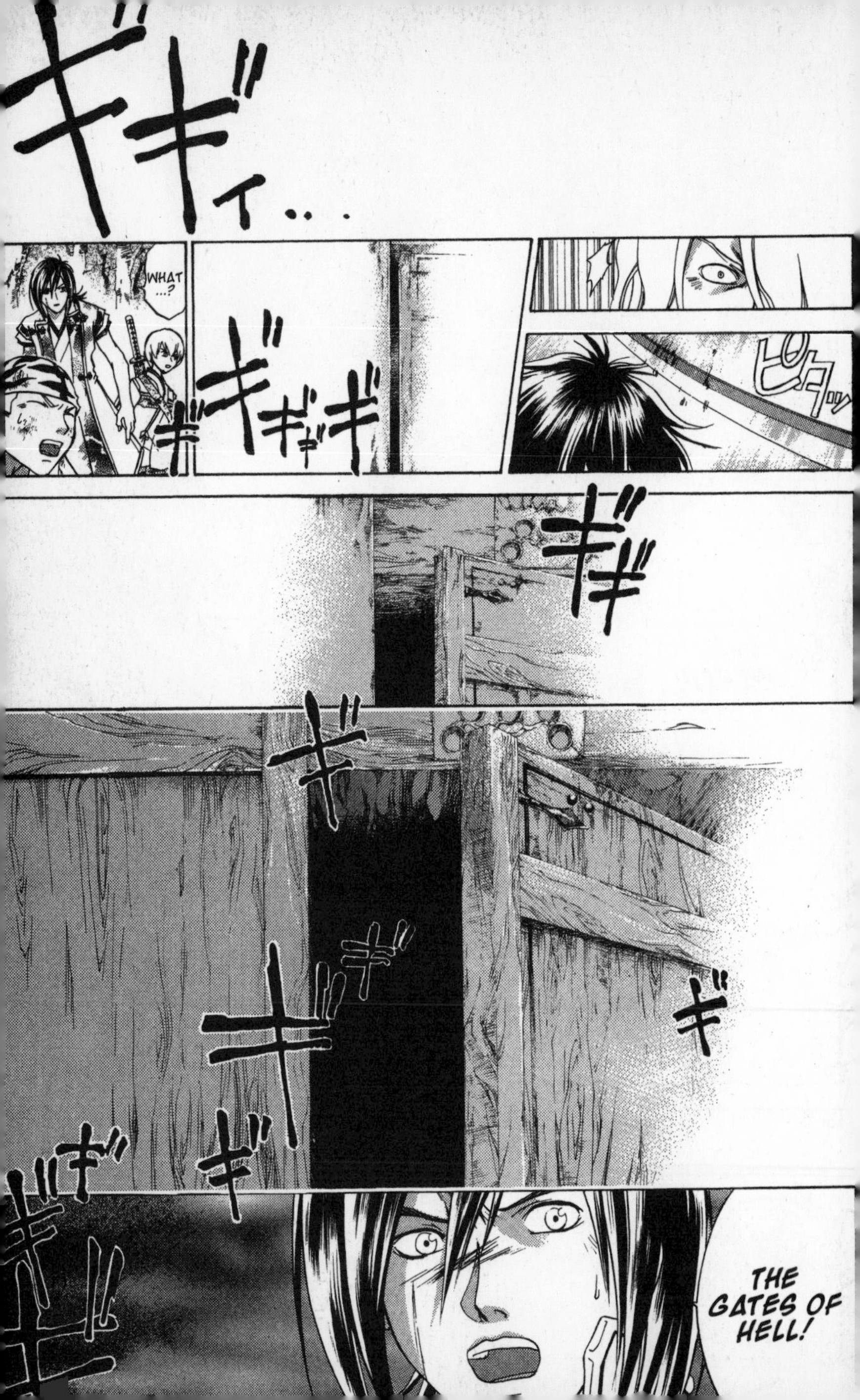
ギギィ...
ピクッ
ギギギギ
WHAT ...?
ギギ
ギギ
ギギギギ
ギギギ!!
THE GATES OF HELL!

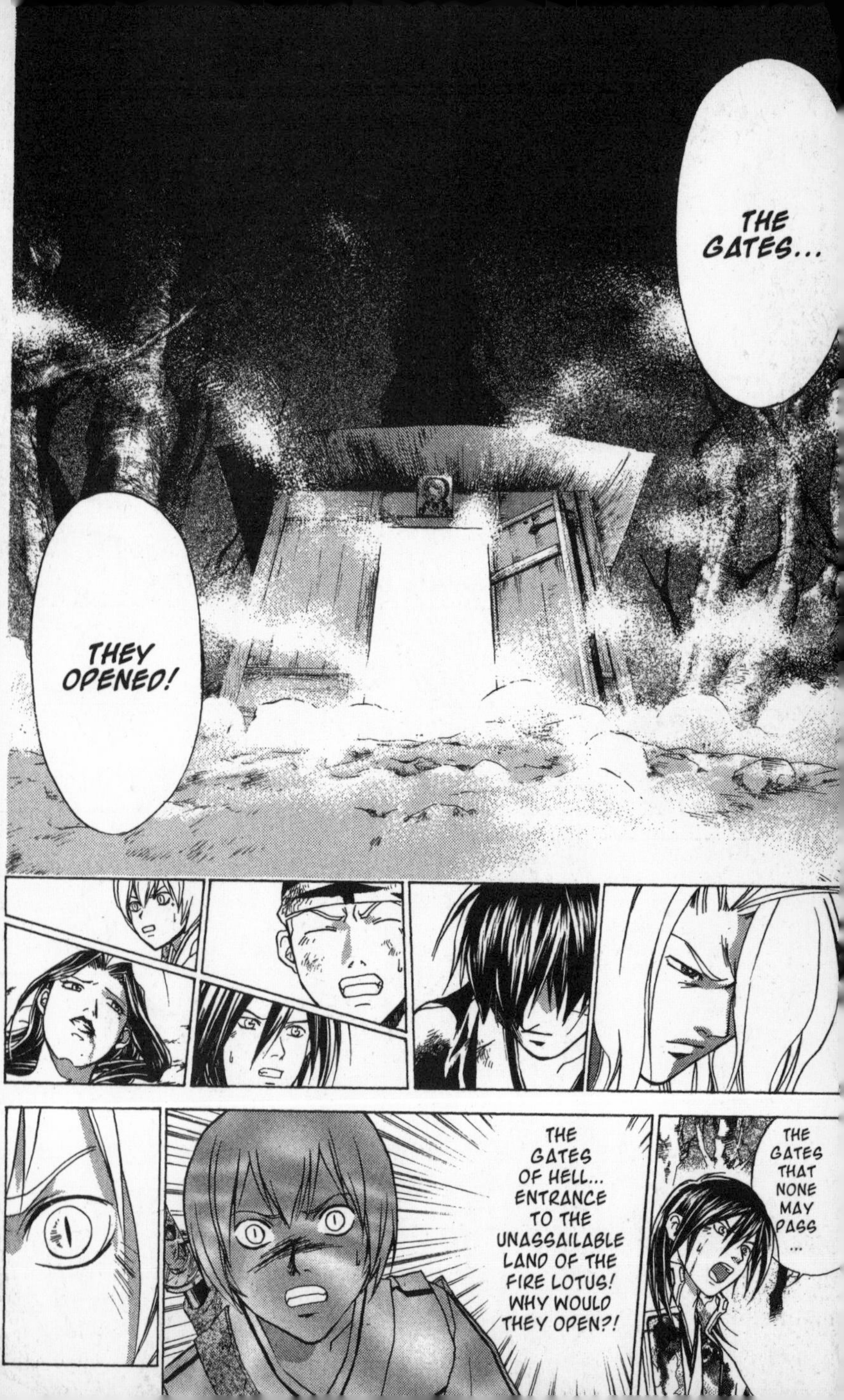
THE GATES...
THEY OPENED!
THE GATES THAT NONE MAY PASS ...
THE GATES OF HELL... ENTRANCE TO THE UNASSAILABLE LAND OF THE FIRE LOTUS! WHY WOULD THEY OPEN?!

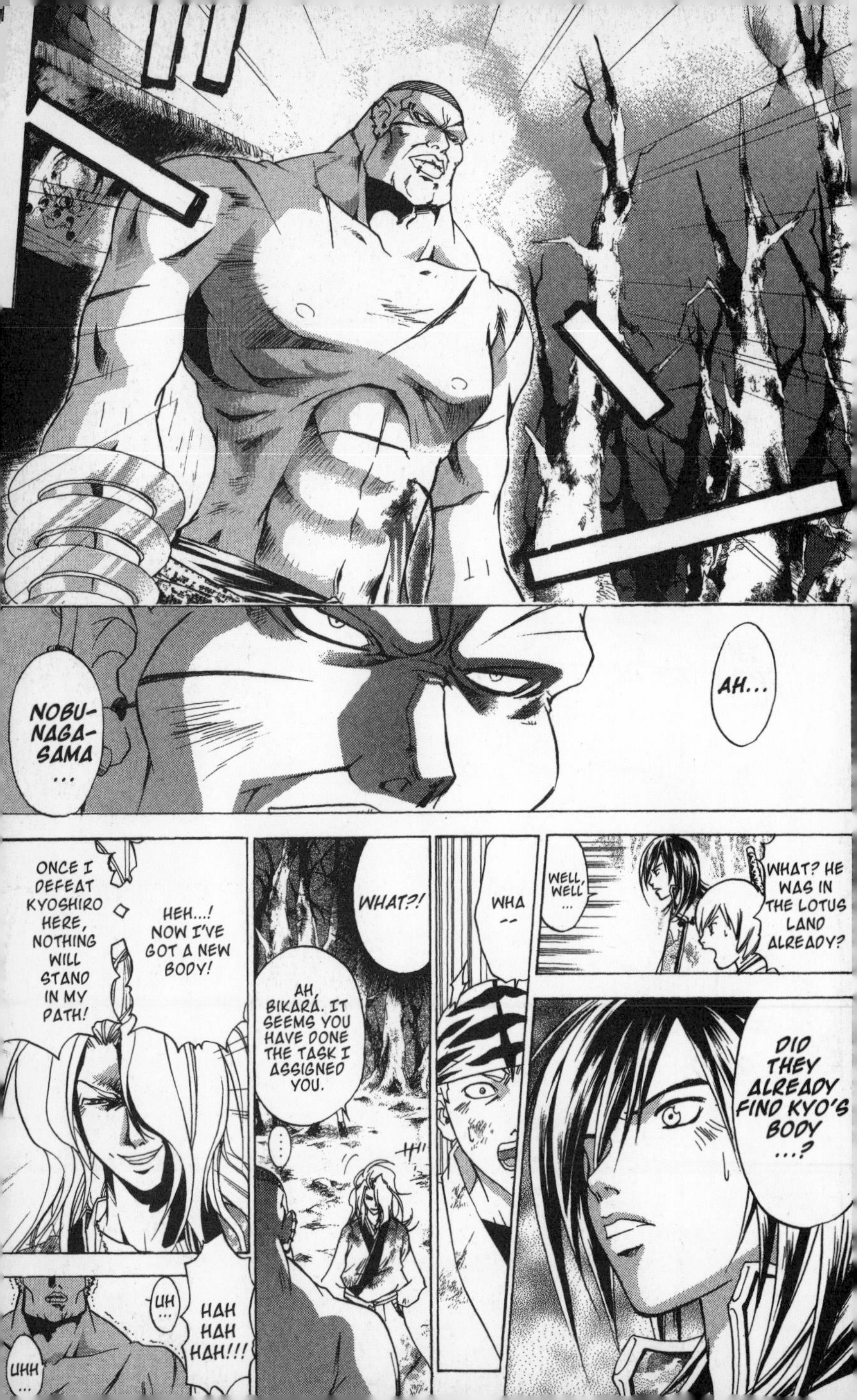
AH...
NOBUNAGA-SAMA...
WHAT? HE WAS IN THE LOTUS LAND ALREADY?
WELL, WELL...
DID THEY ALREADY FIND KYO'S BODY...?
WHA--
WHAT?!
AH, BIKARÁ. IT SEEMS YOU HAVE DONE THE TASK I ASSIGNED YOU.
...
HEH...! NOW I'VE GOT A NEW BODY!
ONCE I DEFEAT KYOSHIRO HERE, NOTHING WILL STAND IN MY PATH!
HAH HAH HAH!!!
UH...
UHH...

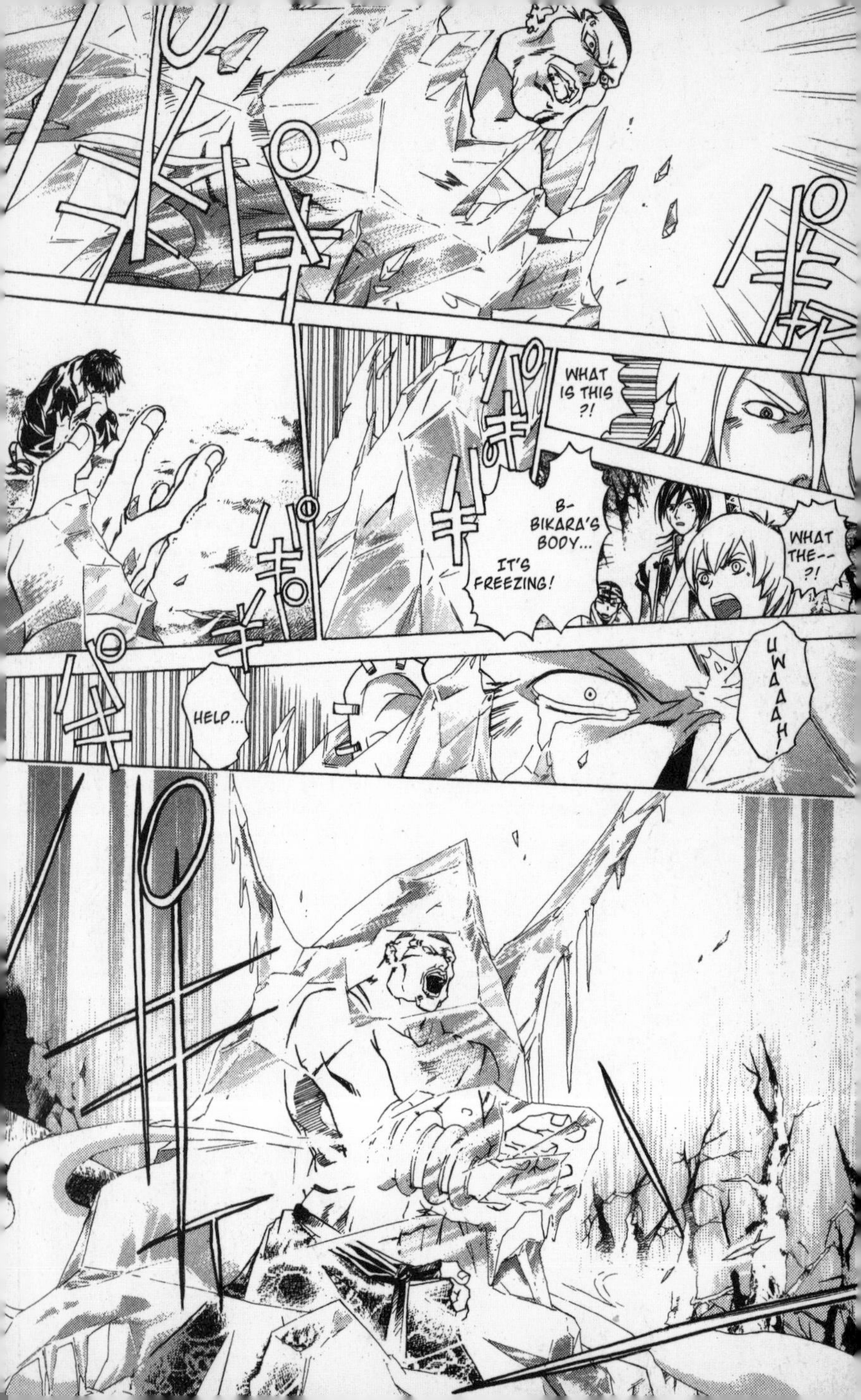
WHAT IS THIS ?!
WHAT THE--?!
B-BIKARA'S BODY...
IT'S FREEZING!
UWAAAH!
HELP...

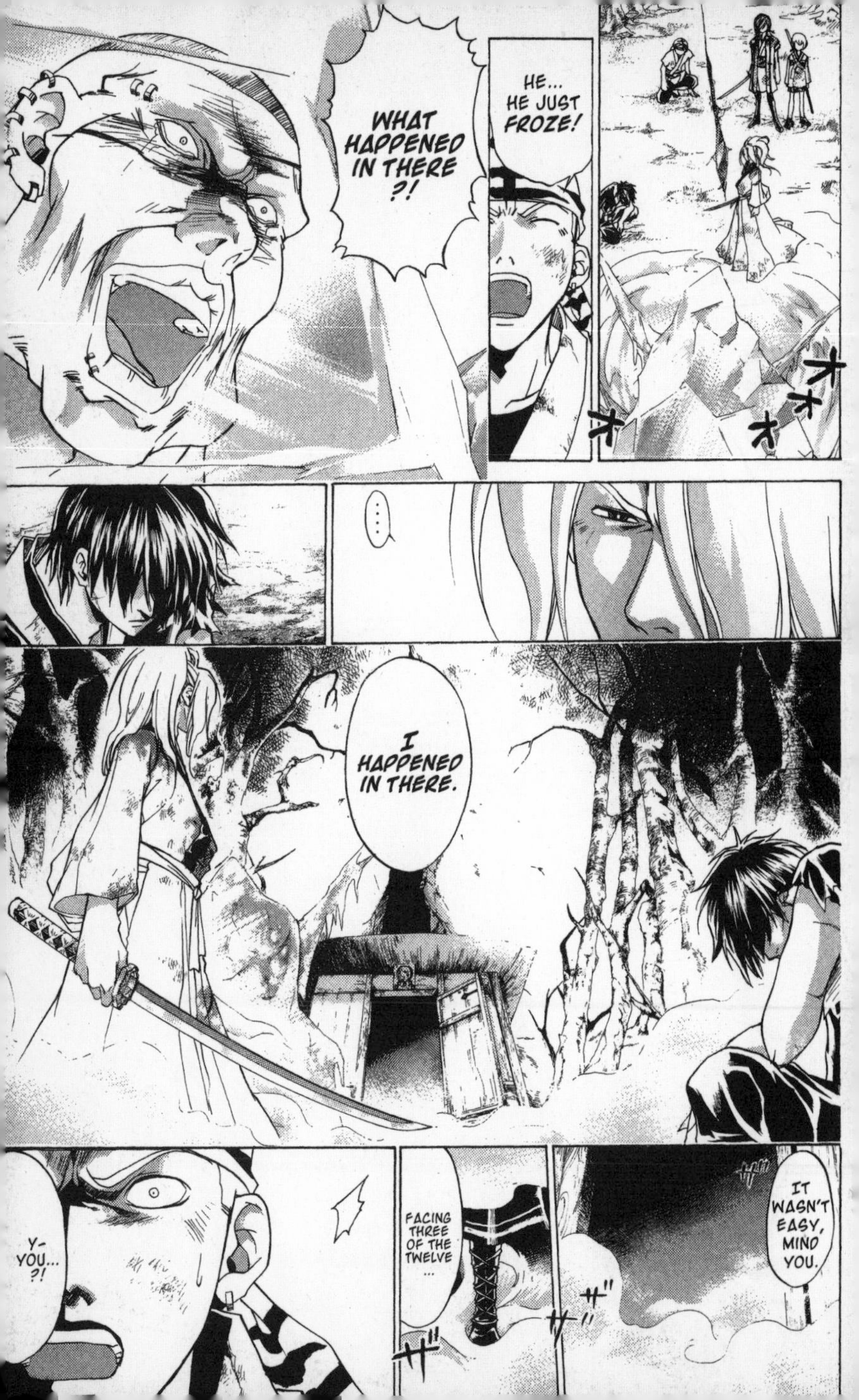
HE... HE JUST FROZE!
WHAT HAPPENED IN THERE?!
....
I HAPPENED IN THERE.
IT WASN'T EASY, MIND YOU.
FACING THREE OF THE TWELVE ...
Y-YOU...?!

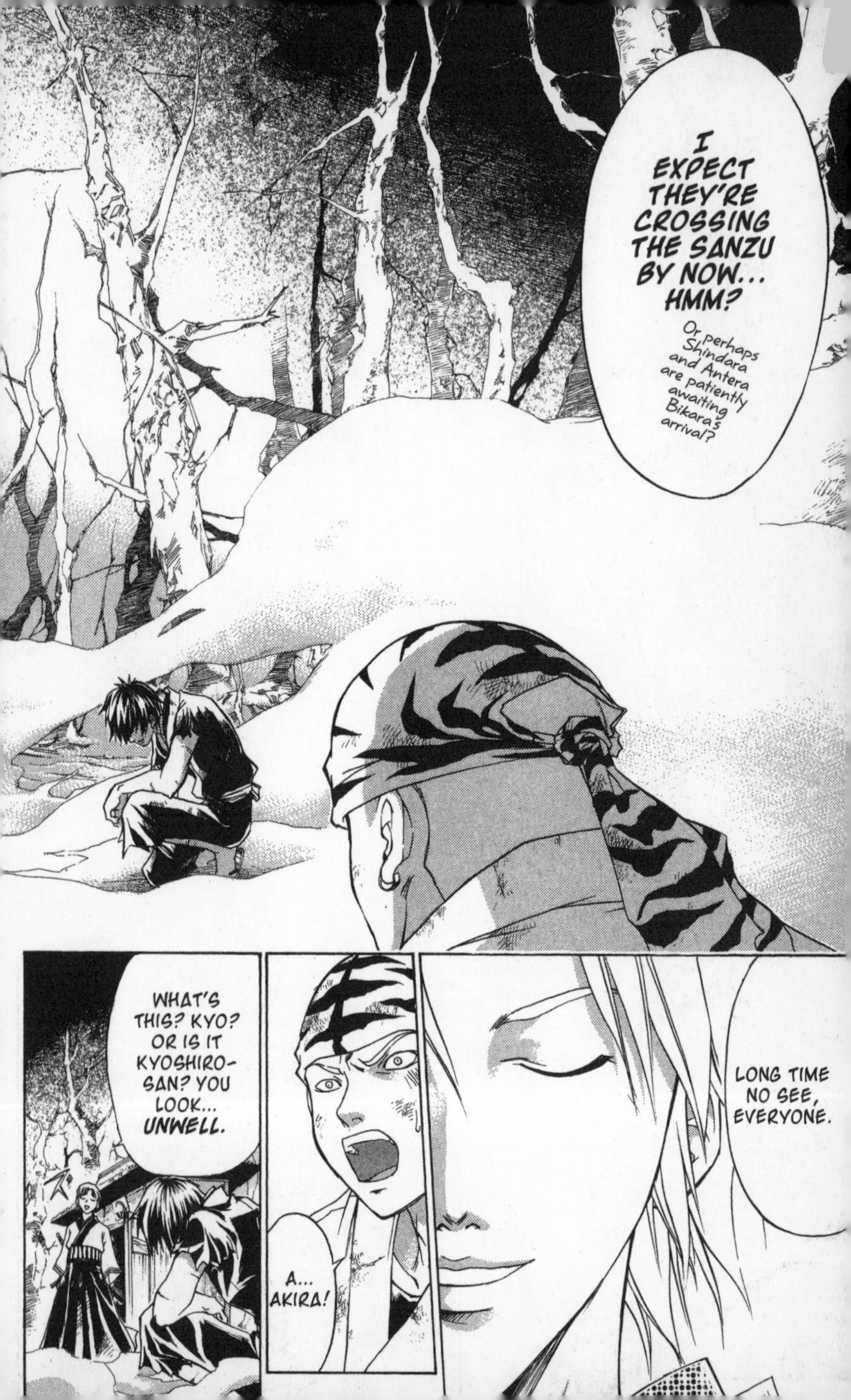
I EXPECT THEY'RE CROSSING THE SANZU BY NOW... HMM?
Or perhaps Shindara and Antera are patiently awaiting Bikara's arrival?
LONG TIME NO SEE, EVERYONE.
A... AKIRA!
WHAT'S THIS? KYO? OR IS IT KYOSHIRO-SAN? YOU LOOK... **UNWELL.**

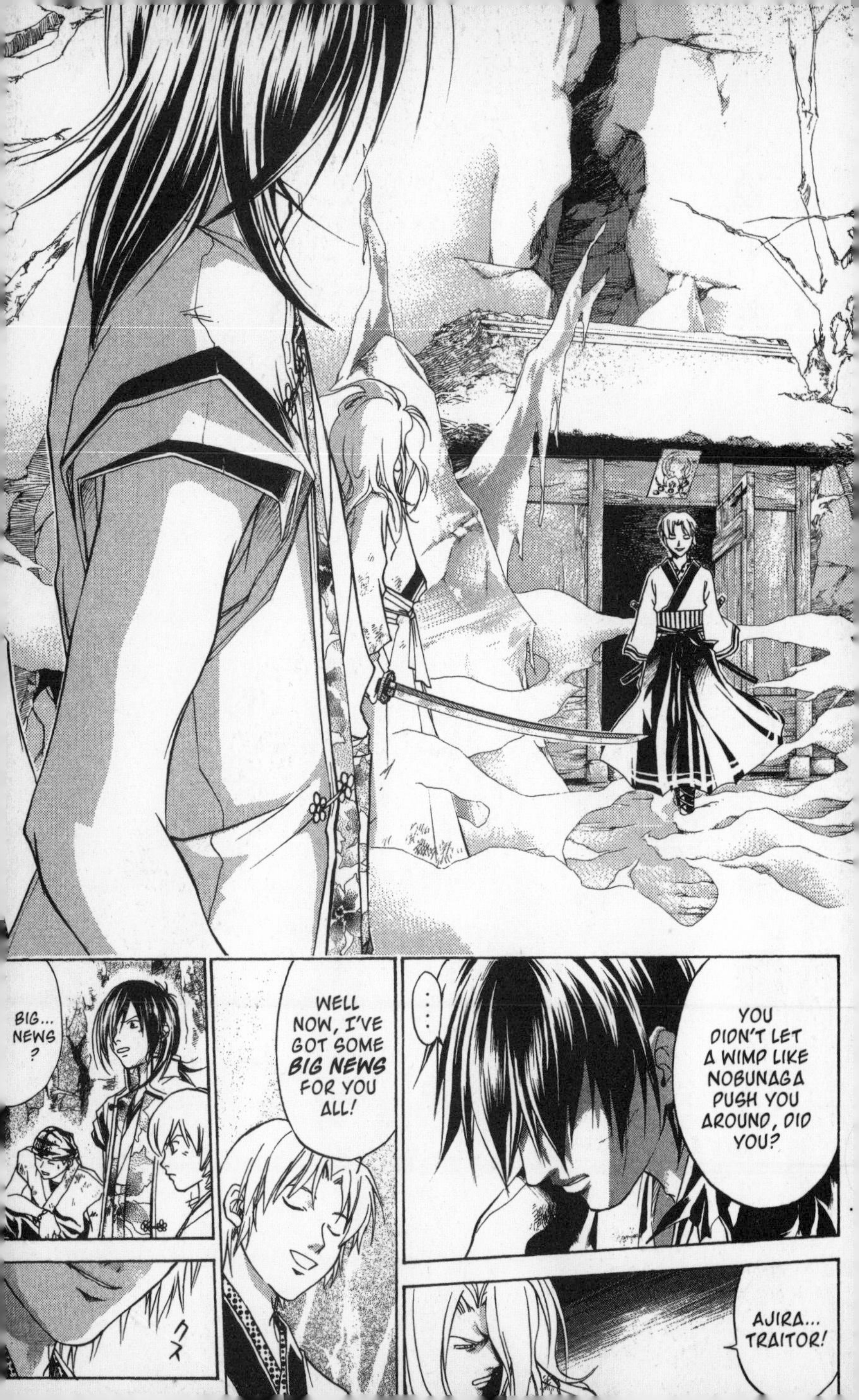
...
YOU DIDN'T LET A WIMP LIKE NOBUNAGA PUSH YOU AROUND, DID YOU?
AJIRA... TRAITOR!
WELL NOW, I'VE GOT SOME **BIG NEWS** FOR YOU ALL!
BIG... NEWS?
クス

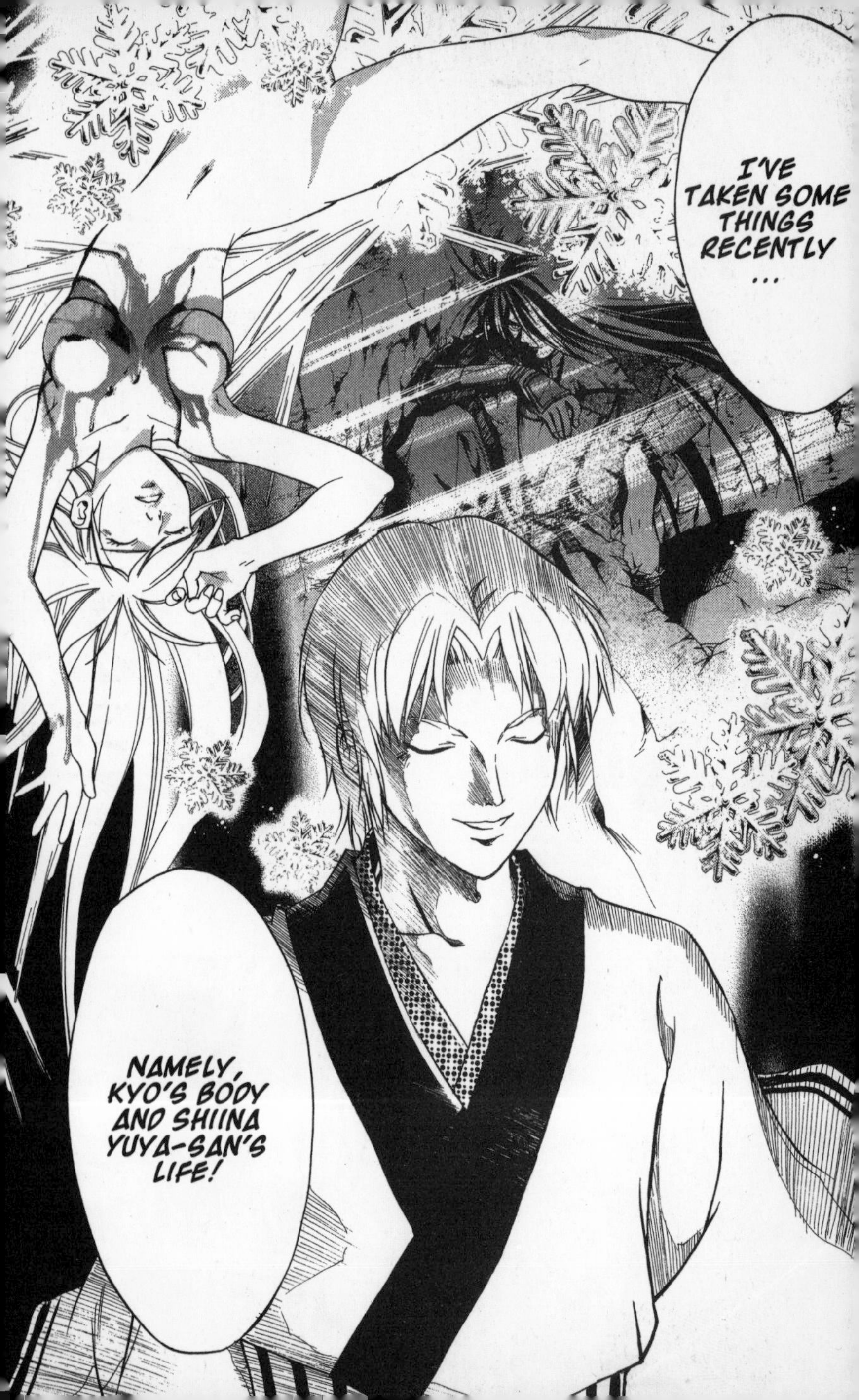
I'VE TAKEN SOME THINGS RECENTLY ...
NAMELY, KYO'S BODY AND SHIINA YUYA-SAN'S LIFE!

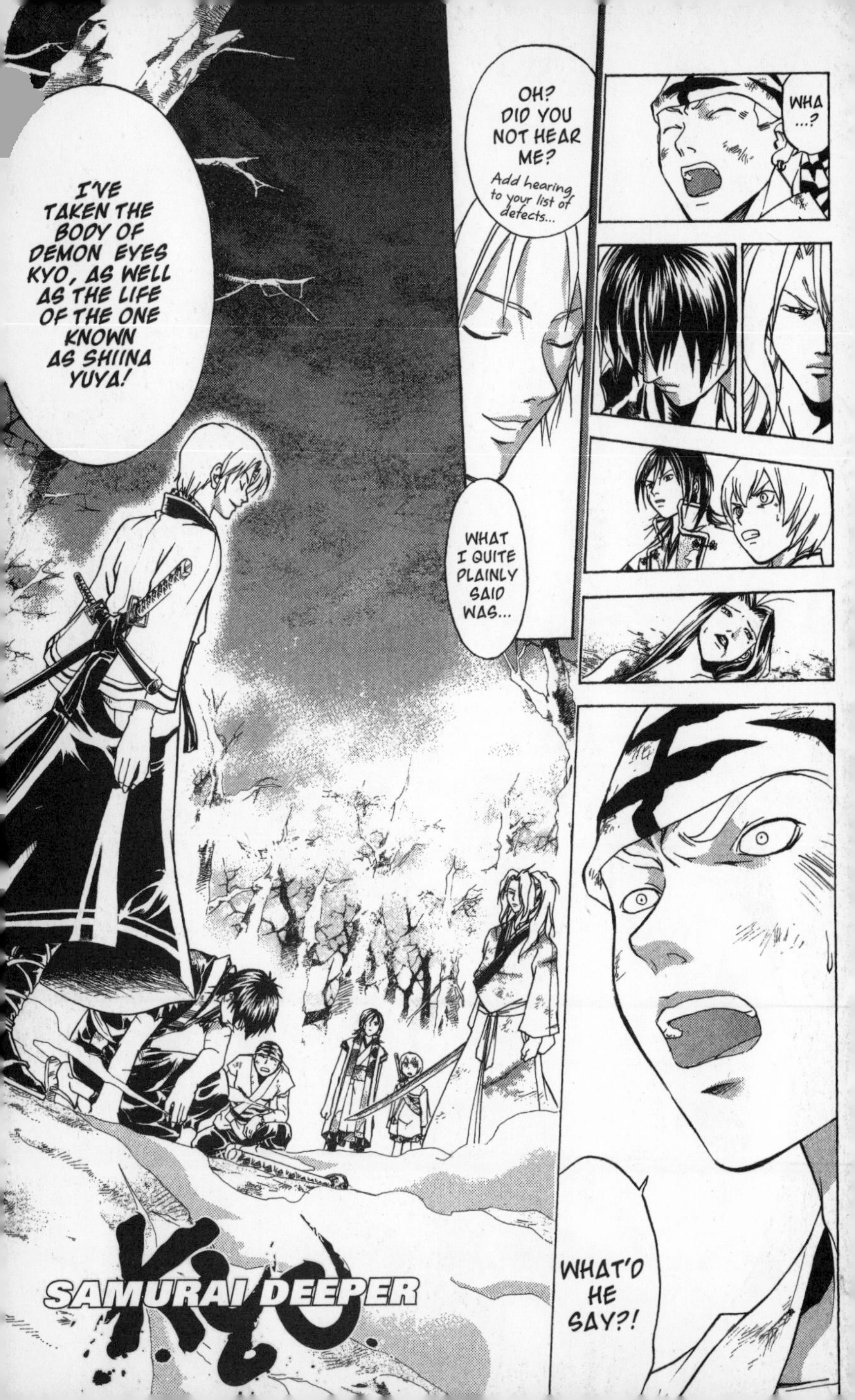
WHA ...?
WHAT'D HE SAY?!
OH? DID YOU NOT HEAR ME?
Add hearing to your list of defects...
WHAT I QUITE PLAINLY SAID WAS...
I'VE TAKEN THE BODY OF DEMON EYES KYO, AS WELL AS THE LIFE OF THE ONE KNOWN AS SHIINA YUYA!
SAMURAI DEEPER KYO

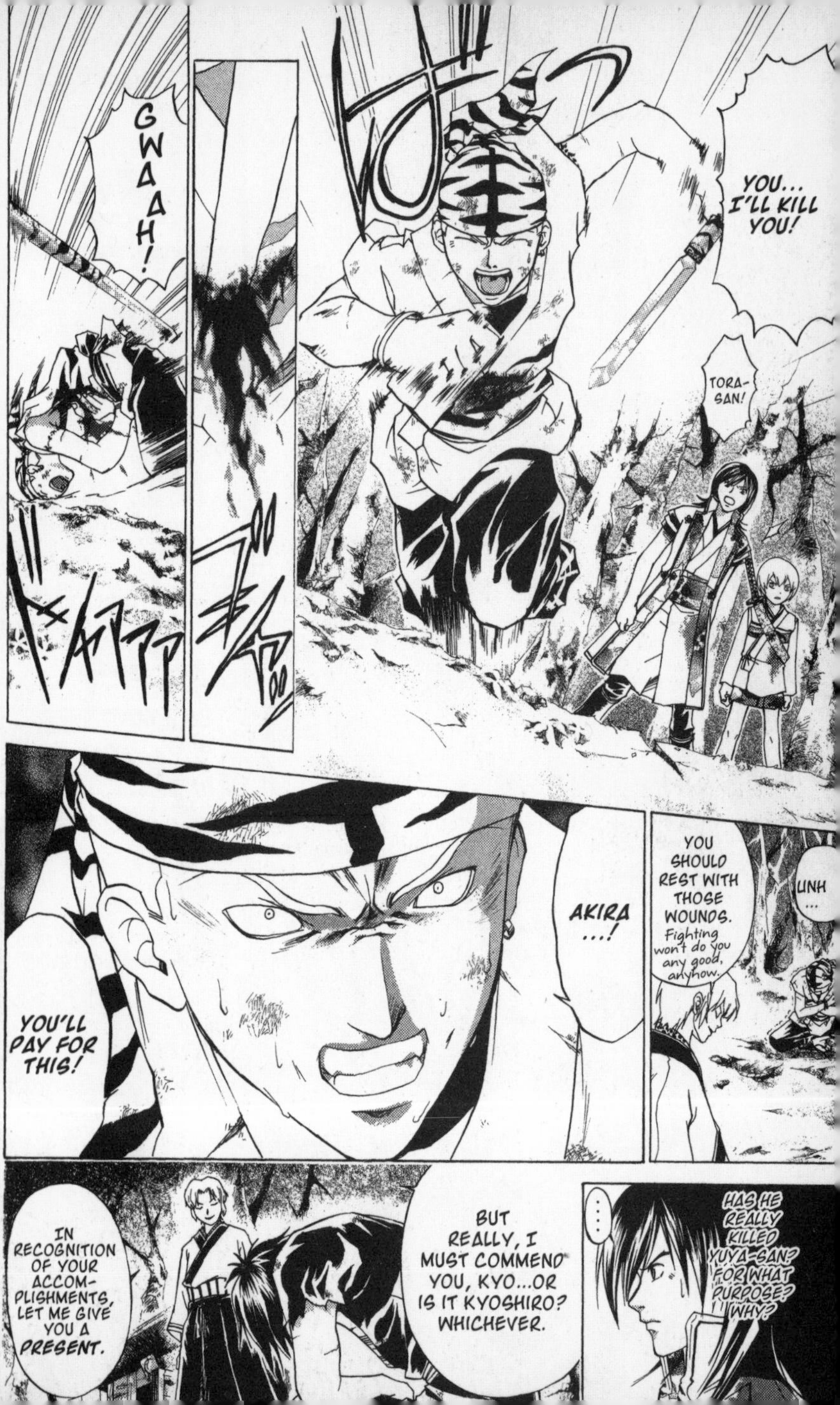
YOU... I'LL KILL YOU!
TORA-SAN!
GWAAAH!
UNH ...
YOU SHOULD REST WITH THOSE WOUNDS. Fighting won't do you any good, anyhow.
AKIRA ...!
YOU'LL PAY FOR THIS!
....
HAS HE REALLY KILLED YUYA-SAN? FOR WHAT PURPOSE? WHY?
BUT REALLY, I MUST COMMEND YOU, KYO...OR IS IT KYOSHIRO? WHICHEVER.
IN RECOGNITION OF YOUR ACCOMPLISHMENTS, LET ME GIVE YOU A PRESENT.

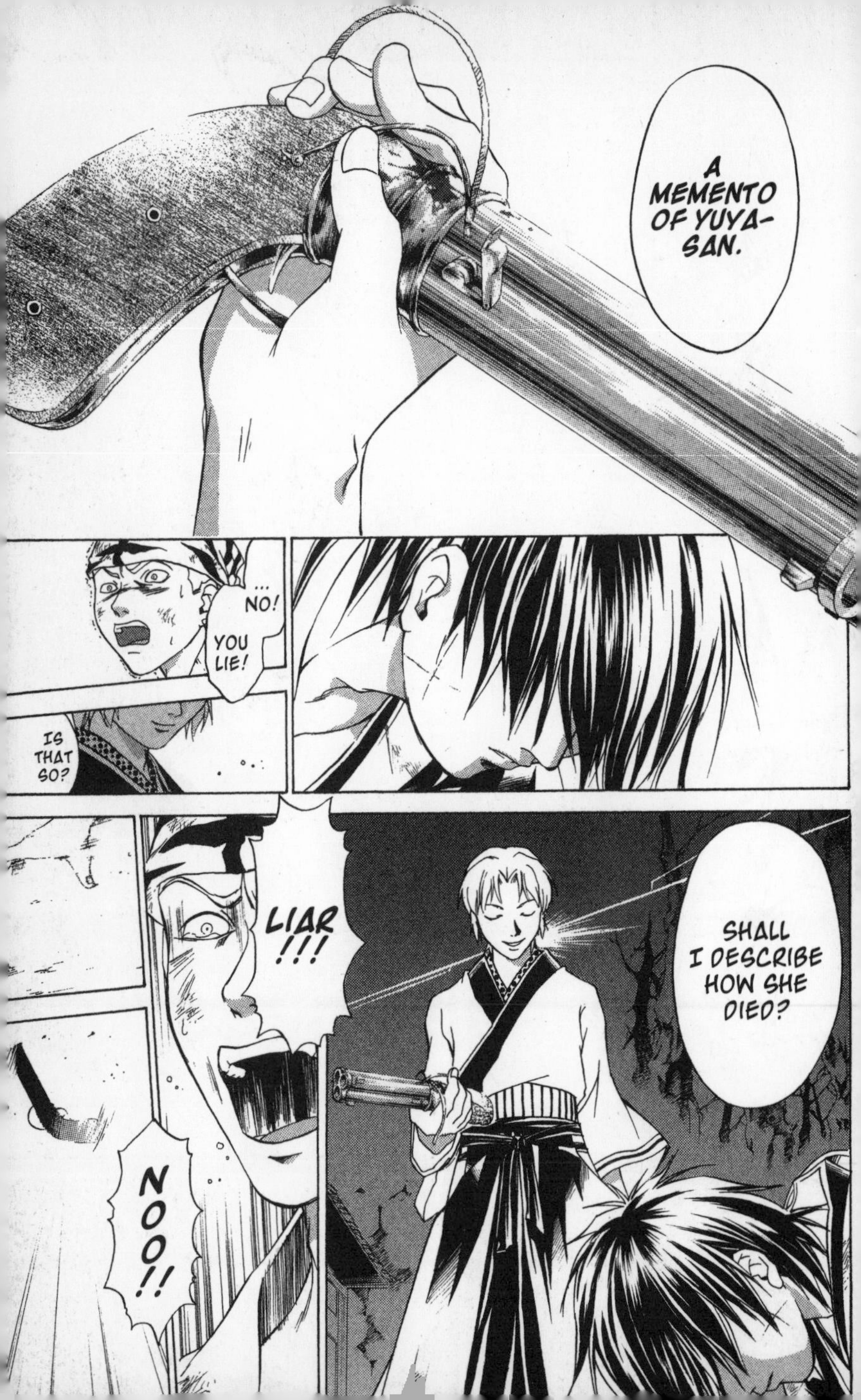
A MEMENTO OF YUYA-SAN.
... NO! YOU LIE!
IS THAT SO?
SHALL I DESCRIBE HOW SHE DIED?
LIAR!!!
NOOO!!

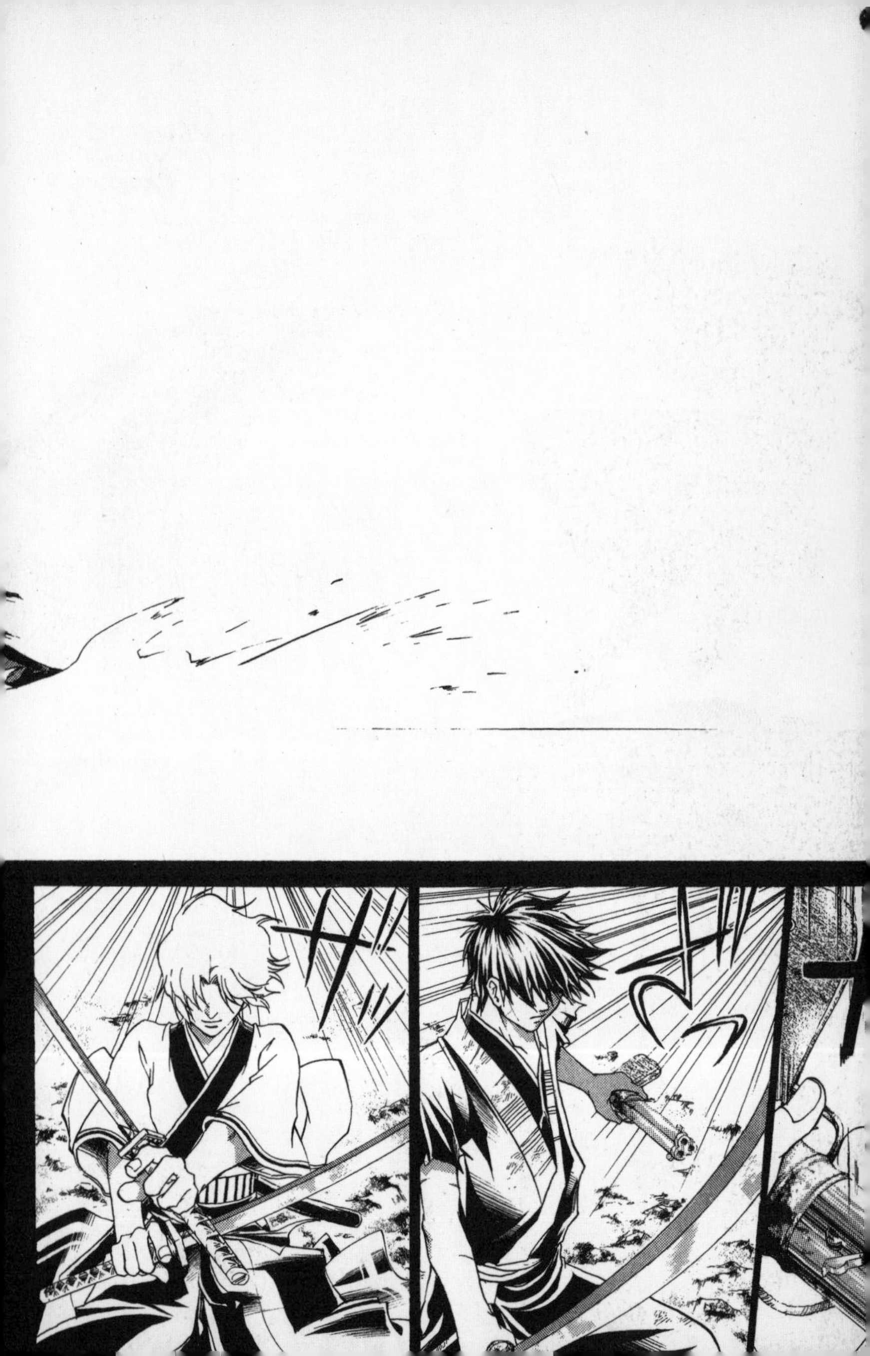

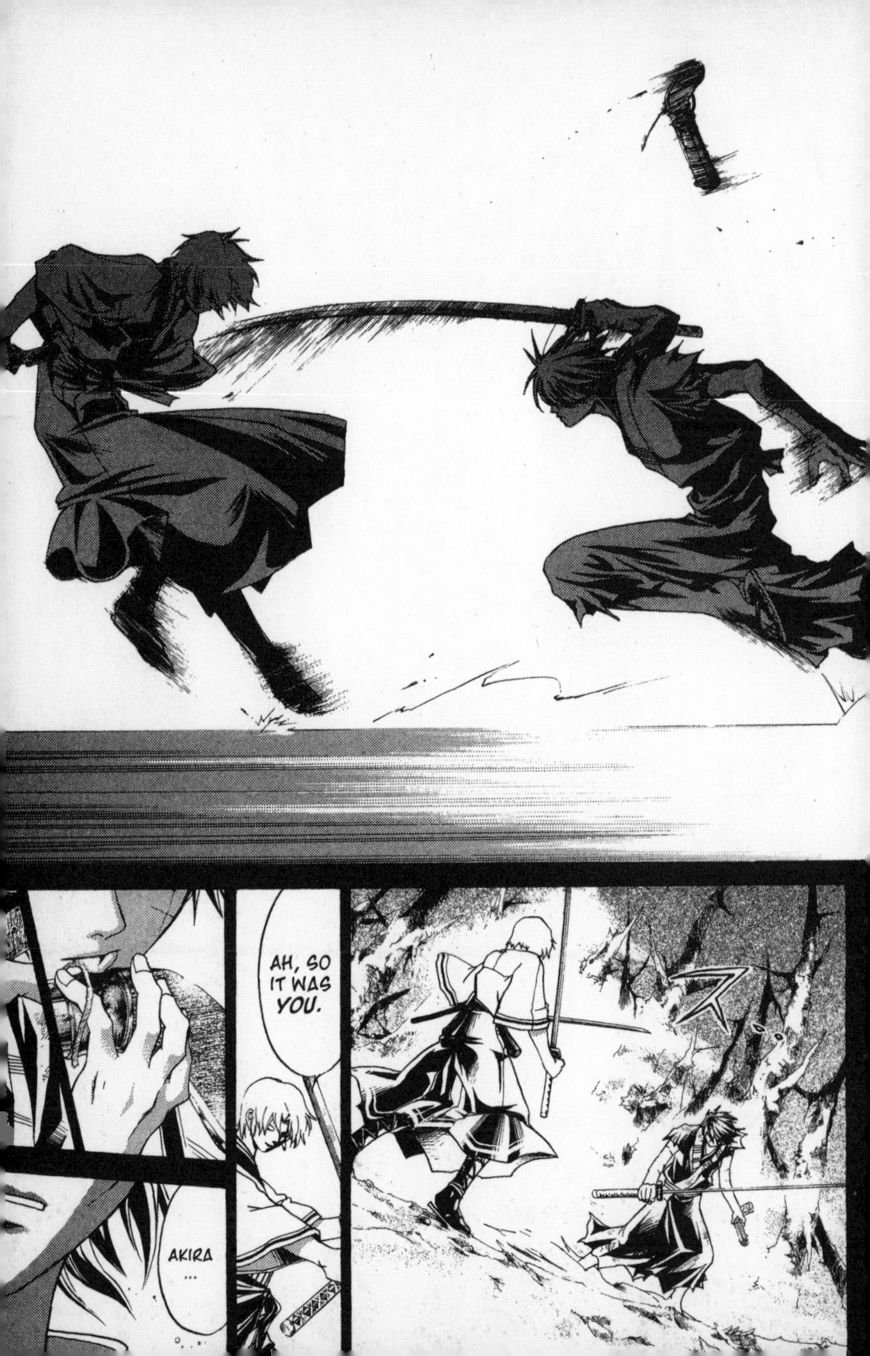
AH, SO IT WAS YOU.
AKIRA ...

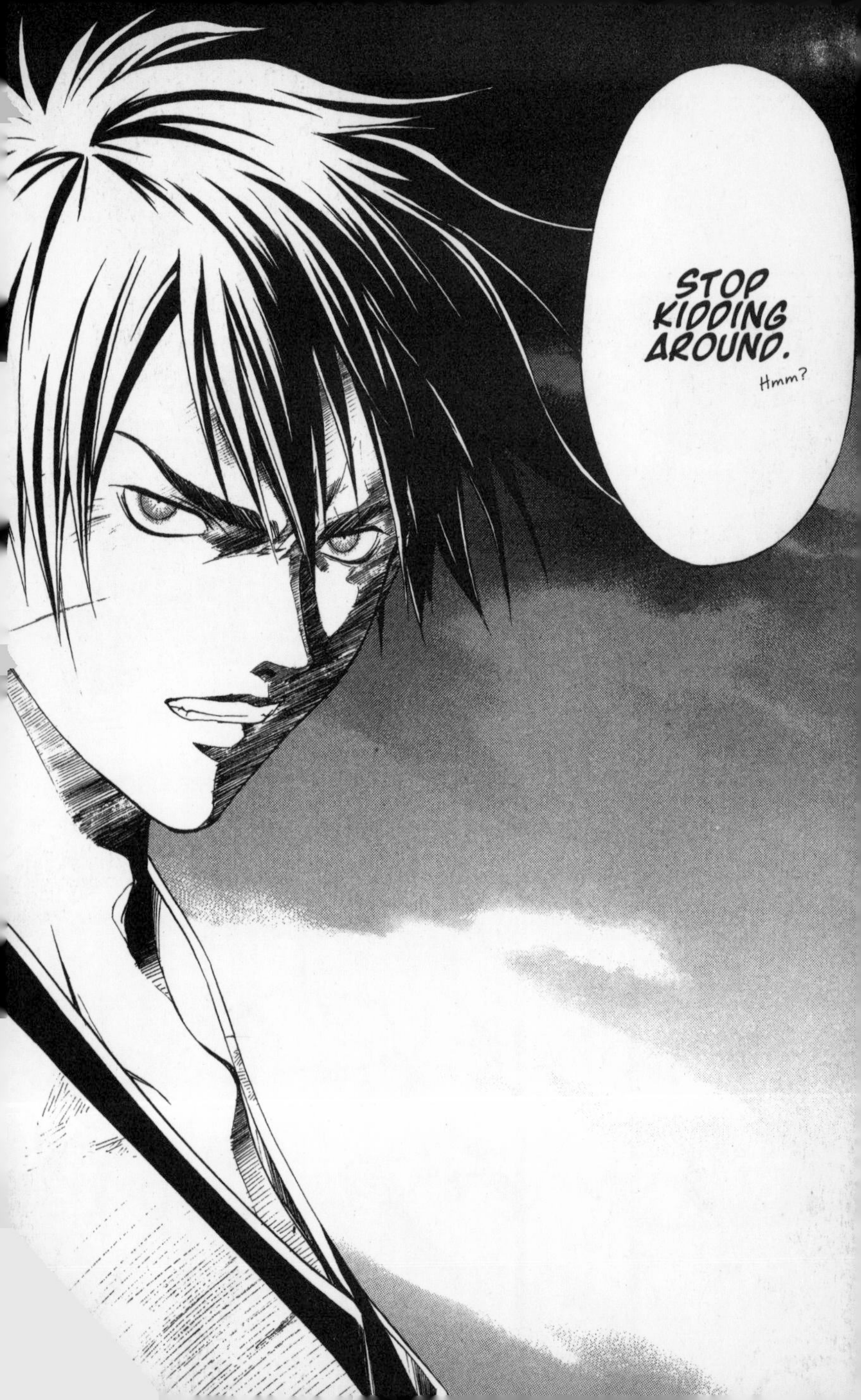
STOP KIDDING AROUND.
Hmm?

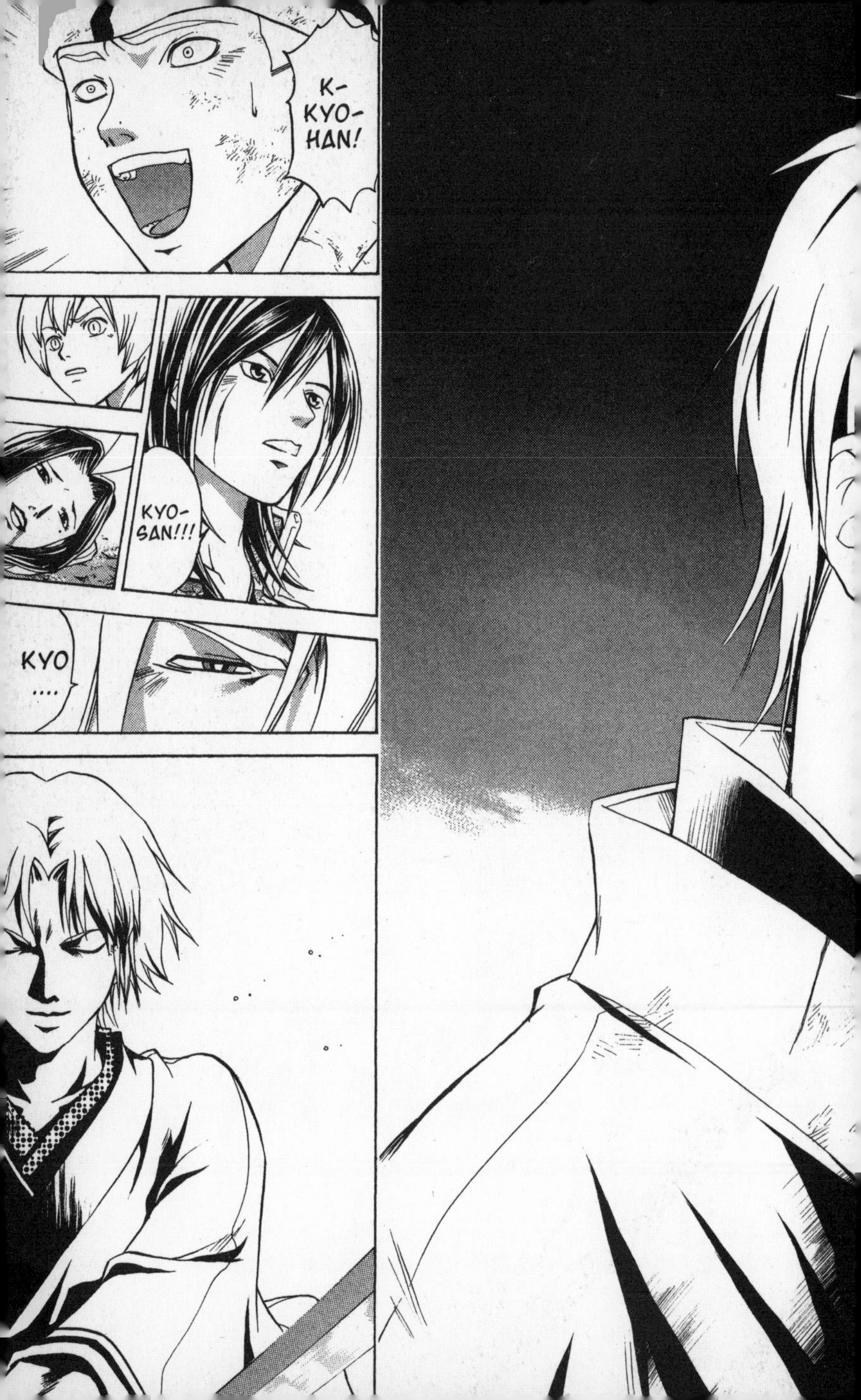
K-KYO-HAN!
KYO-SAN!!!
KYO ....

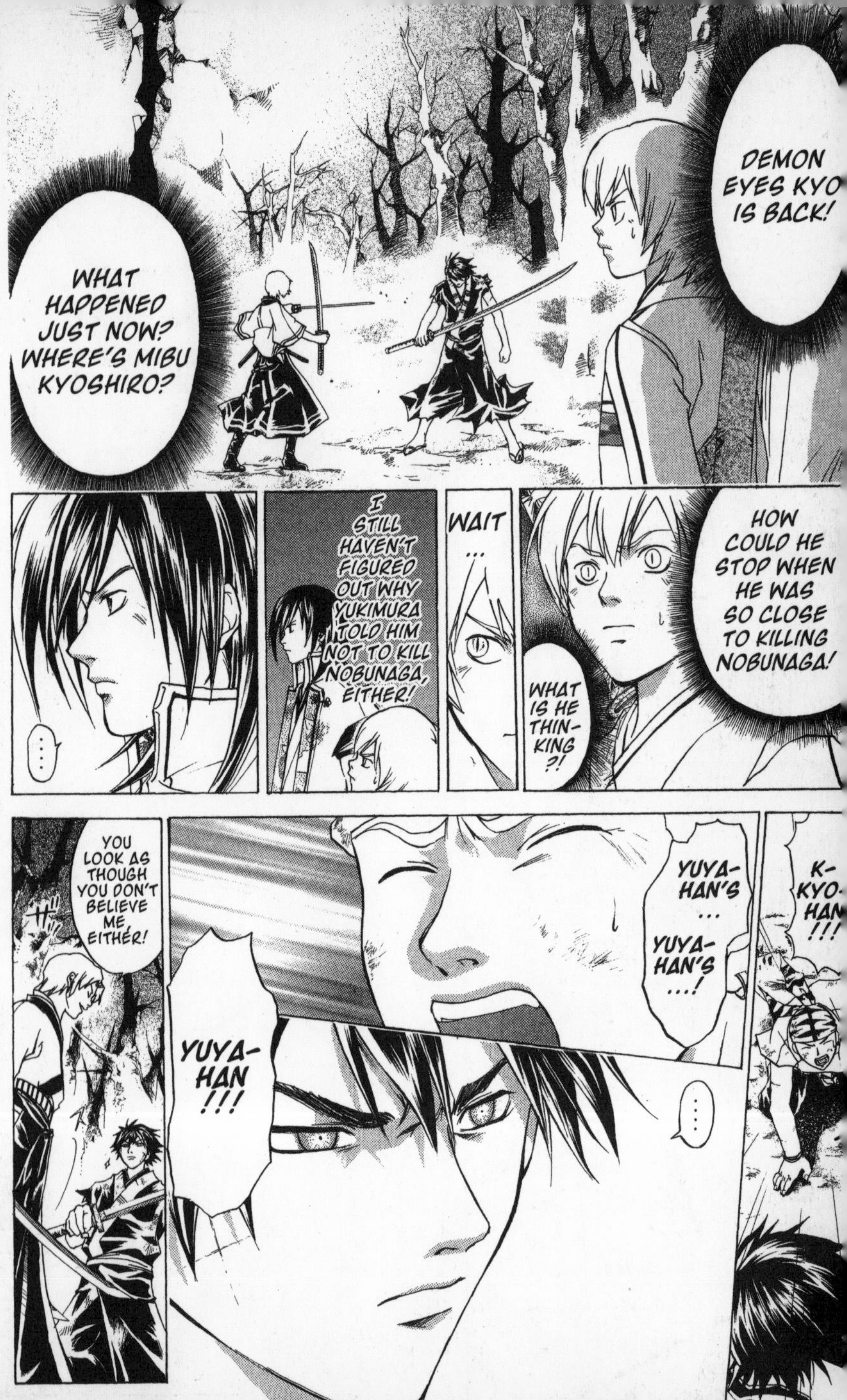
DEMON EYES KYO IS BACK!
WHAT HAPPENED JUST NOW? WHERE'S MIBU KYOSHIRO?
HOW COULD HE STOP WHEN HE WAS SO CLOSE TO KILLING NOBUNAGA!
WHAT IS HE THINKING ?!
WAIT ...
I STILL HAVEN'T FIGURED OUT WHY YUKIMURA TOLD HIM NOT TO KILL NOBUNAGA, EITHER!
....
K-KYO-HAN!!!
YUYA-HAN'S ... YUYA-HAN'S ...!
....
YUYA-HAN!!!
YOU LOOK AS THOUGH YOU DON'T BELIEVE ME EITHER!

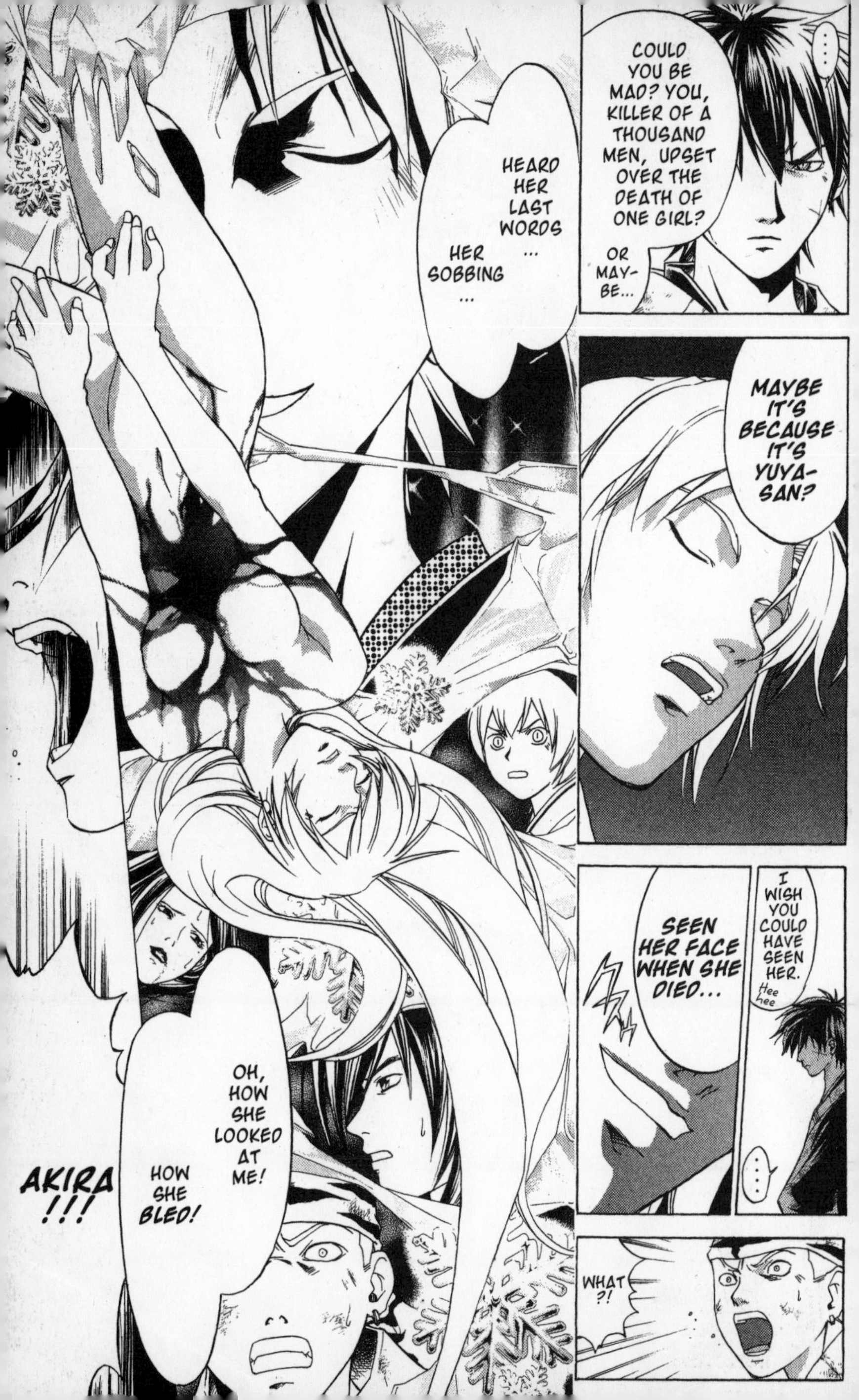

...
COULD YOU BE MAD? YOU, KILLER OF A THOUSAND MEN, UPSET OVER THE DEATH OF ONE GIRL?
OR MAYBE...
MAYBE IT'S BECAUSE IT'S YUYA-SAN?
I WISH YOU COULD HAVE SEEN HER.
Hee hee
SEEN HER FACE WHEN SHE DIED...
...
WHAT ?!
HEARD HER LAST WORDS ...
HER SOBBING ...
OH, HOW SHE LOOKED AT ME!
HOW SHE BLED!
AKIRA !!!

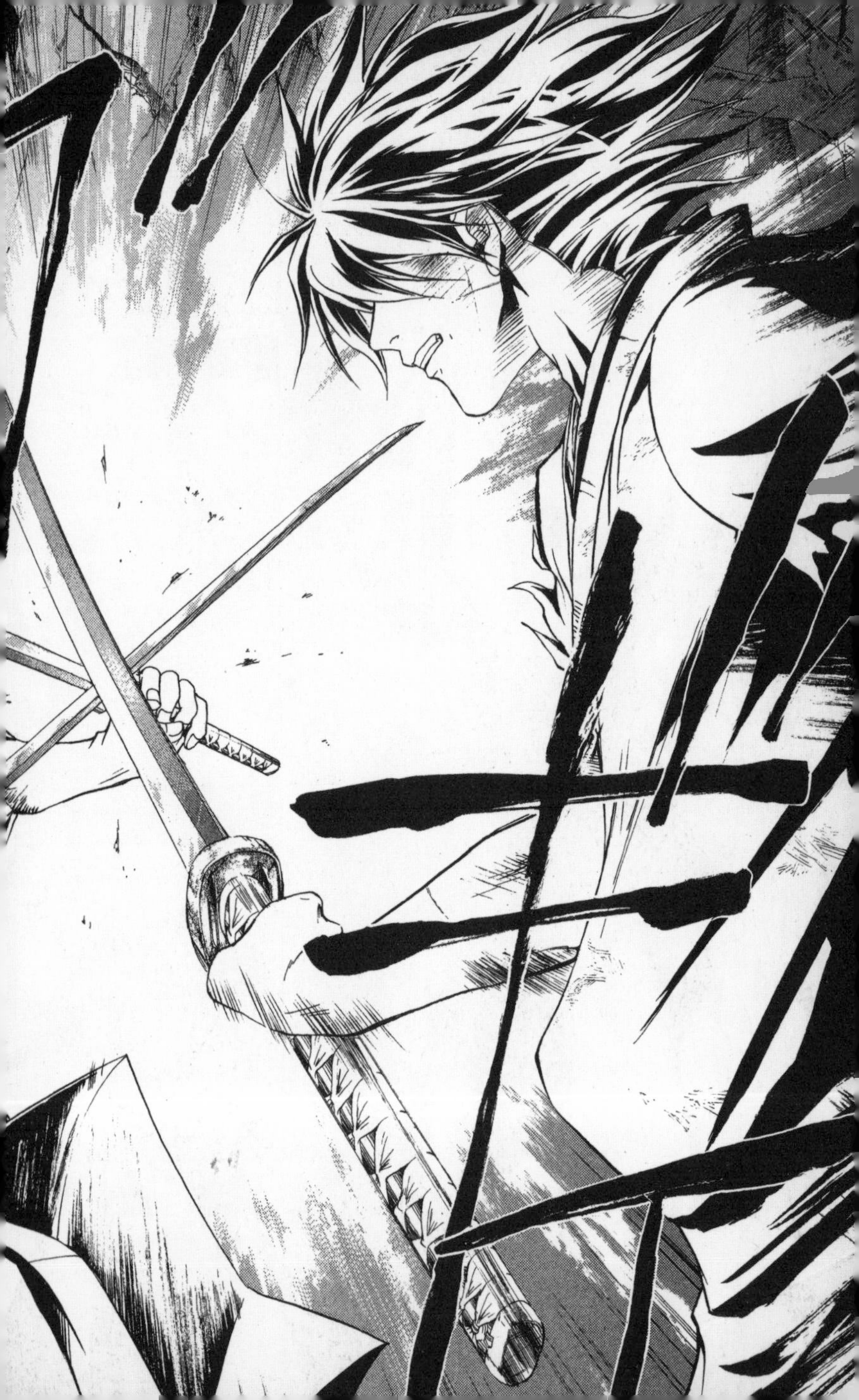

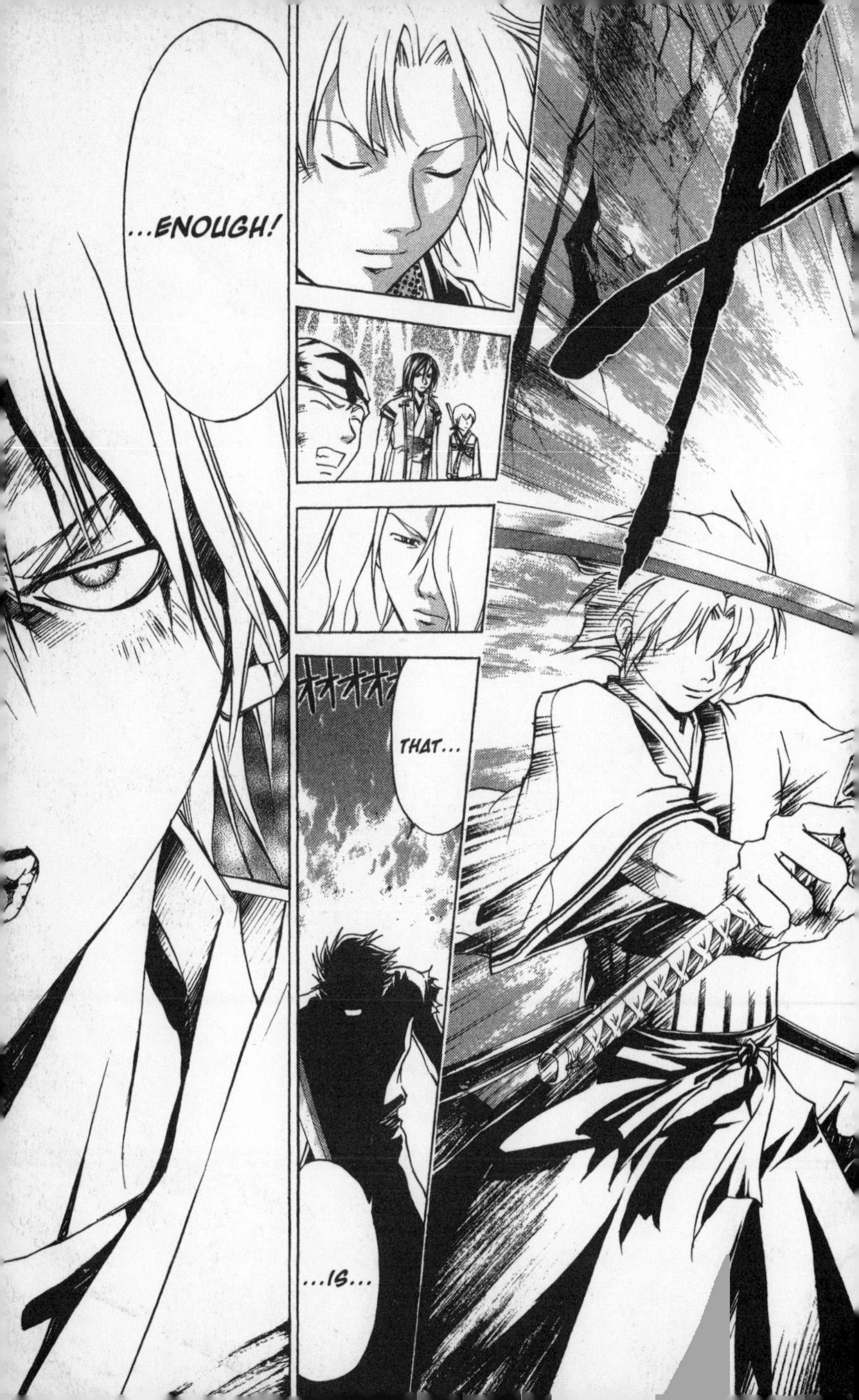
オオオオ
THAT...
...IS...
...ENOUGH!

KYO-SAN.
WHAT'S GOING ON--?
HE WAS NEAR DEATH AFTER THE FIGHT WITH NOBUNAGA ...
BUT NOW...
WHY DO I FEEL THE SAME TERROR NOW THAT I FELT WHEN I SAW THOSE GLOWING CRIMON EYES AT SEKIGAHARA?
IS IT BECAUSE OF YUYA-SAN, AS AKIRA-SAN SAYS? OR IS IT JUST HIS SAMURAI SPIRIT RISING TO MEET A WORTHY ADVERSARY?
AT LAST, RE-SULTS!
I'VE BEEN WAIT-ING.
AND I'M MORE THAN READY!
Heh heh.

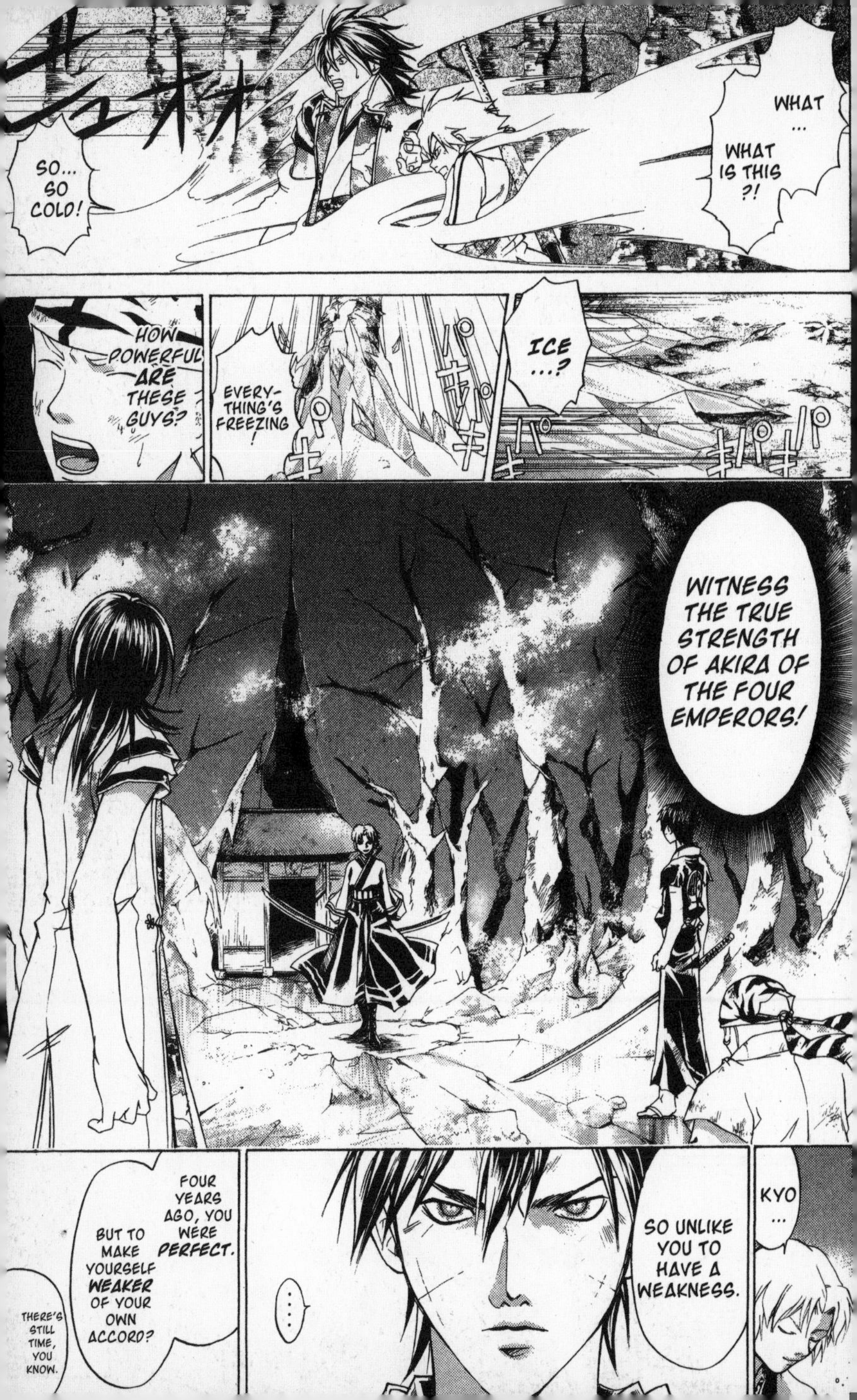
WHAT... WHAT IS THIS?!
SO... SO COLD!
ICE...?
EVERYTHING'S FREEZING!
HOW POWERFUL ARE THESE GUYS?
WITNESS THE TRUE STRENGTH OF AKIRA OF THE FOUR EMPERORS!
KYO...
SO UNLIKE YOU TO HAVE A WEAKNESS.
....
FOUR YEARS AGO, YOU WERE PERFECT.
BUT TO MAKE YOURSELF WEAKER OF YOUR OWN ACCORD?
THERE'S STILL TIME, YOU KNOW.

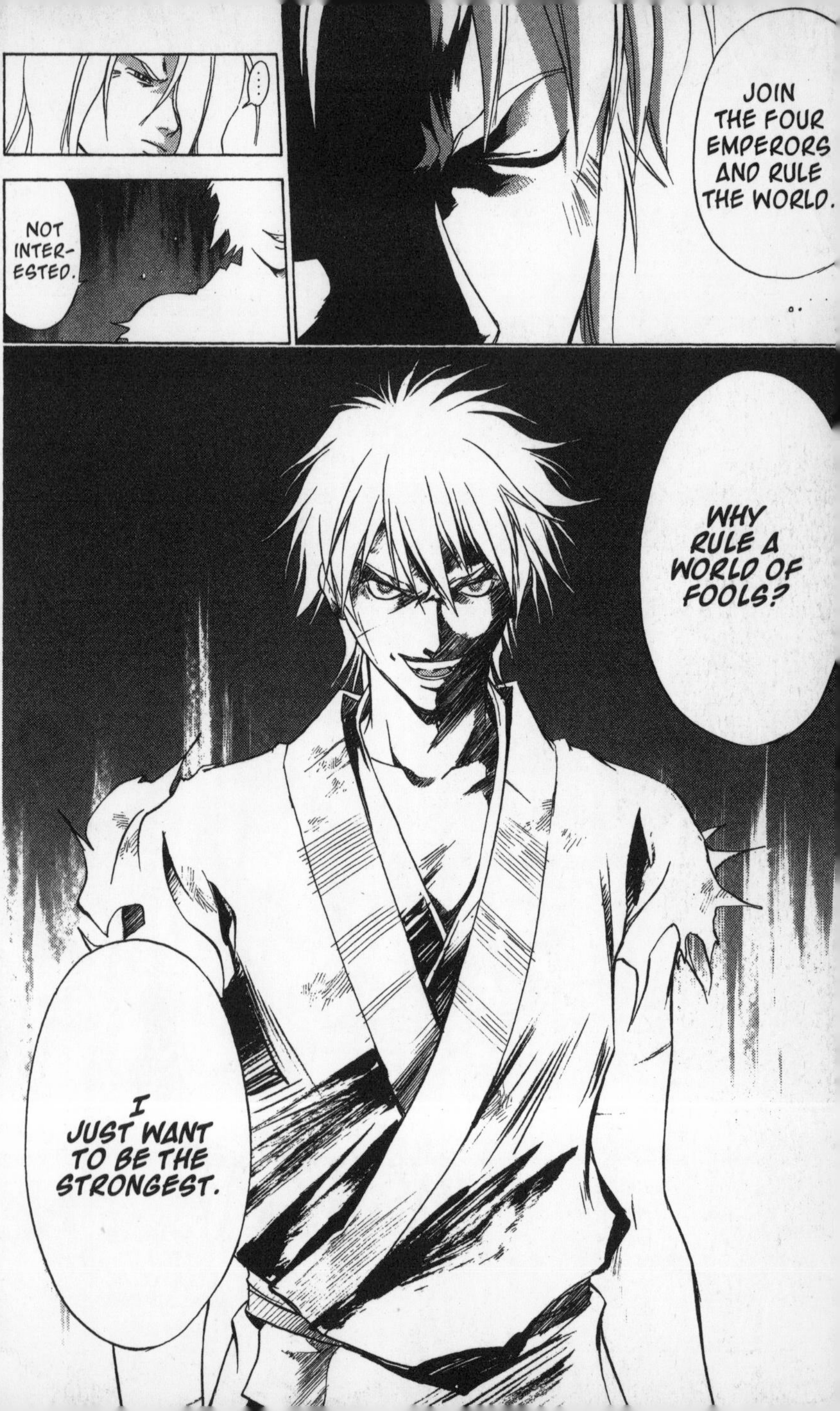

JOIN THE FOUR EMPERORS AND RULE THE WORLD.
...
NOT INTER-ESTED.
WHY RULE A WORLD OF FOOLS?
I JUST WANT TO BE THE STRONGEST.

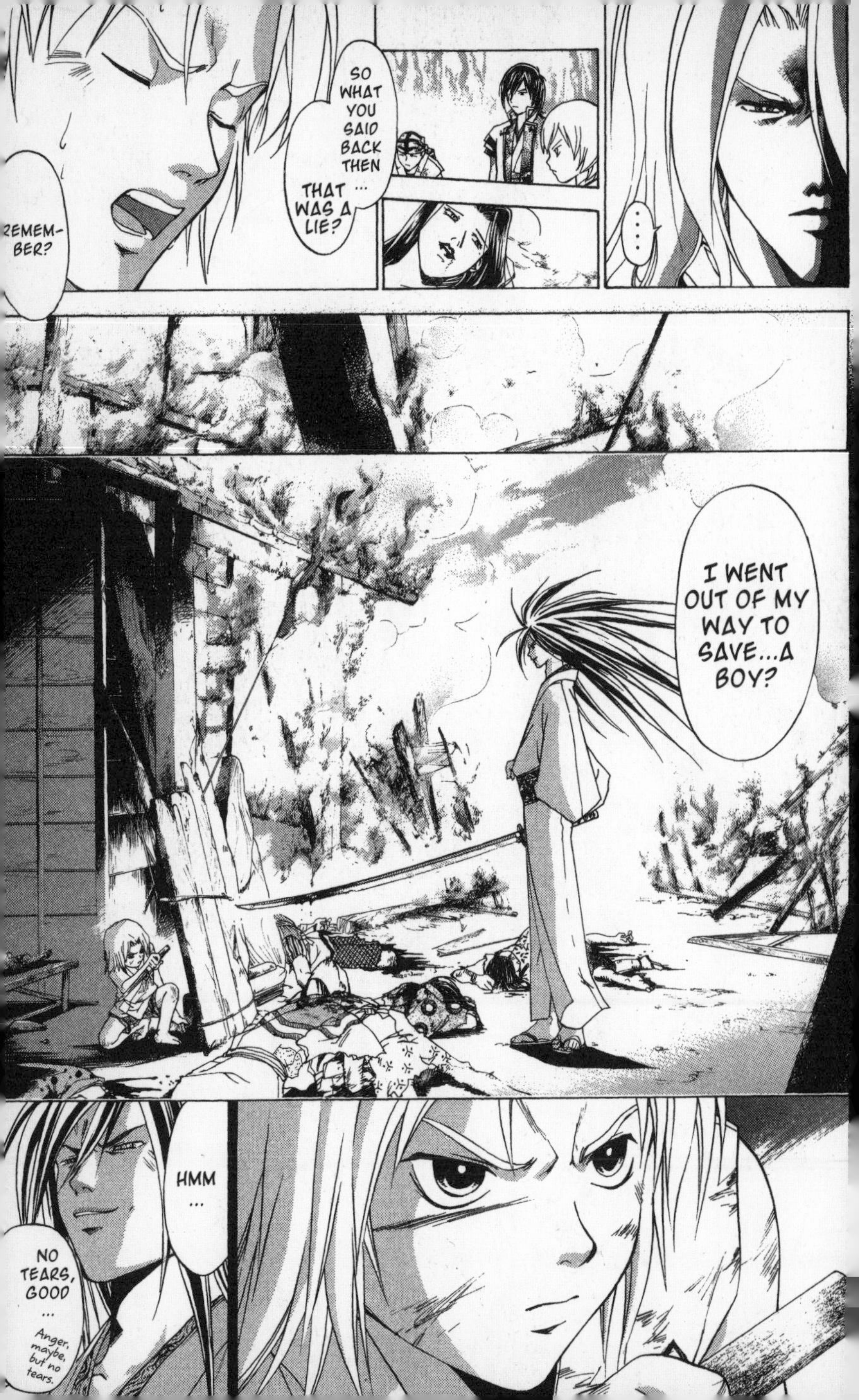

•••
SO WHAT YOU SAID BACK THEN ... THAT WAS A LIE?
REMEMBER?
I WENT OUT OF MY WAY TO SAVE...A BOY?
HMM ...
NO TEARS, GOOD ...
Anger, maybe, but no tears.

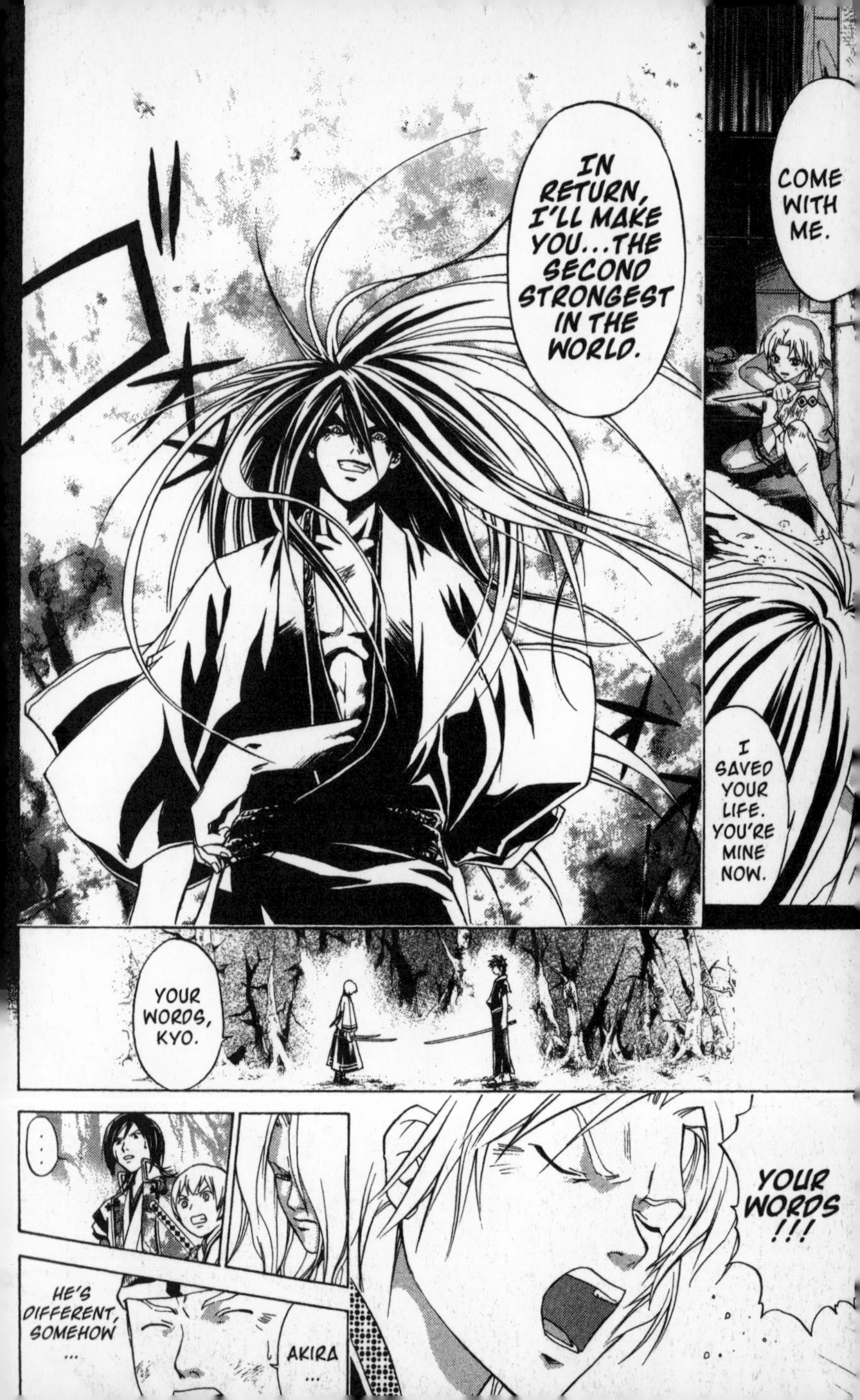

COME WITH ME.
I SAVED YOUR LIFE. YOU'RE MINE NOW.
IN RETURN, I'LL MAKE YOU...THE SECOND STRONGEST IN THE WORLD.
YOUR WORDS, KYO.
YOUR WORDS!!!
...
...
HE'S DIFFERENT, SOMEHOW ...
AKIRA ...

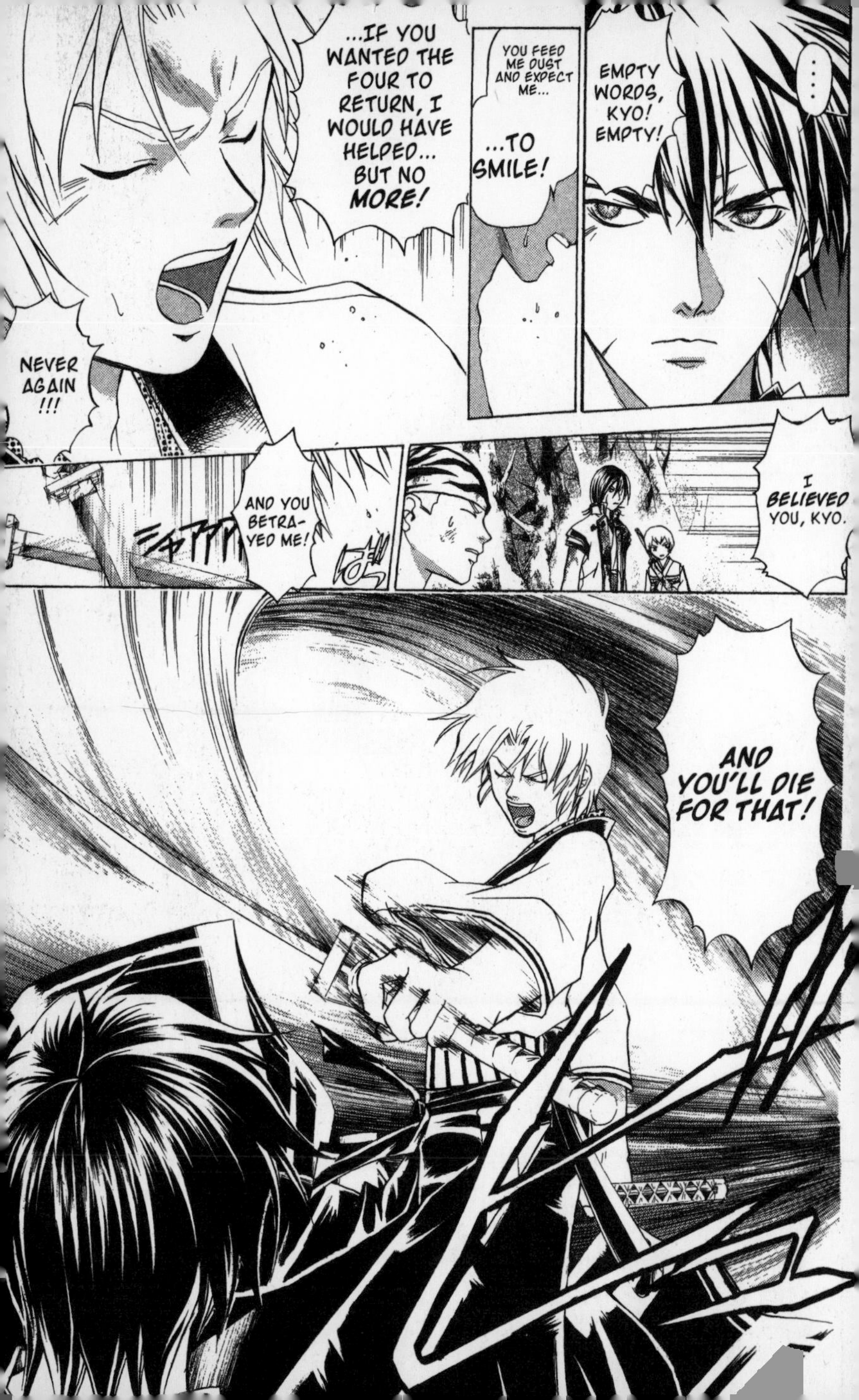
....
EMPTY WORDS, KYO! EMPTY!
YOU FEED ME DUST AND EXPECT ME...
...TO SMILE!
...IF YOU WANTED THE FOUR TO RETURN, I WOULD HAVE HELPED... BUT NO MORE!
NEVER AGAIN!!!
I BELIEVED YOU, KYO.
AND YOU BETRA-YED ME!
AND YOU'LL DIE FOR THAT!

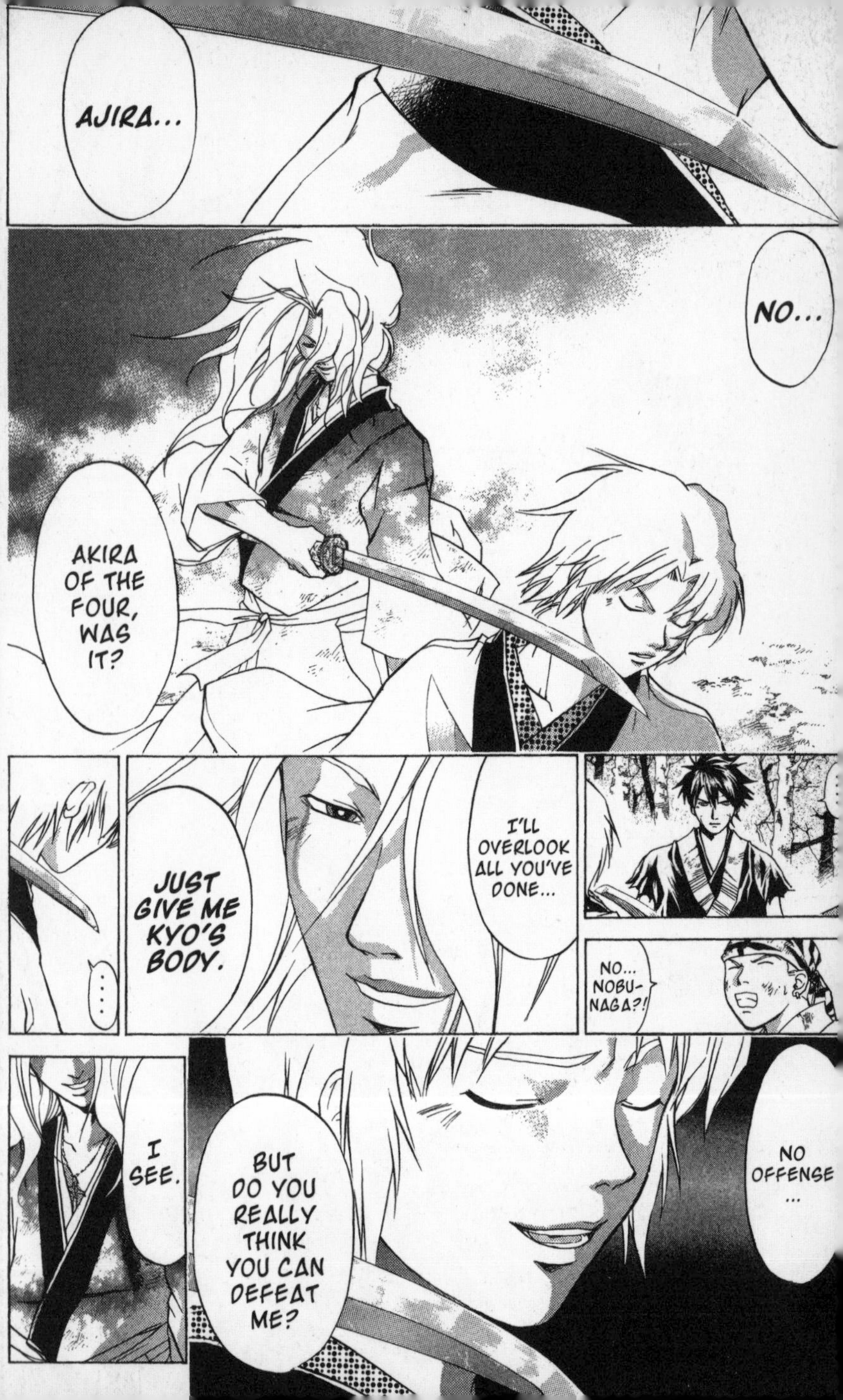
AJIRA...
NO...
AKIRA OF THE FOUR, WAS IT?
...
NO... NOBUNAGA?!
I'LL OVERLOOK ALL YOU'VE DONE...
JUST GIVE ME KYO'S BODY.
...
NO OFFENSE ...
BUT DO YOU REALLY THINK YOU CAN DEFEAT ME?
I SEE.

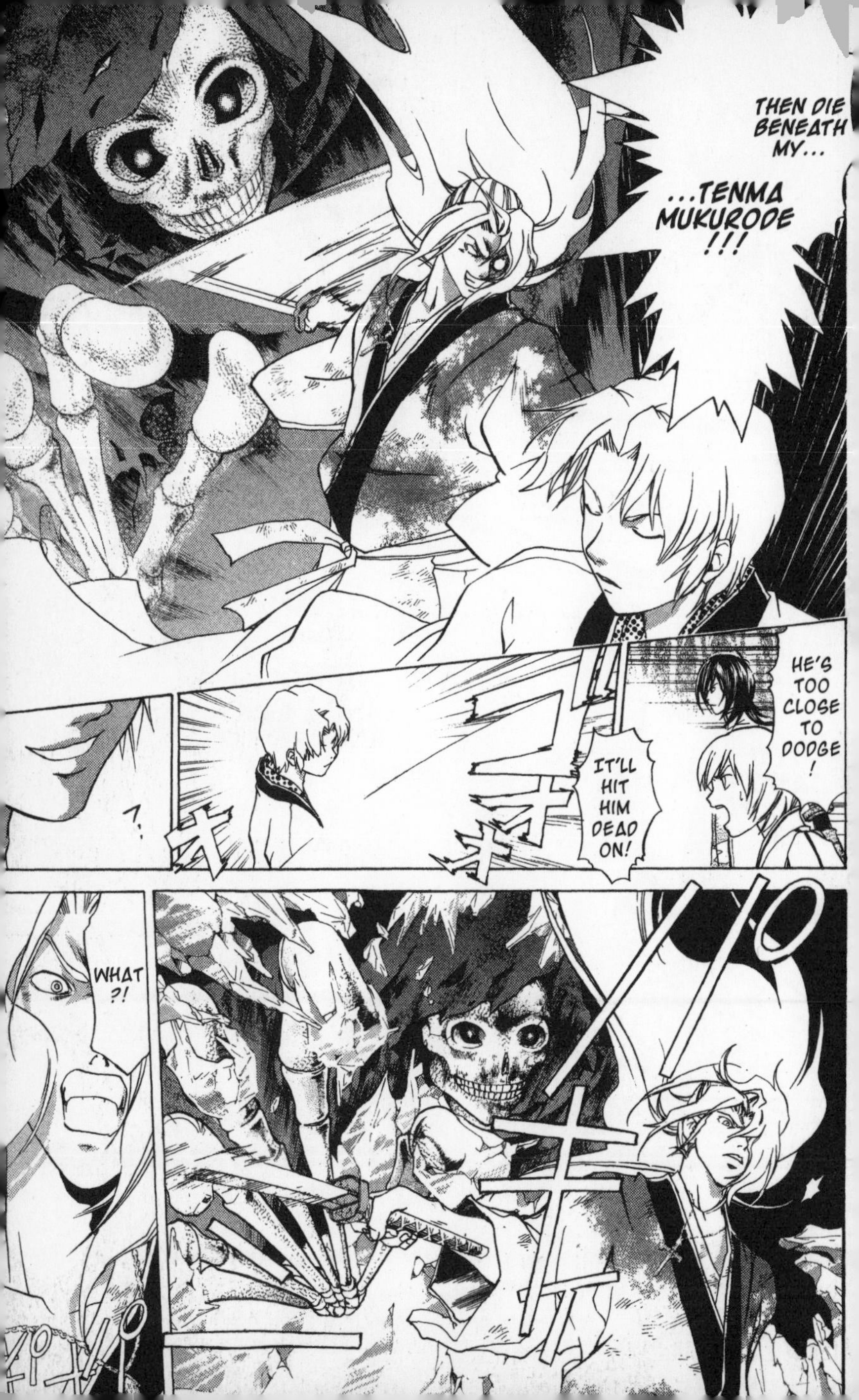
THEN DIE BENEATH MY...
...TENMA MUKURODE!!!
HE'S TOO CLOSE TO DODGE!
IT'LL HIT HIM DEAD ON!
?!
WHAT?!

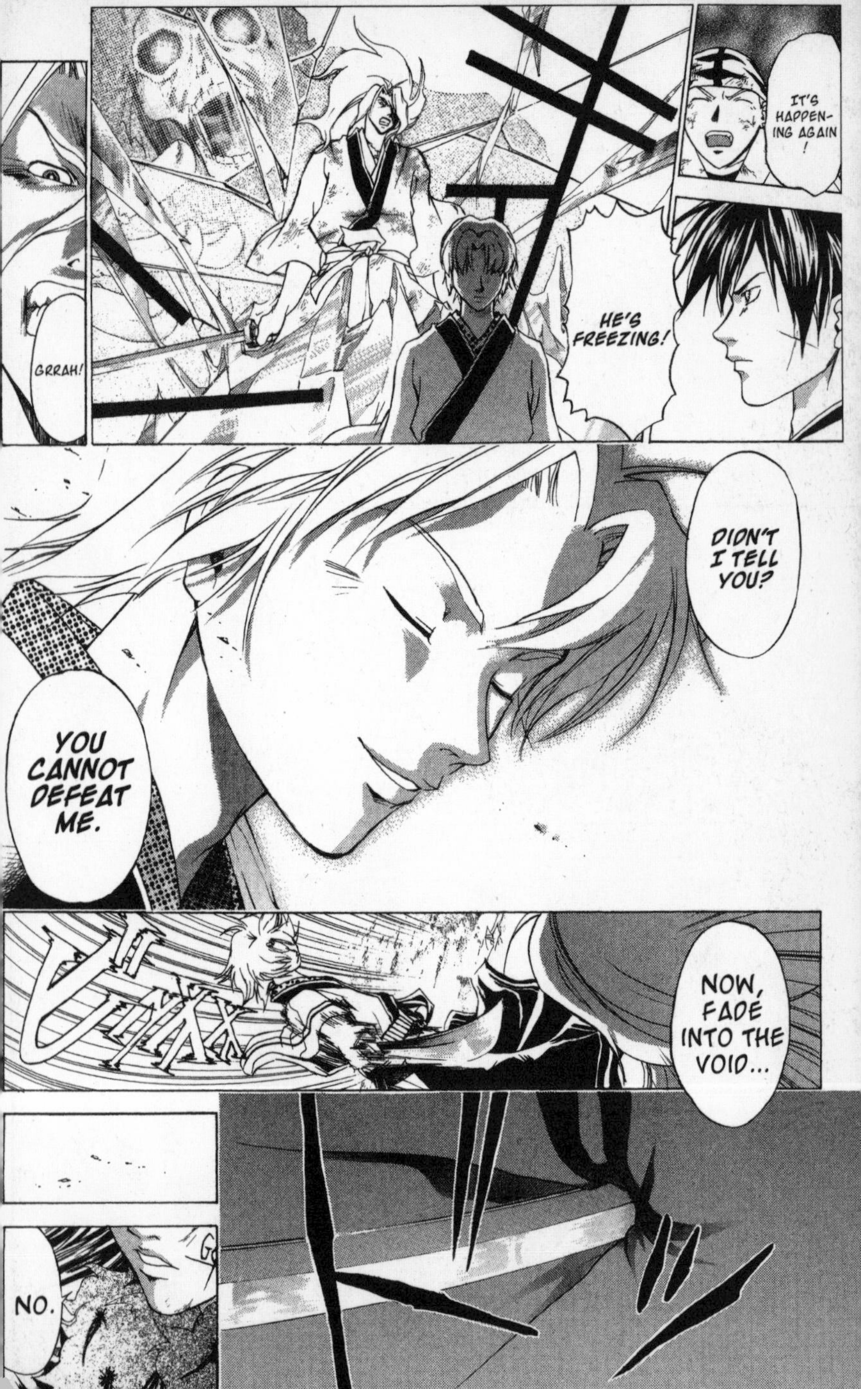
IT'S HAPPEN-ING AGAIN!
HE'S FREEZING!
GRRAH!
DIDN'T I TELL YOU?
YOU CANNOT DEFEAT ME.
NOW, FADE INTO THE VOID...
NO.

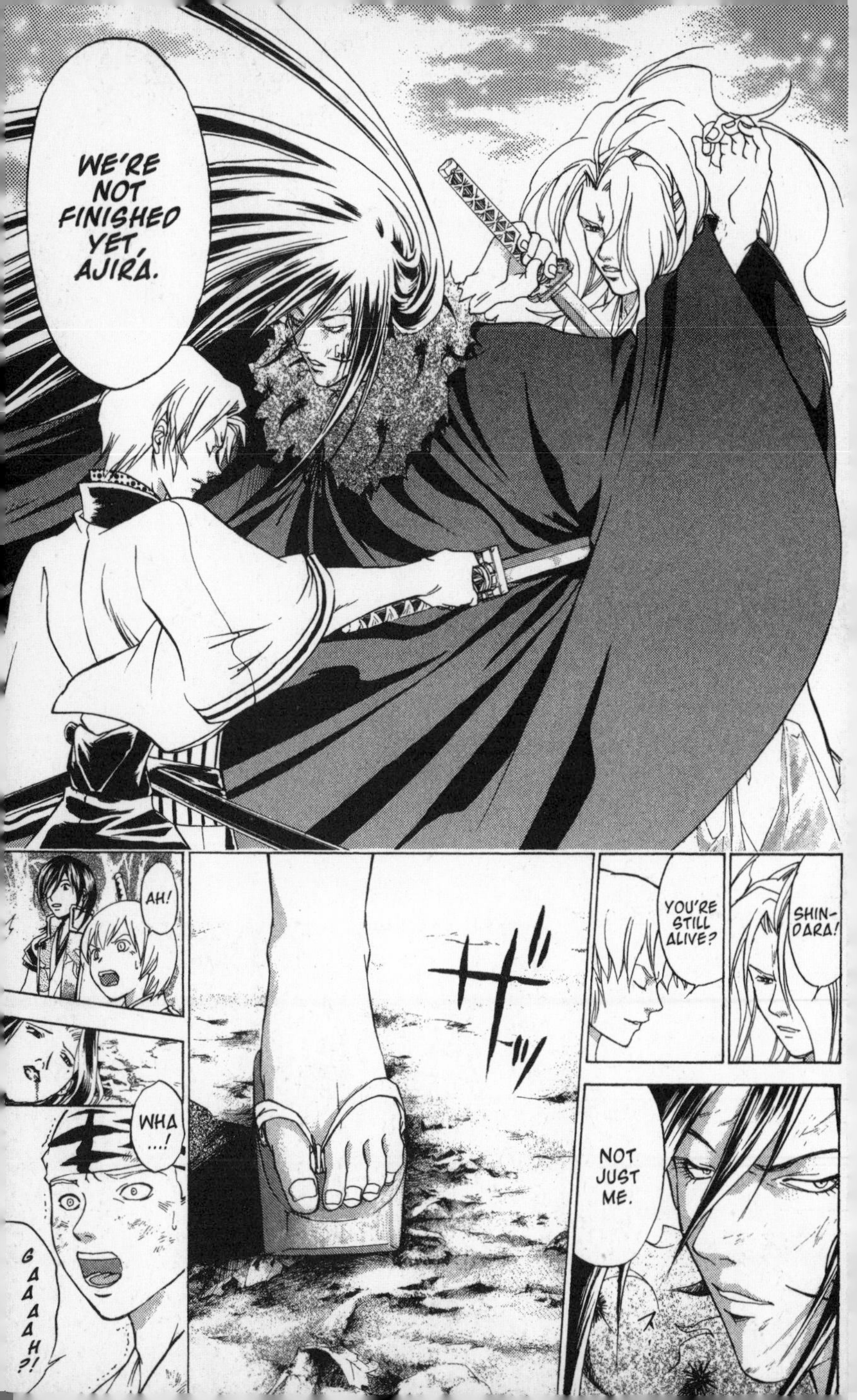
WE'RE NOT FINISHED YET, AJIRA.
SHIN-DARA!
YOU'RE STILL ALIVE?
NOT JUST ME.
AH!
WHA ...!
GAAAAAH?!

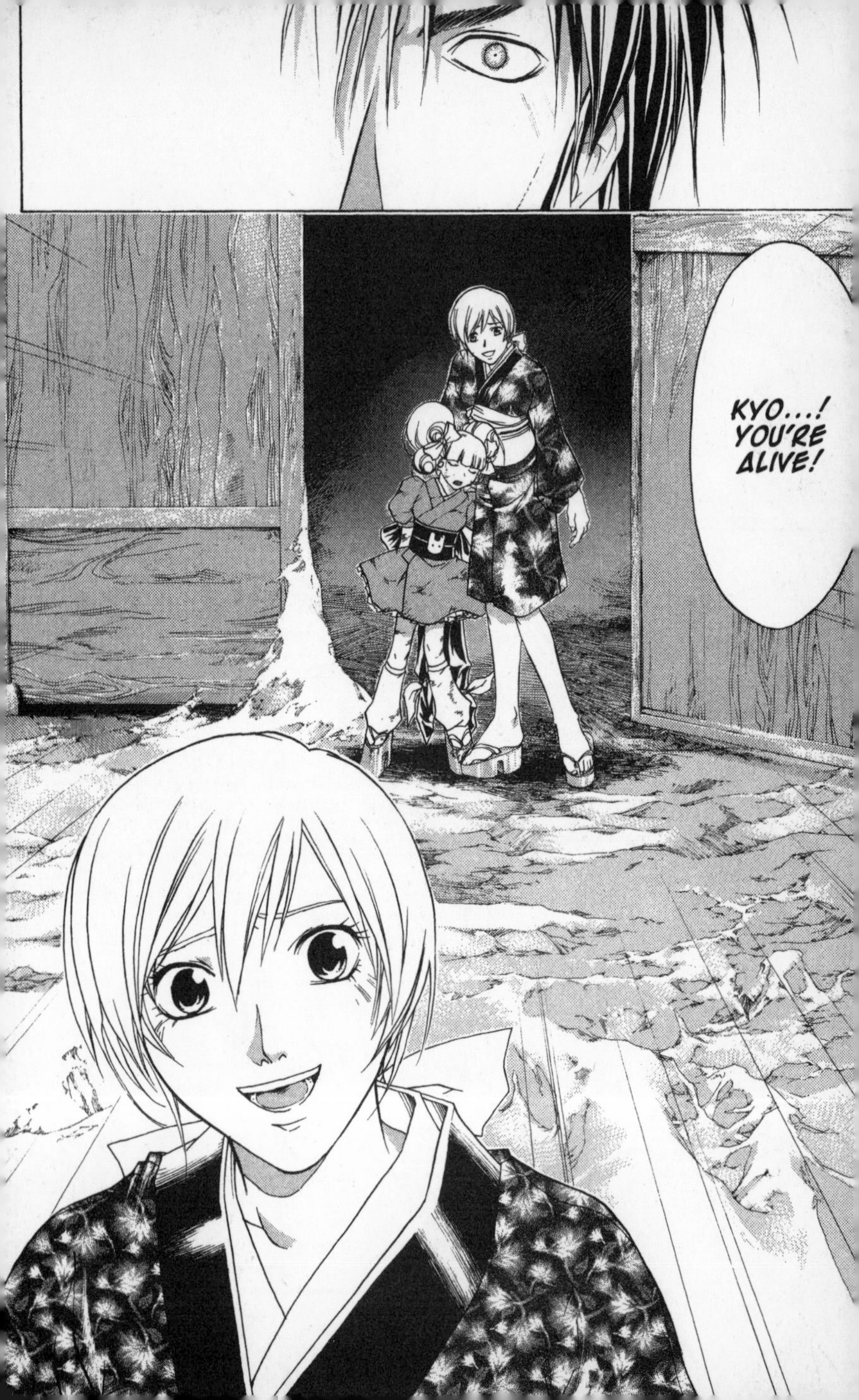
KYO...! YOU'RE ALIVE!

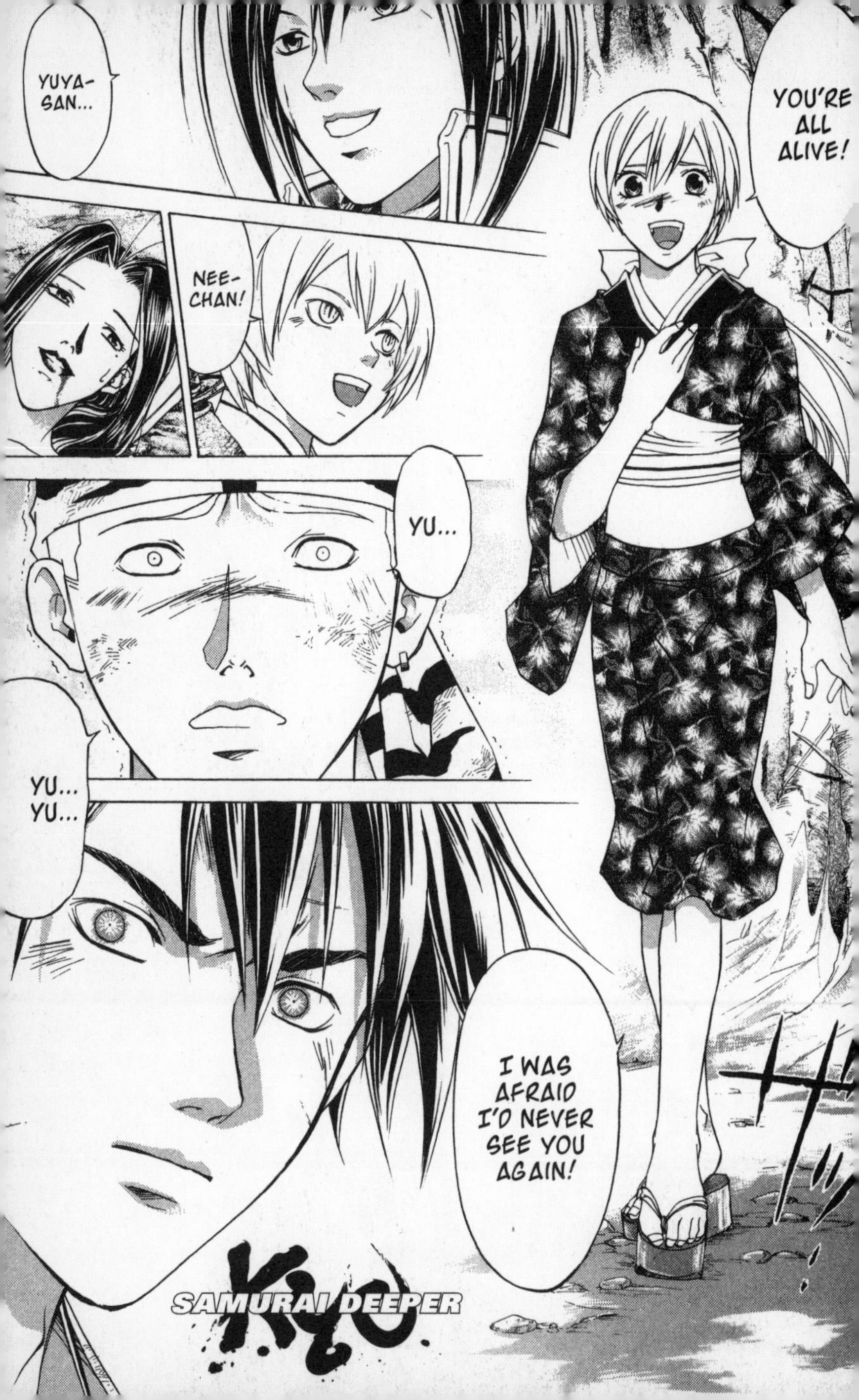
YOU'RE ALL ALIVE!
I WAS AFRAID I'D NEVER SEE YOU AGAIN!
YUYA-SAN...
NEE-CHAN!
YU...
YU... YU...
SAMURAI DEEPER KYO

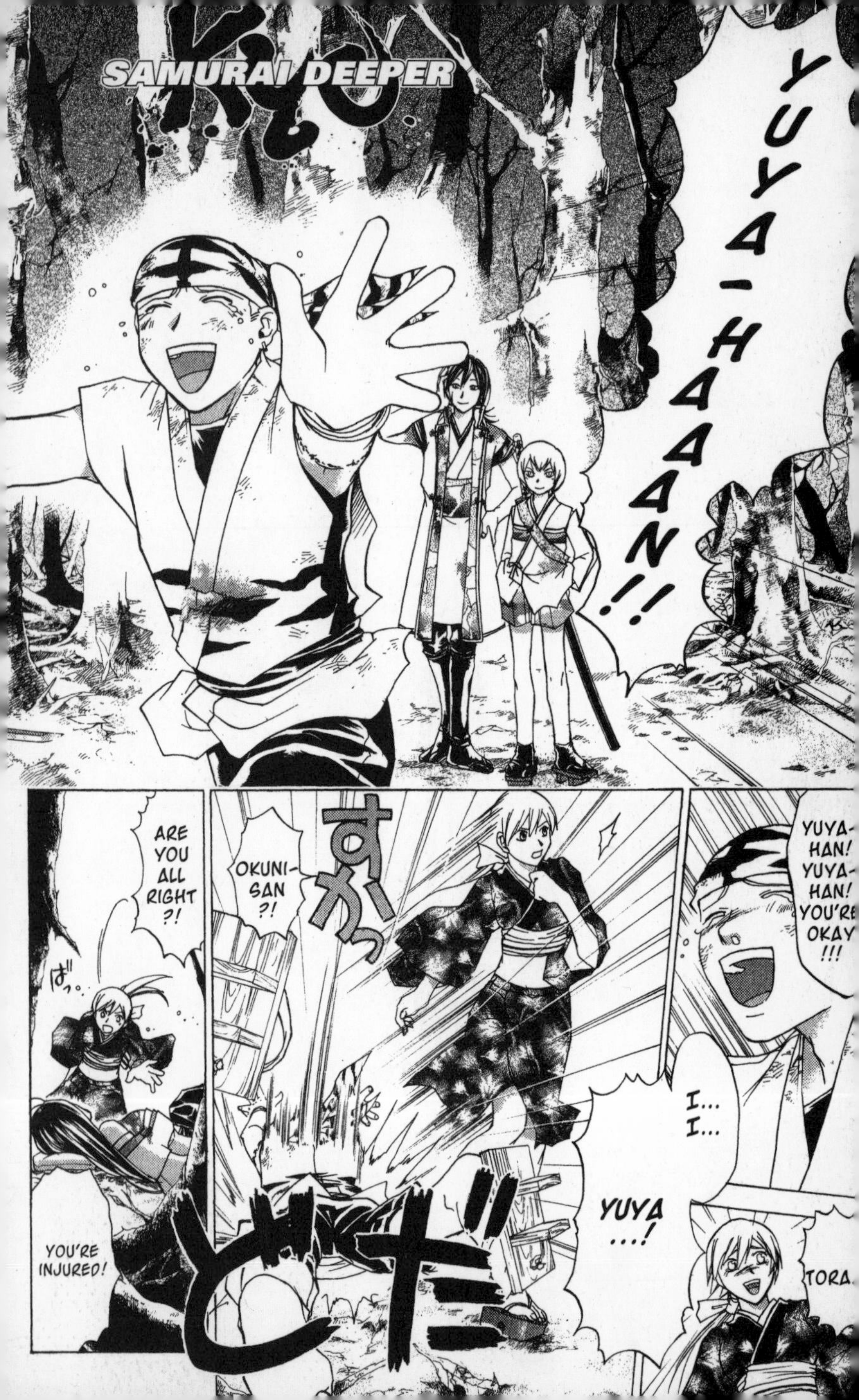
SAMURAI DEEPER
YUYA-HAAAAAN!!
YUYA-HAN! YUYA-HAN! YOU'RE OKAY!!!
I... I...
TORA...
すかっ
OKUNI-SAN?!
YUYA...!
どサ
ARE YOU ALL RIGHT?!
ばっ
YOU'RE INJURED!

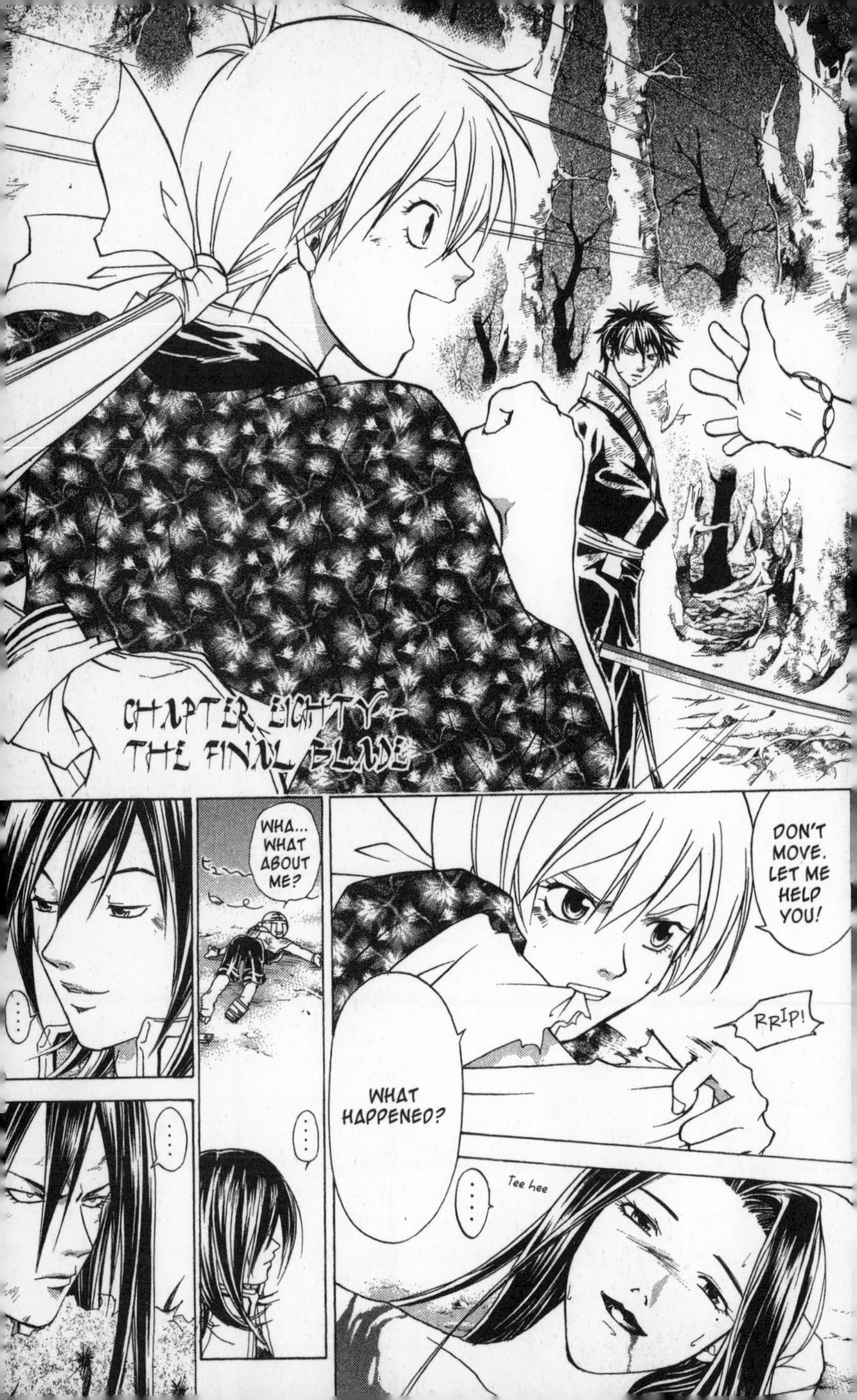
CHAPTER EIGHTY-
THE FINAL BLADE
DON'T MOVE. LET ME HELP YOU!
RRIP!
WHAT HAPPENED?
WHA... WHAT ABOUT ME?
....
....
Tee hee
....
....

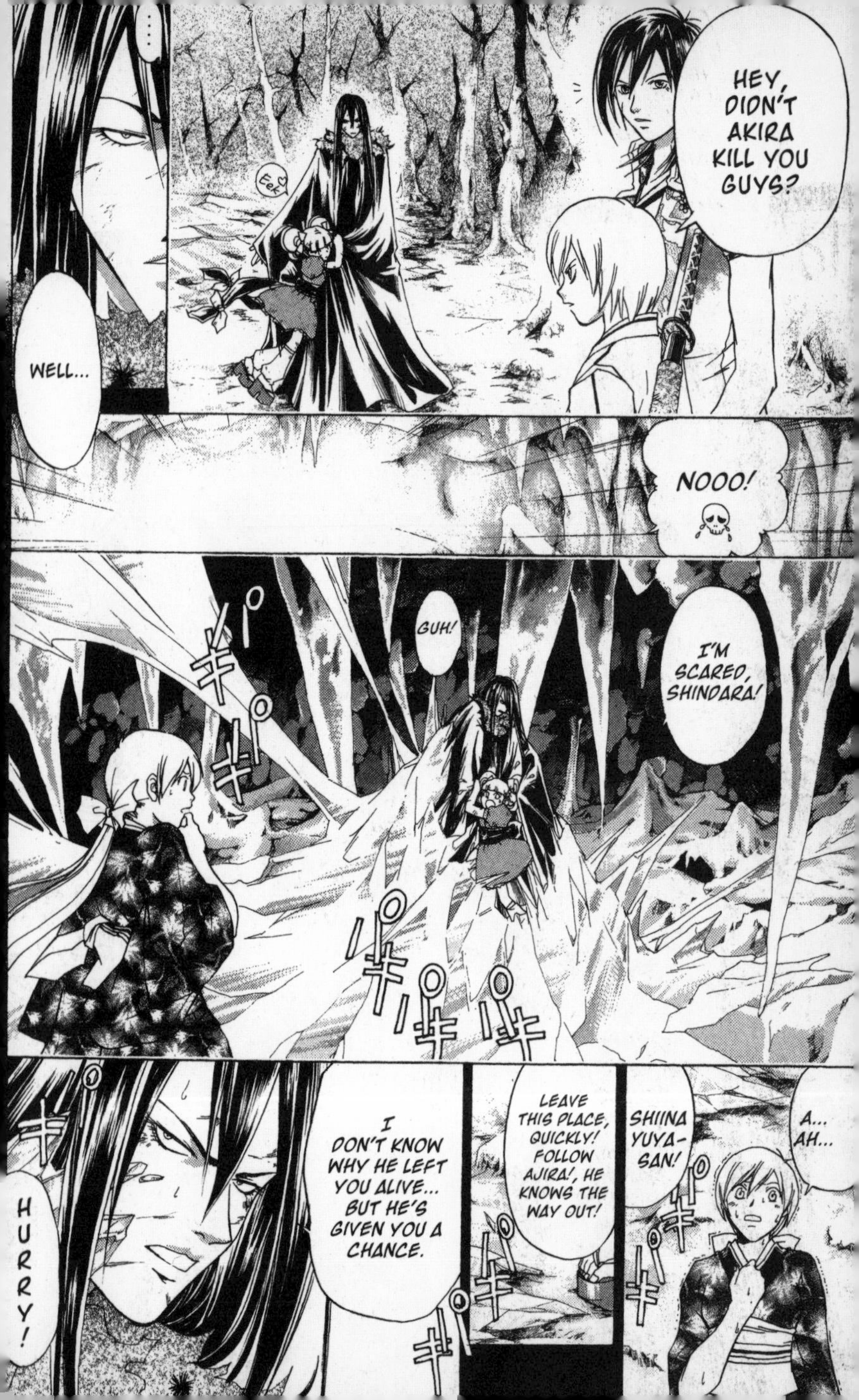
HEY, DIDN'T AKIRA KILL YOU GUYS?
Eek
...
WELL...
NOOO!
I'M SCARED, SHINDARA!
GUH!
A... AH...
SHIINA YUYA-SAN!
LEAVE THIS PLACE, QUICKLY! FOLLOW AJIRA!, HE KNOWS THE WAY OUT!
I DON'T KNOW WHY HE LEFT YOU ALIVE... BUT HE'S GIVEN YOU A CHANCE.
HURRY!

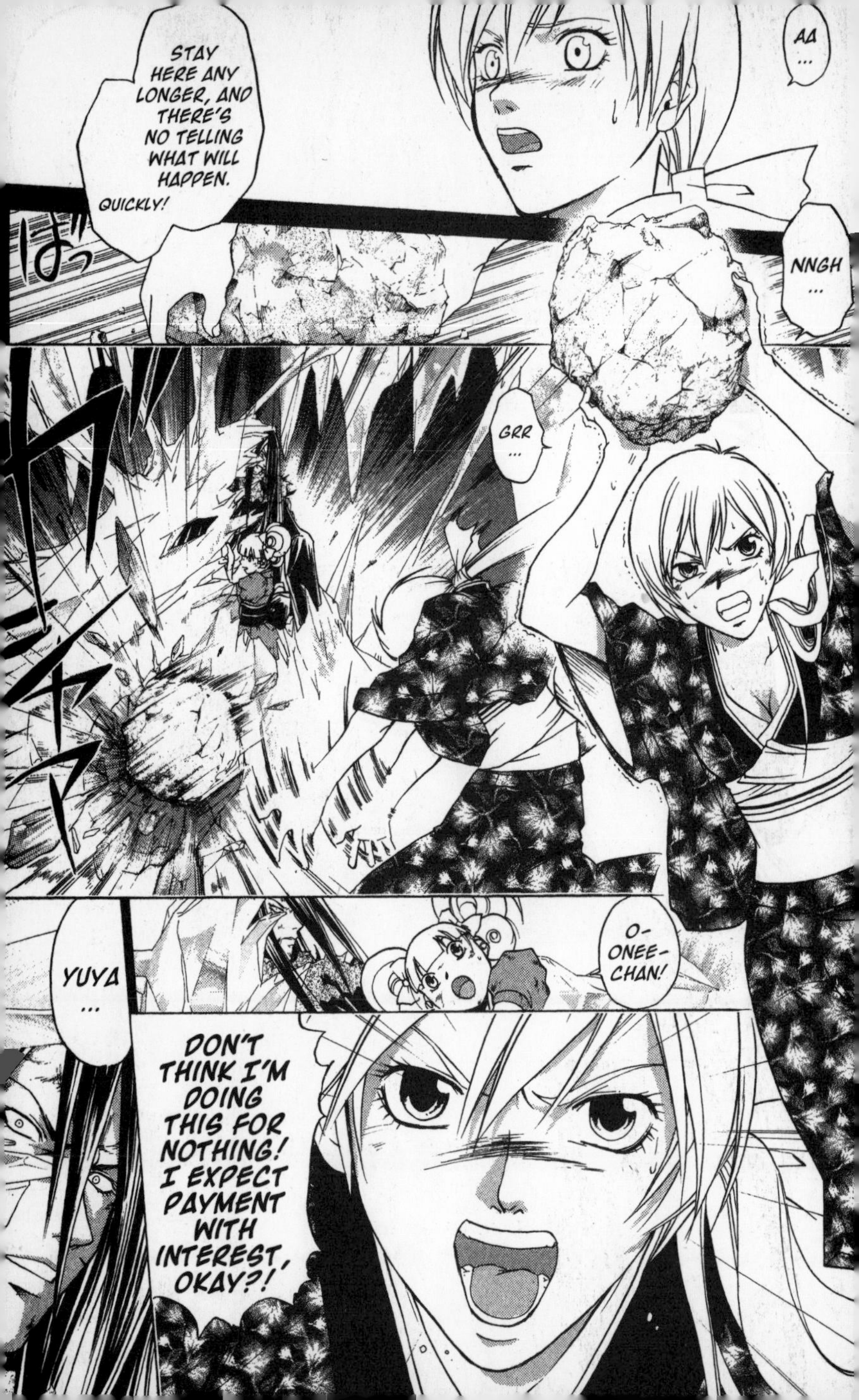
AA ...
STAY HERE ANY LONGER, AND THERE'S NO TELLING WHAT WILL HAPPEN.
QUICKLY!
NNGH ...
ばっ
GRR ...
O-ONEE-CHAN!
YUYA ...
DON'T THINK I'M DOING THIS FOR NOTHING! I EXPECT PAYMENT WITH INTEREST, OKAY?!

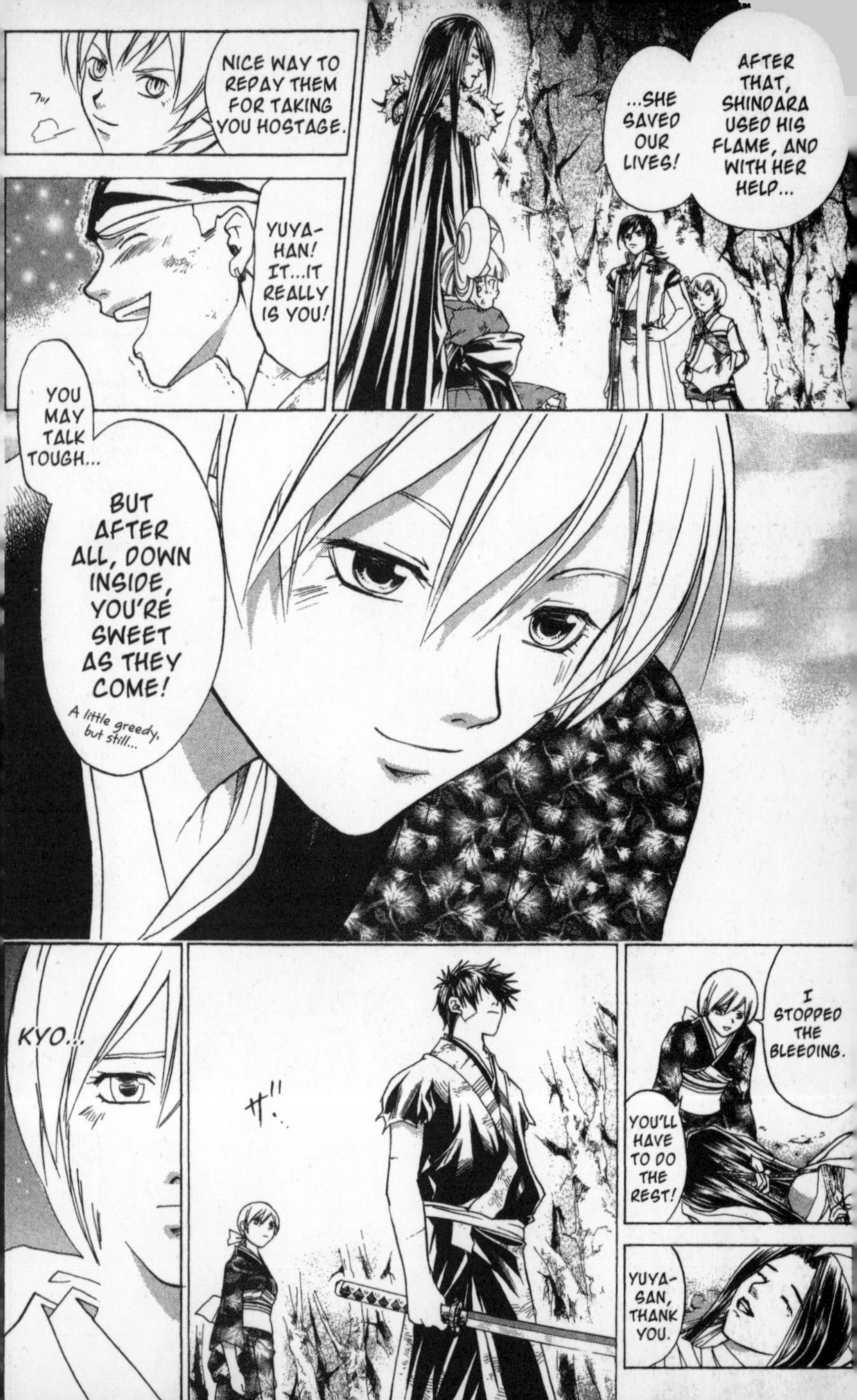
AFTER THAT, SHINDARA USED HIS FLAME, AND WITH HER HELP...
...SHE SAVED OUR LIVES!
フッ
NICE WAY TO REPAY THEM FOR TAKING YOU HOSTAGE.
YUYA-HAN! IT...IT REALLY IS YOU!
YOU MAY TALK TOUGH...
BUT AFTER ALL, DOWN INSIDE, YOU'RE SWEET AS THEY COME!
A little greedy, but still...
I STOPPED THE BLEEDING.
YOU'LL HAVE TO DO THE REST!
YUYA-SAN, THANK YOU.
ザ!!..
KYO...

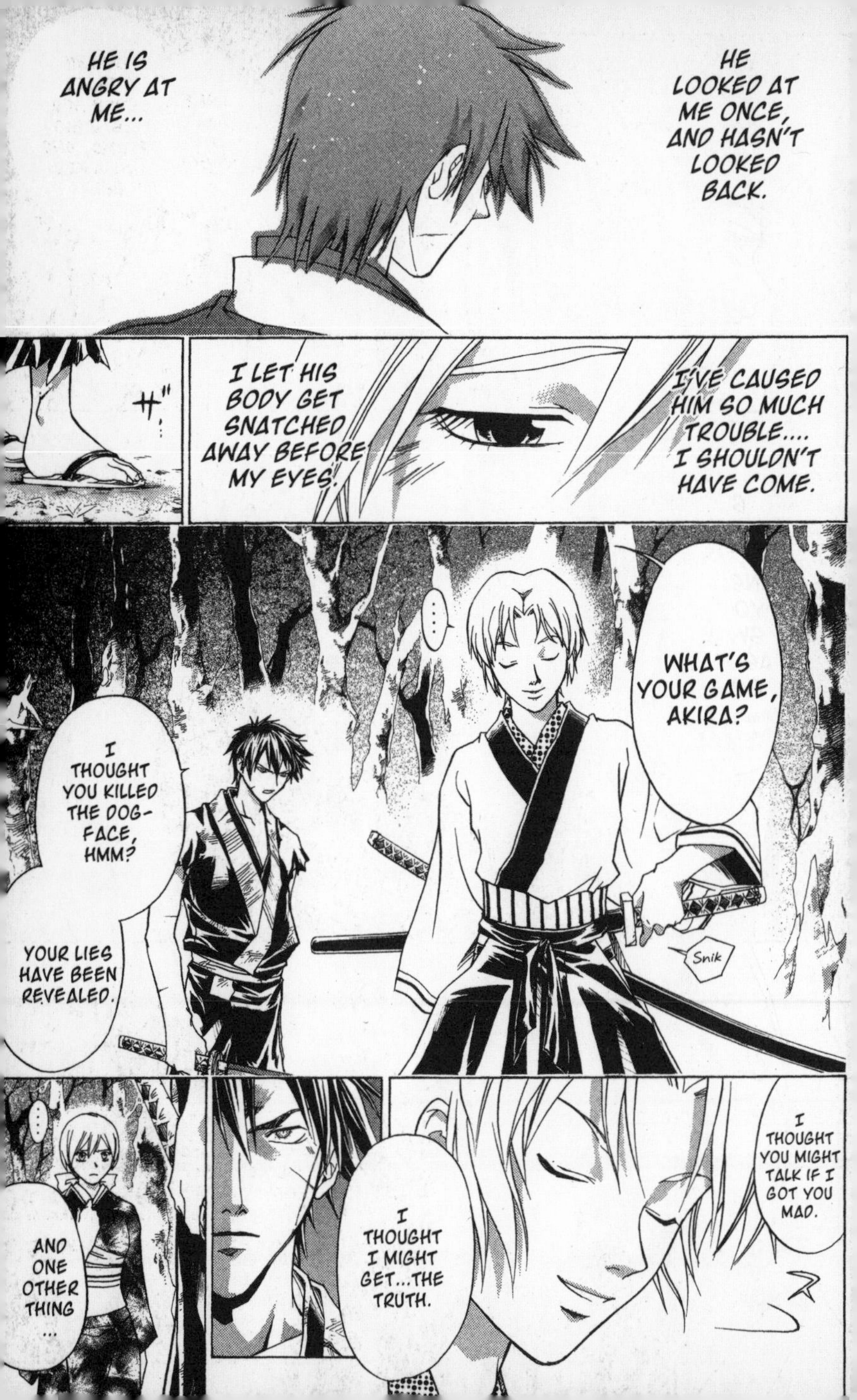
HE LOOKED AT ME ONCE, AND HASN'T LOOKED BACK.
HE IS ANGRY AT ME...
I'VE CAUSED HIM SO MUCH TROUBLE.... I SHOULDN'T HAVE COME.
I LET HIS BODY GET SNATCHED AWAY BEFORE MY EYES.
WHAT'S YOUR GAME, AKIRA?
...
Snik
I THOUGHT YOU KILLED THE DOG-FACE, HMM?
YOUR LIES HAVE BEEN REVEALED.
I THOUGHT YOU MIGHT TALK IF I GOT YOU MAD.
I THOUGHT I MIGHT GET...THE TRUTH.
...
AND ONE OTHER THING ...

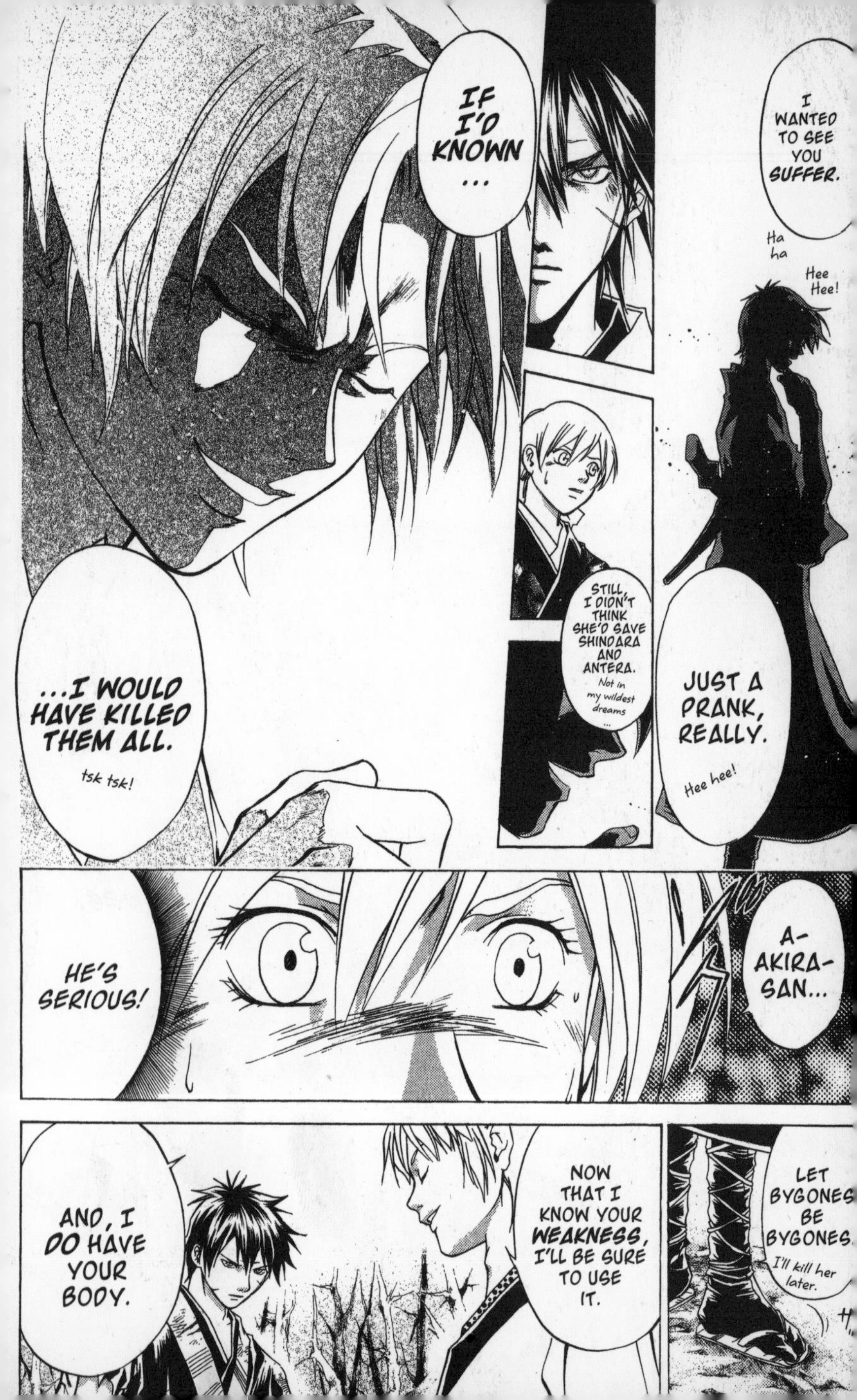

I WANTED TO SEE YOU SUFFER.
Ha ha
Hee Hee!
JUST A PRANK, REALLY.
Hee hee!
IF I'D KNOWN...
STILL, I DIDN'T THINK SHE'D SAVE SHINDARA AND ANTERA.
Not in my wildest dreams...
...I WOULD HAVE KILLED THEM ALL.
tsk tsk!
A-AKIRA-SAN...
HE'S SERIOUS!
LET BYGONES BE BYGONES.
I'll kill her later.
NOW THAT I KNOW YOUR WEAKNESS, I'LL BE SURE TO USE IT.
AND, I DO HAVE YOUR BODY.

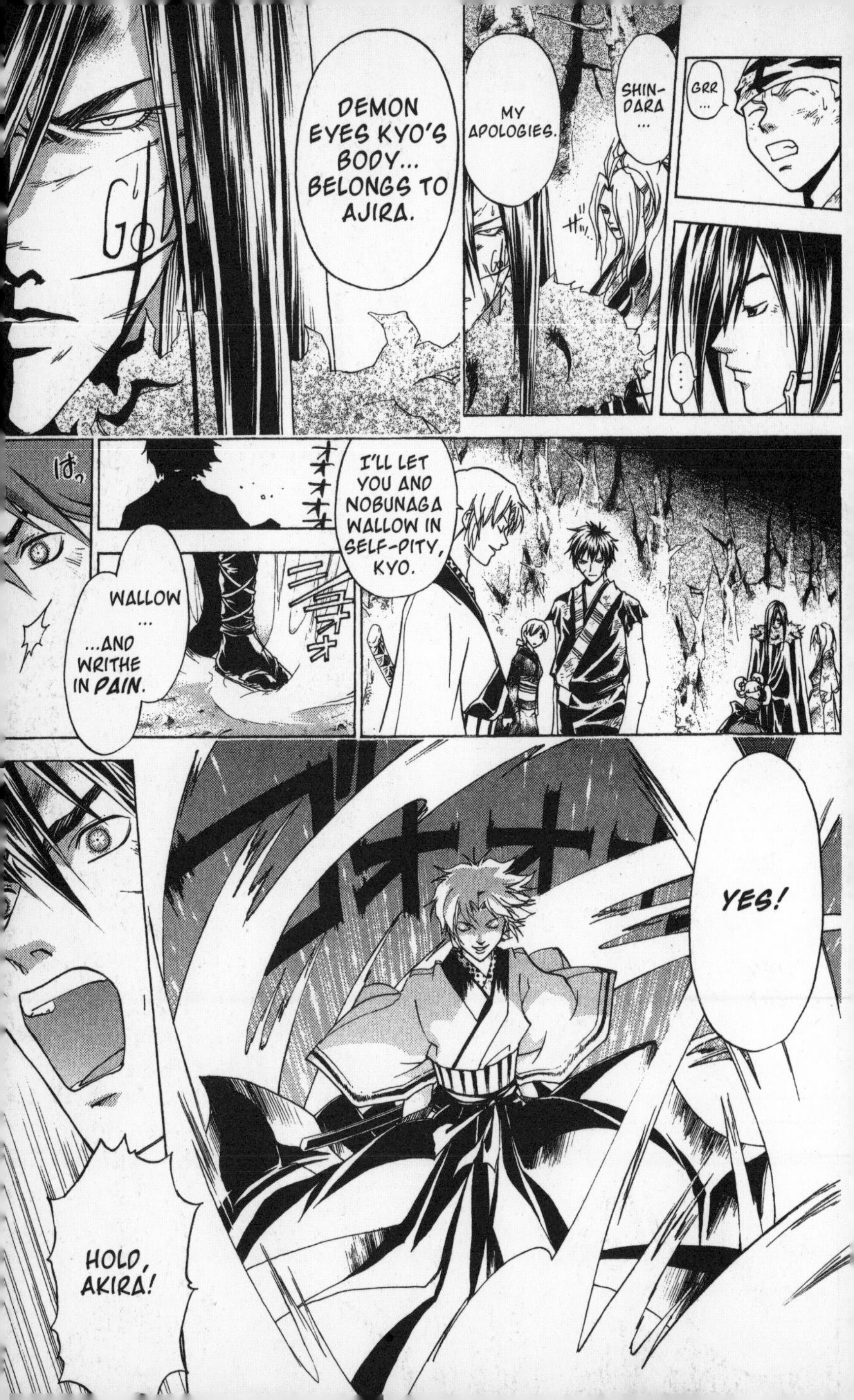
GRR ...
...
SHIN-DARA ...
MY APOLOGIES.
DEMON EYES KYO'S BODY... BELONGS TO AJIRA.
I'LL LET YOU AND NOBUNAGA WALLOW IN SELF-PITY, KYO.
...
WALLOW ... ...AND WRITHE IN PAIN.
はっ
YES!
HOLD, AKIRA!

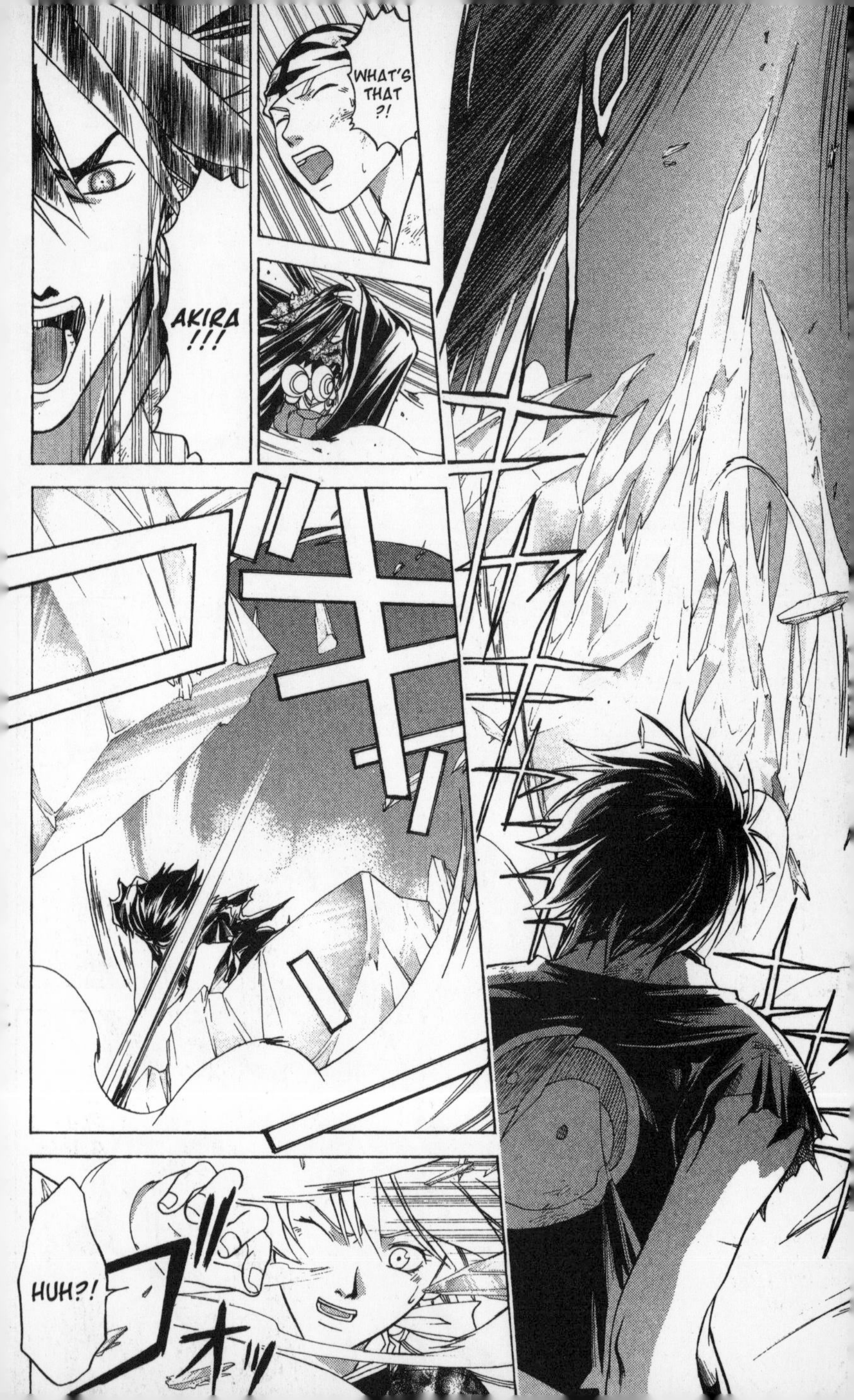
WHAT'S THAT ?!
AKIRA !!!
HUH?!

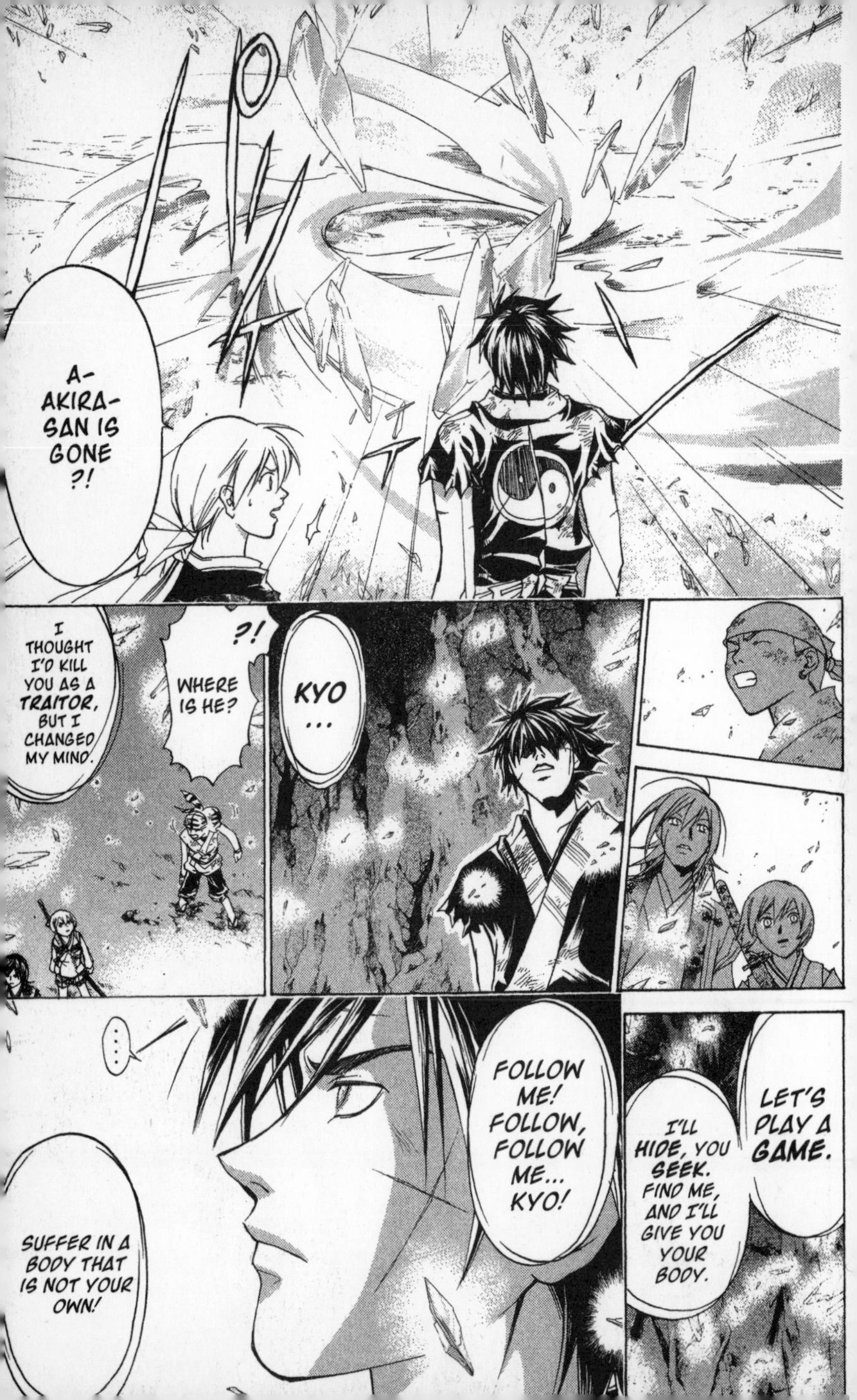
A-AKIRA-SAN IS GONE?!
KYO...
?!
WHERE IS HE?
I THOUGHT I'D KILL YOU AS A TRAITOR, BUT I CHANGED MY MIND.
LET'S PLAY A GAME.
I'LL HIDE, YOU SEEK. FIND ME, AND I'LL GIVE YOU YOUR BODY.
FOLLOW ME! FOLLOW, FOLLOW ME... KYO!
...
SUFFER IN A BODY THAT IS NOT YOUR OWN!

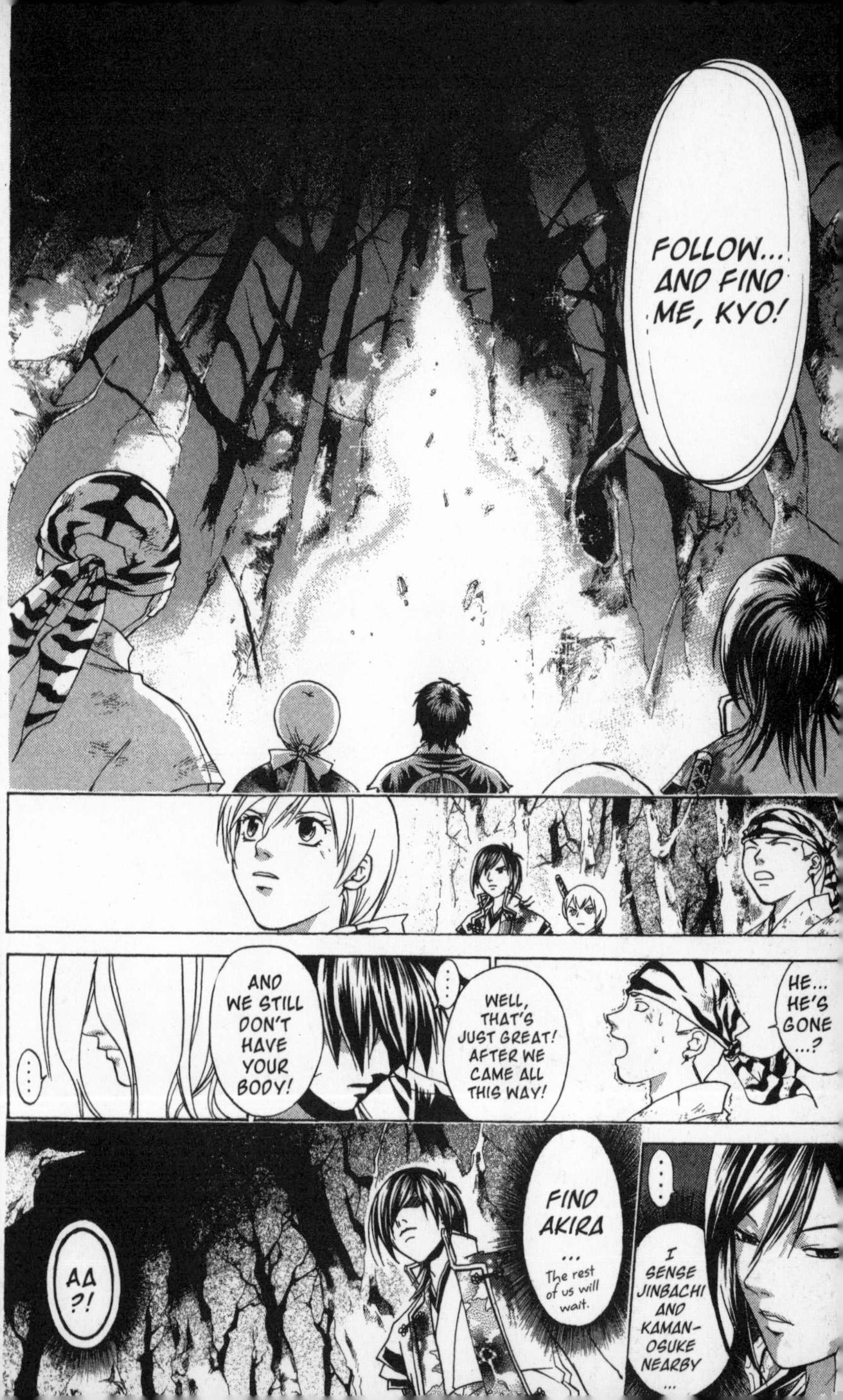
FOLLOW... AND FIND ME, KYO!
HE... HE'S GONE ...?
WELL, THAT'S JUST GREAT! AFTER WE CAME ALL THIS WAY!
...
AND WE STILL DON'T HAVE YOUR BODY!
...
...
I SENSE JINBACHI AND KAMANOSUKE NEARBY ...
FIND AKIRA ...
The rest of us will wait.
AA ?!

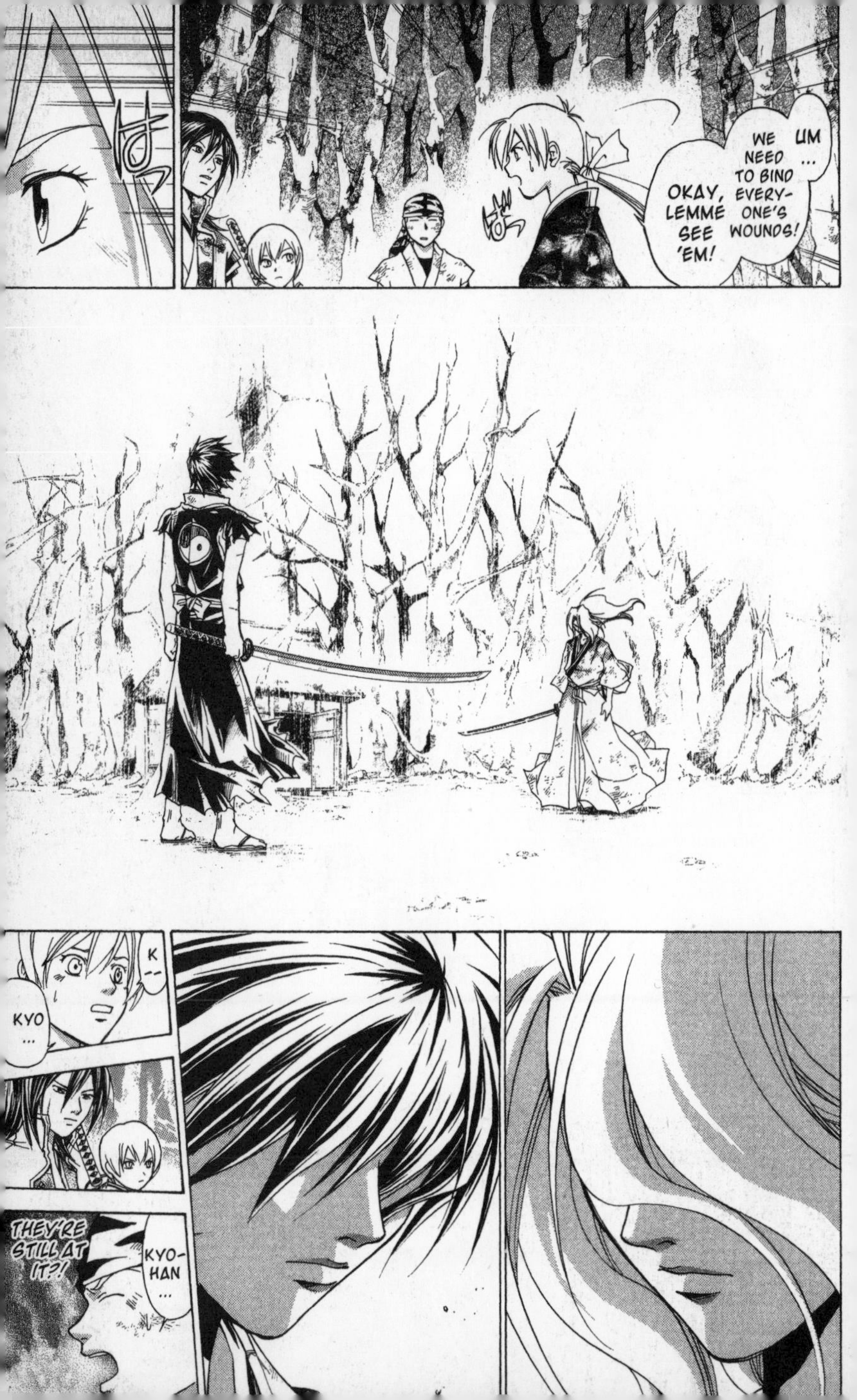
UM ...
WE NEED TO BIND EVERYONE'S WOUNDS!
OKAY, LEMME SEE 'EM!
K--
KYO ...
KYO-HAN ...
THEY'RE STILL AT IT?!

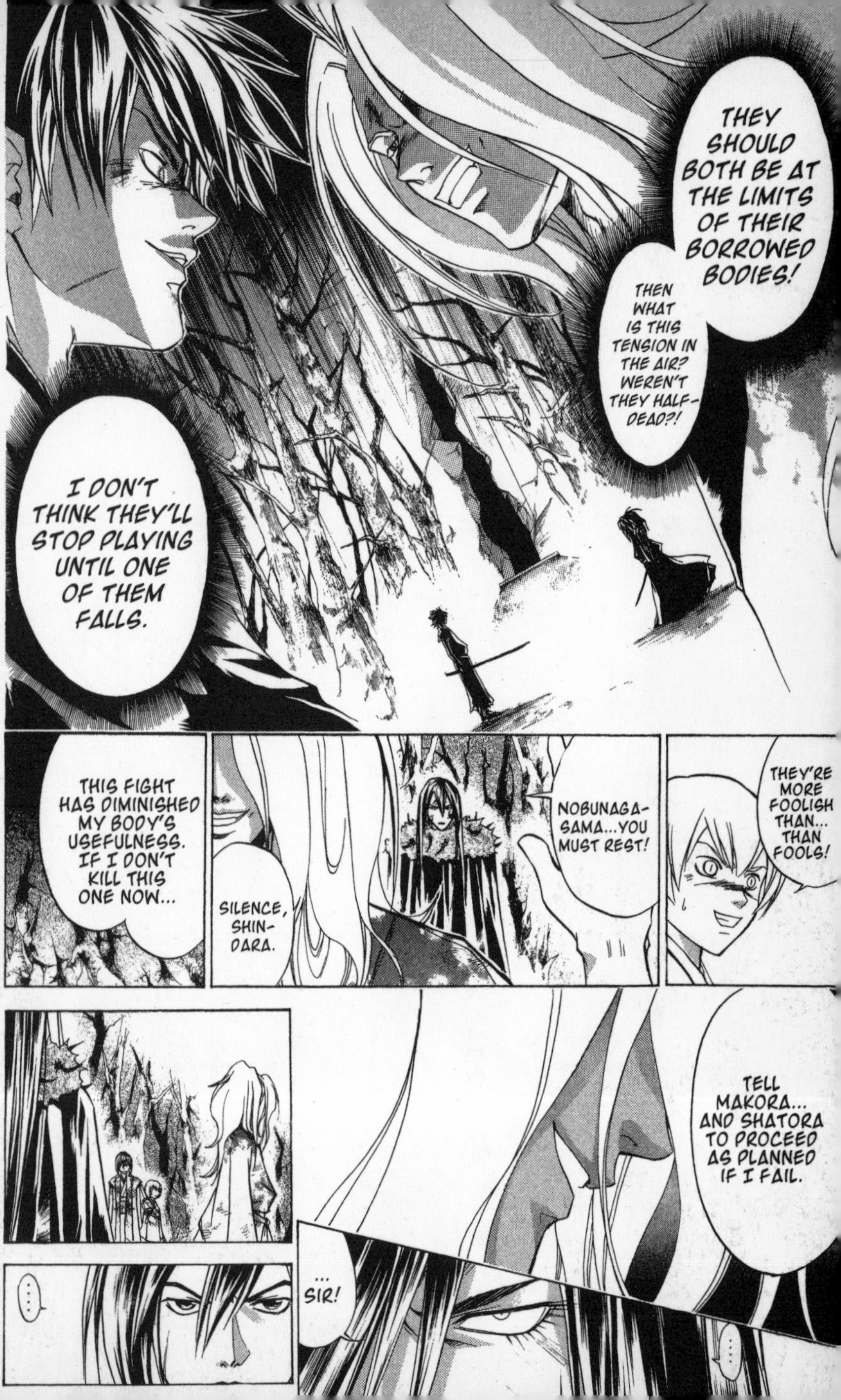
THEY SHOULD BOTH BE AT THE LIMITS OF THEIR BORROWED BODIES!
THEN WHAT IS THIS TENSION IN THE AIR? WEREN'T THEY HALF-DEAD?!
I DON'T THINK THEY'LL STOP PLAYING UNTIL ONE OF THEM FALLS.
THEY'RE MORE FOOLISH THAN... THAN FOOLS!
NOBUNAGA-SAMA...YOU MUST REST!
SILENCE, SHIN-DARA.
THIS FIGHT HAS DIMINISHED MY BODY'S USEFULNESS. IF I DON'T KILL THIS ONE NOW...
TELL MAKORA... AND SHATORA TO PROCEED AS PLANNED IF I FAIL.
...
...SIR!
...

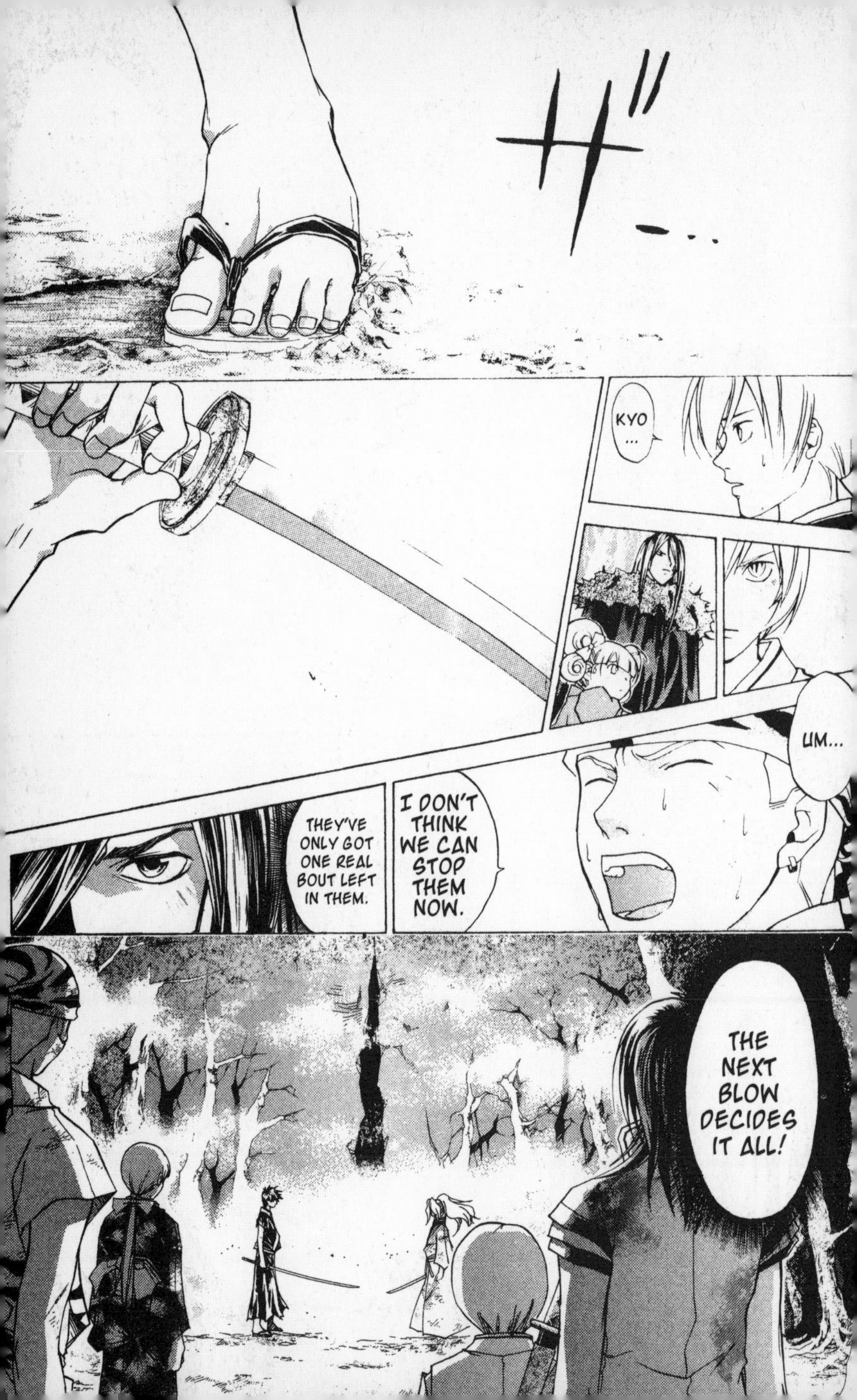
ザ
KYO...
UM...
I DON'T THINK WE CAN STOP THEM NOW.
THEY'VE ONLY GOT ONE REAL BOUT LEFT IN THEM.
THE NEXT BLOW DECIDES IT ALL!

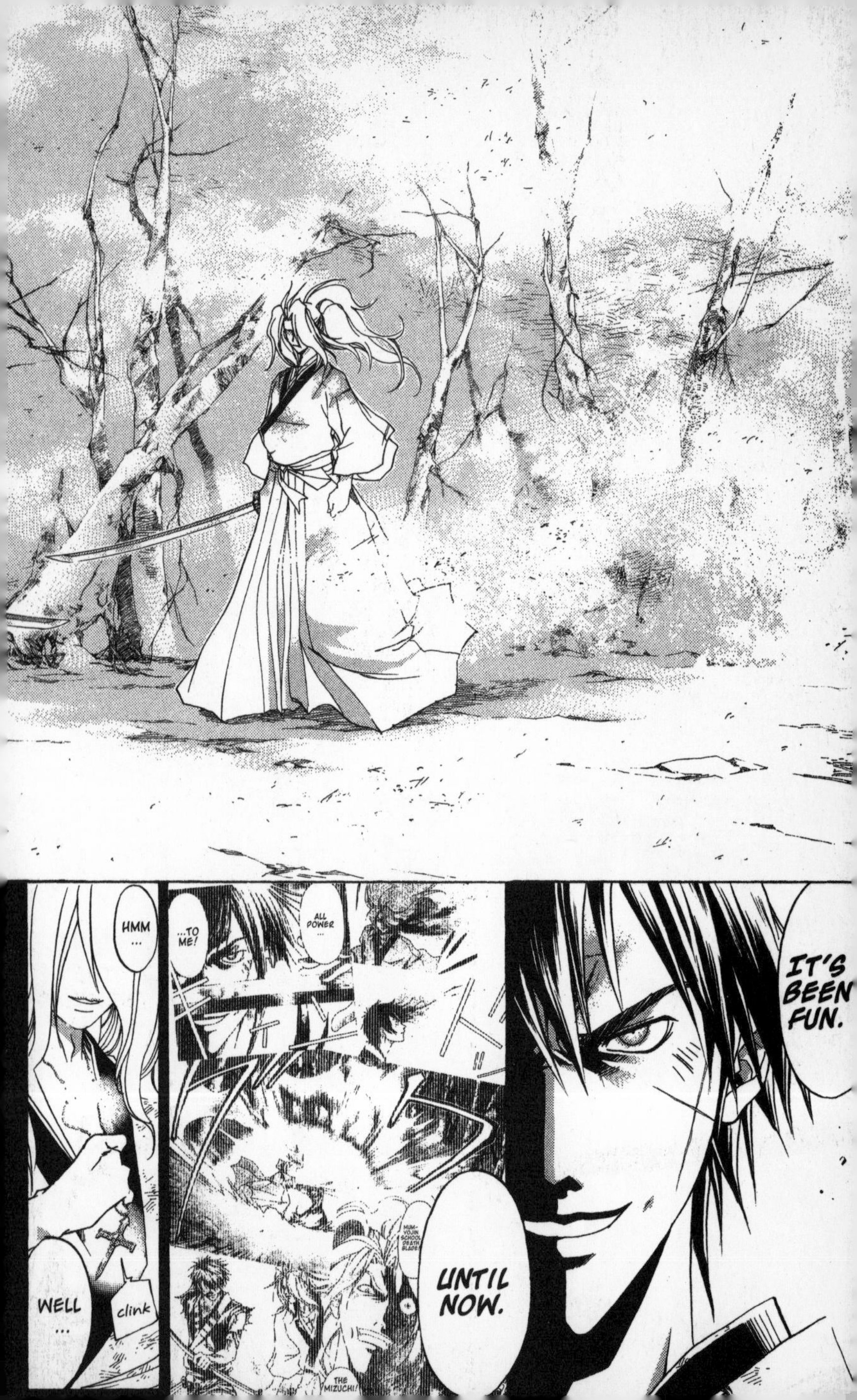
IT'S BEEN FUN.
UNTIL NOW.
ALL POWER ...
...TO ME!
MUM-VOJIN SCHOOL DEATH BLADE!
THE MIZUCHI!!
HMM ...
clink
WELL ...

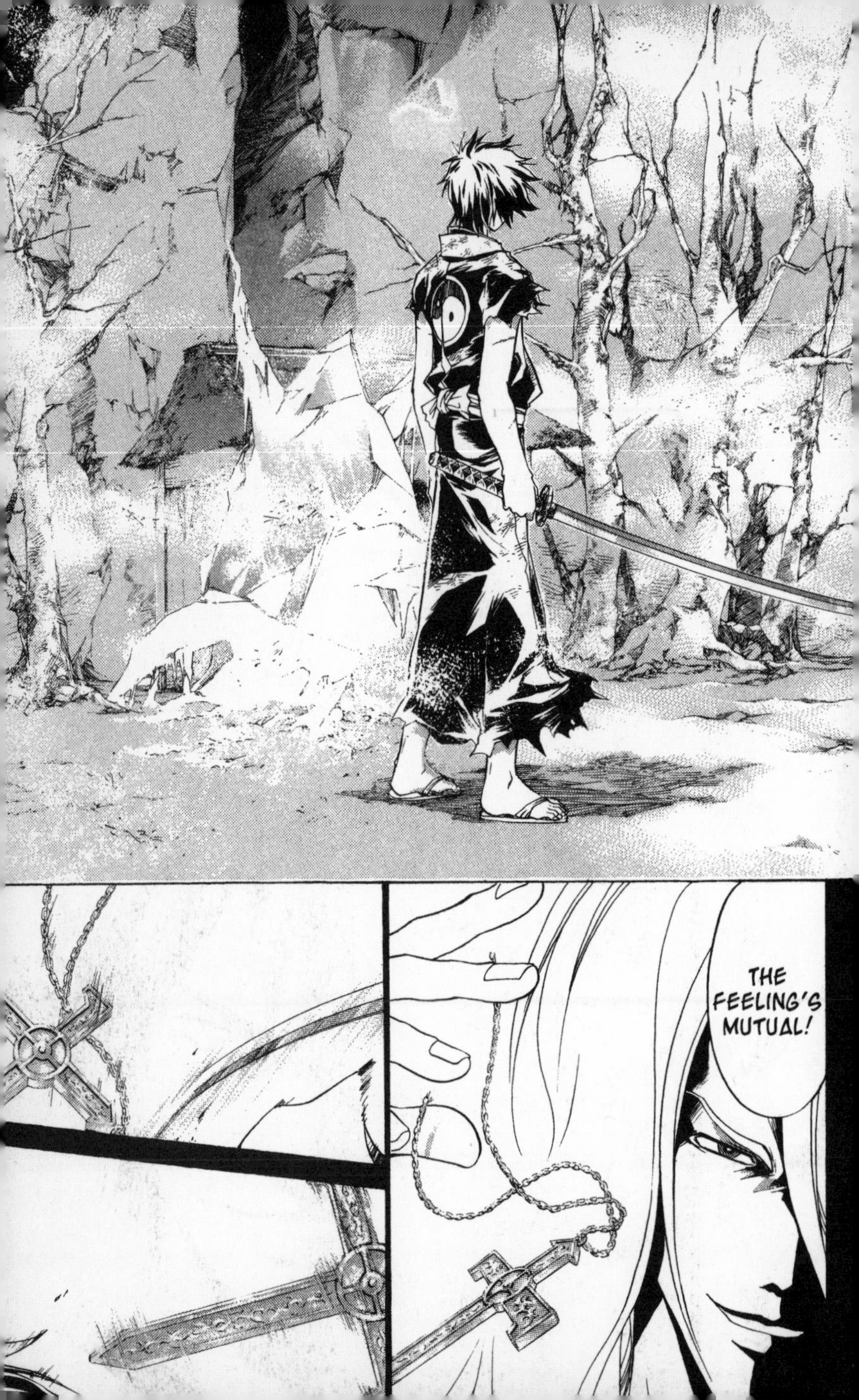
THE FEELING'S MUTUAL!

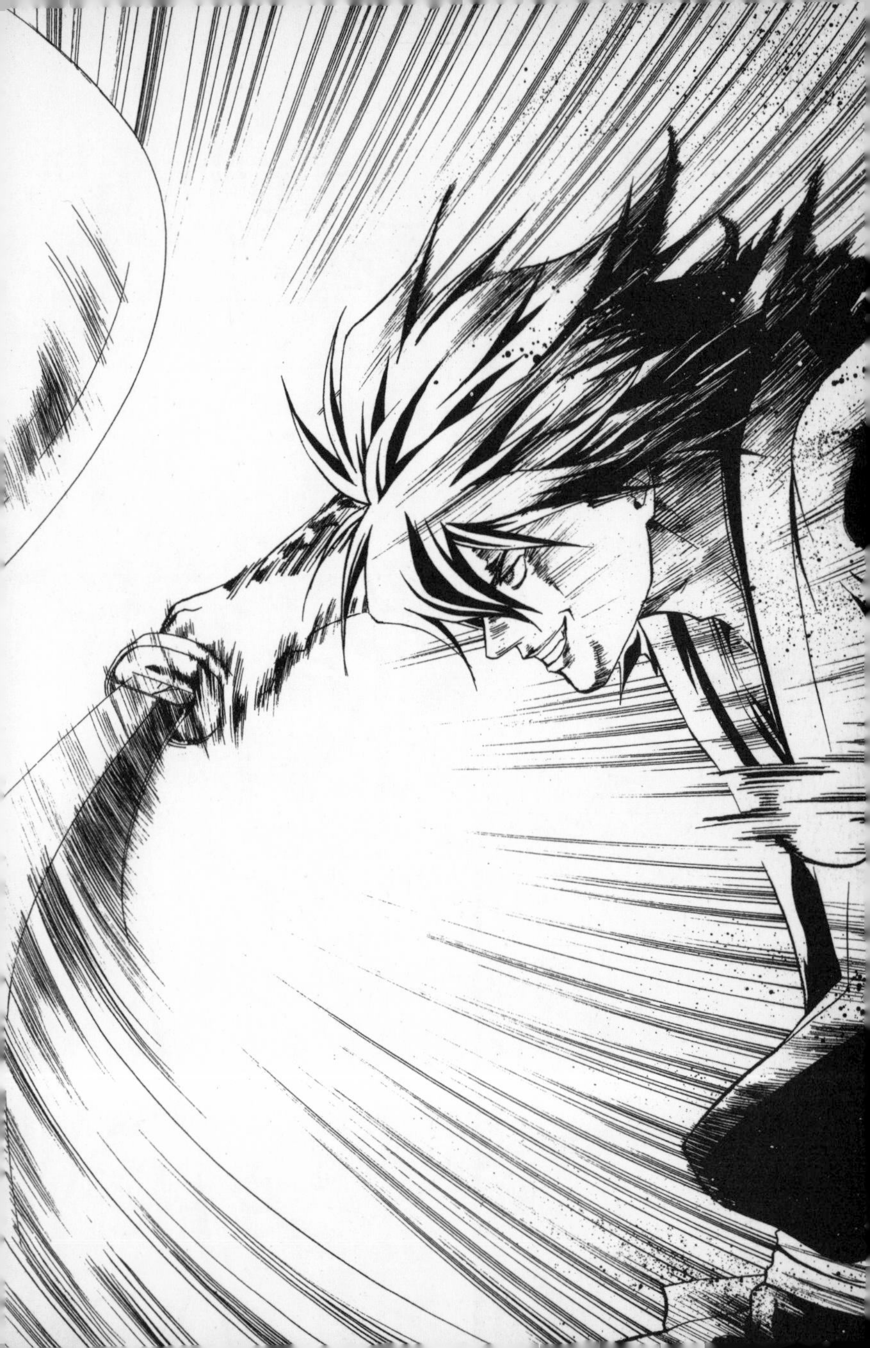

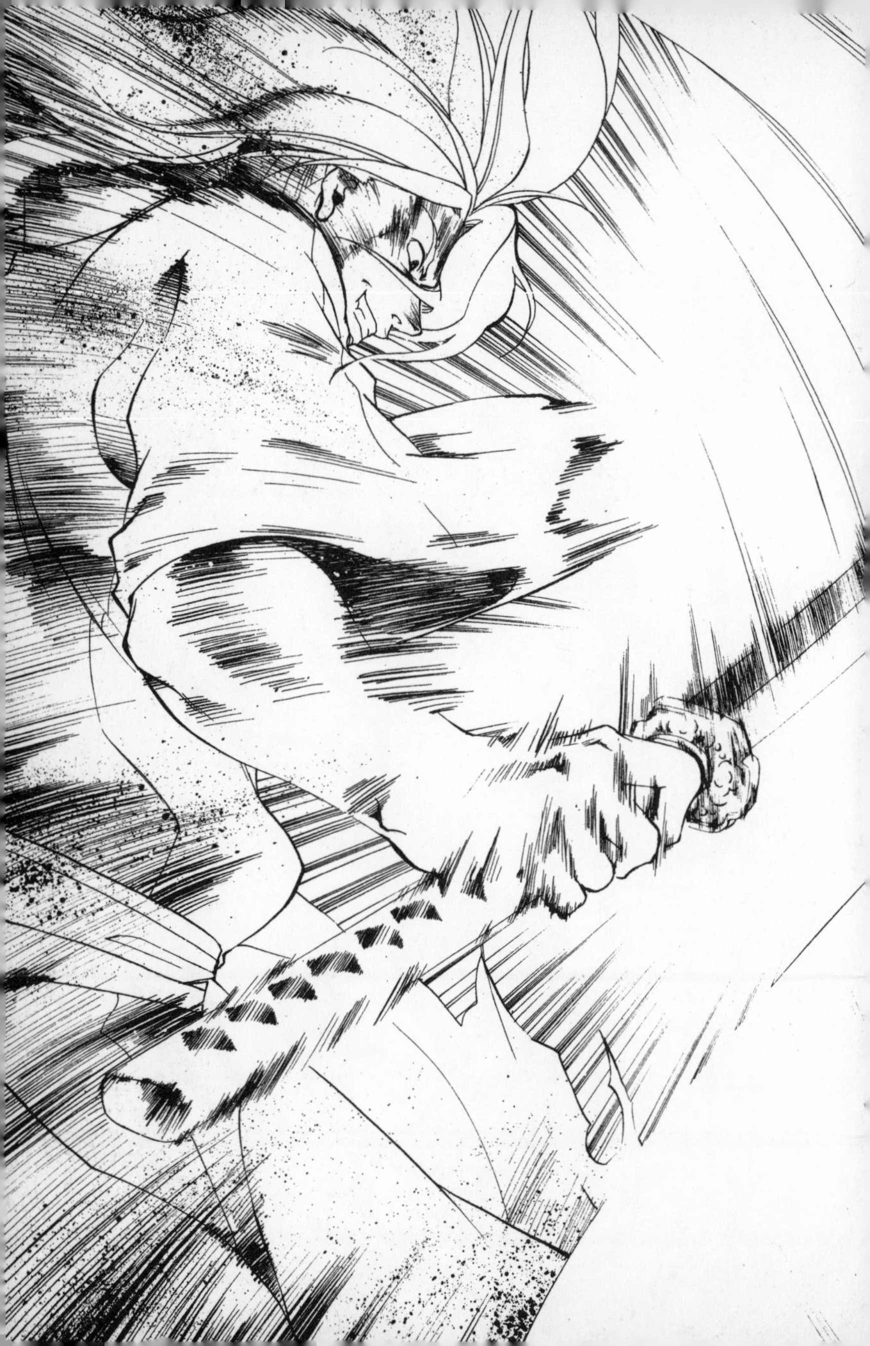

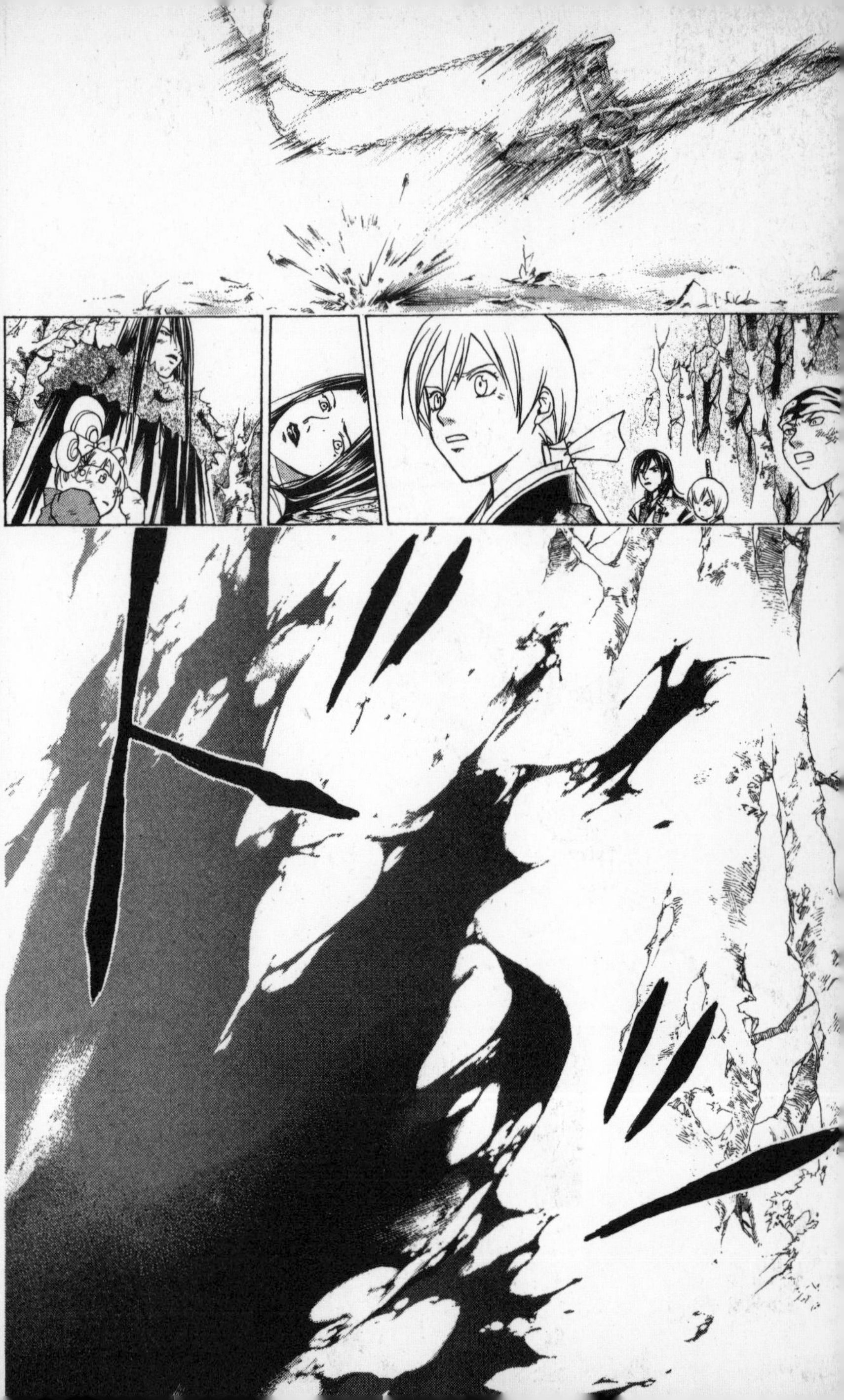
ドッ

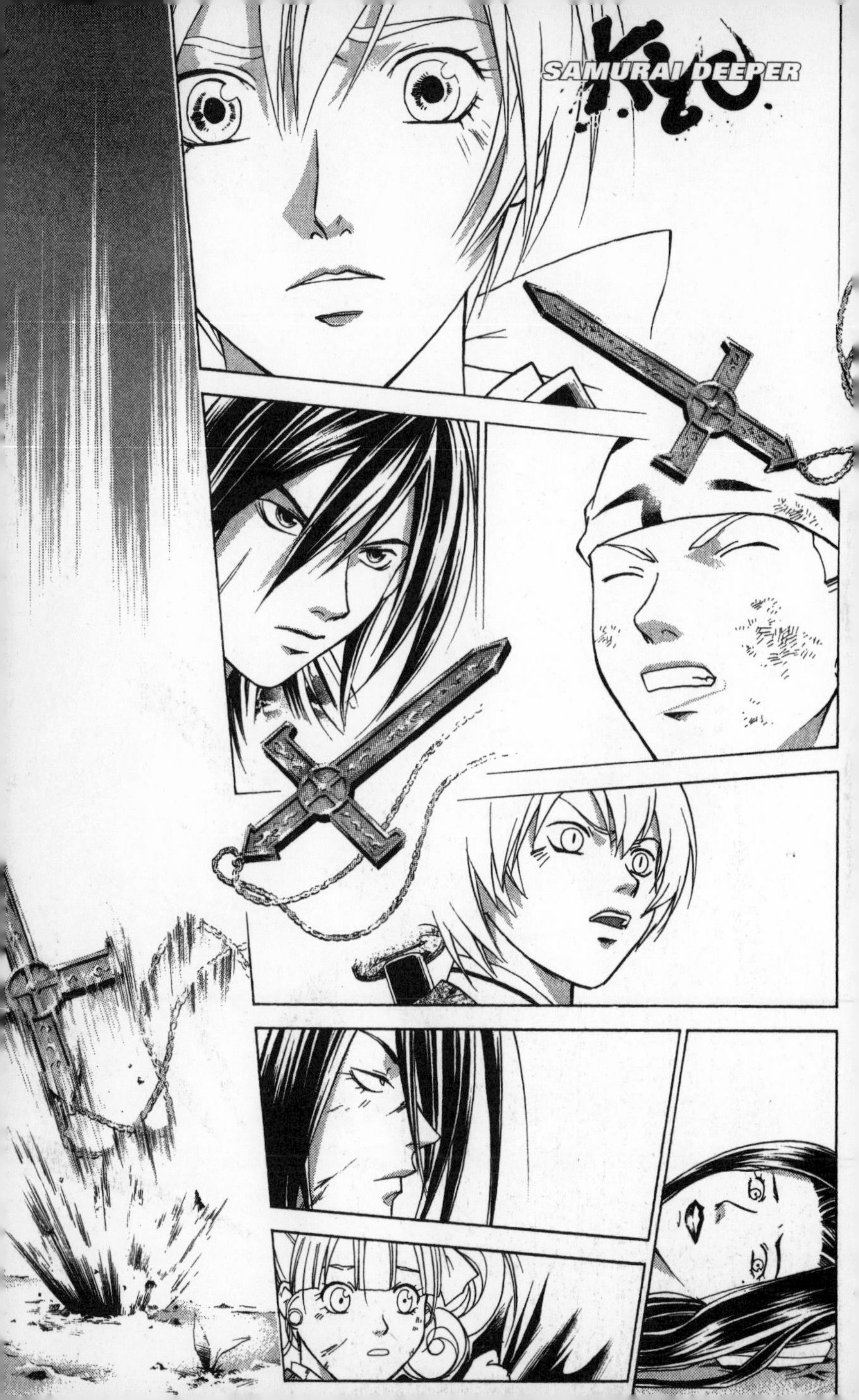
SAMURAI DEEPER KYO

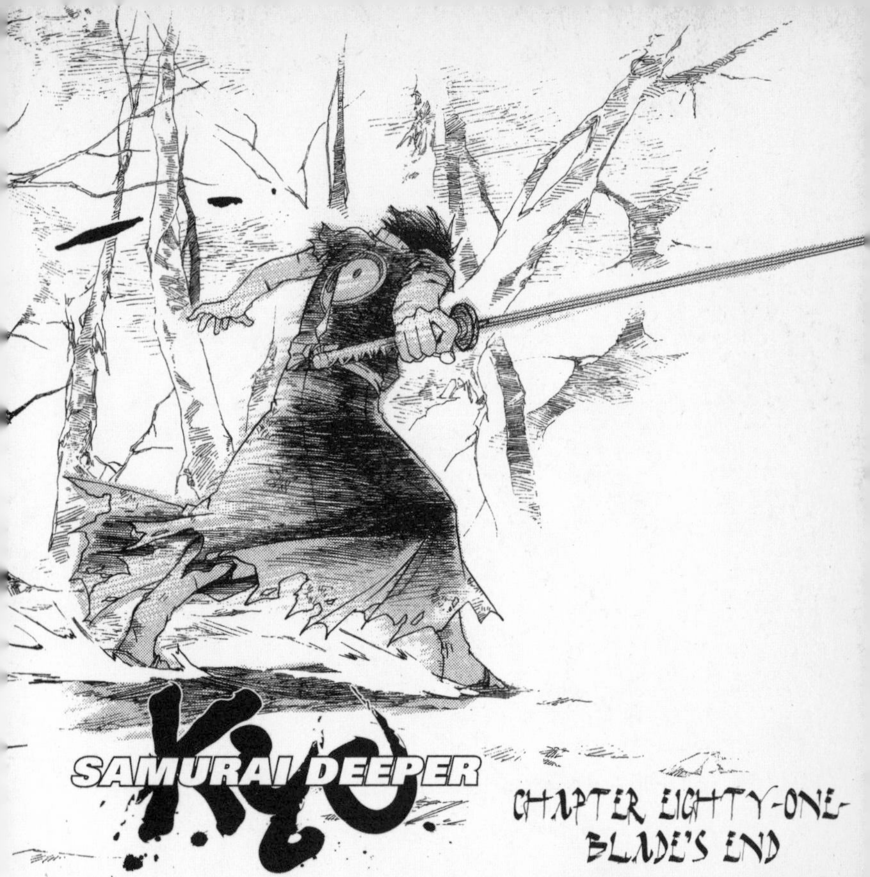
SAMURAI DEEPER KYO
CHAPTER EIGHTY-ONE-
BLADE'S END

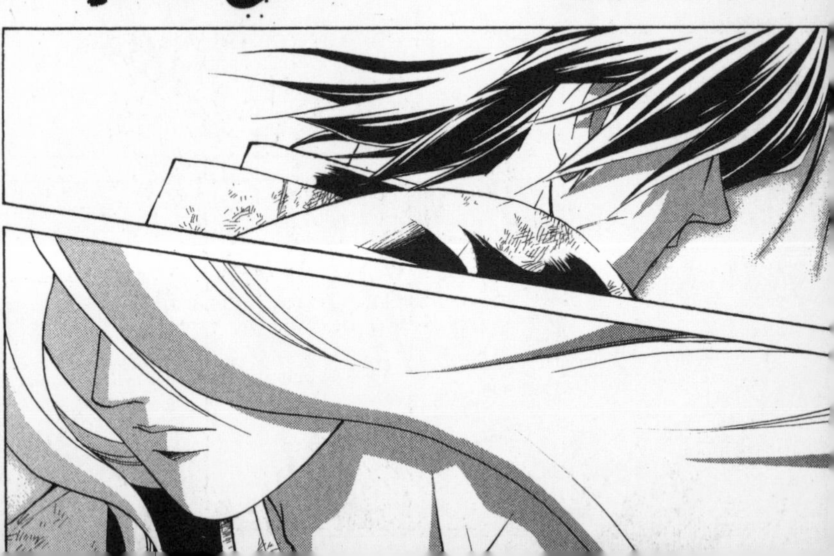

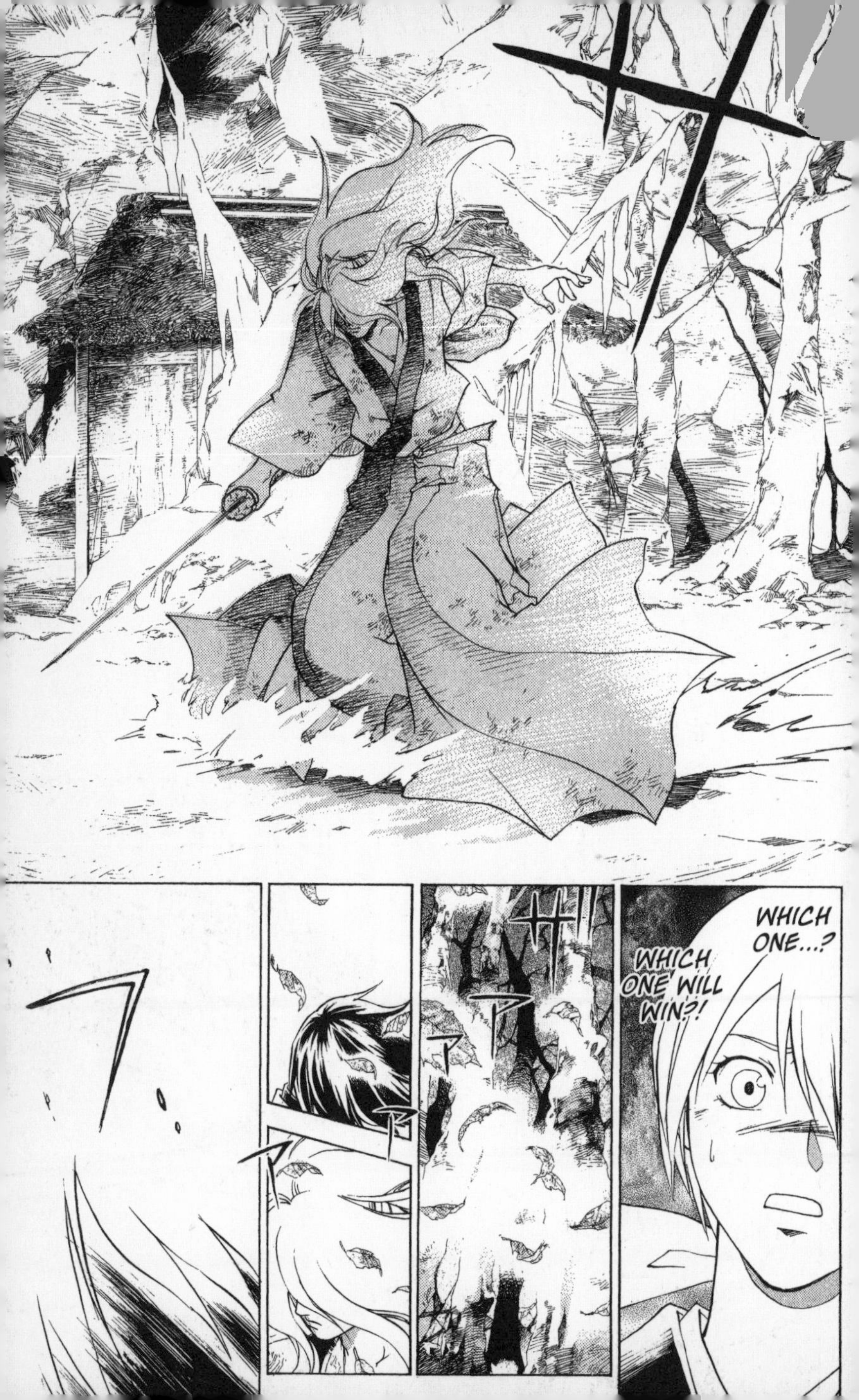
WHICH ONE...?
WHICH ONE WILL WIN?!

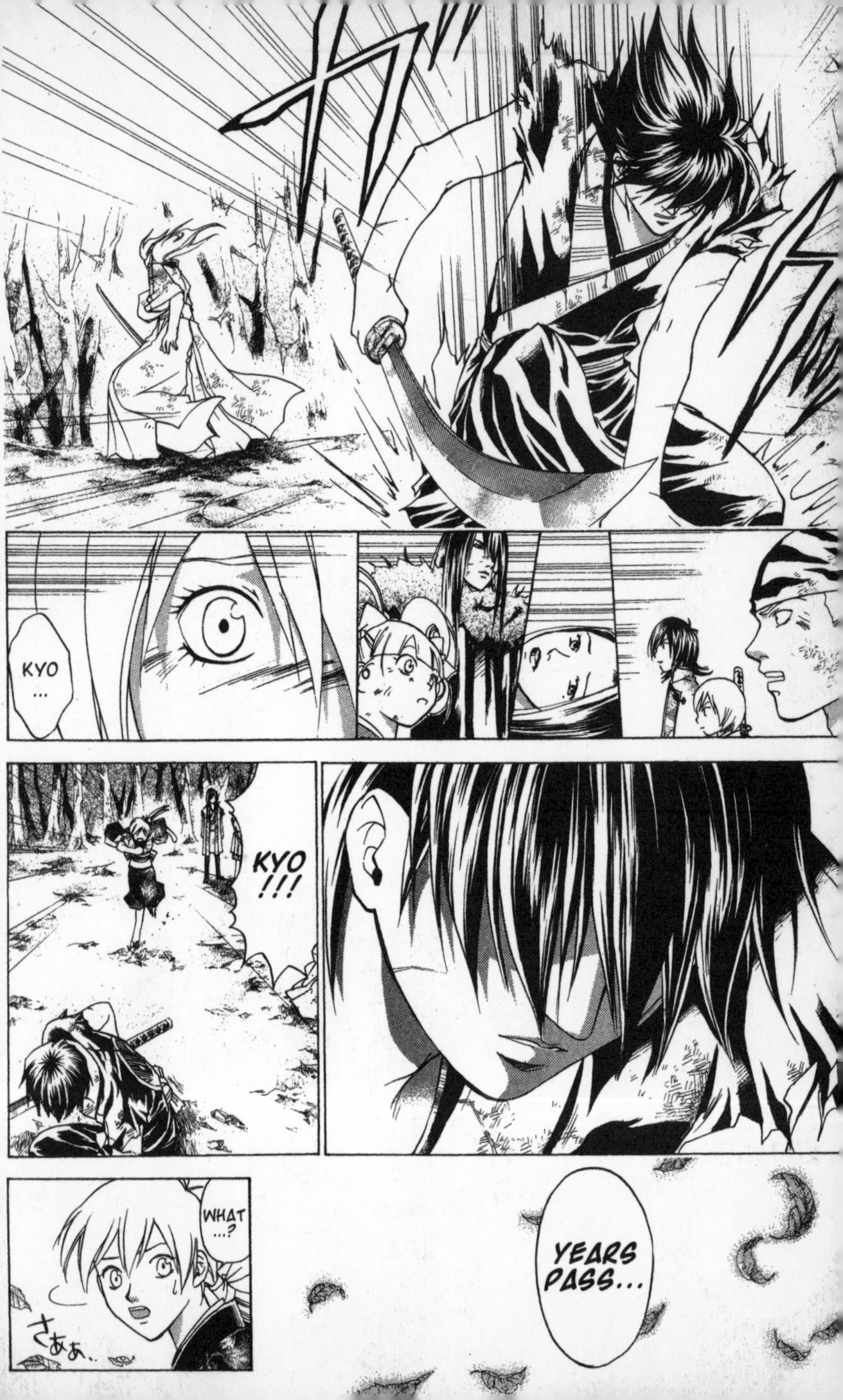
KYO ...
KYO !!!
YEARS PASS...
WHAT ...?
さあぁ..

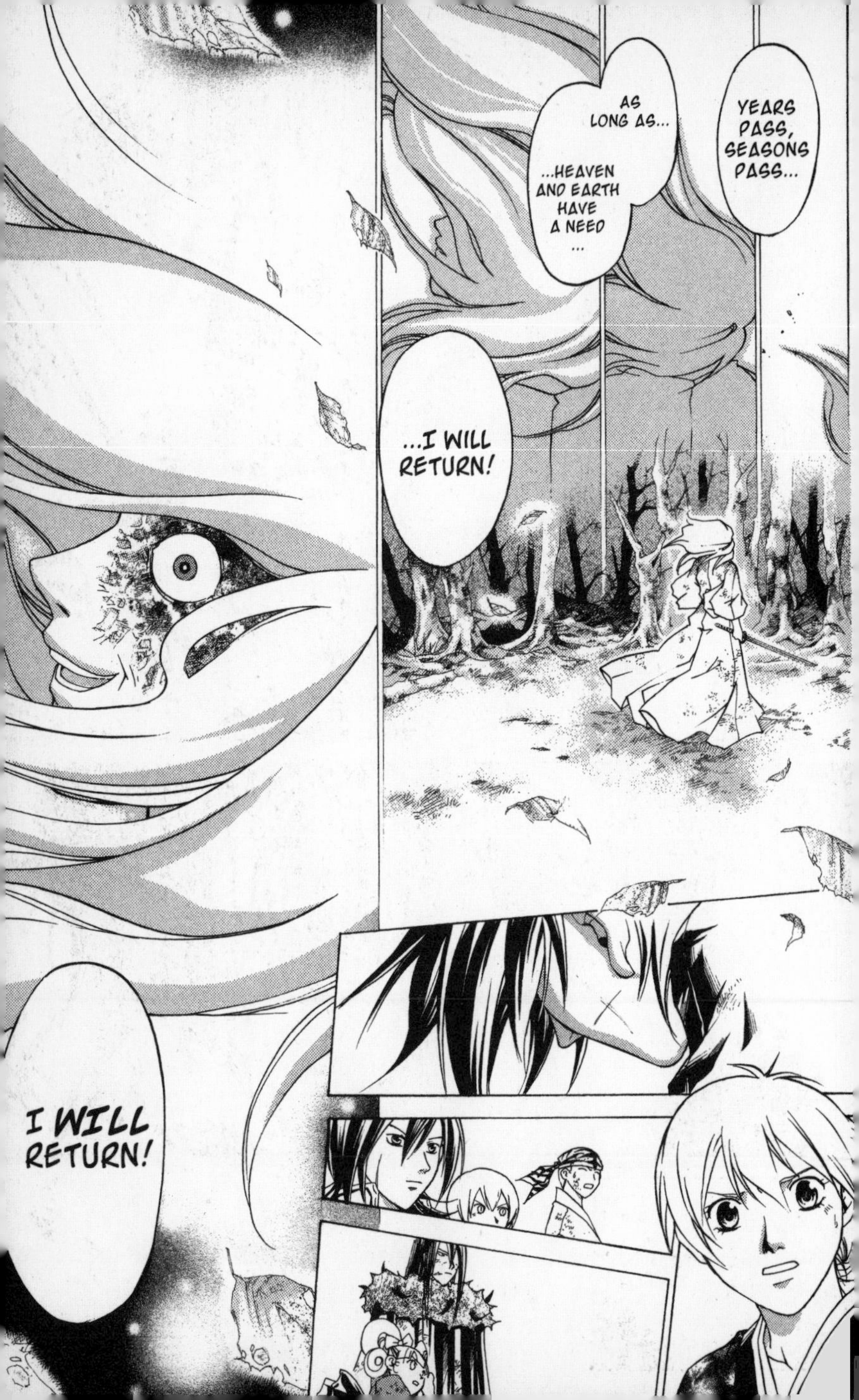
YEARS PASS, SEASONS PASS...
AS LONG AS...
...HEAVEN AND EARTH HAVE A NEED ...
...I WILL RETURN!
I WILL RETURN!

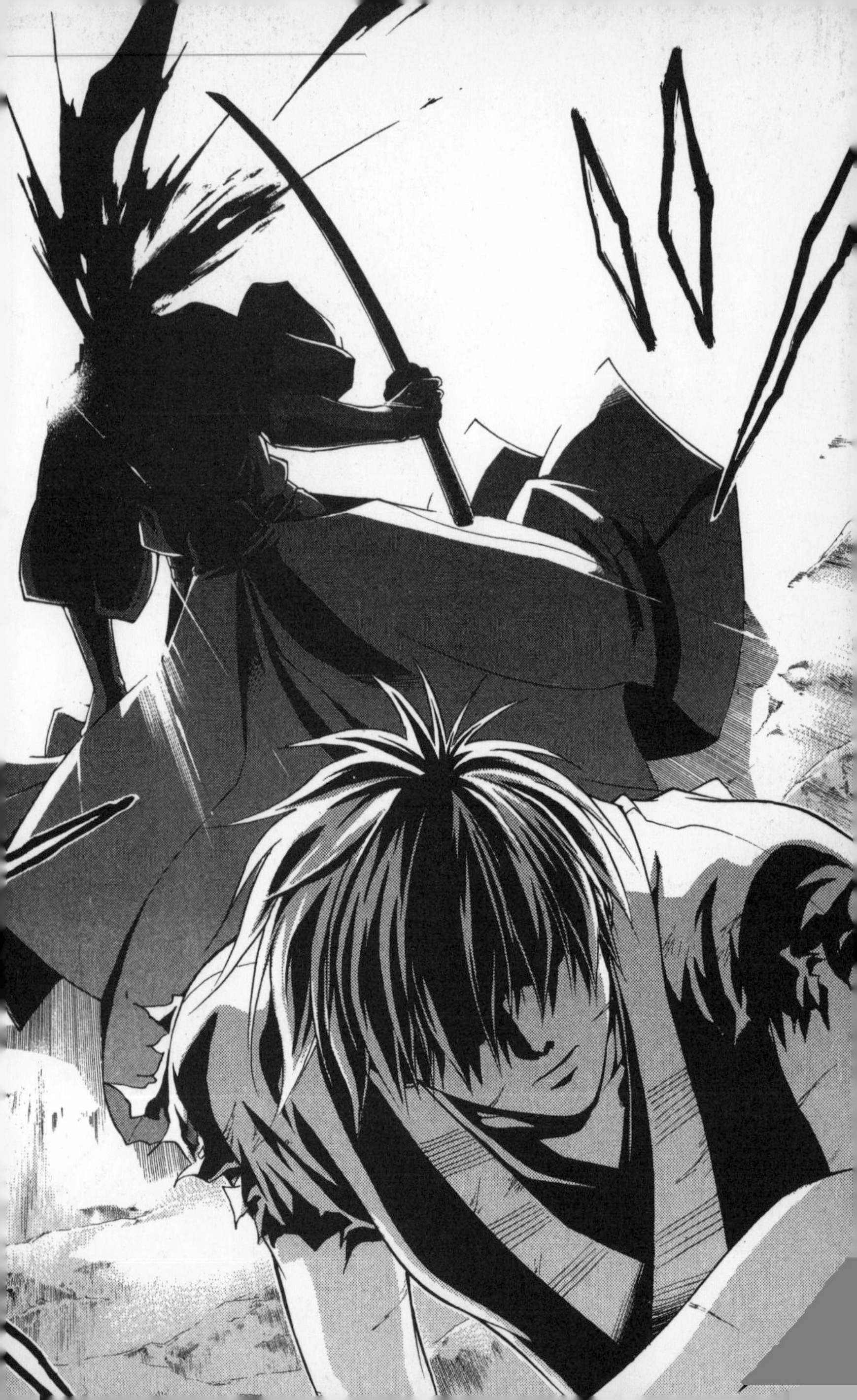

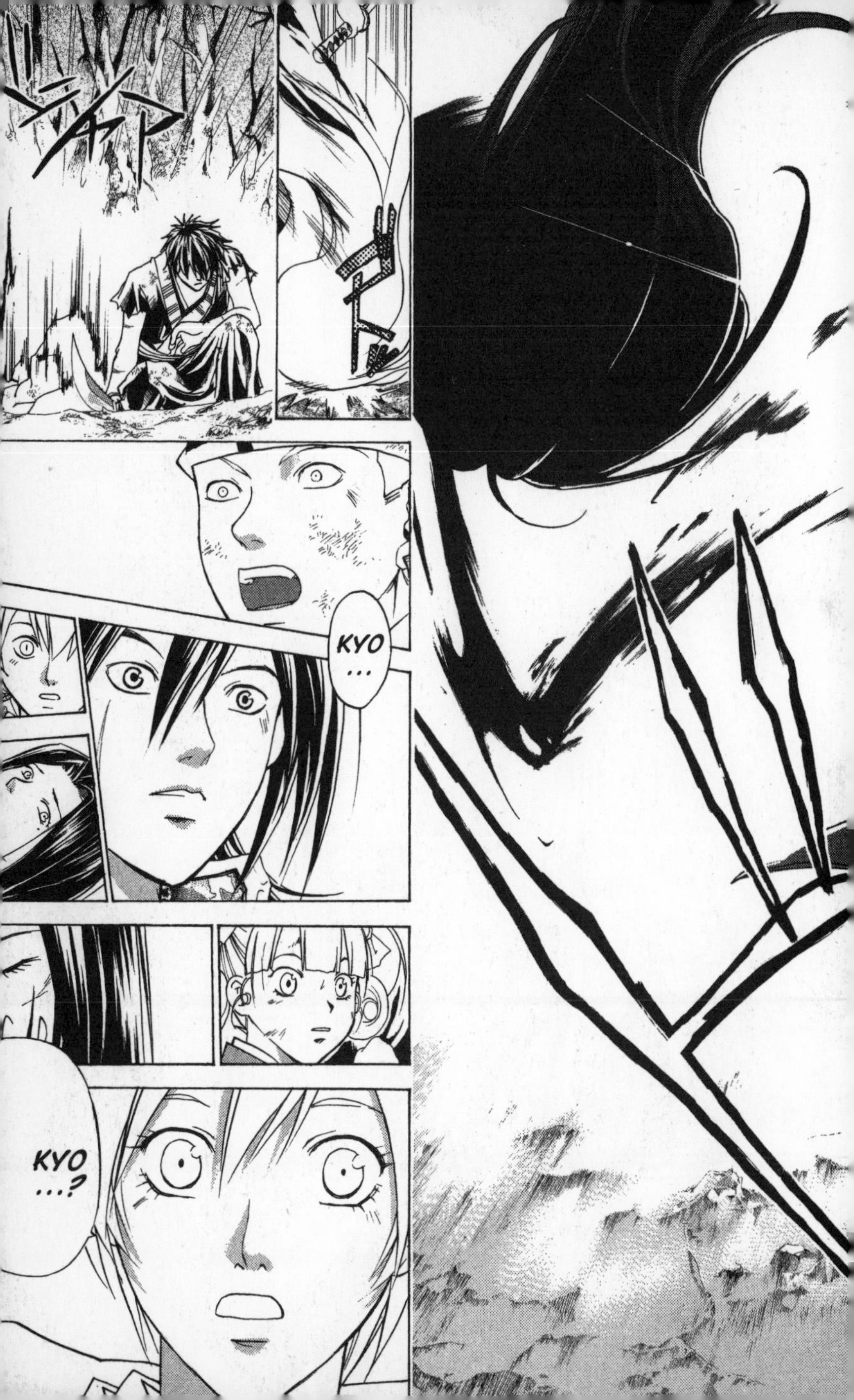
KYO ...
KYO ...?

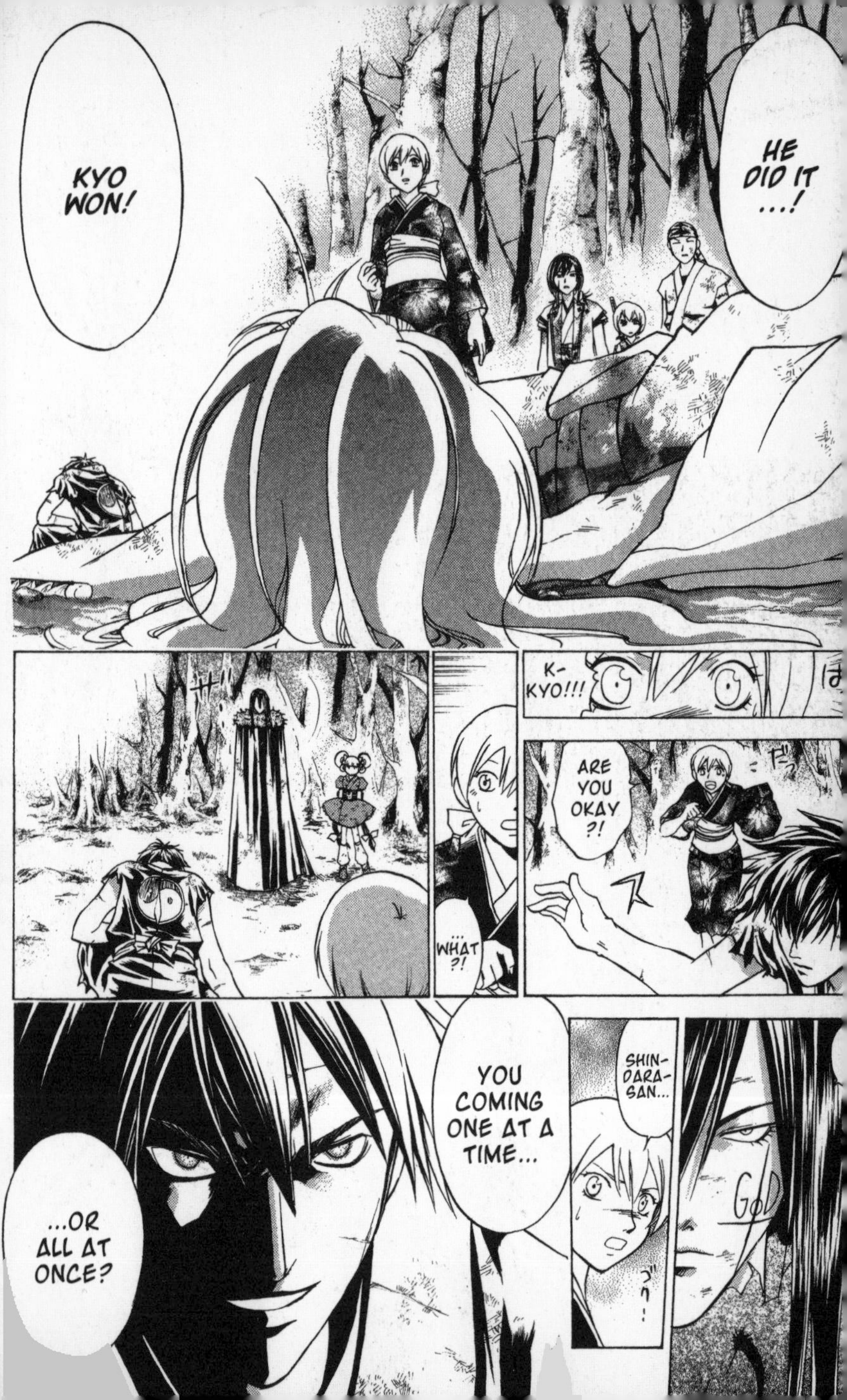
HE DID IT ...!
KYO WON!
K-KYO!!!
ARE YOU OKAY ?!
... WHAT ?!
SHIN-DARA-SAN...
YOU COMING ONE AT A TIME...
...OR ALL AT ONCE?

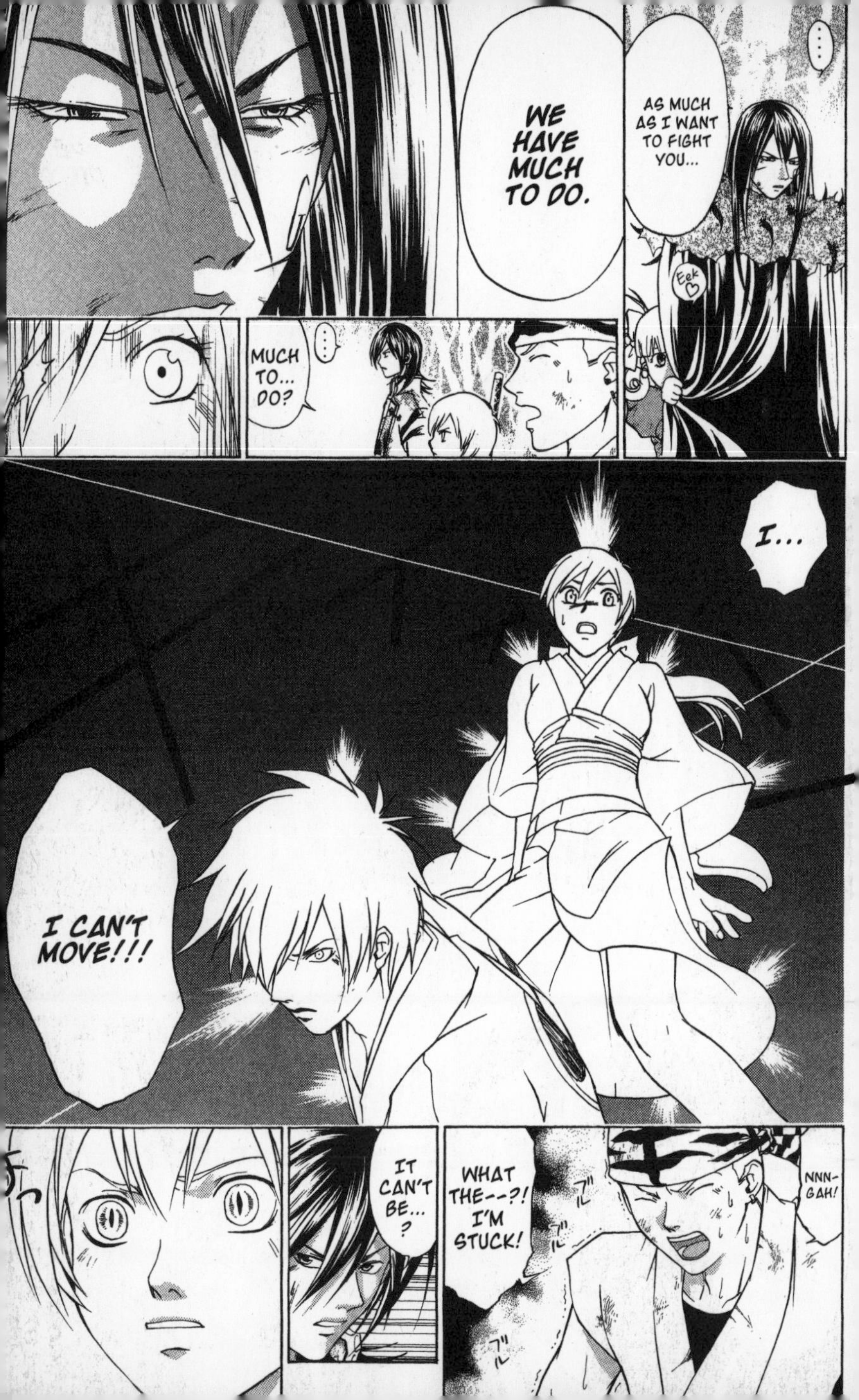
. . .
AS MUCH AS I WANT TO FIGHT YOU...
Eek ♡
WE HAVE MUCH TO DO.
. . .
MUCH TO... DO?
I...
I CAN'T MOVE!!!
NNN-GAH!
WHAT THE--?! I'M STUCK!
IT CAN'T BE...?

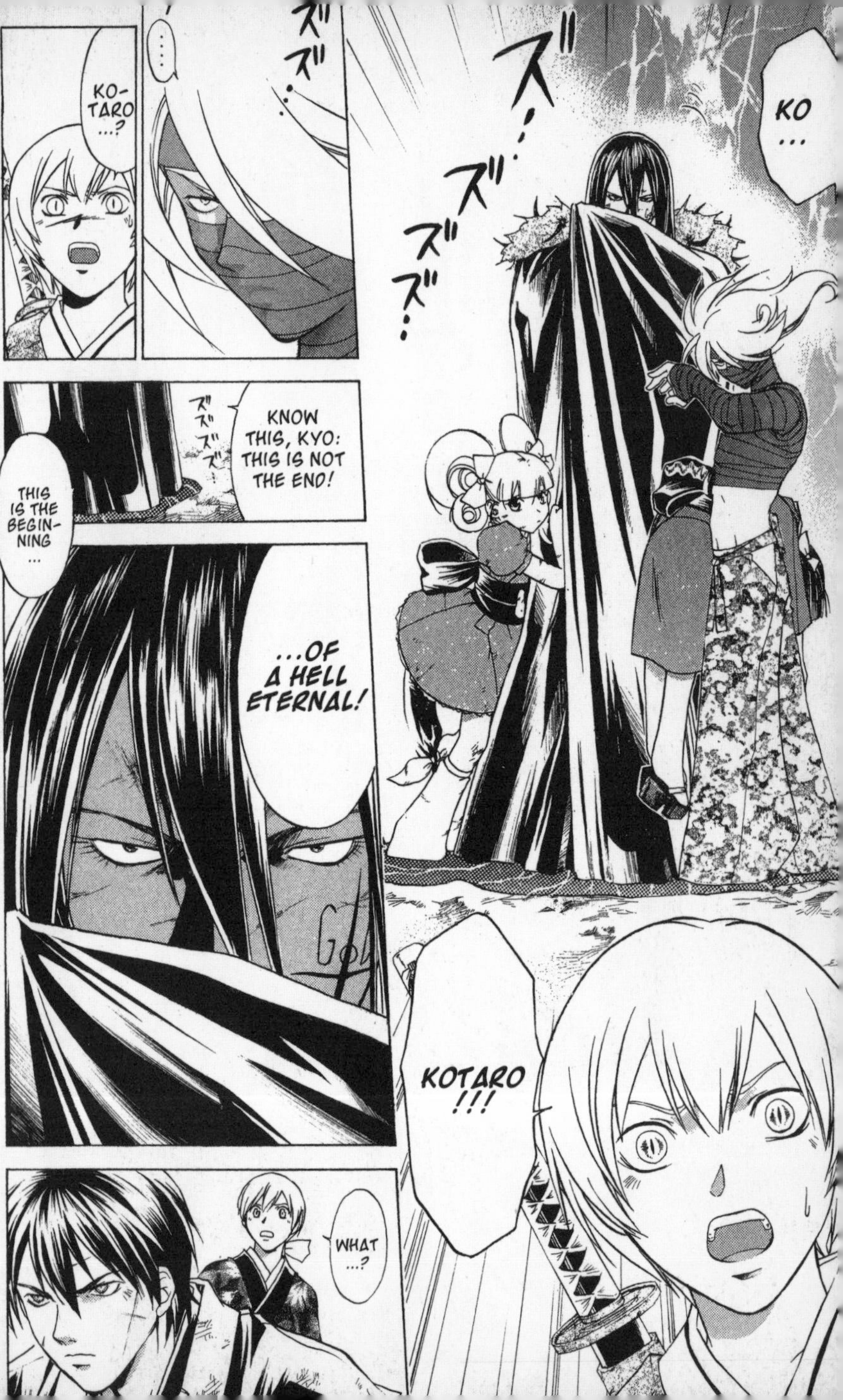
KO ...
ズ...ズズズ...
......
KO-TARO ...?
ズズズズ
KNOW THIS, KYO: THIS IS NOT THE END!
THIS IS THE BEGIN-NING ...
...OF A HELL ETERNAL!
KOTARO !!!
WHAT ...?

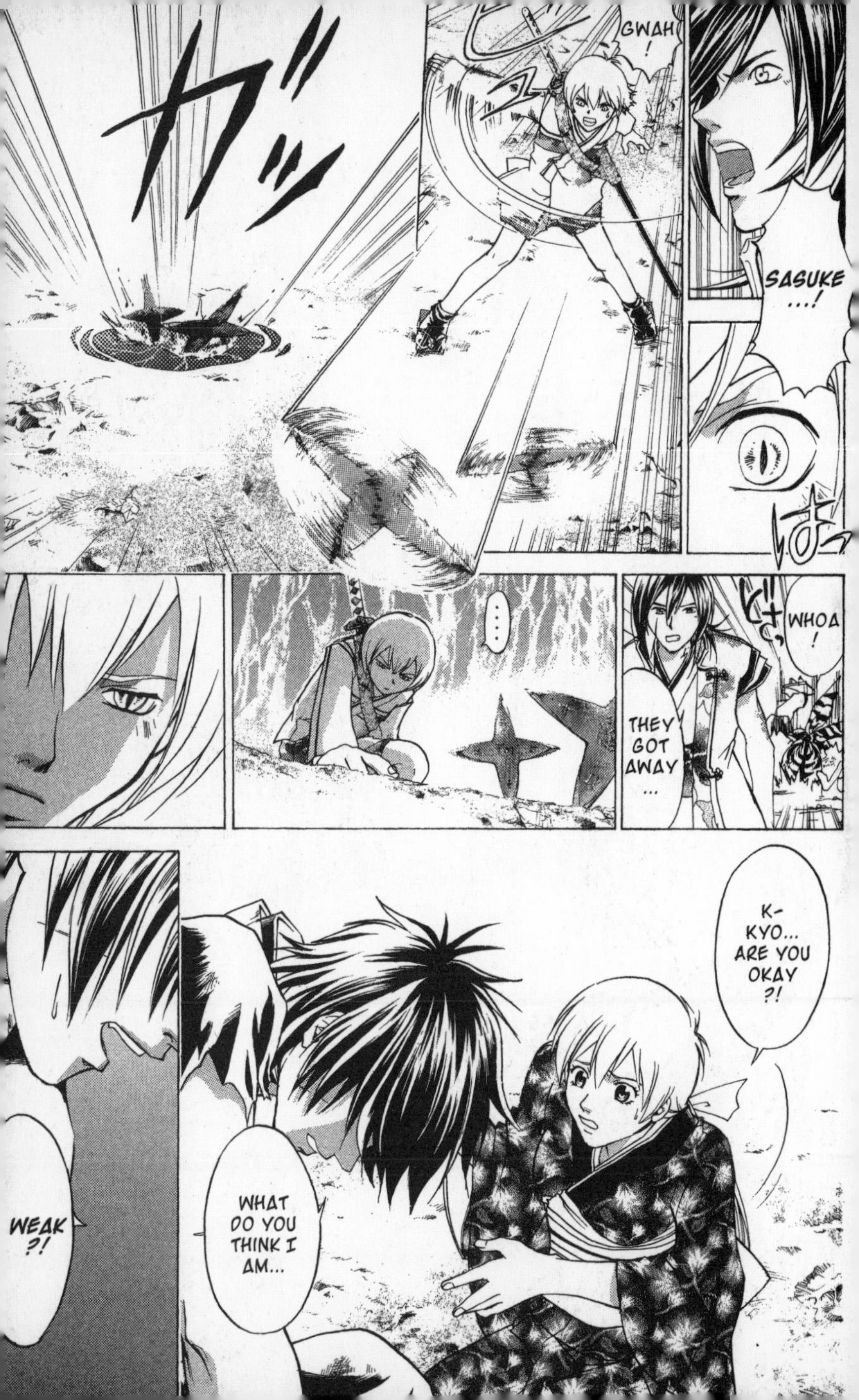
SASUKE ...!
はっ
GWAH!
ガッ
WHOA!
THEY GOT AWAY ...
...
K-KYO... ARE YOU OKAY ?!
WHAT DO YOU THINK I AM...
WEAK ?!

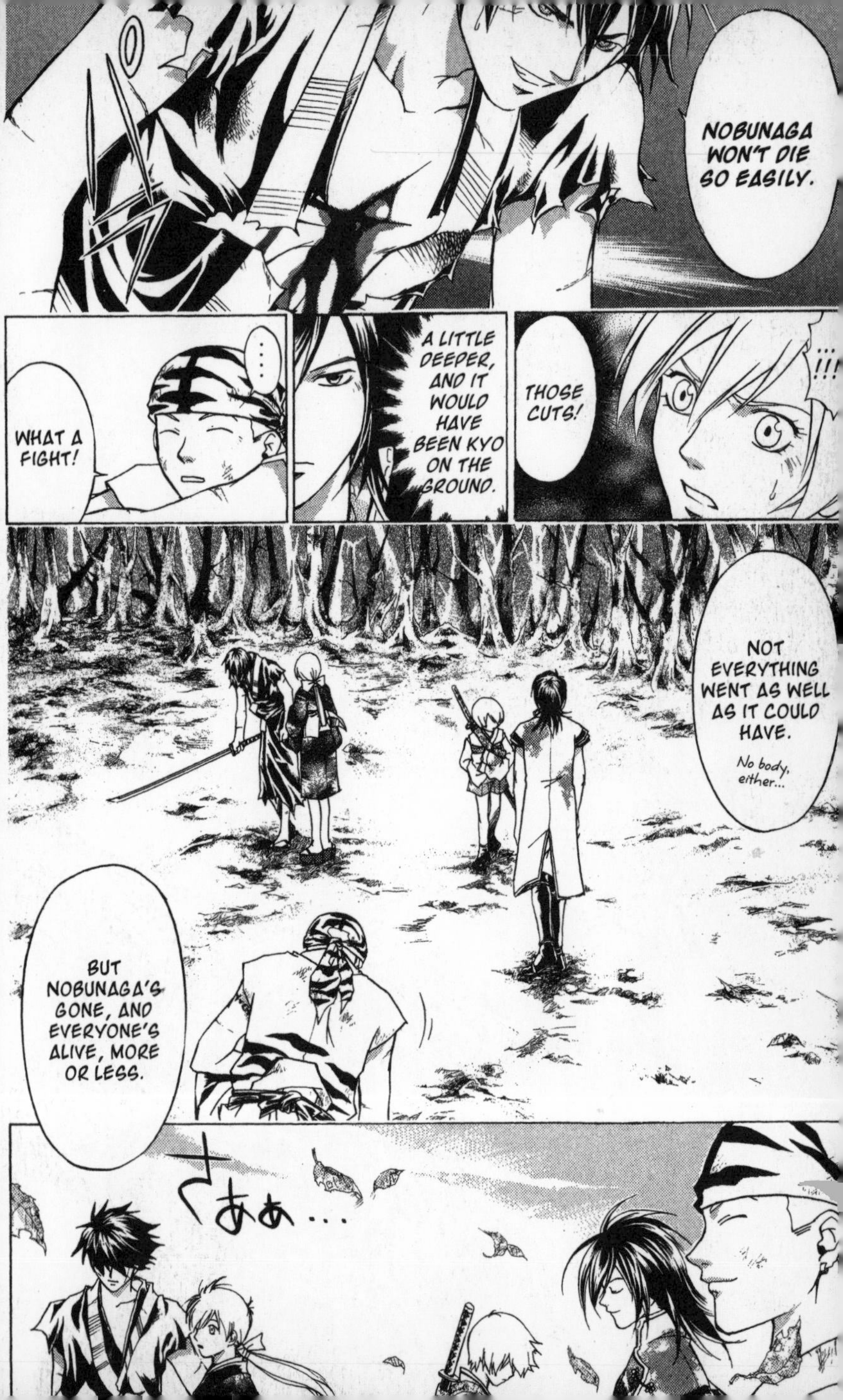
NOBUNAGA WON'T DIE SO EASILY.
!!!
THOSE CUTS!
A LITTLE DEEPER, AND IT WOULD HAVE BEEN KYO ON THE GROUND.
....
WHAT A FIGHT!
NOT EVERYTHING WENT AS WELL AS IT COULD HAVE.
No body, either...
BUT NOBUNAGA'S GONE, AND EVERYONE'S ALIVE, MORE OR LESS.
さあぁ...

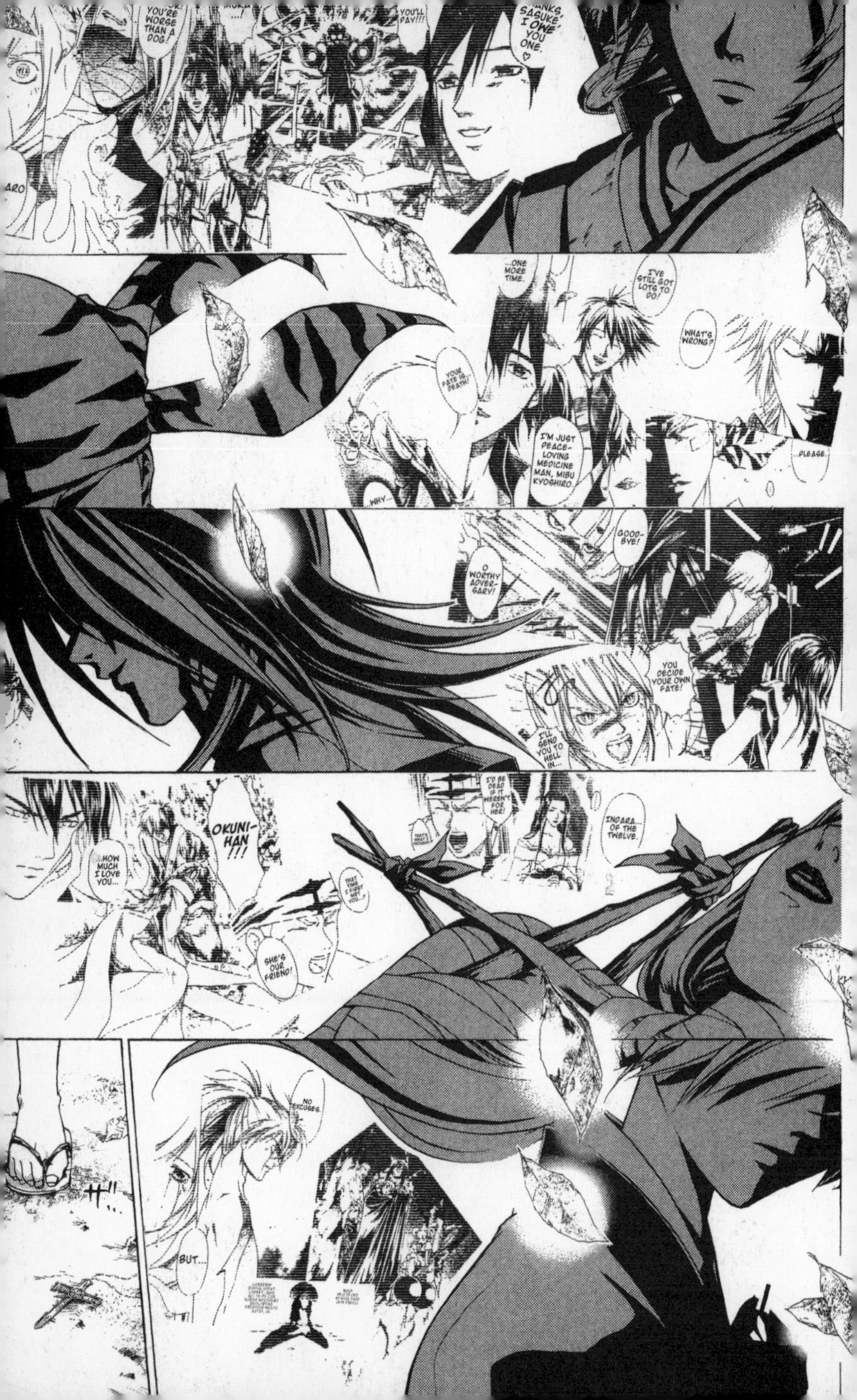

THANKS, SASUKE, I OWE YOU ONE. ♡
YOU'LL PAY!!!
...!
YOU'RE WORSE THAN A DOG!
ARO
...PLEASE.
WHAT'S WRONG?
I'VE STILL GOT LOTS TO DO!
...ONE MORE TIME.
I'M JUST PEACE-LOVING MEDICINE MAN, MIBU KYOSHIRO.
YOUR FATE IS... DEATH!
...WHY...
GOOD-BYE!
YOU DECIDE YOUR OWN FATE!
I'LL SEND YOU TO HELL IN...
O WORTHY ADVERSARY!
INDARA... OF THE TWELVE.
I'D BE DEAD IF IT WEREN'T FOR HER!
THAT TIME I FIRST MET YOU...?
SHE'S OUR FRIEND!
OKUNI-HAN!!!
...HOW MUCH I LOVE YOU...
NO EXCUSES.
BUT...
!!...

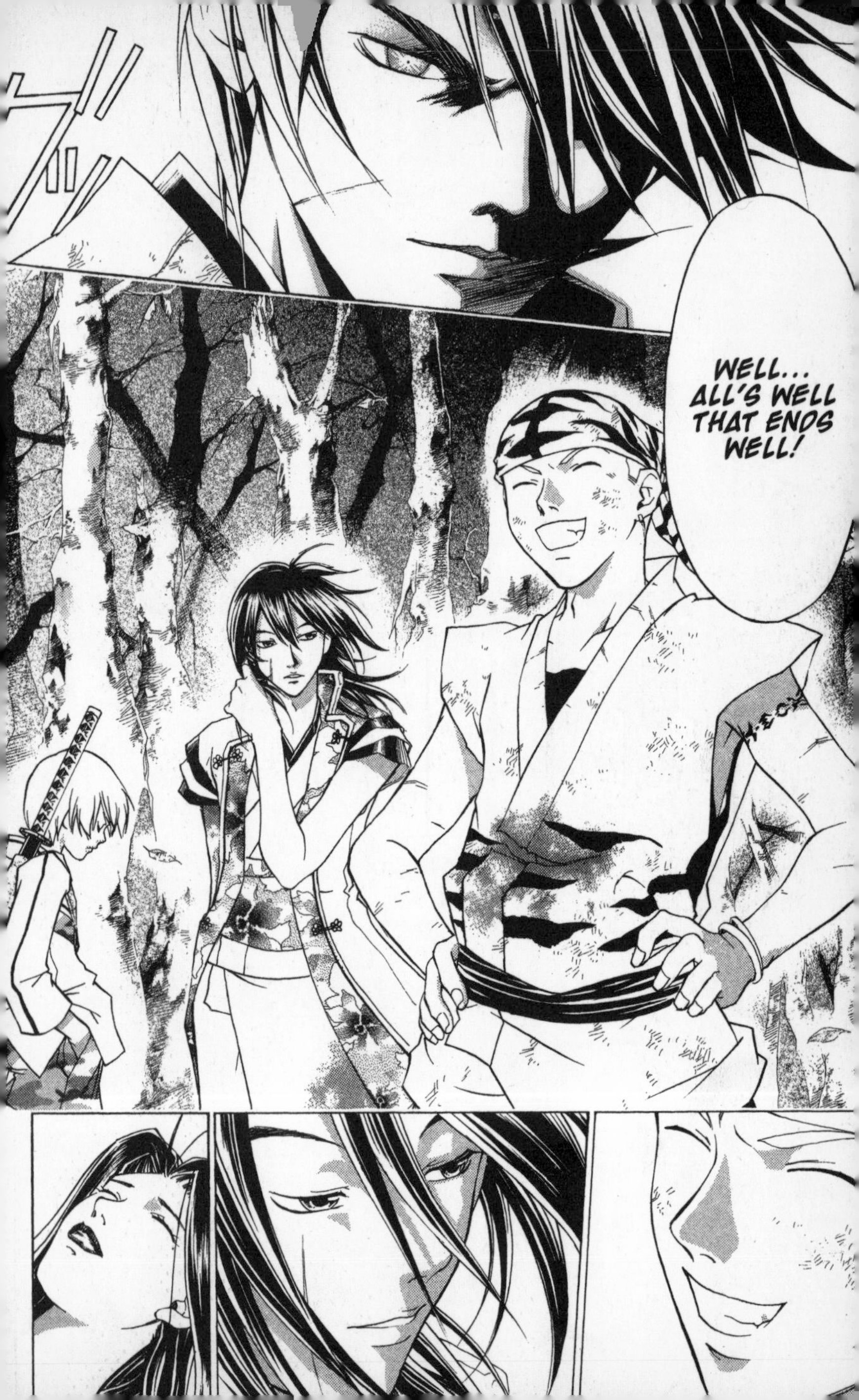
WELL... ALL'S WELL THAT ENDS WELL!

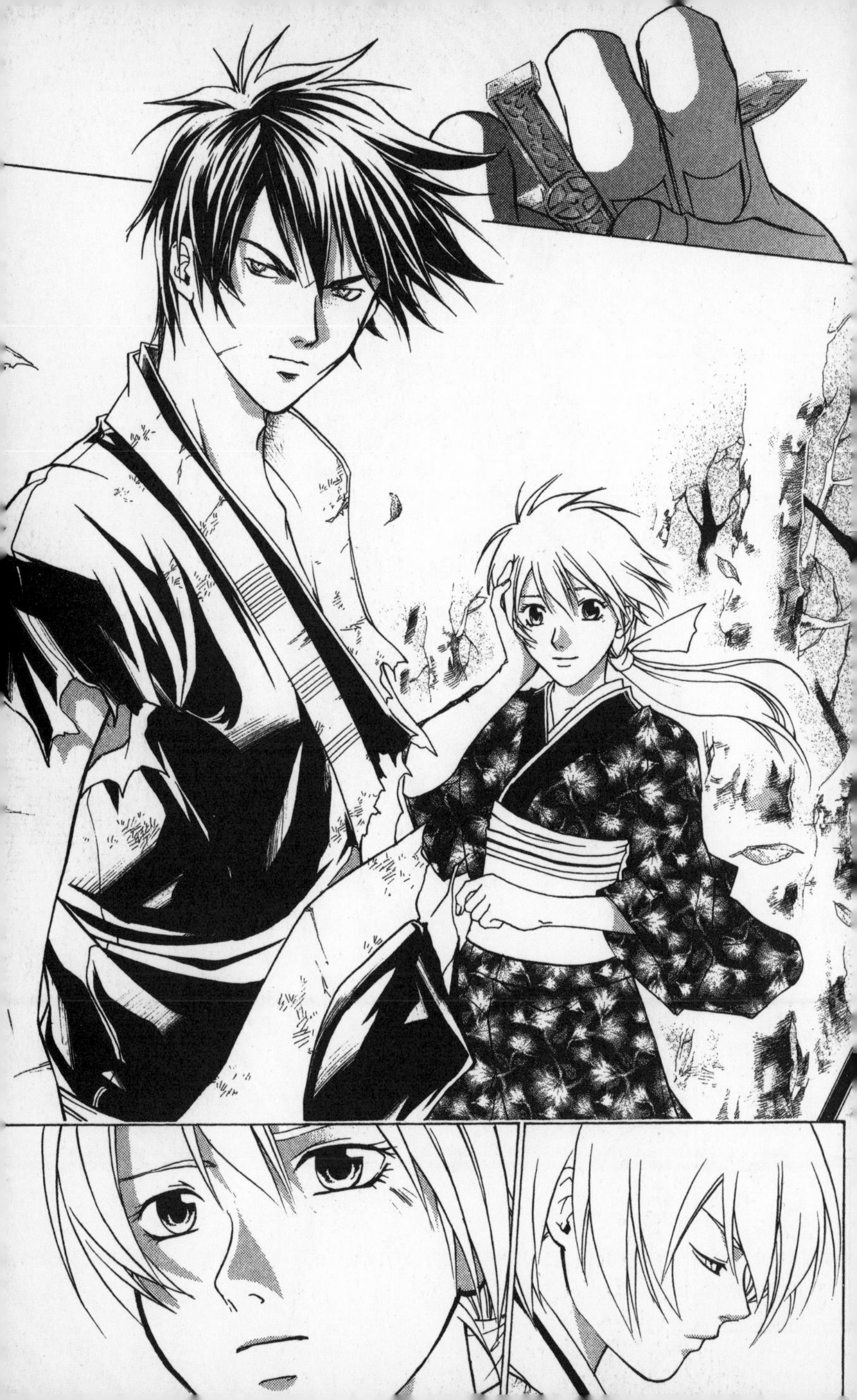

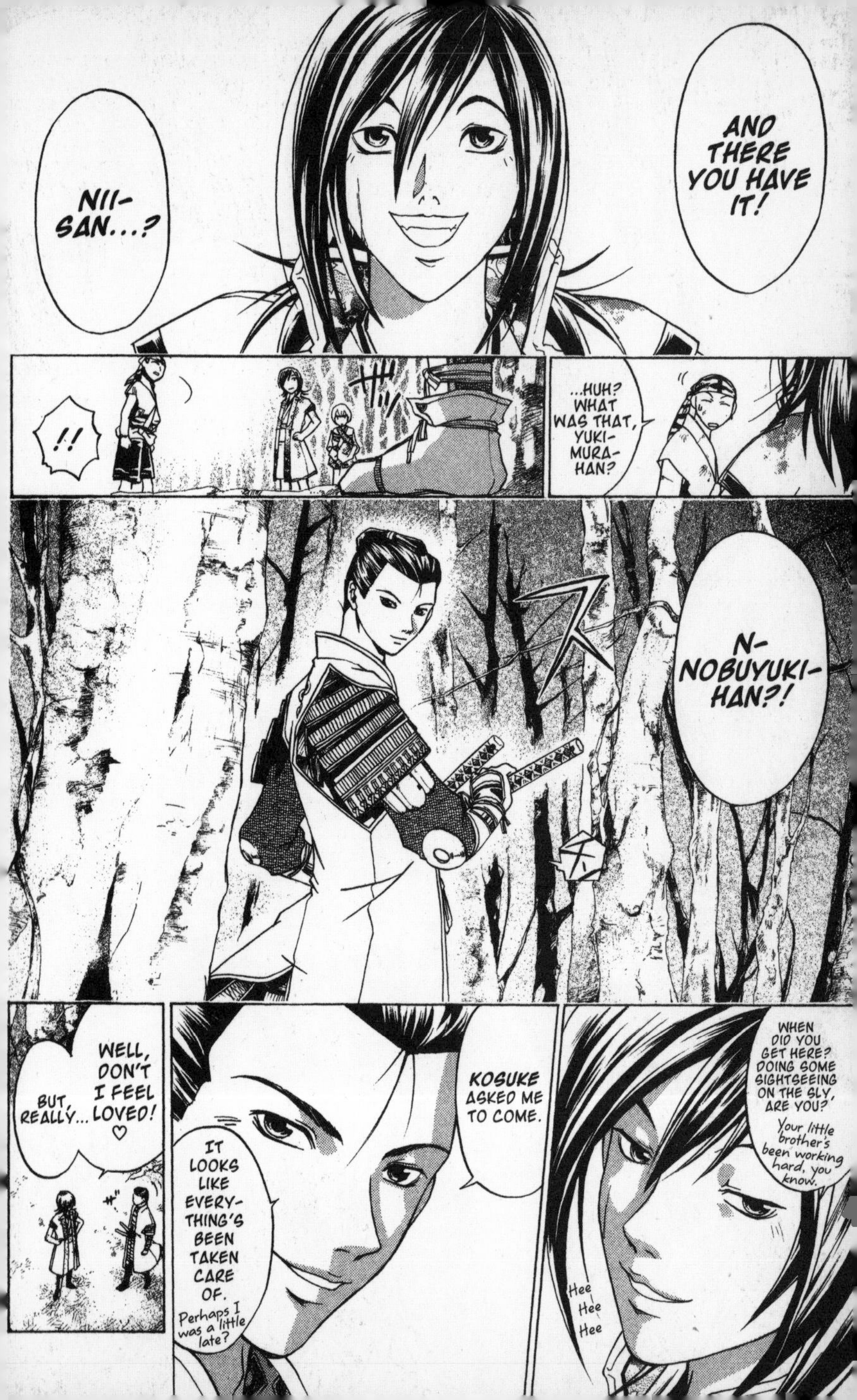
AND THERE YOU HAVE IT!
NII-SAN...?
...HUH? WHAT WAS THAT, YUKI-MURA-HAN?
!!
N-NOBUYUKI-HAN?!
WHEN DID YOU GET HERE? DOING SOME SIGHTSEEING ON THE SLY, ARE YOU?
Your little brother's been working hard, you know.
Hee Hee Hee
KOSUKE ASKED ME TO COME.
IT LOOKS LIKE EVERY-THING'S BEEN TAKEN CARE OF.
Perhaps I was a little late?
WELL, DON'T I FEEL LOVED! ♡
BUT, REALLY...

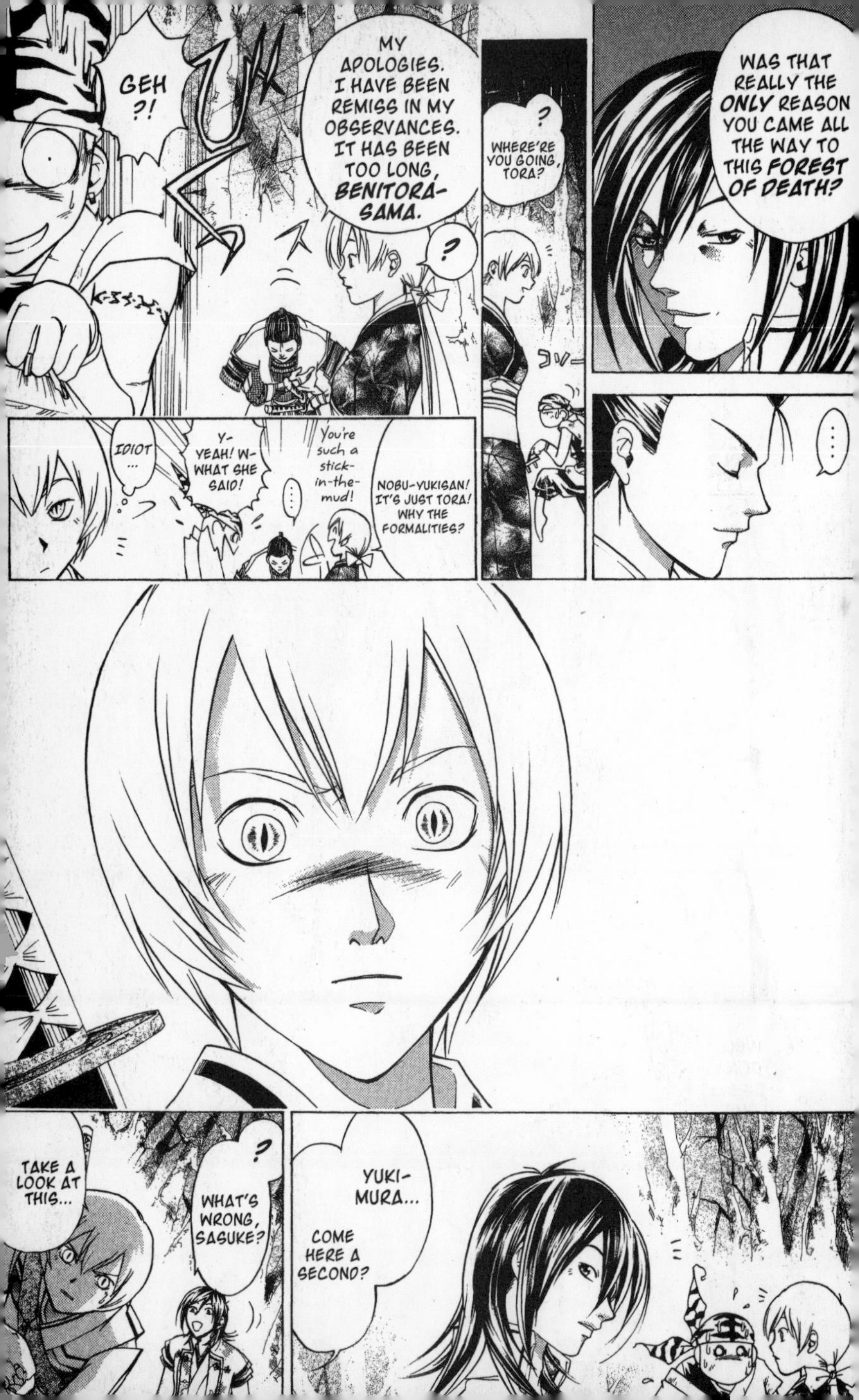
WAS THAT REALLY THE ONLY REASON YOU CAME ALL THE WAY TO THIS FOREST OF DEATH?
....
?
WHERE'RE YOU GOING, TORA?
コソー
MY APOLOGIES. I HAVE BEEN REMISS IN MY OBSERVANCES. IT HAS BEEN TOO LONG, BENITORA-SAMA.
?
GEH ?!
NOBU-YUKISAN! IT'S JUST TORA! WHY THE FORMALITIES?
You're such a stick-in-the-mud!
....
Y-YEAH! W-WHAT SHE SAID!
IDIOT ...
YUKI-MURA...
COME HERE A SECOND?
?
WHAT'S WRONG, SASUKE?
TAKE A LOOK AT THIS...

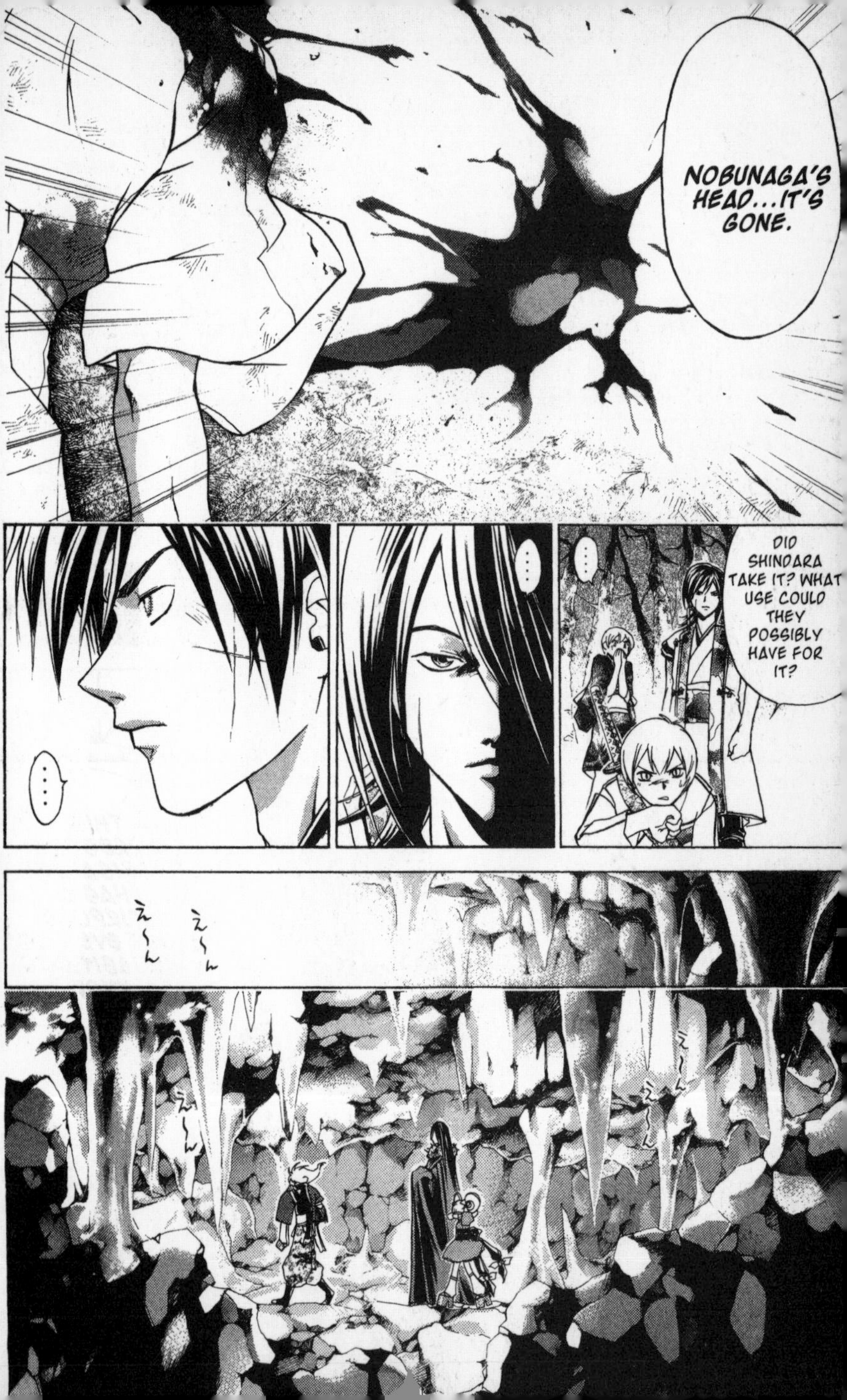
NOBUNAGA'S HEAD...IT'S GONE.
DID SHINDARA TAKE IT? WHAT USE COULD THEY POSSIBLY HAVE FOR IT?
...
...
....
え～ん
え～ん
え～ん
え～ん
え～ん

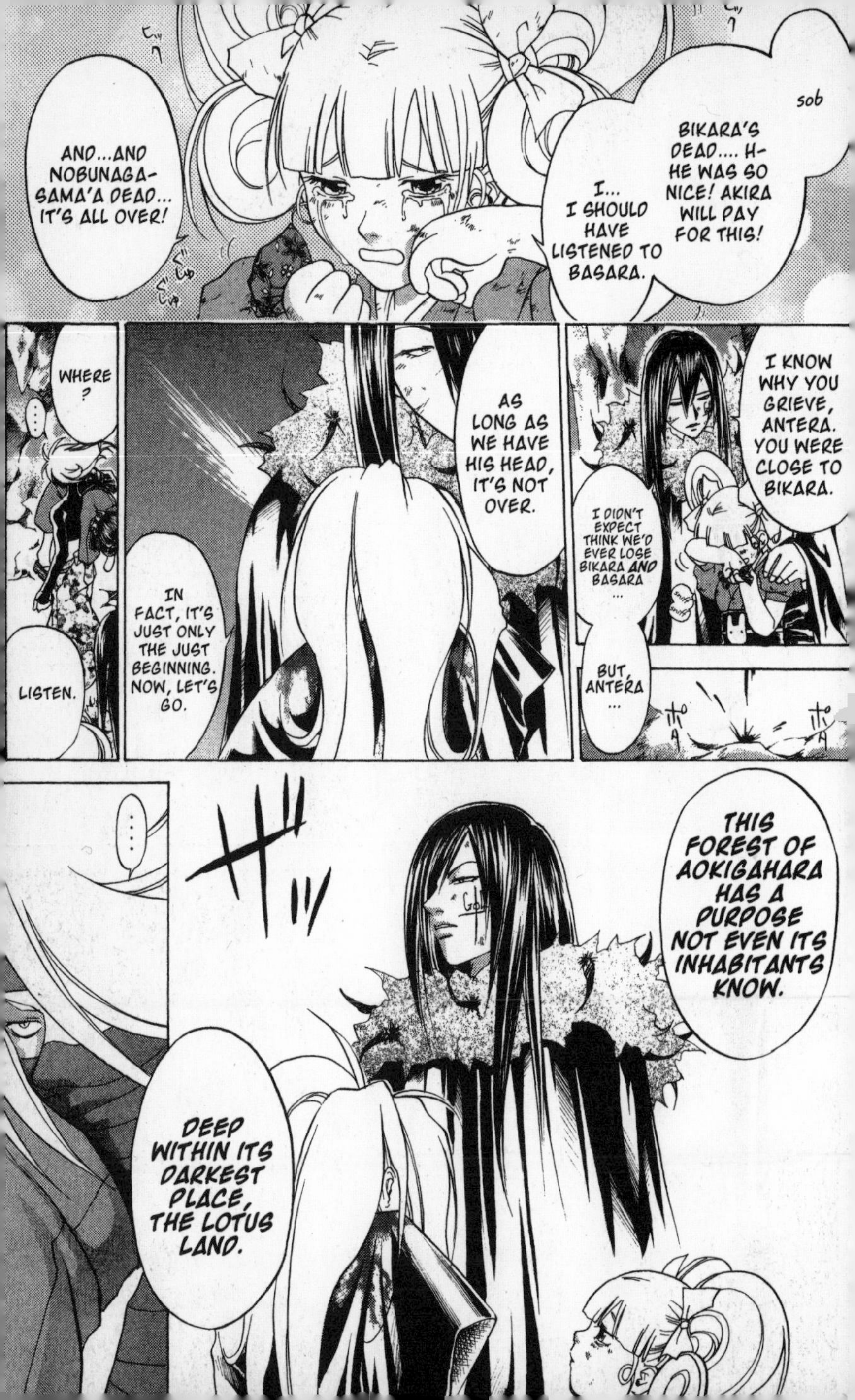
sob
BIKARA'S DEAD.... H-HE WAS SO NICE! AKIRA WILL PAY FOR THIS!
I... I SHOULD HAVE LISTENED TO BASARA.
AND...AND NOBUNAGA-SAMA'A DEAD... IT'S ALL OVER!
I KNOW WHY YOU GRIEVE, ANTERA. YOU WERE CLOSE TO BIKARA.
I DIDN'T EXPECT THINK WE'D EVER LOSE BIKARA AND BASARA ...
BUT, ANTERA ...
AS LONG AS WE HAVE HIS HEAD, IT'S NOT OVER.
IN FACT, IT'S JUST ONLY THE JUST BEGINNING. NOW, LET'S GO.
WHERE ?
...
LISTEN.
THIS FOREST OF AOKIGAHARA HAS A PURPOSE NOT EVEN ITS INHABITANTS KNOW.
....
DEEP WITHIN ITS DARKEST PLACE, THE LOTUS LAND.

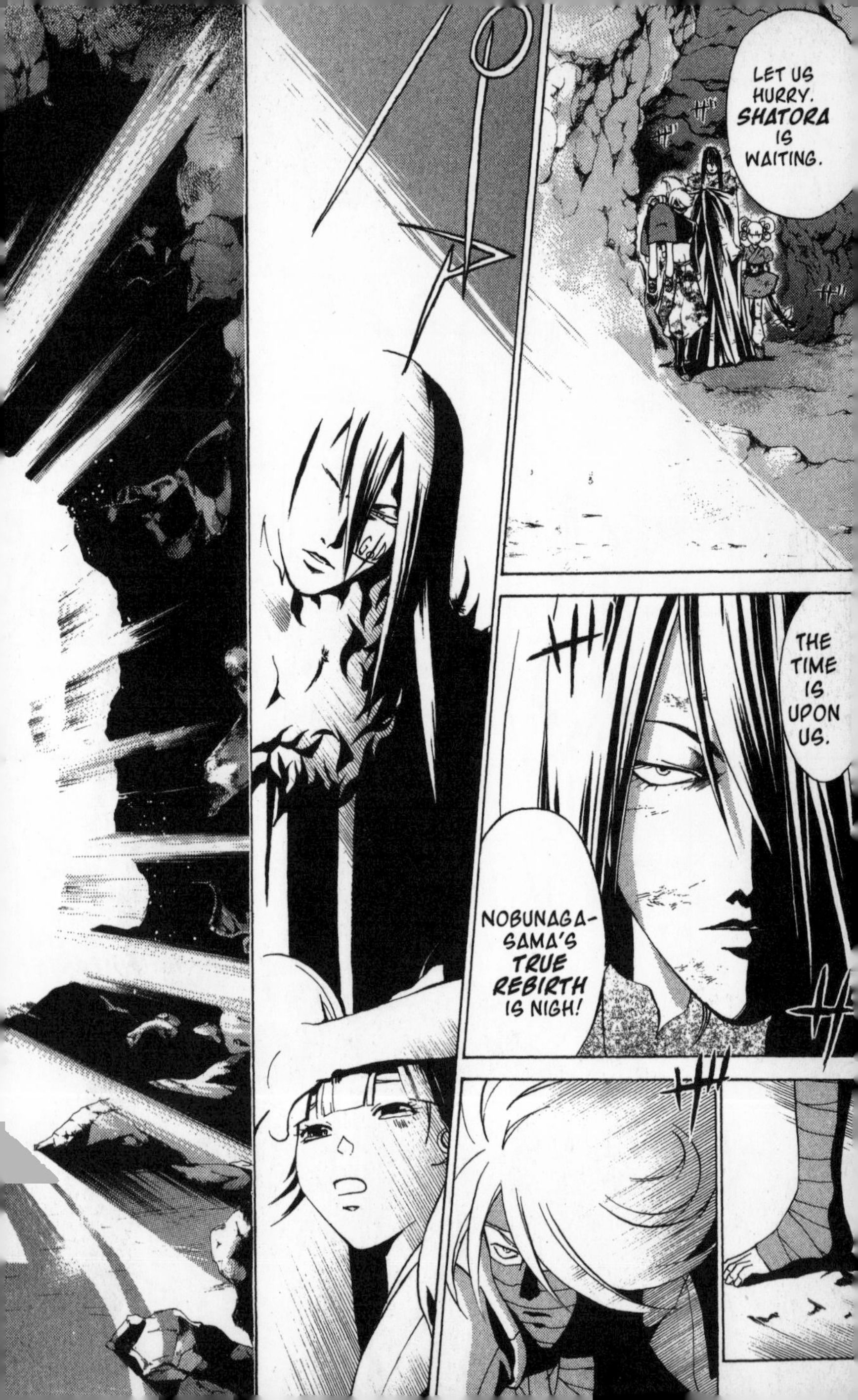
LET US HURRY. SHATORA IS WAITING.
THE TIME IS UPON US.
NOBUNAGA-SAMA'S TRUE REBIRTH IS NIGH!

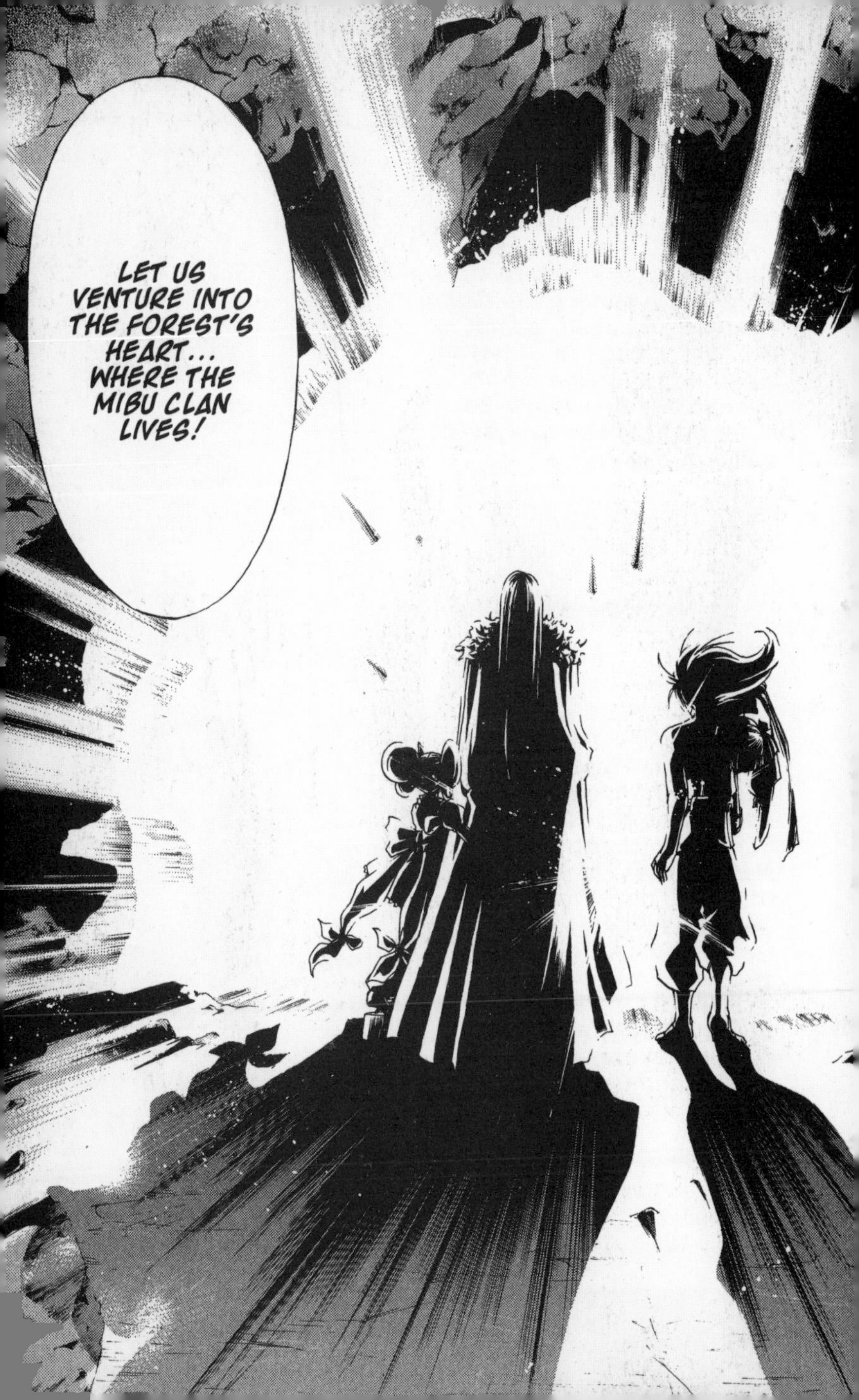
LET US VENTURE INTO THE FOREST'S HEART... WHERE THE MIBU CLAN LIVES!

上条事情 Kamijyo Circumstances

READING AT THE MAGAZINE STAND

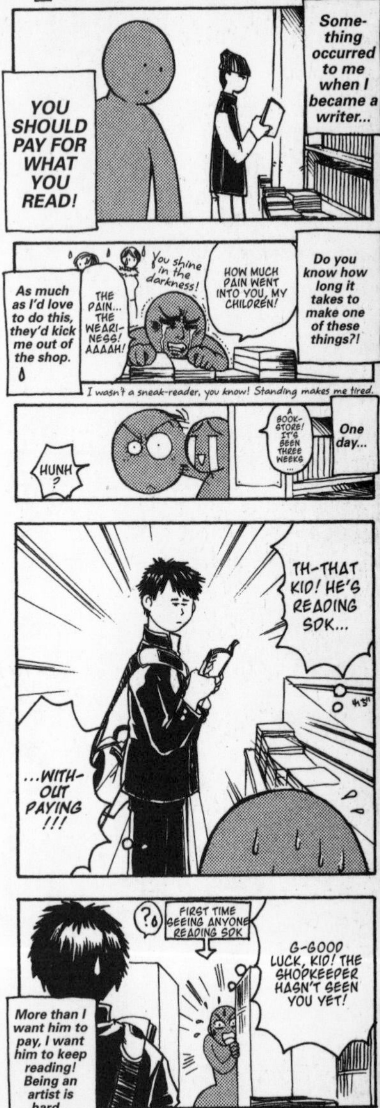
Something occurred to me when I became a writer...
YOU SHOULD PAY FOR WHAT YOU READ!
Do you know how long it takes to make one of these things?!
HOW MUCH PAIN WENT INTO YOU, MY CHILDREN!
You shine in the darkness!
THE PAIN... THE WEARINESS! AAAAH!
As much as I'd love to do this, they'd kick me out of the shop.
I wasn't a sneak-reader, you know! Standing makes me tired.
One day...
A BOOKSTORE! IT'S BEEN THREE WEEKS...
HUNH?
TH-THAT KID! HE'S READING SDK...
...WITHOUT PAYING!!!
G-GOOD LUCK, KID! THE SHOPKEEPER HASN'T SEEN YOU YET!
FIRST TIME SEEING ANYONE READING SDK
?
More than I want him to pay, I want him to keep reading! Being an artist is hard...

Hiya! Thanks to you, we've hit volume 10! Sure, the peanut gallery's saying "you're still on 10?!" but when it's you doing the work, it doesn't seem like that, somehow. Anyway, we owe it all to our faithful readers. My thanks will be... more manga! Kamijyo, over and out. See ya!

As of April 2001, our staff headman, Haruno-san is leaving us! Myself and the entire staff wouldn't have known our heads from our tails without you here, Haruno-san! Thank you so much! I'll never forget it! (Really!) Not only have I learned some great technical stuff from Haruno-san, but I also feel he made me a better person. (Really and truly!) I promise to stay true to my manga and to my dreams!

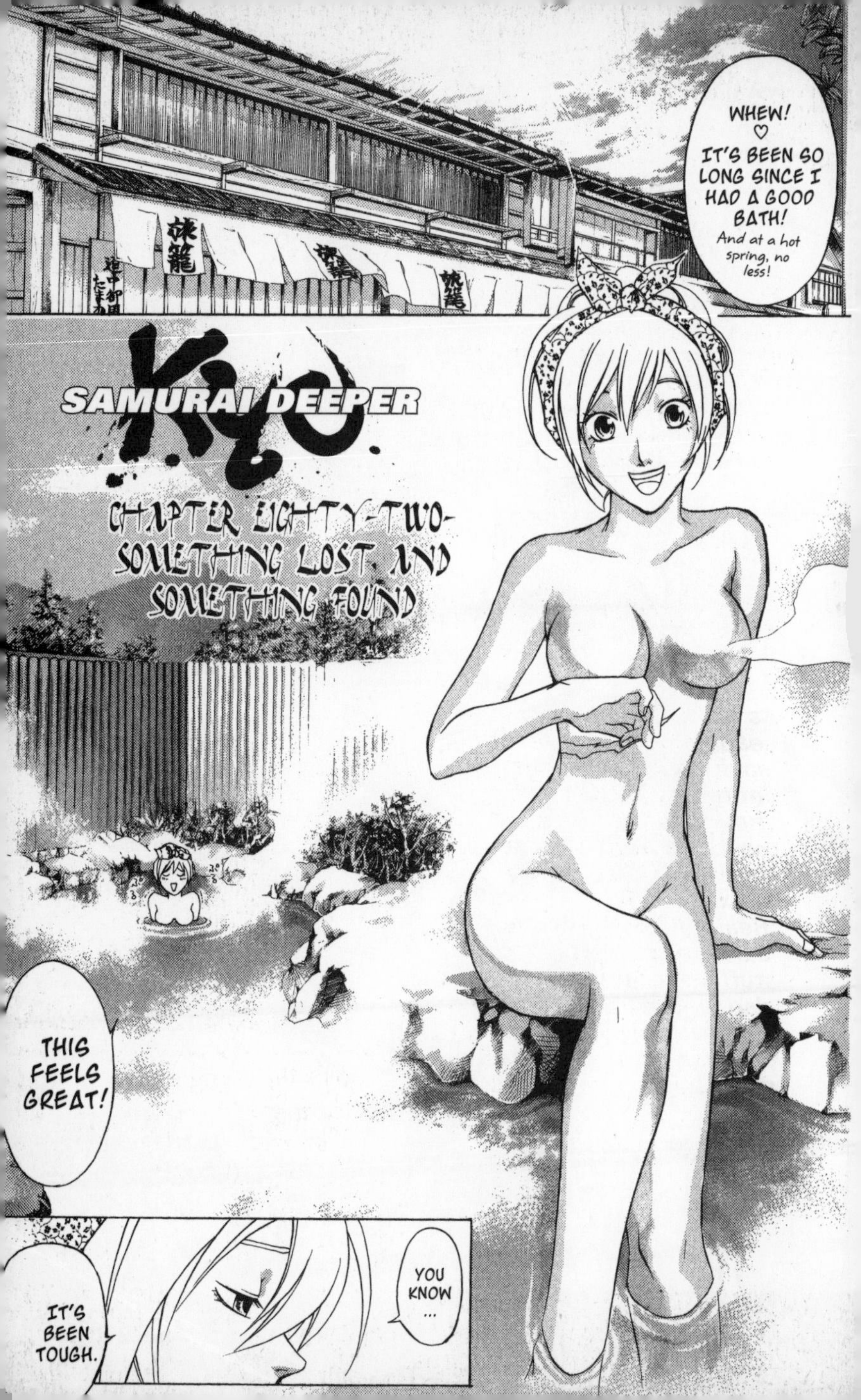
WHEW! ♡ IT'S BEEN SO LONG SINCE I HAD A GOOD BATH!
And at a hot spring, no less!
SAMURAI DEEPER KYO
CHAPTER EIGHTY-TWO- SOMETHING LOST AND SOMETHING FOUND
THIS FEELS GREAT!
YOU KNOW ...
IT'S BEEN TOUGH.

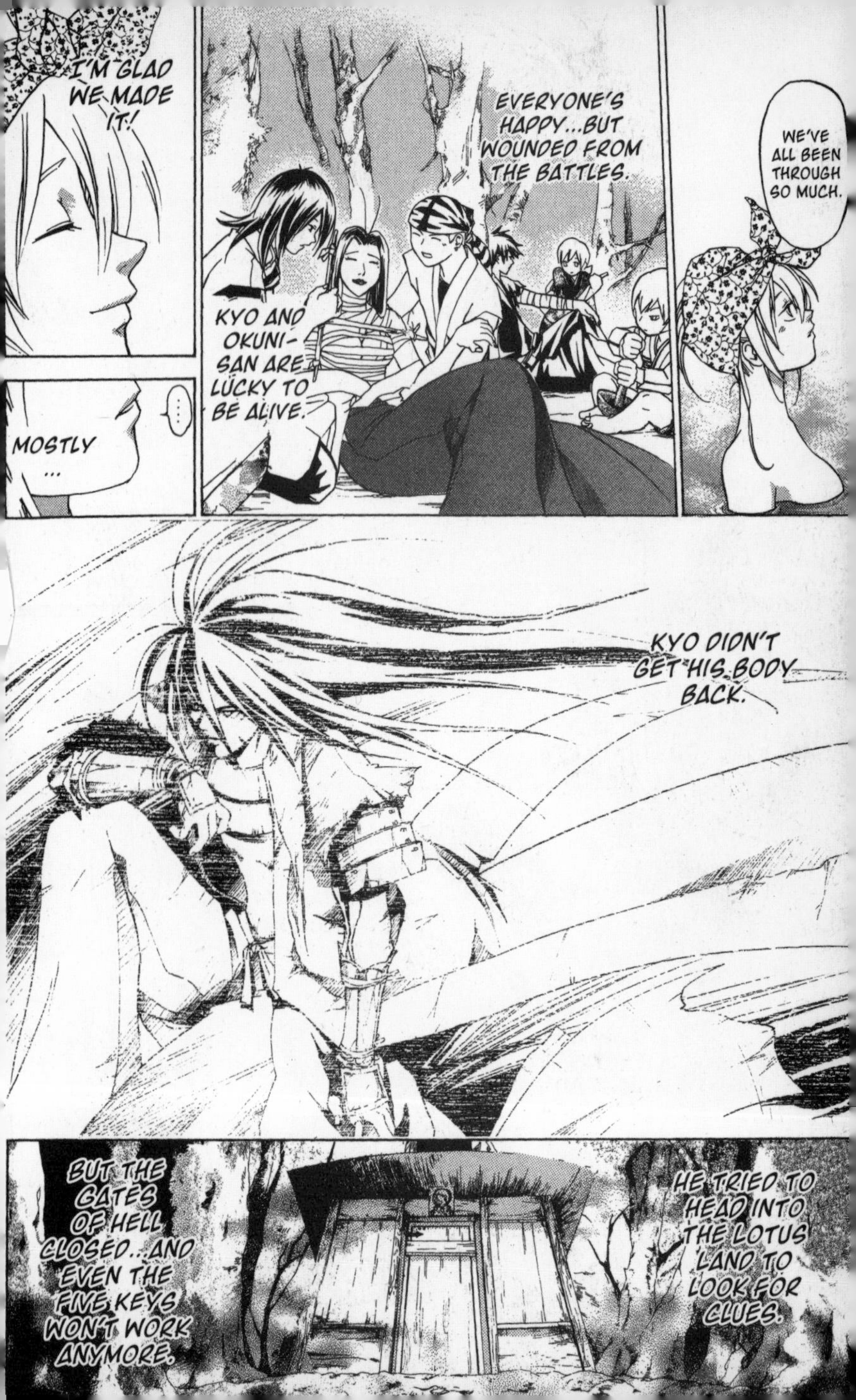
WE'VE ALL BEEN THROUGH SO MUCH.
EVERYONE'S HAPPY...BUT WOUNDED FROM THE BATTLES.
KYO AND OKUNI-SAN ARE LUCKY TO BE ALIVE.
I'M GLAD WE MADE IT!
...
MOSTLY...
KYO DIDN'T GET HIS BODY BACK.
HE TRIED TO HEAD INTO THE LOTUS LAND TO LOOK FOR CLUES.
BUT THE GATES OF HELL CLOSED...AND EVEN THE FIVE KEYS WON'T WORK ANYMORE.

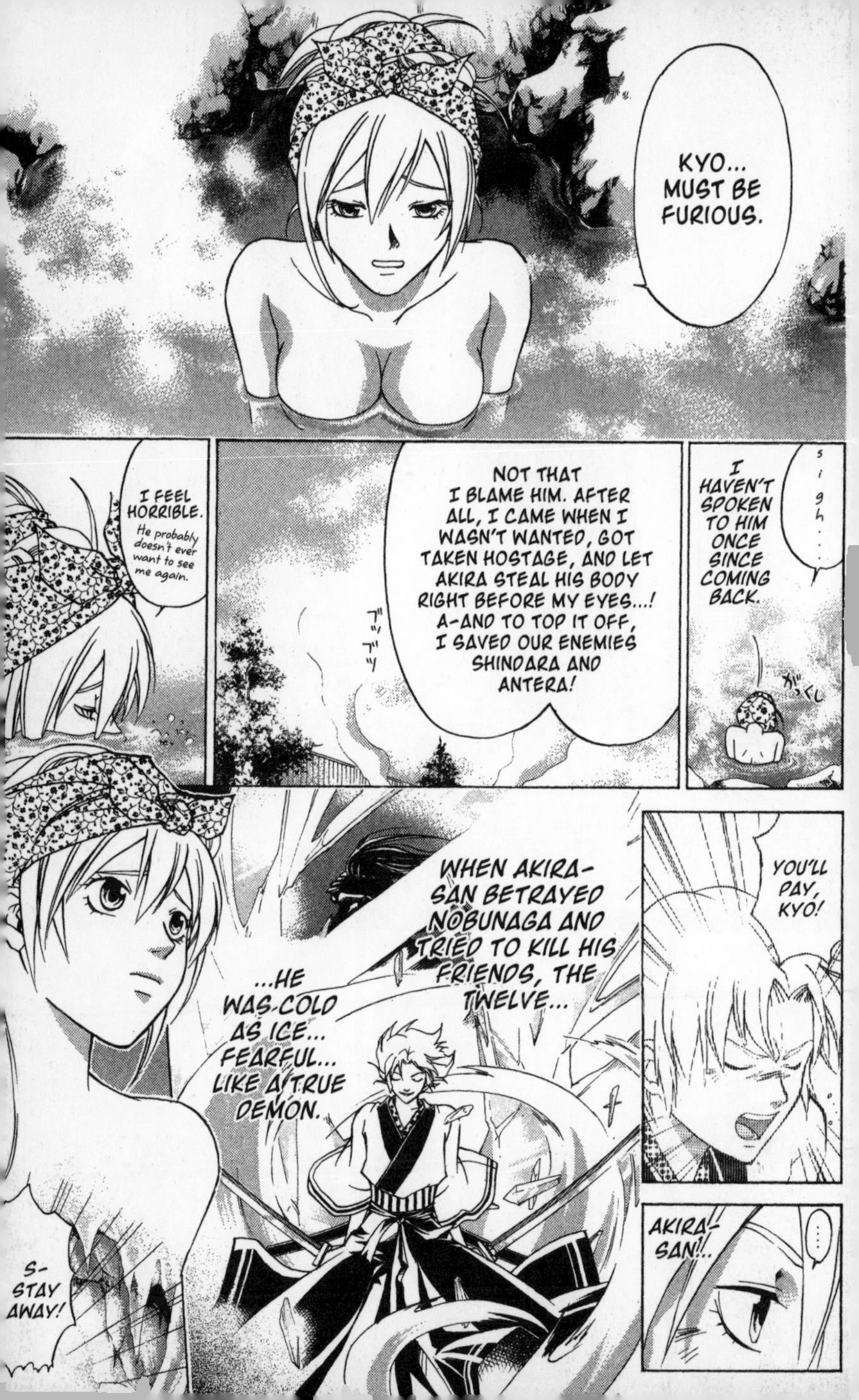
KYO... MUST BE FURIOUS.
s i g h . . .
I HAVEN'T SPOKEN TO HIM ONCE SINCE COMING BACK.
がっくし
NOT THAT I BLAME HIM. AFTER ALL, I CAME WHEN I WASN'T WANTED, GOT TAKEN HOSTAGE, AND LET AKIRA STEAL HIS BODY RIGHT BEFORE MY EYES...! A-AND TO TOP IT OFF, I SAVED OUR ENEMIES SHINDARA AND ANTERA!
ブツブツ
I FEEL HORRIBLE.
He probably doesn't ever want to see me again.
YOU'LL PAY, KYO!
AKIRA-SAN!!
...
WHEN AKIRA-SAN BETRAYED NOBUNAGA AND TRIED TO KILL HIS FRIENDS, THE TWELVE...
...HE WAS COLD AS ICE... FEARFUL... LIKE A TRUE DEMON.
S-STAY AWAY!

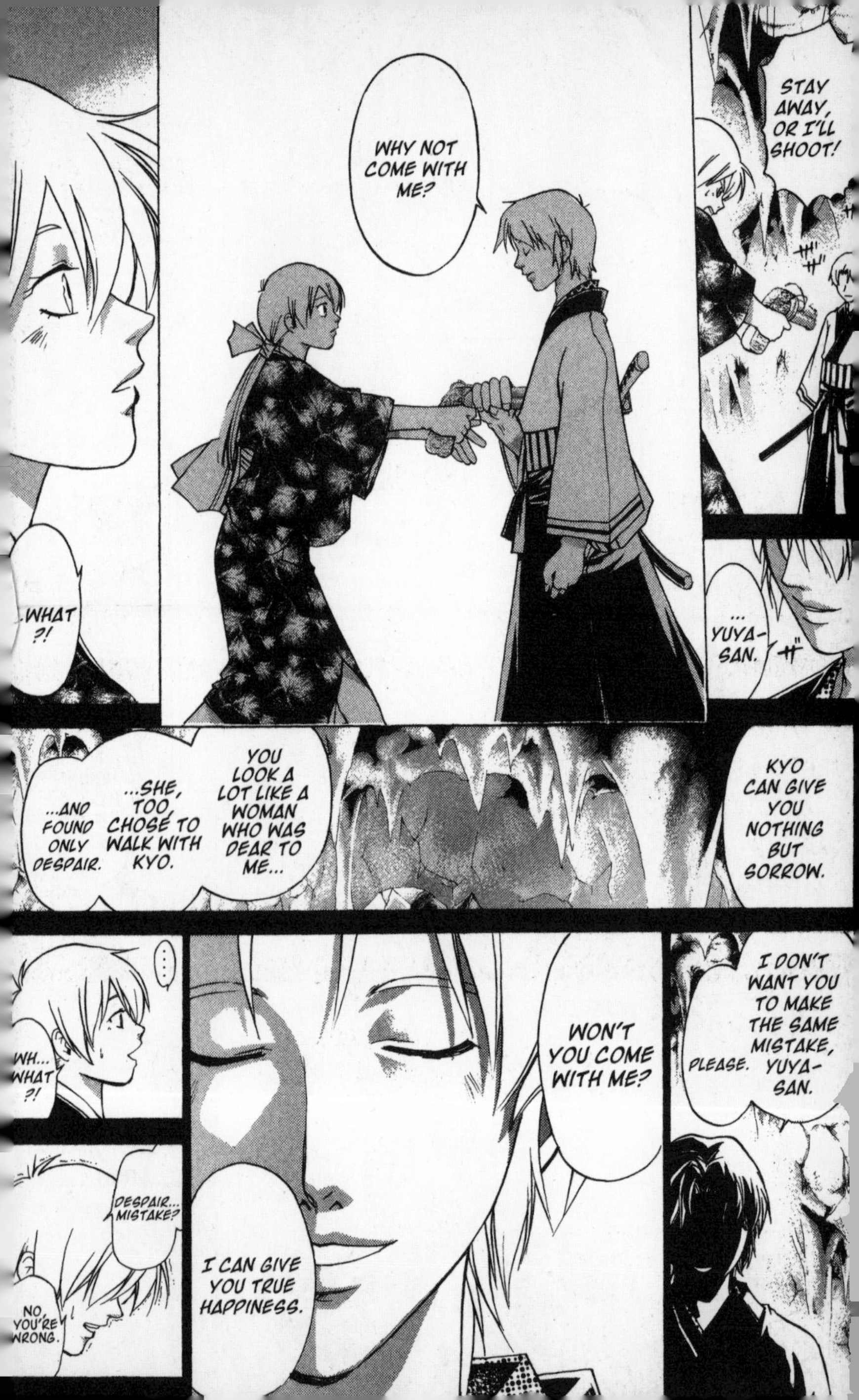
STAY AWAY, OR I'LL SHOOT!
... YUYA-SAN.
WHY NOT COME WITH ME?
...WHAT ?!
KYO CAN GIVE YOU NOTHING BUT SORROW.
YOU LOOK A LOT LIKE A WOMAN WHO WAS DEAR TO ME...
...SHE, TOO, CHOSE TO WALK WITH KYO.
...AND FOUND ONLY DESPAIR.
I DON'T WANT YOU TO MAKE THE SAME MISTAKE, YUYA-SAN.
PLEASE.
WON'T YOU COME WITH ME?
I CAN GIVE YOU TRUE HAPPINESS.
...
WH... WHAT ?!
DESPAIR... MISTAKE?
NO, YOU'RE WRONG.

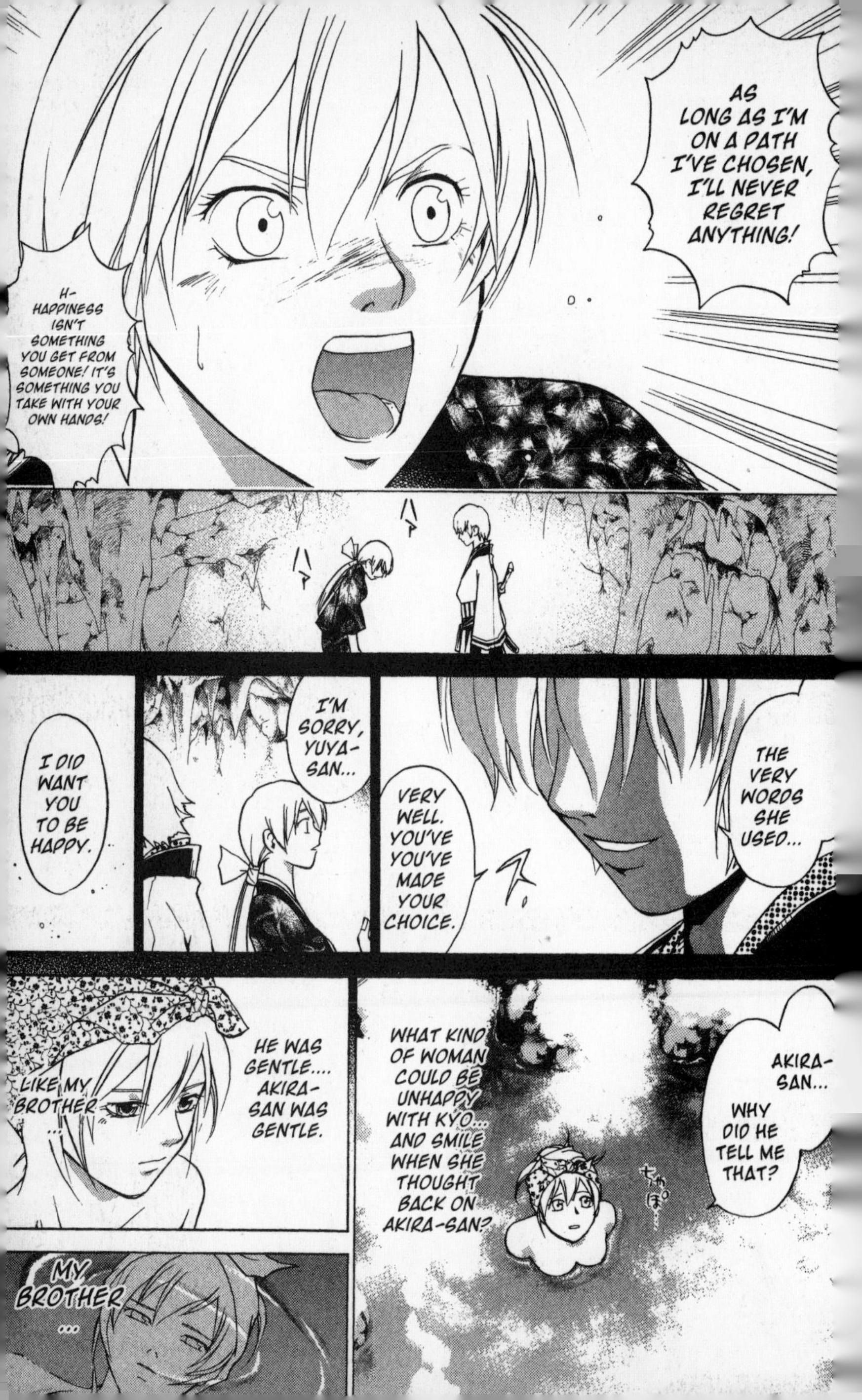
AS LONG AS I'M ON A PATH I'VE CHOSEN, I'LL NEVER REGRET ANYTHING!
H- HAPPINESS ISN'T SOMETHING YOU GET FROM SOMEONE! IT'S SOMETHING YOU TAKE WITH YOUR OWN HANDS!
ハァ
ハァ
THE VERY WORDS SHE USED...
VERY WELL. YOU'VE YOU'VE MADE YOUR CHOICE.
ス
I'M SORRY, YUYA-SAN...
I DID WANT YOU TO BE HAPPY.
AKIRA-SAN...
WHY DID HE TELL ME THAT?
ちゃぽ...
WHAT KIND OF WOMAN COULD BE UNHAPPY WITH KYO... AND SMILE WHEN SHE THOUGHT BACK ON AKIRA-SAN?
HE WAS GENTLE.... AKIRA-SAN WAS GENTLE.
LIKE MY BROTHER ...
MY BROTHER ...

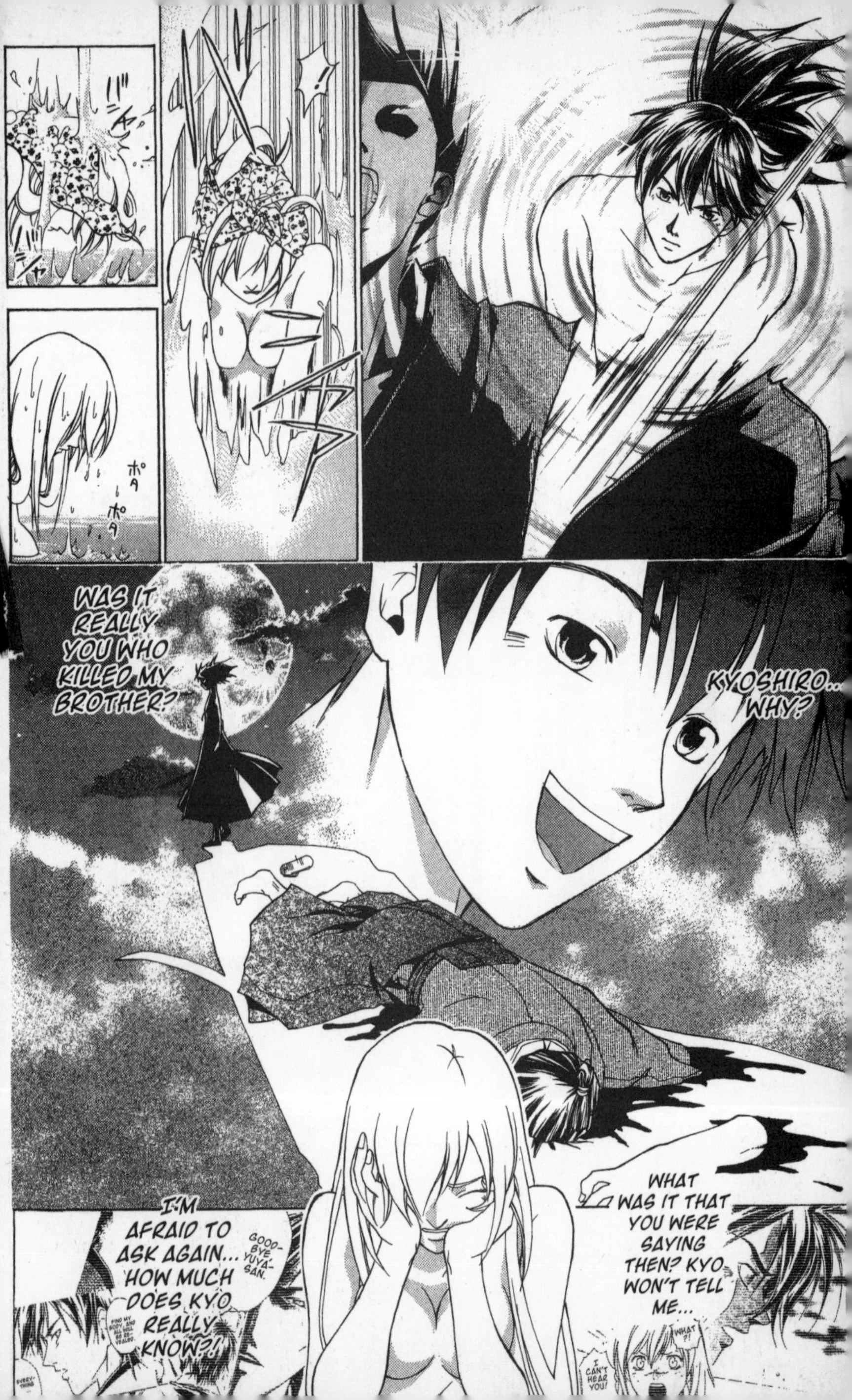
!
バシャ
ポタ ポタ
KYOSHIRO... WHY?
WAS IT REALLY YOU WHO KILLED MY BROTHER?
WHAT WAS IT THAT YOU WERE SAYING THEN? KYO WON'T TELL ME...
WHAT?!
I CAN'T HEAR YOU!
I'M AFRAID TO ASK AGAIN... HOW MUCH DOES KYO REALLY KNOW?!
GOOD-BYE, YUYA-SAN.
FIND MY BODY, AND ALL WILL BE REVEALED.
EVERYTHING

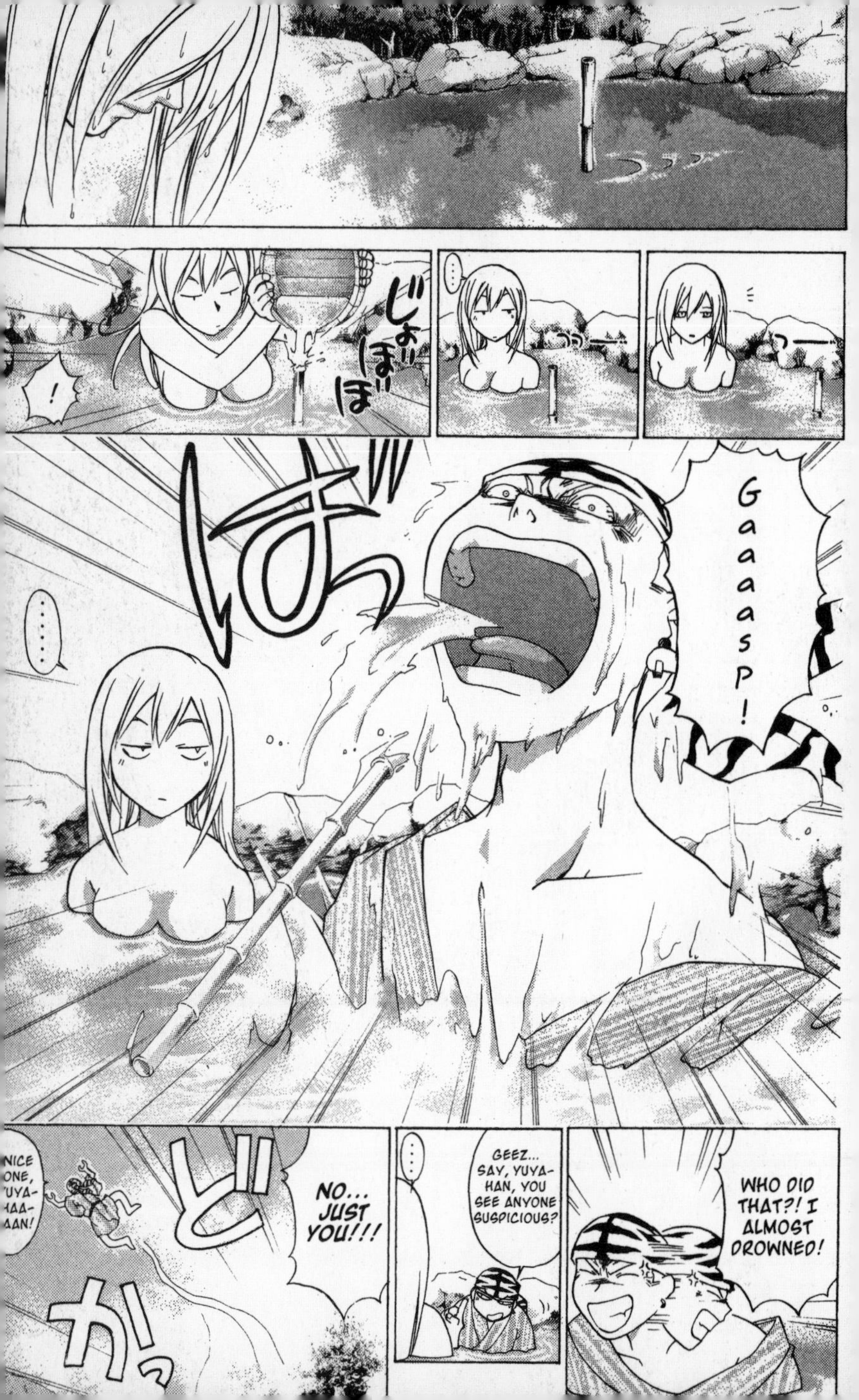
…
!
Gaaaasp!
……
WHO DID THAT?! I ALMOST DROWNED!
GEEZ... SAY, YUYA-HAN, YOU SEE ANYONE SUSPICIOUS?
…
NO… JUST YOU!!!
NICE ONE, YUYA-HAA-AAN!

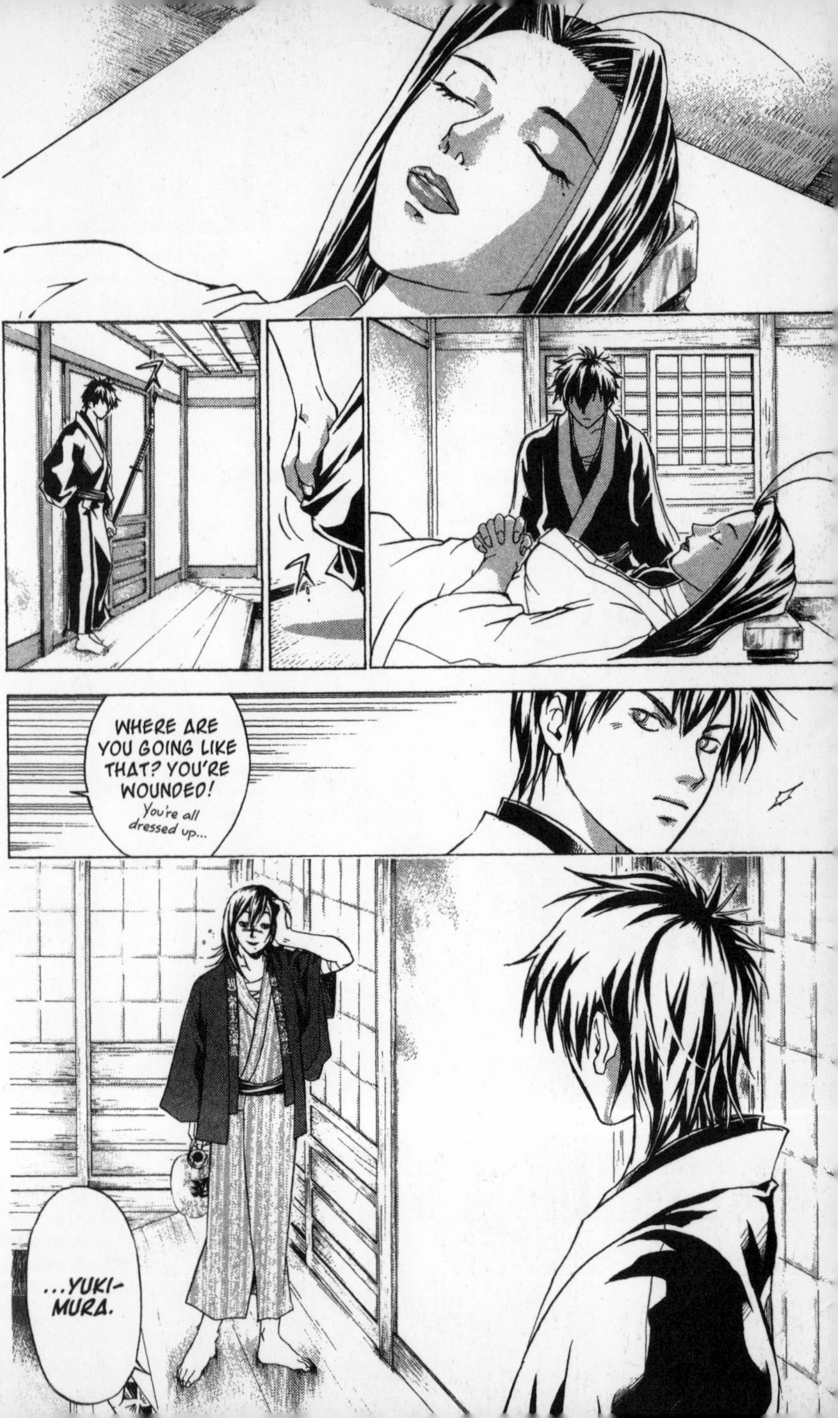
WHERE ARE YOU GOING LIKE THAT? YOU'RE WOUNDED!
You're all dressed up...
...YUKI-MURA.

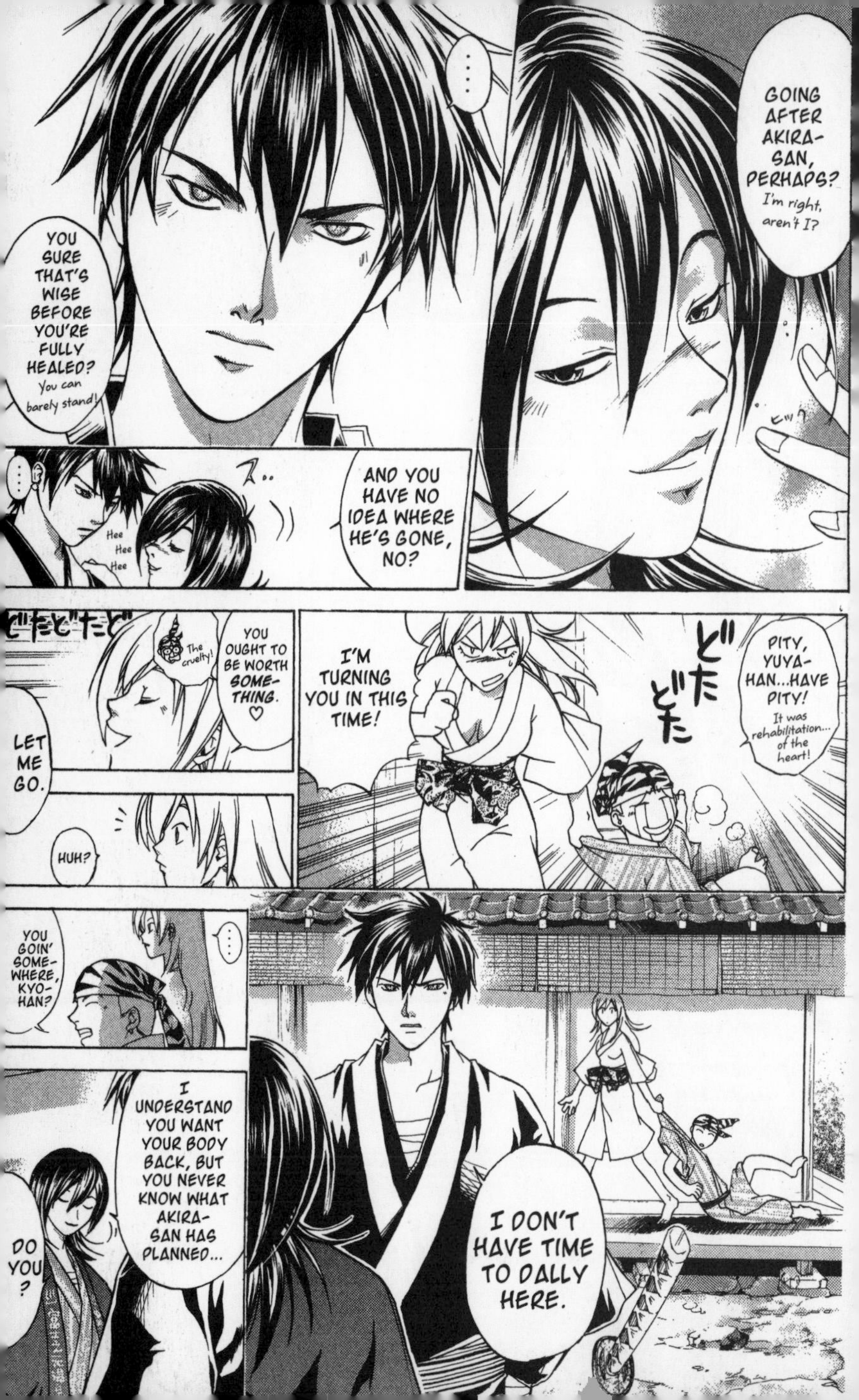
GOING AFTER AKIRA-SAN, PERHAPS?
I'm right, aren't I?
...
YOU SURE THAT'S WISE BEFORE YOU'RE FULLY HEALED?
You can barely stand!
AND YOU HAVE NO IDEA WHERE HE'S GONE, NO?
...
Hee Hee Hee
PITY, YUYA-HAN...HAVE PITY!
It was rehabilitation... of the heart!
どたどた
I'M TURNING YOU IN THIS TIME!
YOU OUGHT TO BE WORTH SOMETHING. ♡
The cruelty!
LET ME GO.
HUH?
I DON'T HAVE TIME TO DALLY HERE.
...
YOU GOIN' SOMEWHERE, KYO-HAN?
I UNDERSTAND YOU WANT YOUR BODY BACK, BUT YOU NEVER KNOW WHAT AKIRA-SAN HAS PLANNED...
DO YOU?

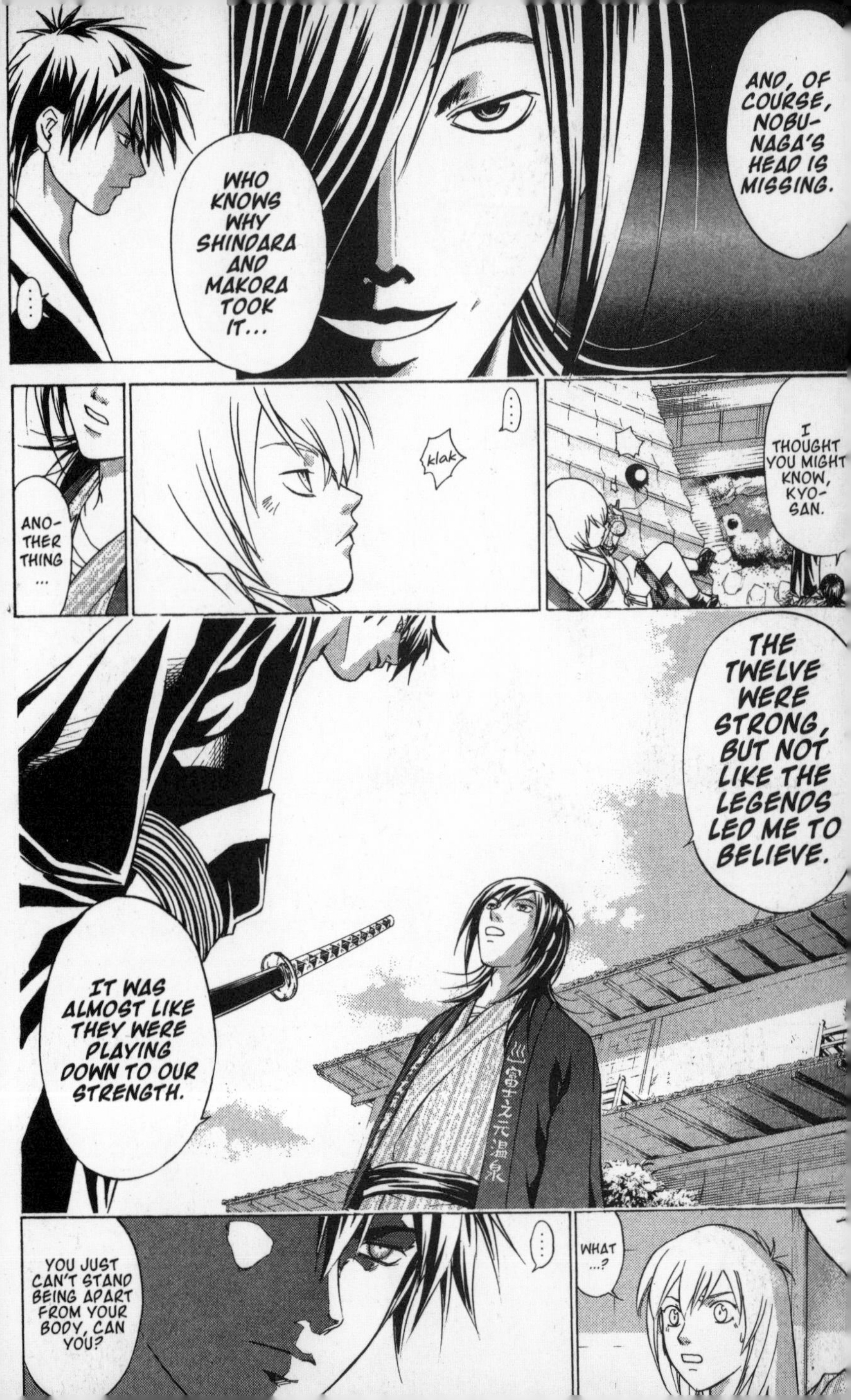
AND, OF COURSE, NOBUNAGA'S HEAD IS MISSING.
WHO KNOWS WHY SHINDARA AND MAKORA TOOK IT...
...
I THOUGHT YOU MIGHT KNOW, KYO-SAN.
...
klak
ANOTHER THING...
THE TWELVE WERE STRONG, BUT NOT LIKE THE LEGENDS LED ME TO BELIEVE.
IT WAS ALMOST LIKE THEY WERE PLAYING DOWN TO OUR STRENGTH.
WHAT...?
...
YOU JUST CAN'T STAND BEING APART FROM YOUR BODY, CAN YOU?

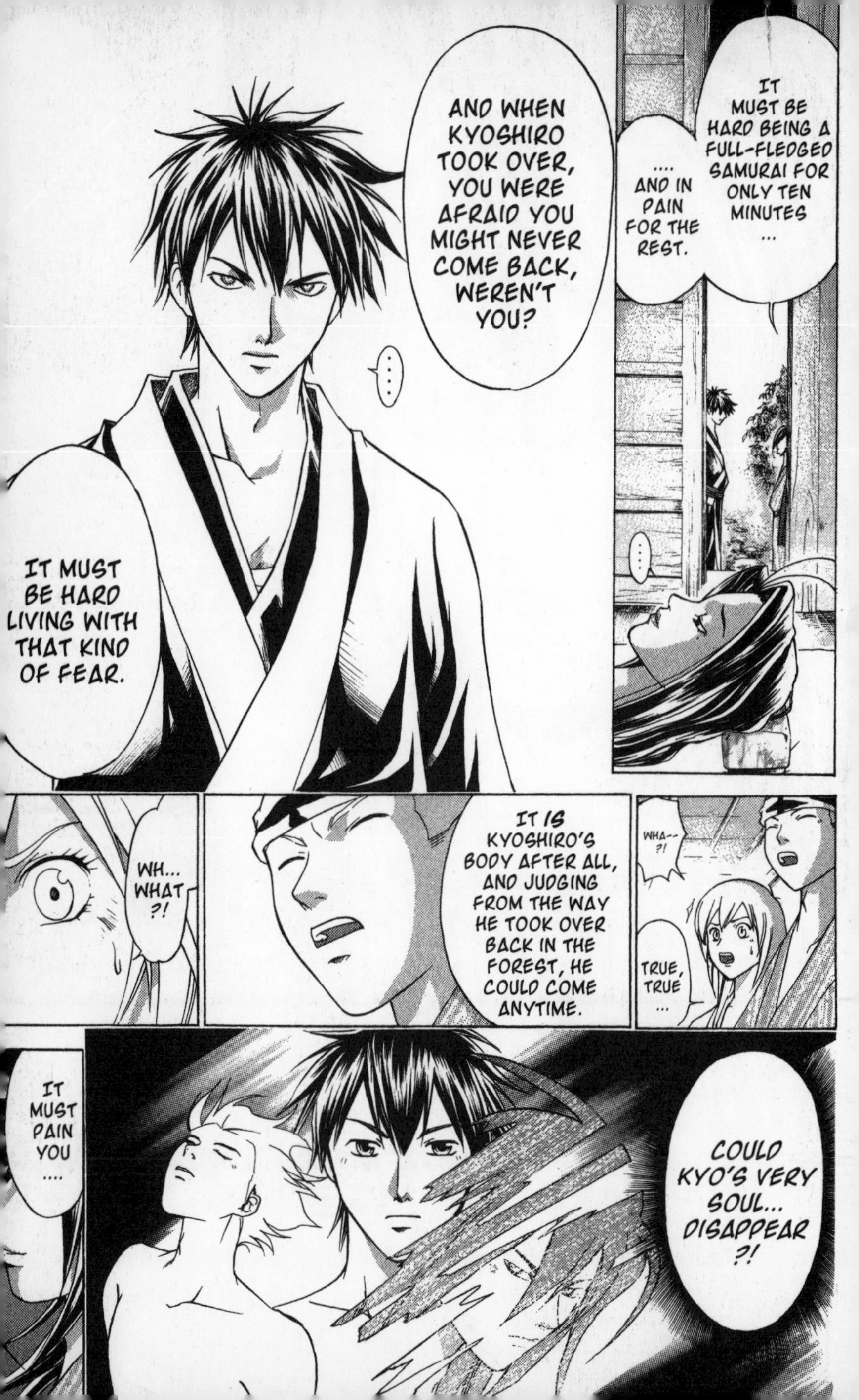
IT MUST BE HARD BEING A FULL-FLEDGED SAMURAI FOR ONLY TEN MINUTES ...
.... AND IN PAIN FOR THE REST.
...
AND WHEN KYOSHIRO TOOK OVER, YOU WERE AFRAID YOU MIGHT NEVER COME BACK, WEREN'T YOU?
...
IT MUST BE HARD LIVING WITH THAT KIND OF FEAR.
WHA-- ?!
TRUE, TRUE ...
IT IS KYOSHIRO'S BODY AFTER ALL, AND JUDGING FROM THE WAY HE TOOK OVER BACK IN THE FOREST, HE COULD COME ANYTIME.
WH... WHAT ?!
COULD KYO'S VERY SOUL... DISAPPEAR ?!
IT MUST PAIN YOU ....

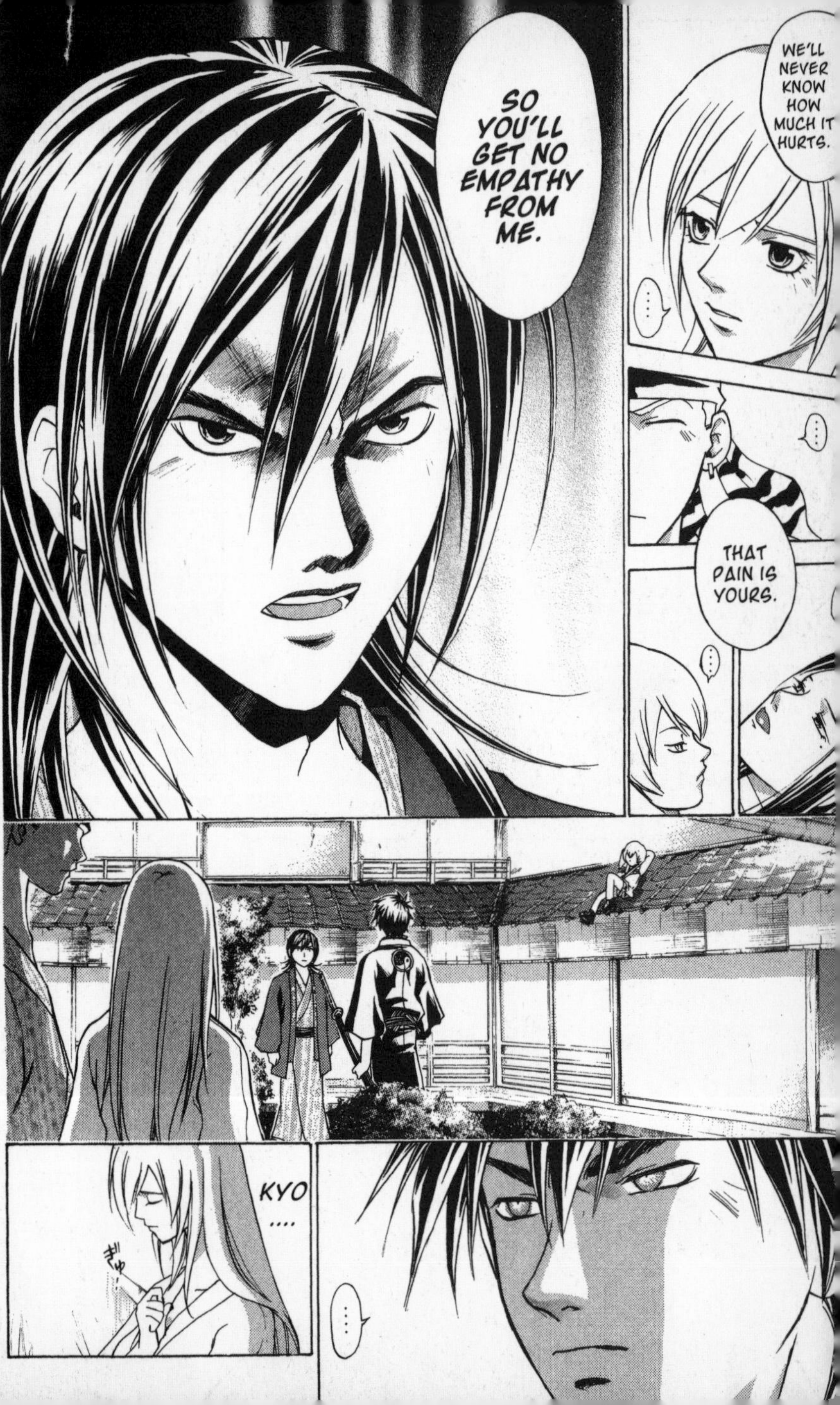
WE'LL NEVER KNOW HOW MUCH IT HURTS.
...
...
THAT PAIN IS YOURS.
...
SO YOU'LL GET NO EMPATHY FROM ME.
....
KYO .....
ぎゅ!

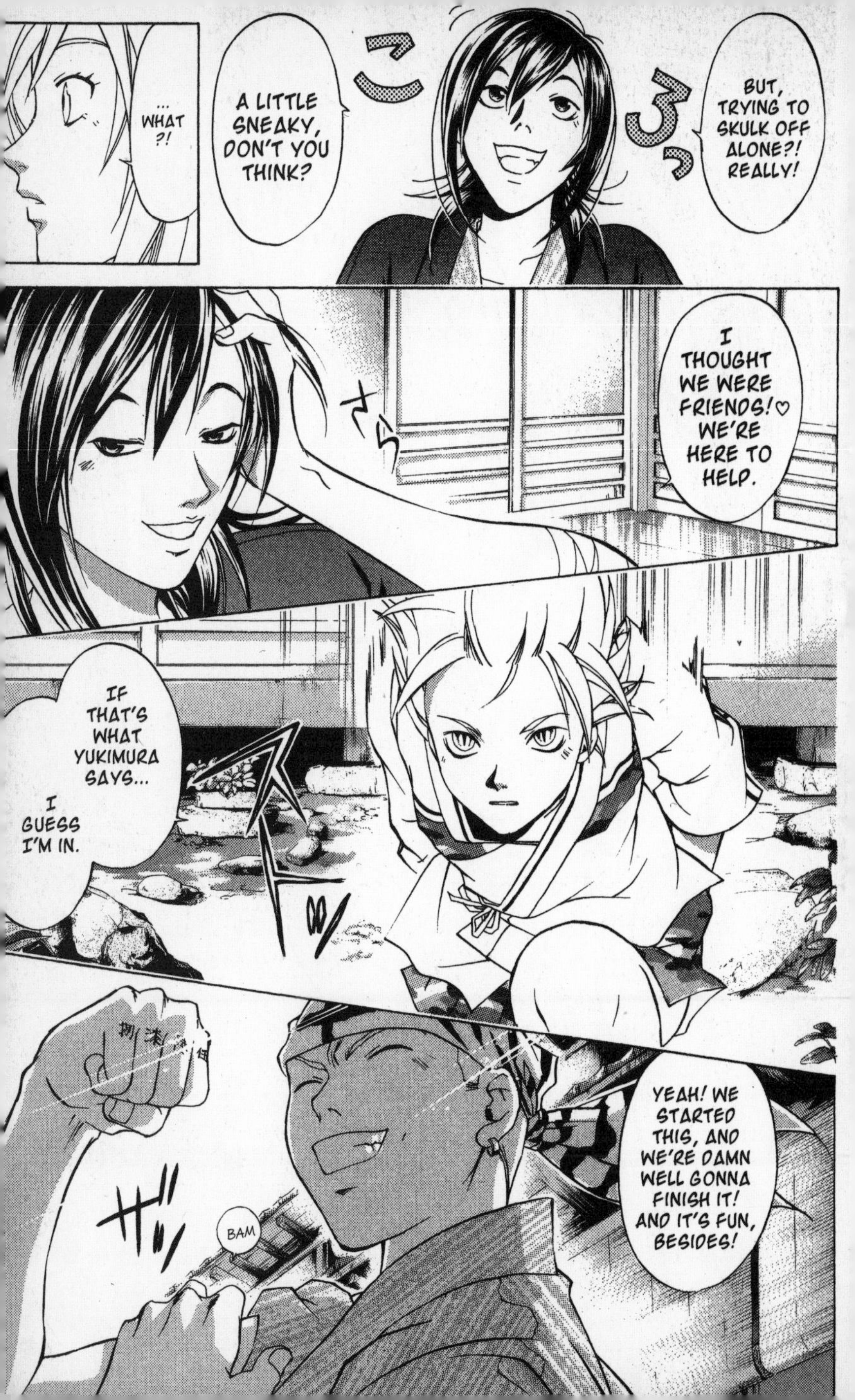

BUT, TRYING TO SKULK OFF ALONE?! REALLY!
A LITTLE SNEAKY, DON'T YOU THINK?
...WHAT?!
I THOUGHT WE WERE FRIENDS!♡ WE'RE HERE TO HELP.
IF THAT'S WHAT YUKIMURA SAYS...
I GUESS I'M IN.
YEAH! WE STARTED THIS, AND WE'RE DAMN WELL GONNA FINISH IT! AND IT'S FUN, BESIDES!
BAM

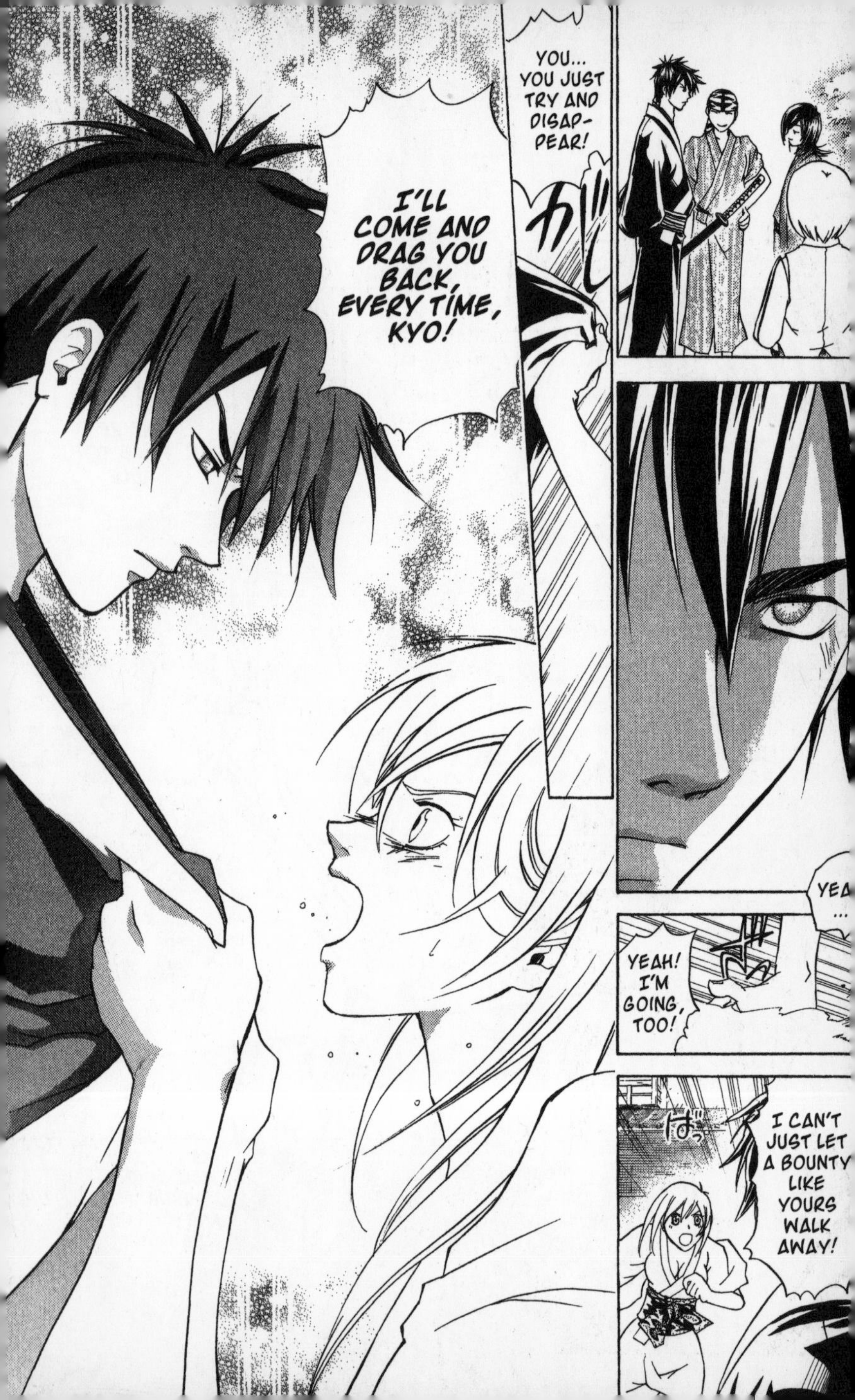
YEA ...
YEAH! I'M GOING, TOO!
I CAN'T JUST LET A BOUNTY LIKE YOURS WALK AWAY!
YOU... YOU JUST TRY AND DISAP-PEAR!
I'LL COME AND DRAG YOU BACK, EVERY TIME, KYO!

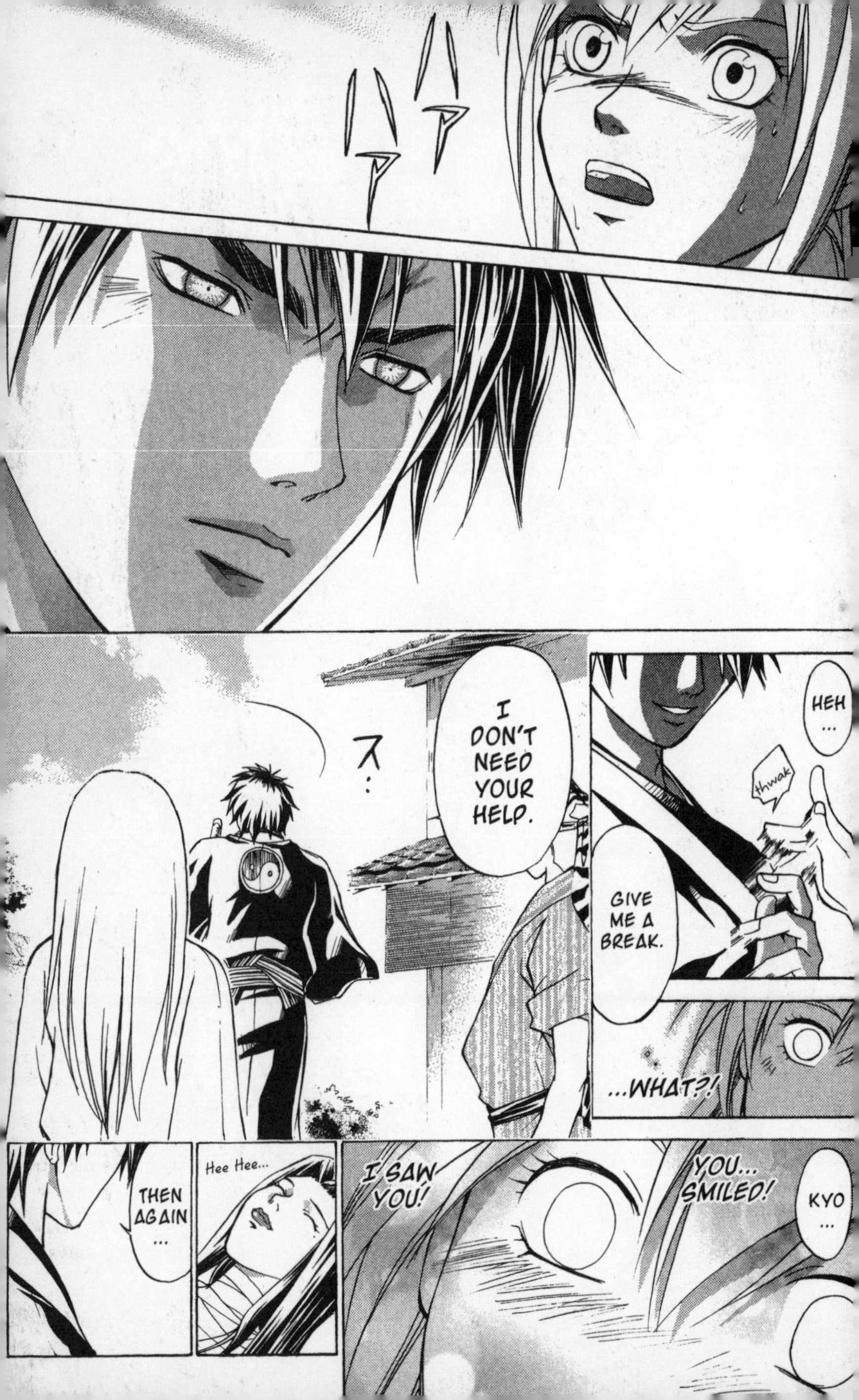
ハァ ハァ
HEH...
thwak
GIVE ME A BREAK.
...WHAT?!
I DON'T NEED YOUR HELP.
ス…
KYO...
YOU... SMILED!
I SAW YOU!
Hee Hee...
THEN AGAIN...

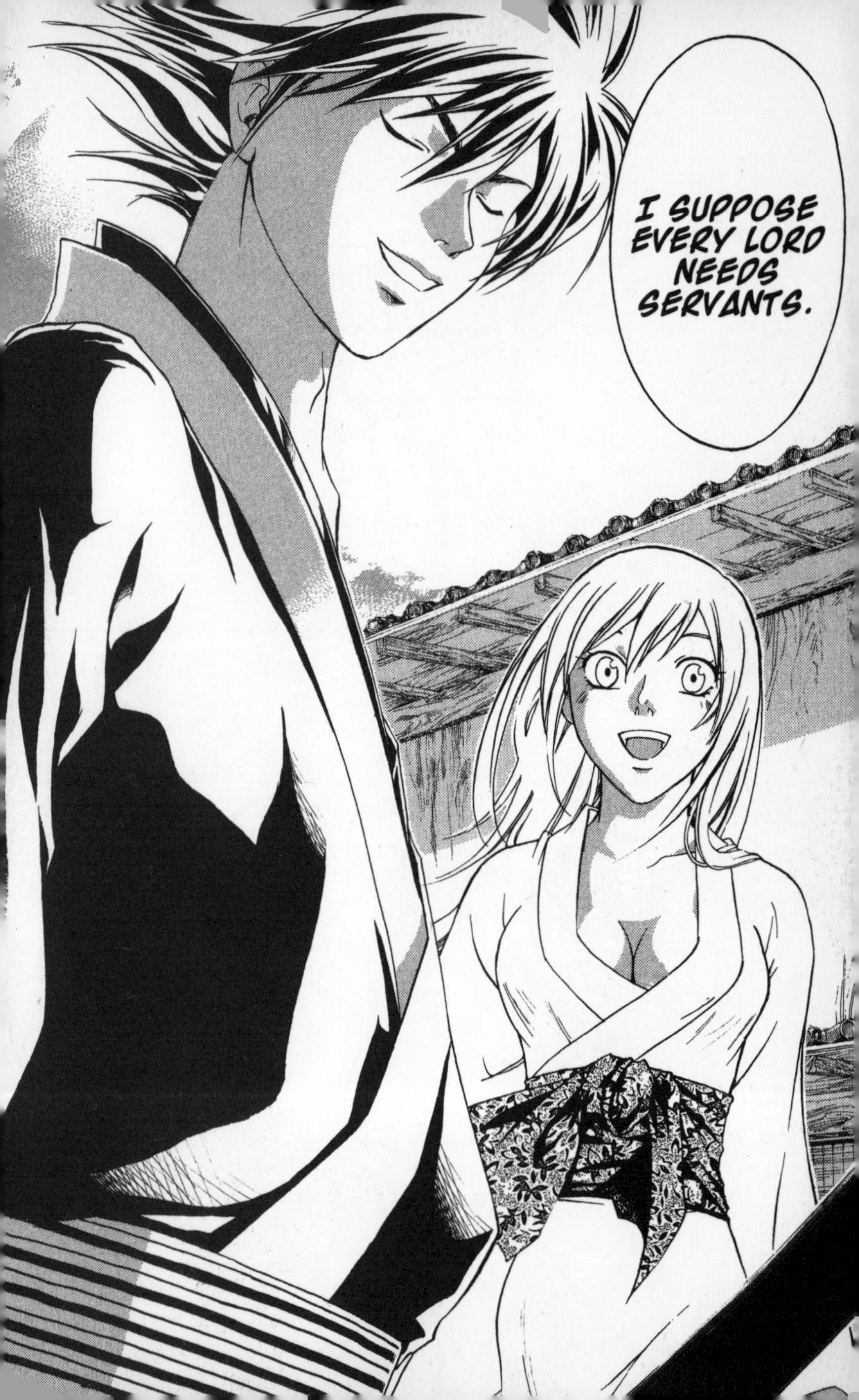
I SUPPOSE EVERY LORD NEEDS SERVANTS.

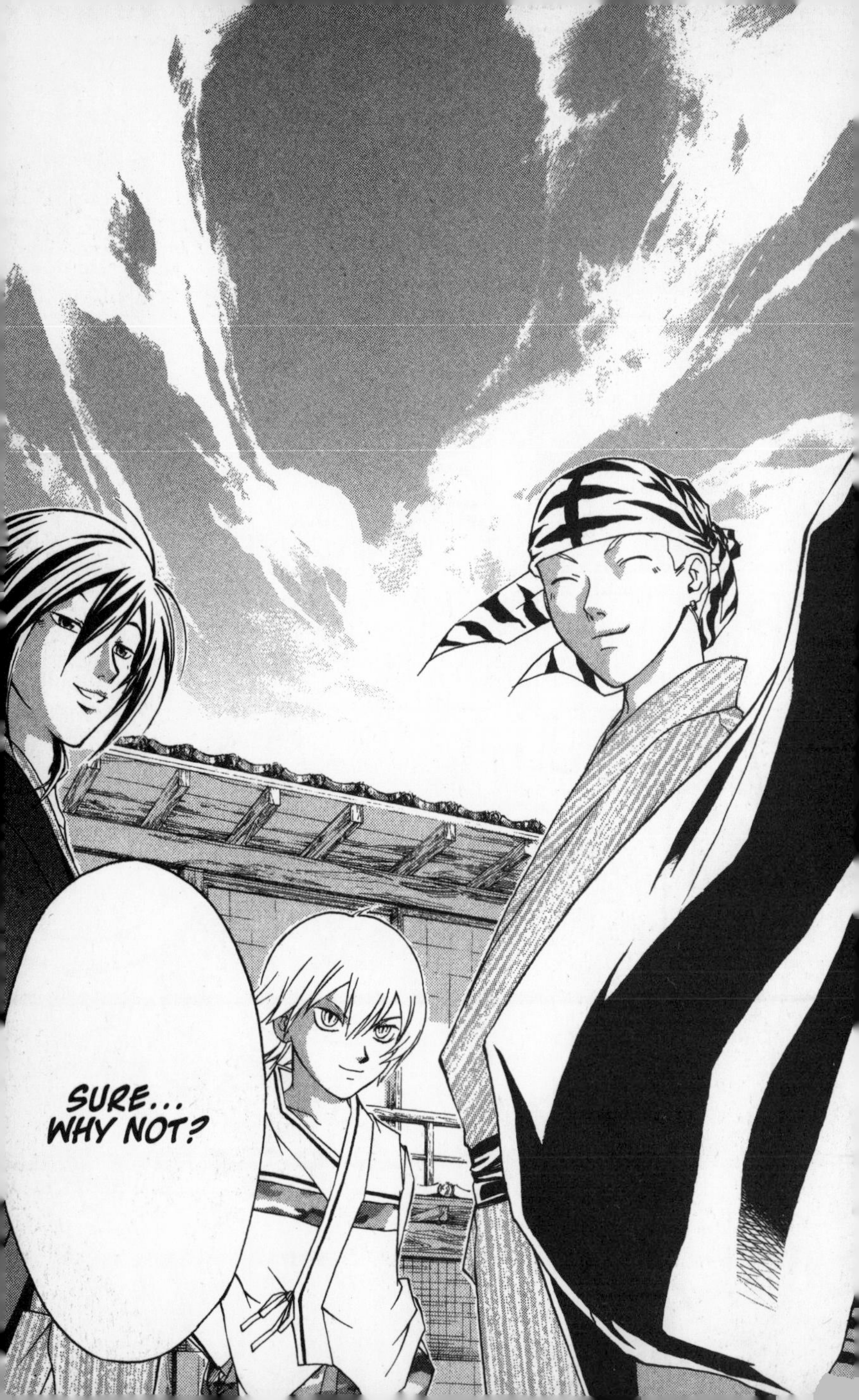
SURE... WHY NOT?

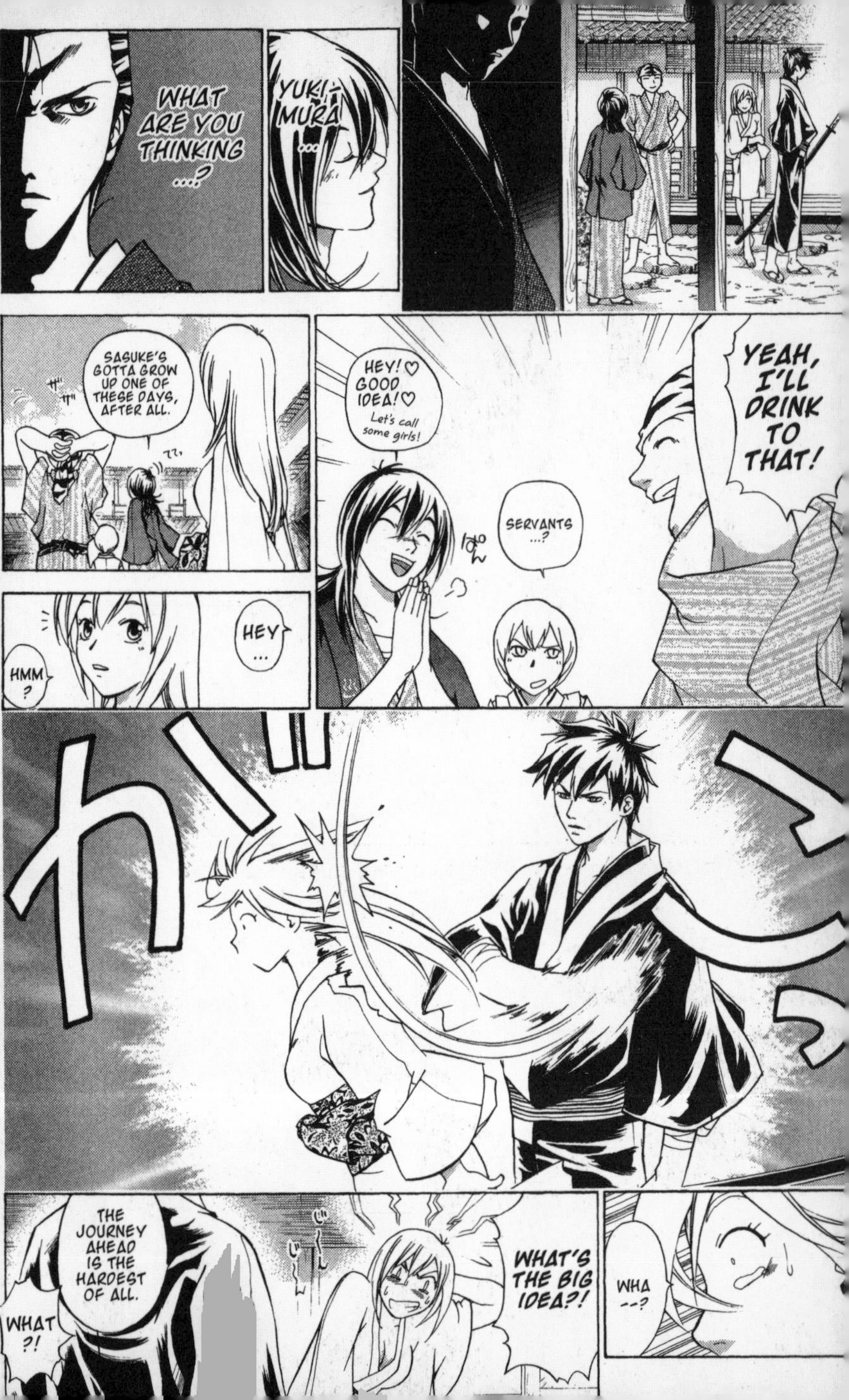
YUKI-MURA...
WHAT ARE YOU THINKING...?
YEAH, I'LL DRINK TO THAT!
HEY! ♡ GOOD IDEA! ♡ Let's call some girls!
SERVANTS...?
SASUKE'S GOTTA GROW UP ONE OF THESE DAYS, AFTER ALL.
HEY...
HMM?
WHA--?
WHAT'S THE BIG IDEA?!
THE JOURNEY AHEAD IS THE HARDEST OF ALL.
WHAT?!

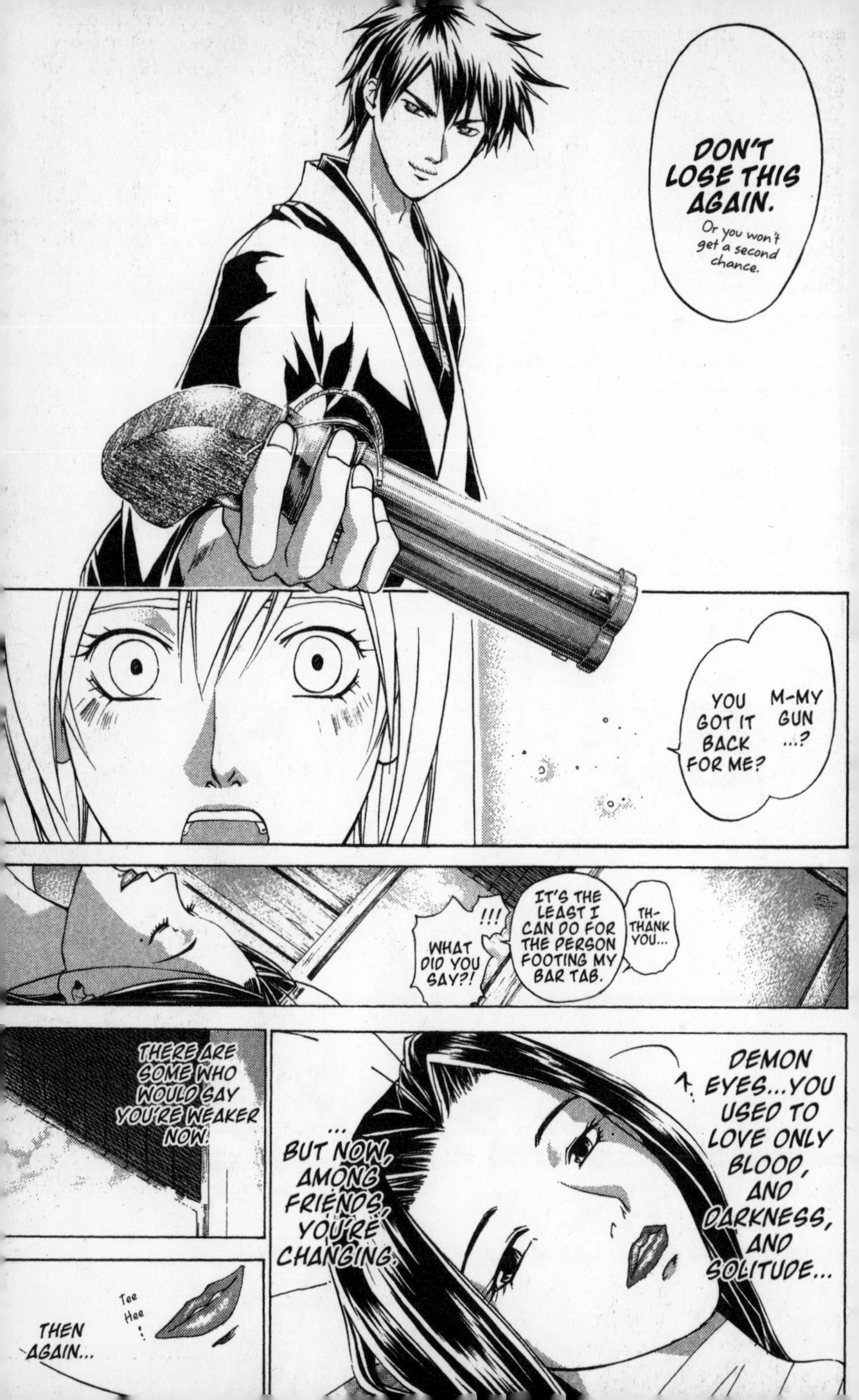
DON'T LOSE THIS AGAIN.
Or you won't get a second chance.
M-MY GUN ...?
YOU GOT IT BACK FOR ME?
TH-THANK YOU...
IT'S THE LEAST I CAN DO FOR THE PERSON FOOTING MY BAR TAB.
!!!
WHAT DID YOU SAY?!
DEMON EYES...YOU USED TO LOVE ONLY BLOOD, AND DARKNESS, AND SOLITUDE...
...BUT NOW, AMONG FRIENDS, YOU'RE CHANGING.
THERE ARE SOME WHO WOULD SAY YOU'RE WEAKER NOW.
Tee Hee
THEN AGAIN...

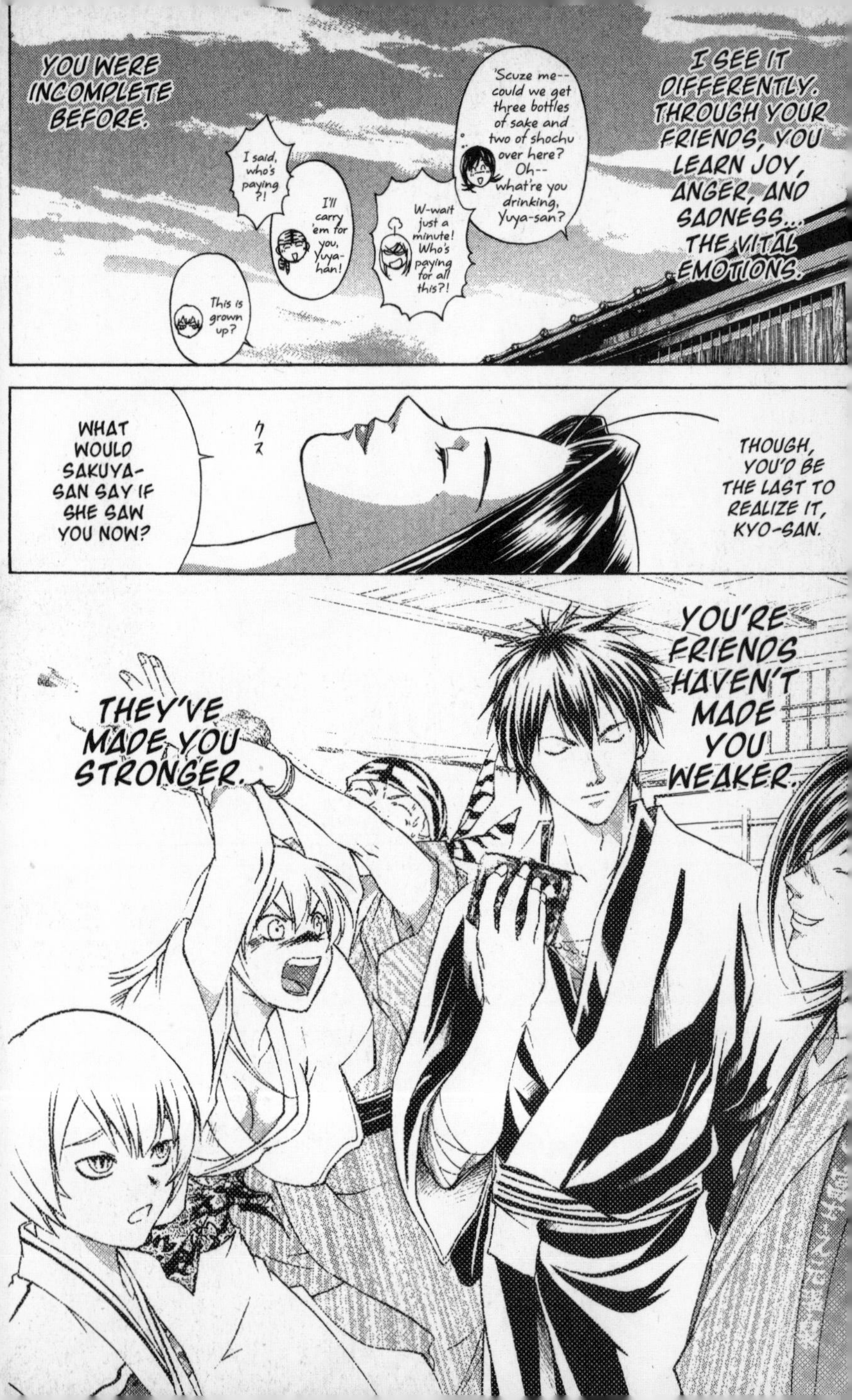
I SEE IT DIFFERENTLY. THROUGH YOUR FRIENDS, YOU LEARN JOY, ANGER, AND SADNESS... THE VITAL EMOTIONS.
'Scuze me--could we get three bottles of sake and two of shochu over here? Oh--what're you drinking, Yuya-san?
W-wait just a minute! Who's paying for all this?!
I said, who's paying?!
I'll carry 'em for you, Yuya-han!
This is grown up?
YOU WERE INCOMPLETE BEFORE.
THOUGH, YOU'D BE THE LAST TO REALIZE IT, KYO-SAN.
クス
WHAT WOULD SAKUYA-SAN SAY IF SHE SAW YOU NOW?
YOU'RE FRIENDS HAVEN'T MADE YOU WEAKER.
THEY'VE MADE YOU STRONGER.

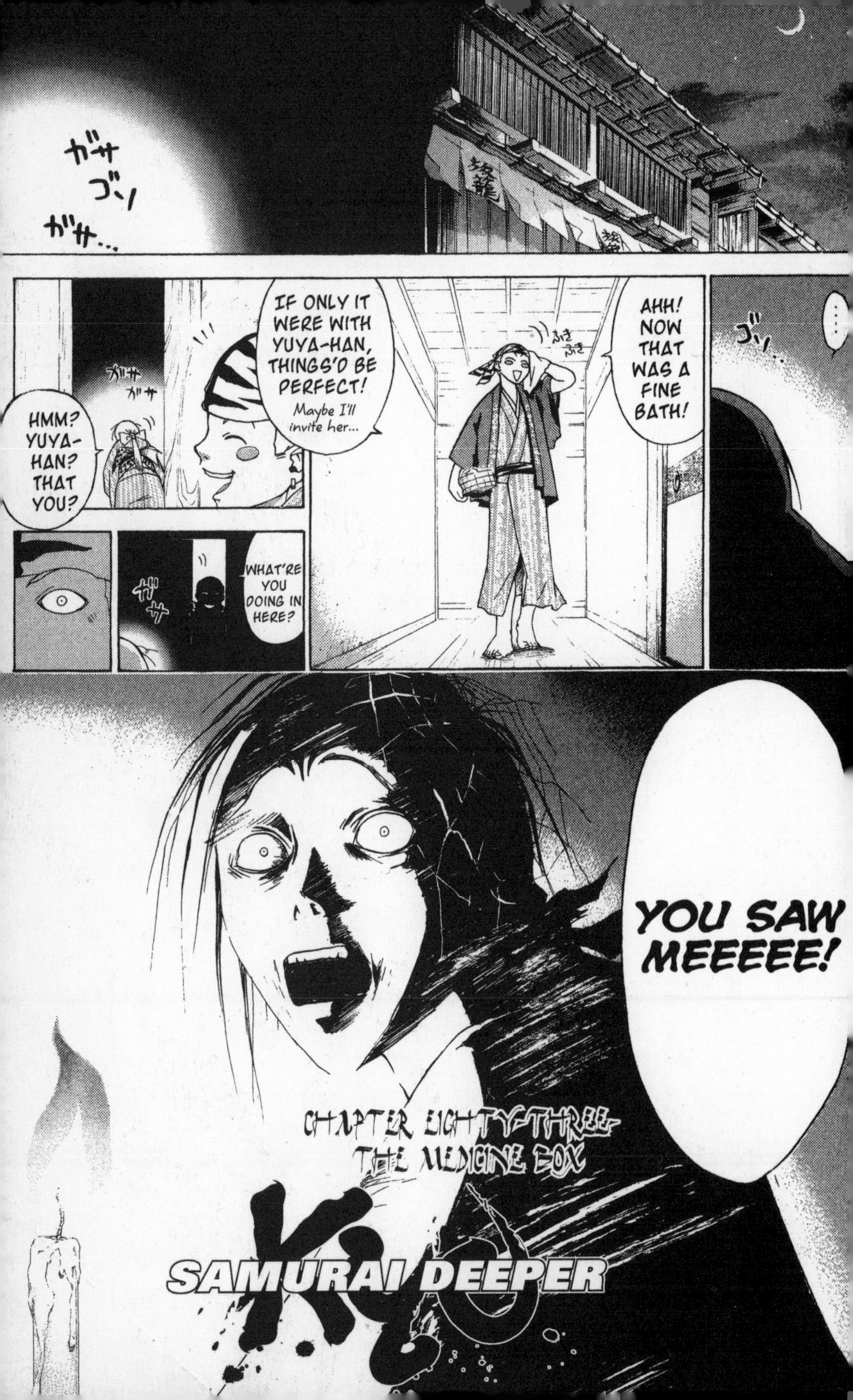
ガサ
ゴソ
ガサ…
…
ゴソ…
AHH! NOW THAT WAS A FINE BATH!
ふきふき
IF ONLY IT WERE WITH YUYA-HAN, THINGS'D BE PERFECT!
Maybe I'll invite her...
ガサガサ
HMM? YUYA-HAN? THAT YOU?
WHAT'RE YOU DOING IN HERE?
ガサ
YOU SAW MEEEEEE!
CHAPTER EIGHTY-THREE: THE MEDICINE BOX
SAMURAI DEEPER

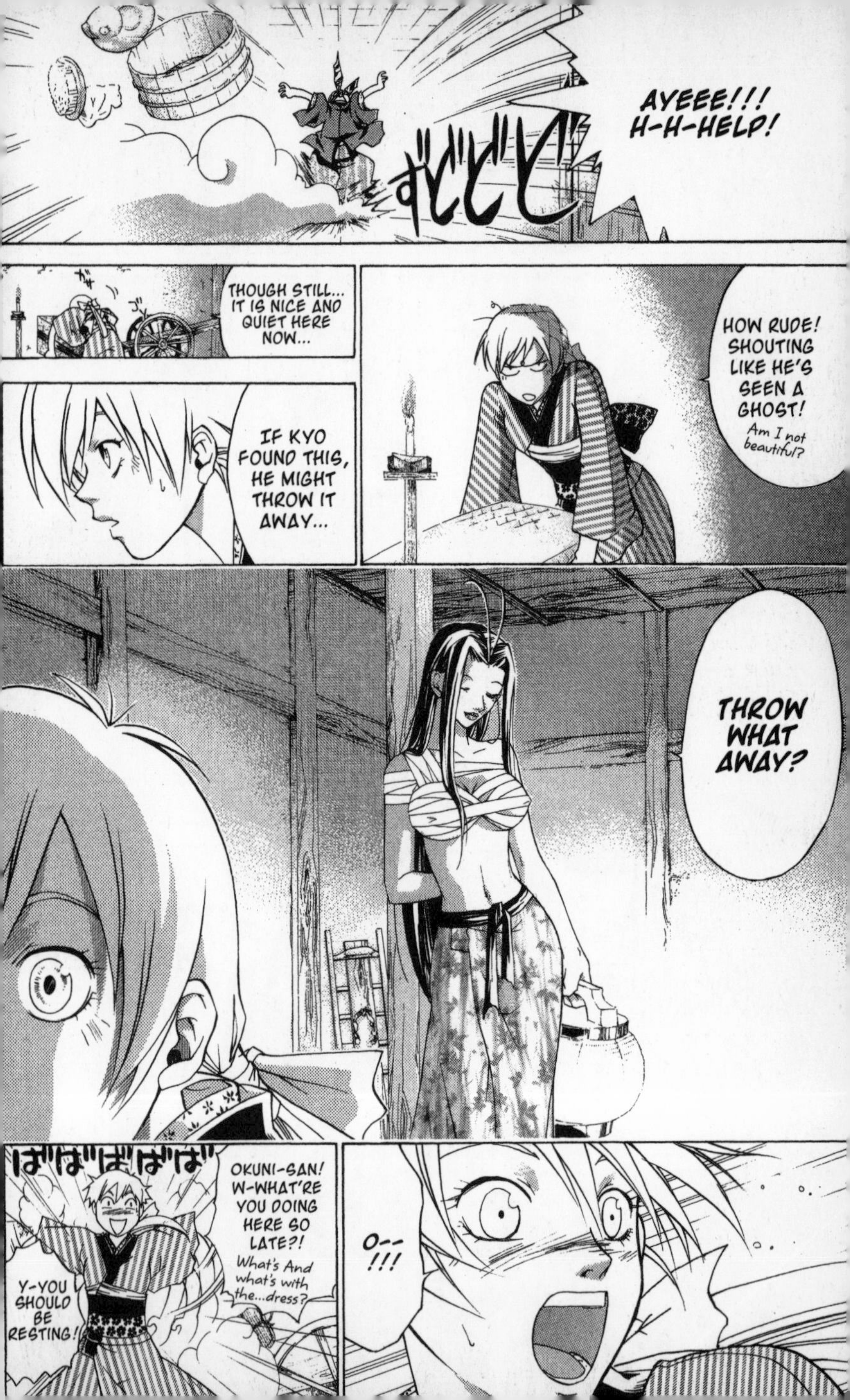
AYEEE!!! H-H-HELP!
ずどどど
HOW RUDE! SHOUTING LIKE HE'S SEEN A GHOST!
Am I not beautiful?
THOUGH STILL... IT IS NICE AND QUIET HERE NOW...
IF KYO FOUND THIS, HE MIGHT THROW IT AWAY...
THROW WHAT AWAY?
O--!!!
ばばばばば
OKUNI-SAN! W-WHAT'RE YOU DOING HERE SO LATE?!
What's And what's with the...dress?
Y-YOU SHOULD BE RESTING!

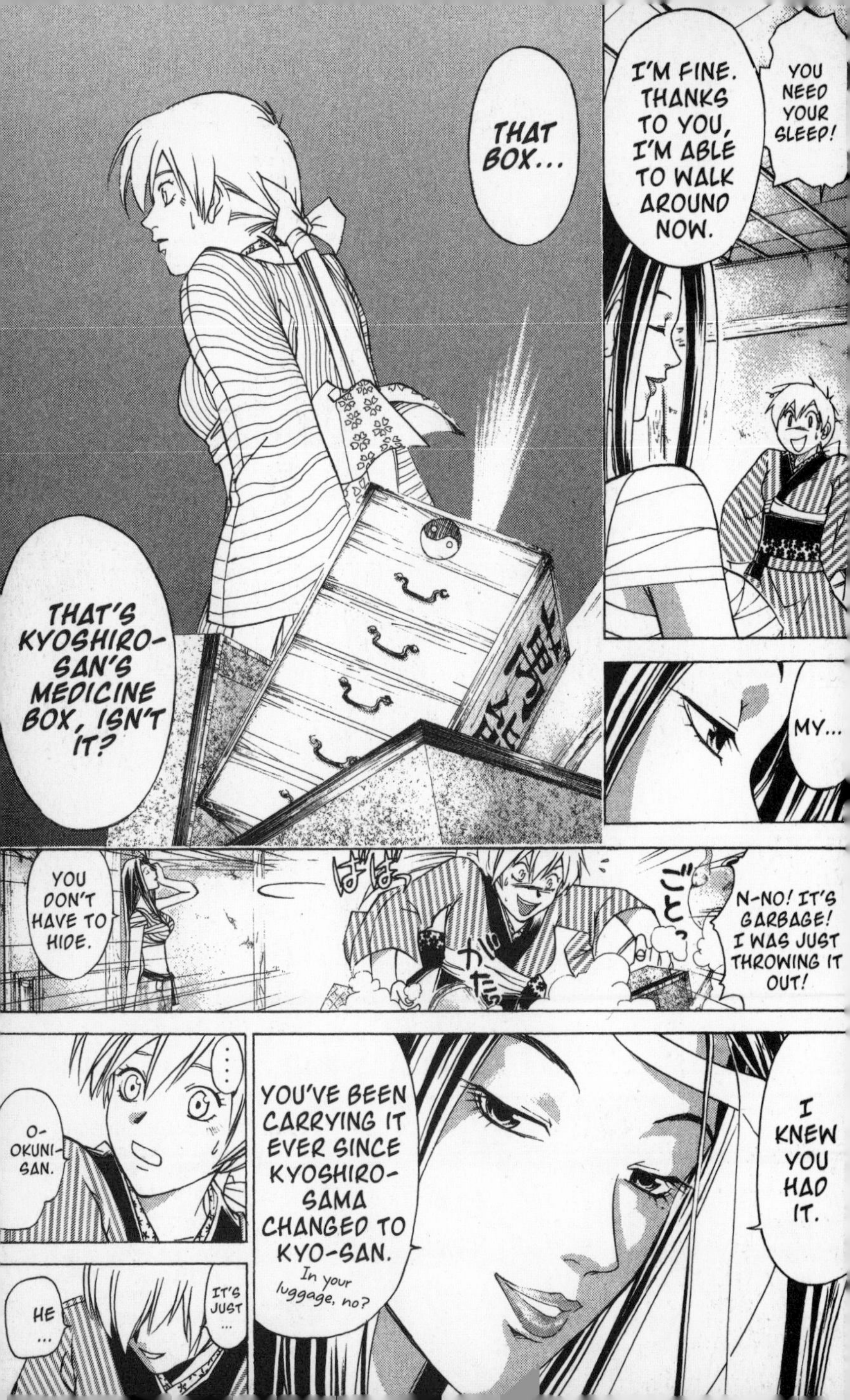
YOU NEED YOUR SLEEP!
I'M FINE. THANKS TO YOU, I'M ABLE TO WALK AROUND NOW.
MY...
THAT BOX...
THAT'S KYOSHIRO-SAN'S MEDICINE BOX, ISN'T IT?
N-NO! IT'S GARBAGE! I WAS JUST THROWING IT OUT!
YOU DON'T HAVE TO HIDE.
I KNEW YOU HAD IT.
YOU'VE BEEN CARRYING IT EVER SINCE KYOSHIRO-SAMA CHANGED TO KYO-SAN.
In your luggage, no?
...
O-OKUNI-SAN.
IT'S JUST ...
HE ...

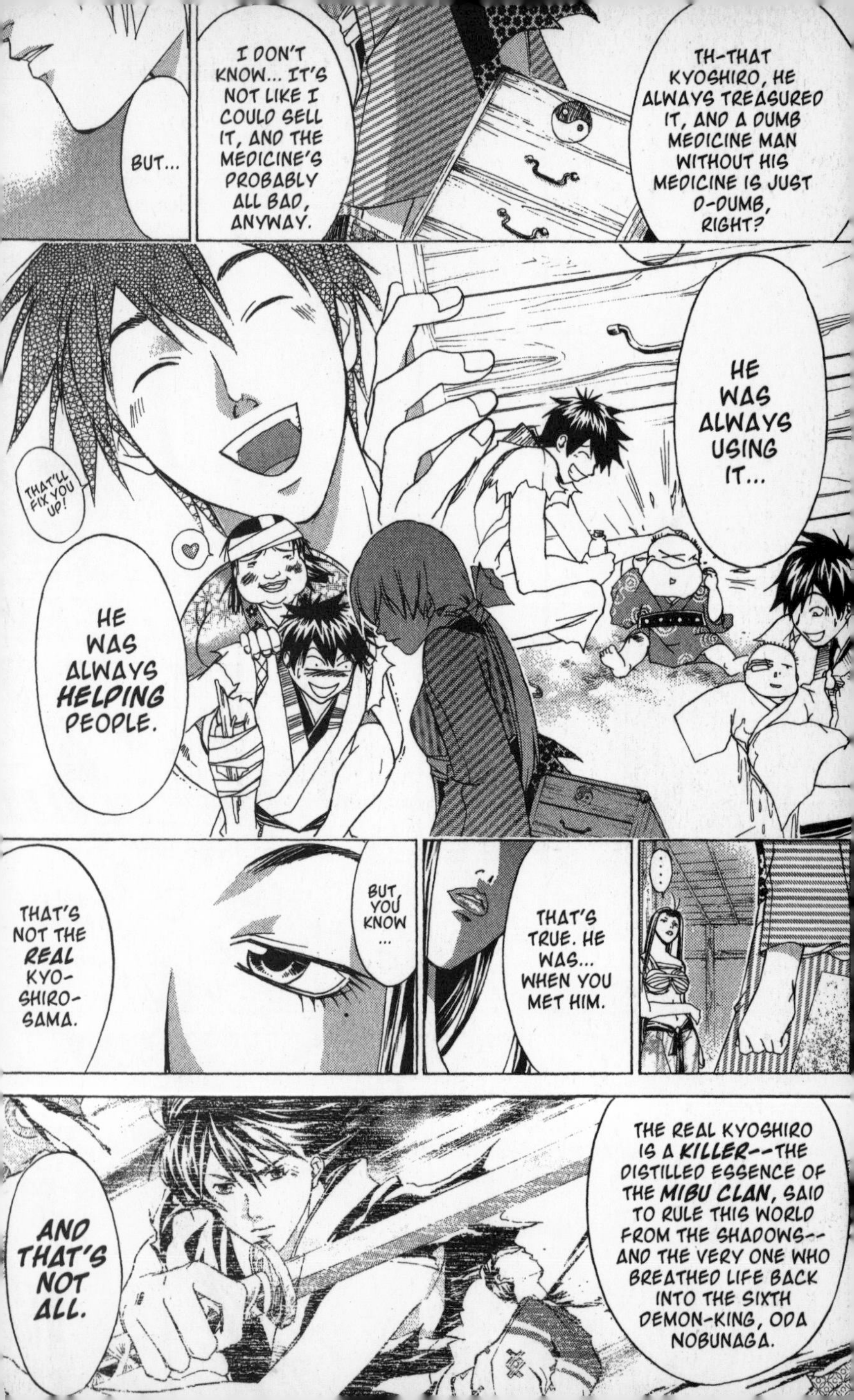

TH-THAT KYOSHIRO, HE ALWAYS TREASURED IT, AND A DUMB MEDICINE MAN WITHOUT HIS MEDICINE IS JUST D-DUMB, RIGHT?
I DON'T KNOW... IT'S NOT LIKE I COULD SELL IT, AND THE MEDICINE'S PROBABLY ALL BAD, ANYWAY.
BUT...
HE WAS ALWAYS USING IT...
THAT'LL FIX YOU UP!
HE WAS ALWAYS **HELPING** PEOPLE.
...
THAT'S TRUE. HE WAS... WHEN YOU MET HIM.
BUT, YOU KNOW ...
THAT'S NOT THE **REAL** KYO-SHIRO-SAMA.
THE REAL KYOSHIRO IS A **KILLER**--THE DISTILLED ESSENCE OF THE **MIBU CLAN**, SAID TO RULE THIS WORLD FROM THE SHADOWS--AND THE VERY ONE WHO BREATHED LIFE BACK INTO THE SIXTH DEMON-KING, ODA NOBUNAGA.
AND THAT'S NOT ALL.

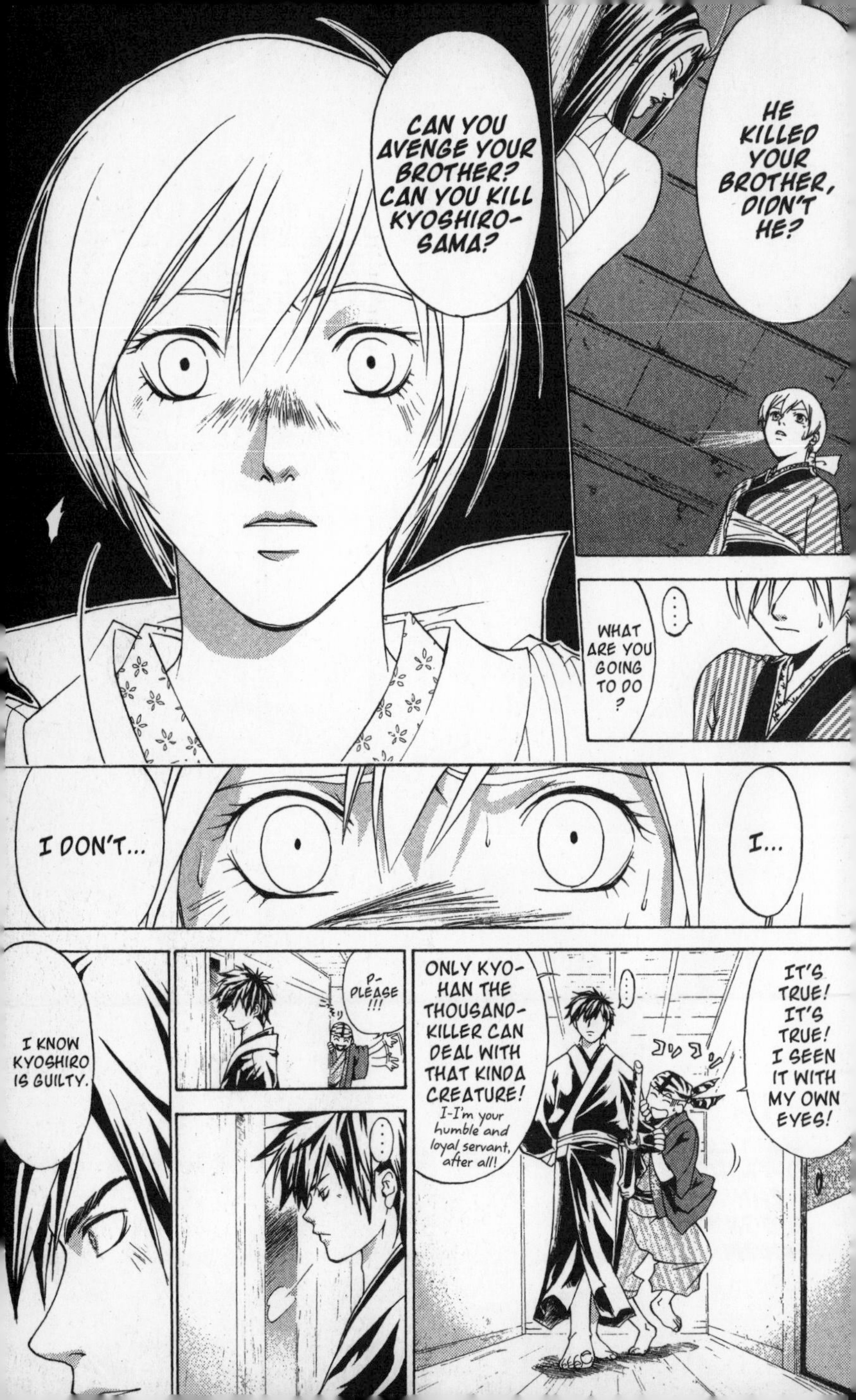
HE KILLED YOUR BROTHER, DIDN'T HE?
CAN YOU AVENGE YOUR BROTHER? CAN YOU KILL KYOSHIRO-SAMA?
...
WHAT ARE YOU GOING TO DO?
I...
I DON'T...
IT'S TRUE! IT'S TRUE! I SEEN IT WITH MY OWN EYES!
...
ONLY KYO-HAN THE THOUSAND-KILLER CAN DEAL WITH THAT KINDA CREATURE!
I-I'm your humble and loyal servant, after all!
P-PLEASE!!!
...
I KNOW KYOSHIRO IS GUILTY.

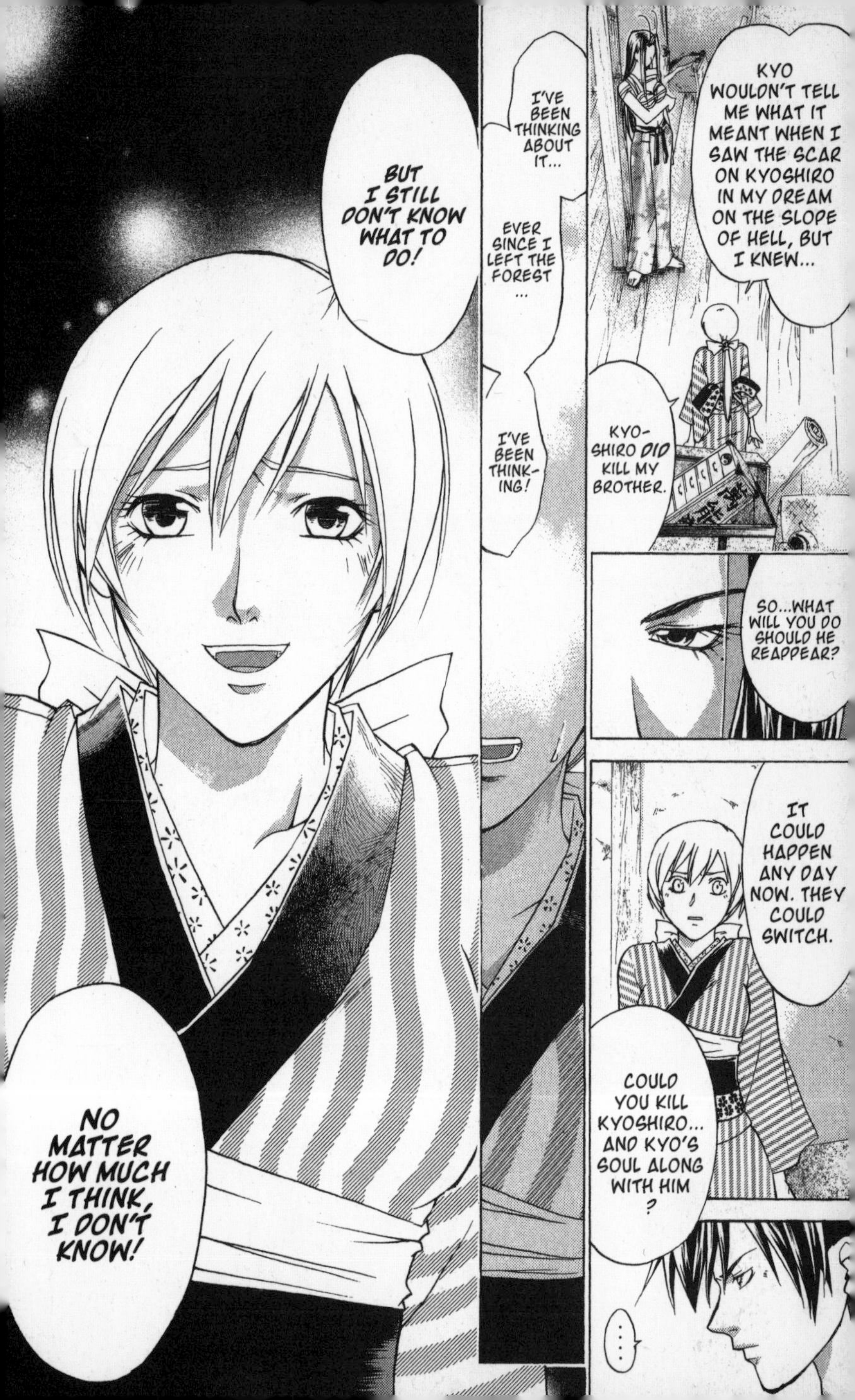
KYO WOULDN'T TELL ME WHAT IT MEANT WHEN I SAW THE SCAR ON KYOSHIRO IN MY DREAM ON THE SLOPE OF HELL, BUT I KNEW...
KYO-SHIRO *DID* KILL MY BROTHER.
SO...WHAT WILL YOU DO SHOULD HE REAPPEAR?
IT COULD HAPPEN ANY DAY NOW. THEY COULD SWITCH.
COULD YOU KILL KYOSHIRO... AND KYO'S SOUL ALONG WITH HIM ?
...
I'VE BEEN THINKING ABOUT IT...
EVER SINCE I LEFT THE FOREST ...
I'VE BEEN THINK-ING!
BUT I STILL DON'T KNOW WHAT TO DO!
NO MATTER HOW MUCH I THINK, I DON'T KNOW!

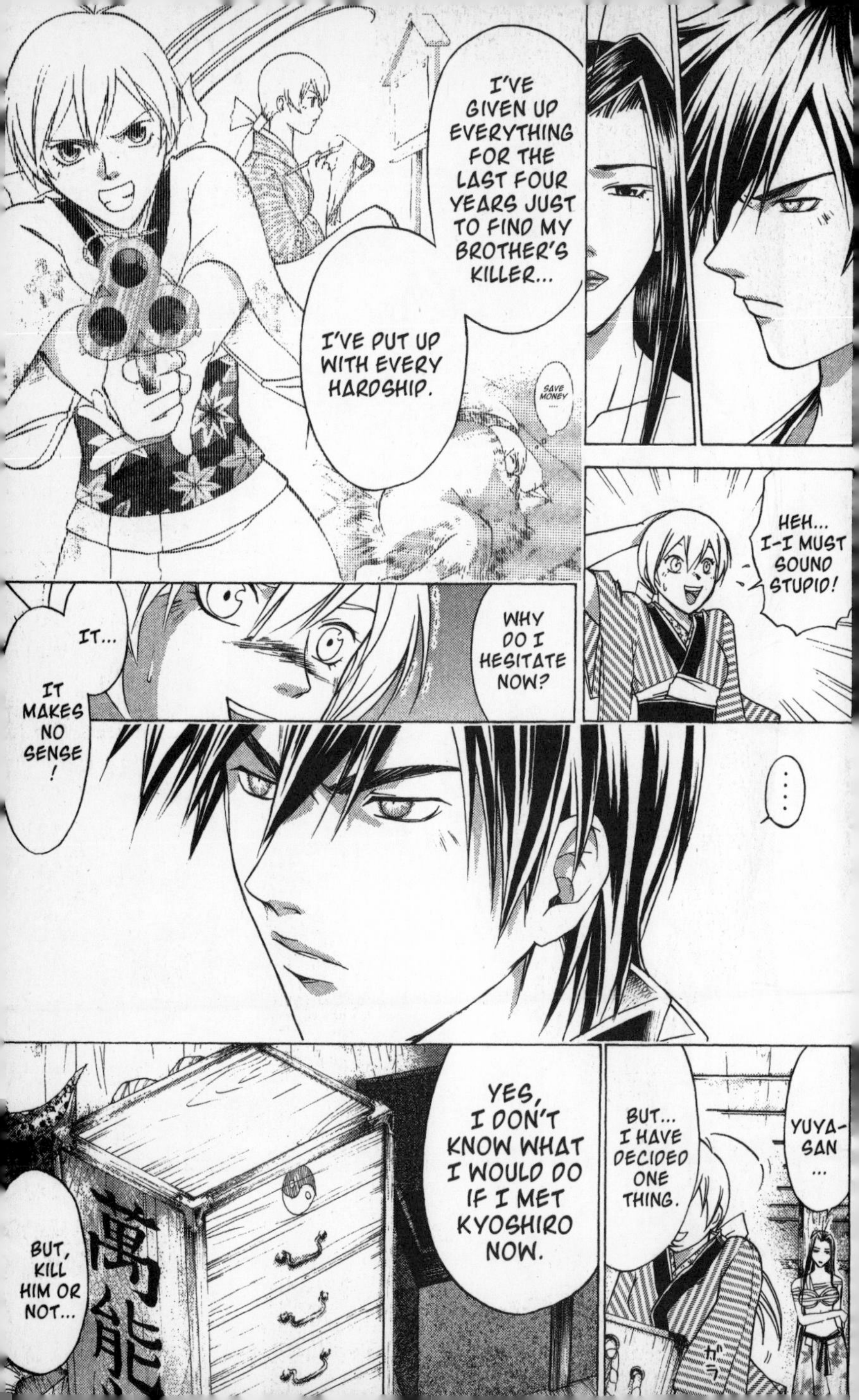

I'VE GIVEN UP EVERYTHING FOR THE LAST FOUR YEARS JUST TO FIND MY BROTHER'S KILLER...
I'VE PUT UP WITH EVERY HARDSHIP.
SAVE MONEY...
HEH... I-I MUST SOUND STUPID!
WHY DO I HESITATE NOW?
IT...
IT MAKES NO SENSE!
....
YUYA-SAN...
ガラ
BUT... I HAVE DECIDED ONE THING.
YES, I DON'T KNOW WHAT I WOULD DO IF I MET KYOSHIRO NOW.
萬能
BUT, KILL HIM OR NOT...

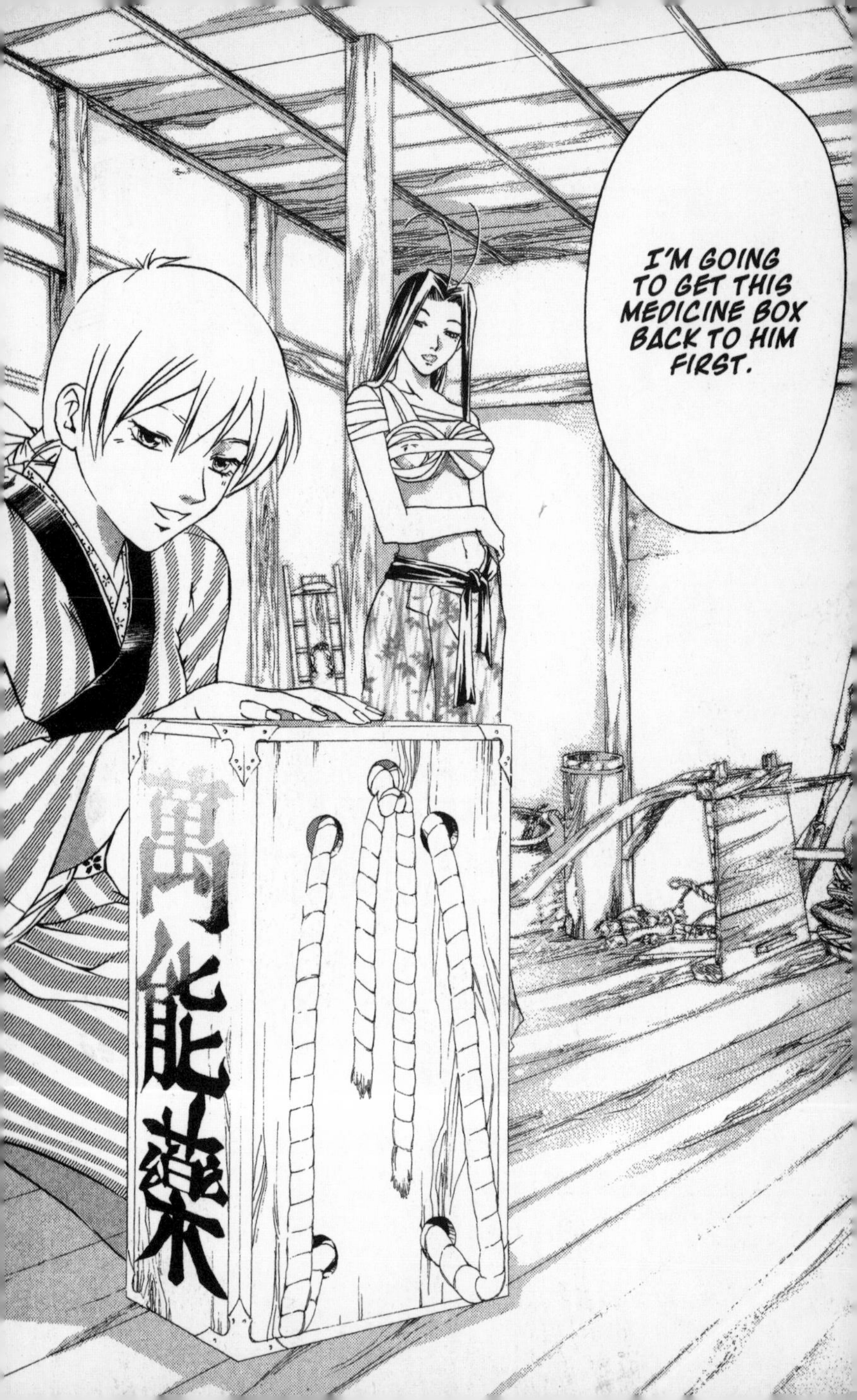
I'M GOING TO GET THIS MEDICINE BOX BACK TO HIM FIRST.
萬能藥

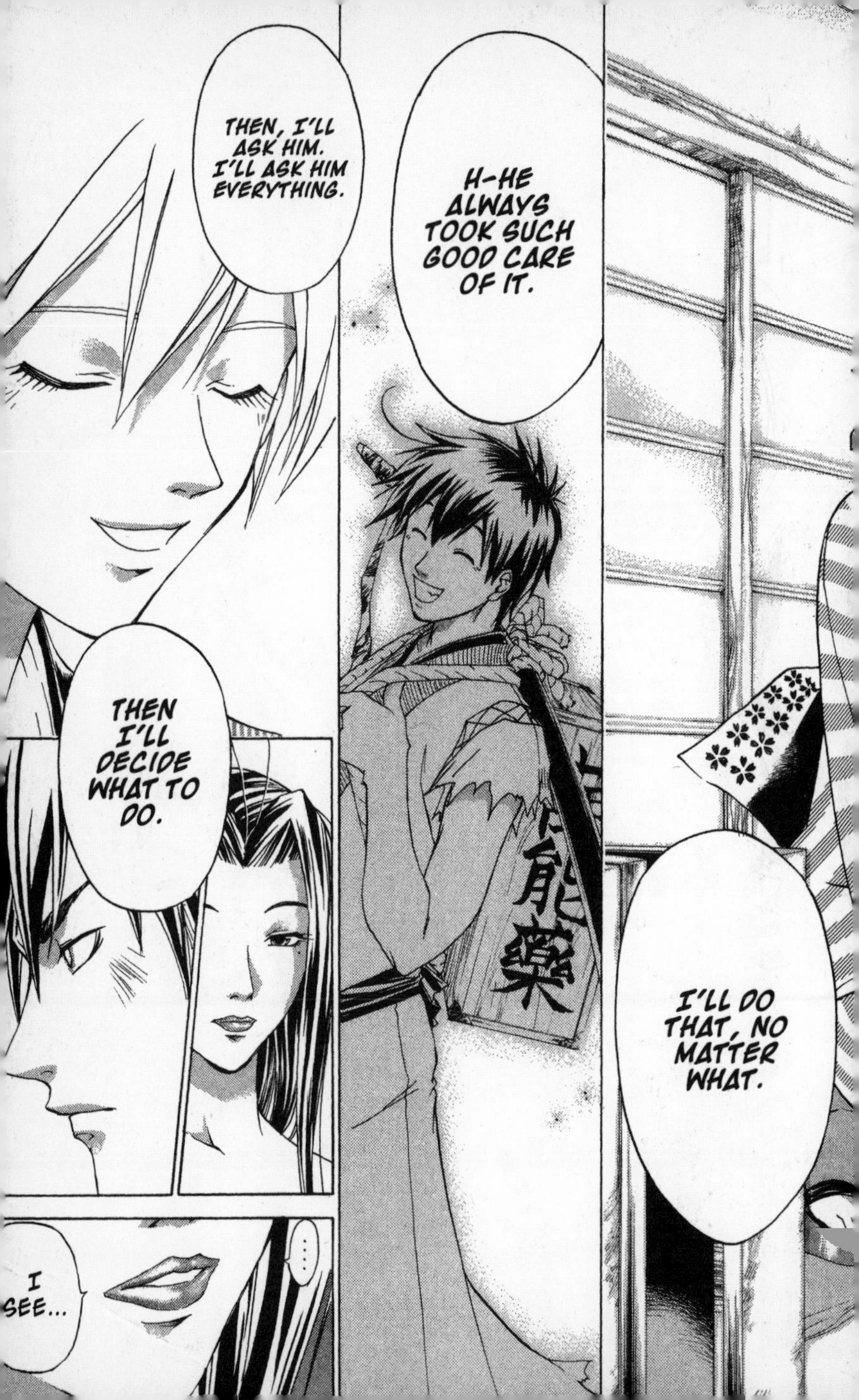
I'LL DO THAT, NO MATTER WHAT.
H-HE ALWAYS TOOK SUCH GOOD CARE OF IT.
THEN, I'LL ASK HIM. I'LL ASK HIM EVERYTHING.
THEN I'LL DECIDE WHAT TO DO.
....
I SEE...

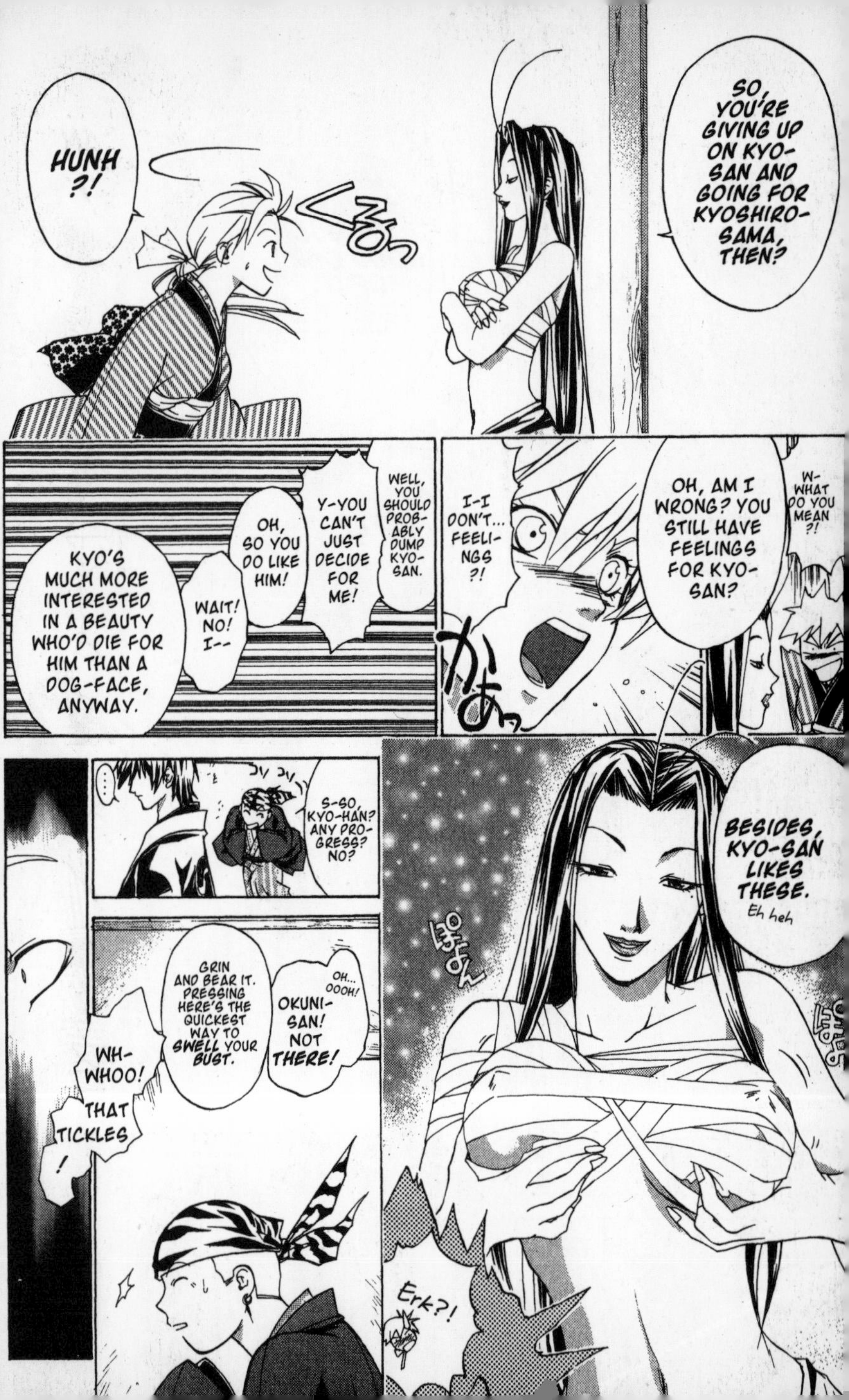
SO, YOU'RE GIVING UP ON KYO-SAN AND GOING FOR KYOSHIRO-SAMA, THEN?
HUNH ?!
W-WHAT DO YOU MEAN ?!
OH, AM I WRONG? YOU STILL HAVE FEELINGS FOR KYO-SAN?
I-I DON'T... FEELINGS ?!
WELL, YOU SHOULD PROBABLY DUMP KYO-SAN.
Y-YOU CAN'T JUST DECIDE FOR ME!
OH, SO YOU DO LIKE HIM!
WAIT! NO! I--
KYO'S MUCH MORE INTERESTED IN A BEAUTY WHO'D DIE FOR HIM THAN A DOG-FACE, ANYWAY.
BESIDES, KYO-SAN LIKES THESE.
Eh heh
Erk?!
S-SO, KYO-HAN? ANY PROGRESS? NO?
....
OH... OOOH!
OKUNI-SAN! NOT THERE!
GRIN AND BEAR IT. PRESSING HERE'S THE QUICKEST WAY TO SWELL YOUR BUST.
WH-WHOO! THAT TICKLES!

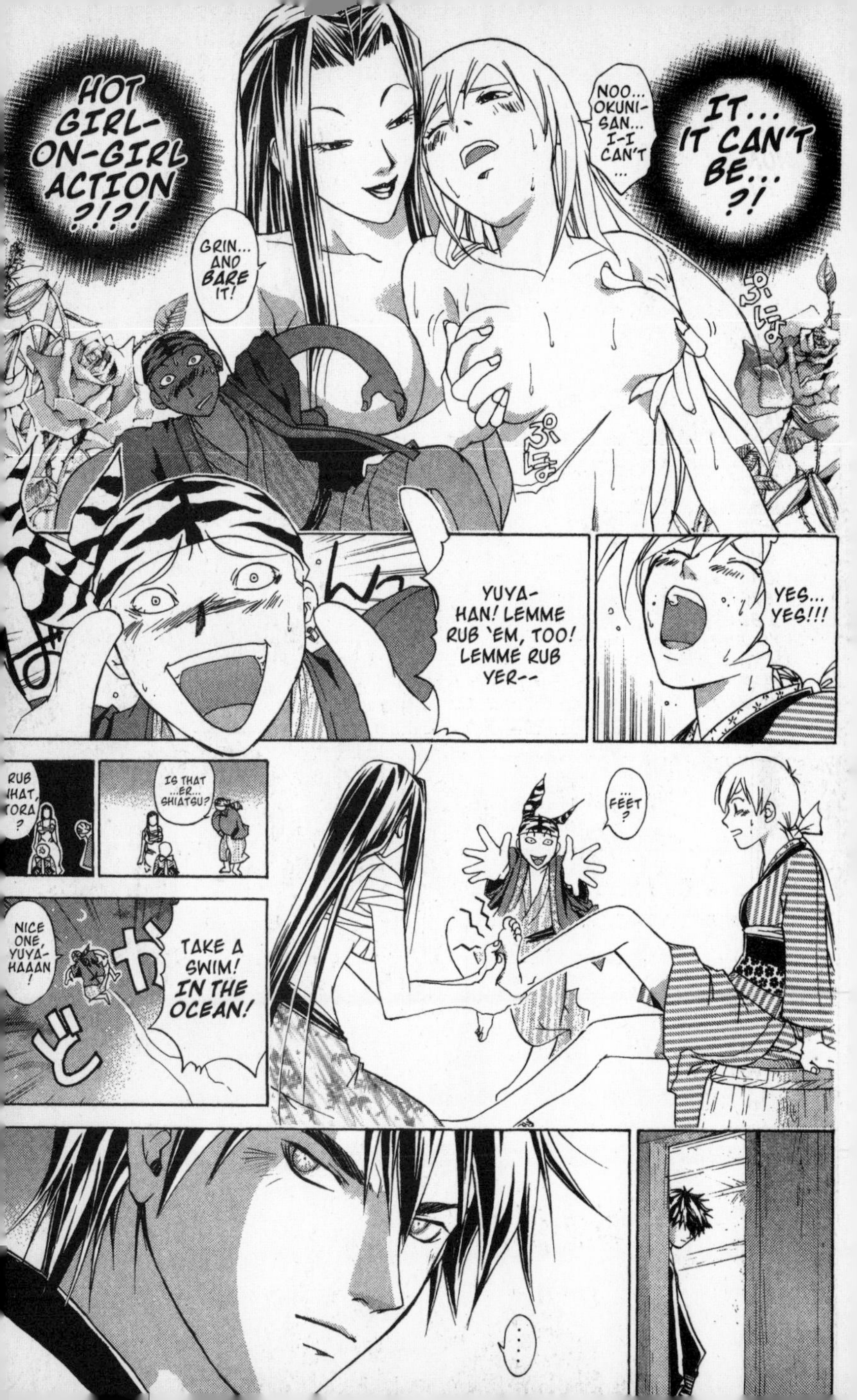
IT... IT CAN'T BE...?!
NOO... OKUNI-SAN... I-I CAN'T...
GRIN... AND BARE IT!
HOT GIRL-ON-GIRL ACTION?!?!
ぷにょ
ぷにょ
YES... YES!!!
YUYA-HAN! LEMME RUB 'EM, TOO! LEMME RUB YER--
...FEET?
IS THAT ...ER... SHIATSU?
RUB HAT, TORA?
TAKE A SWIM! IN THE OCEAN!
NICE ONE, YUYA-HAAAN!
...

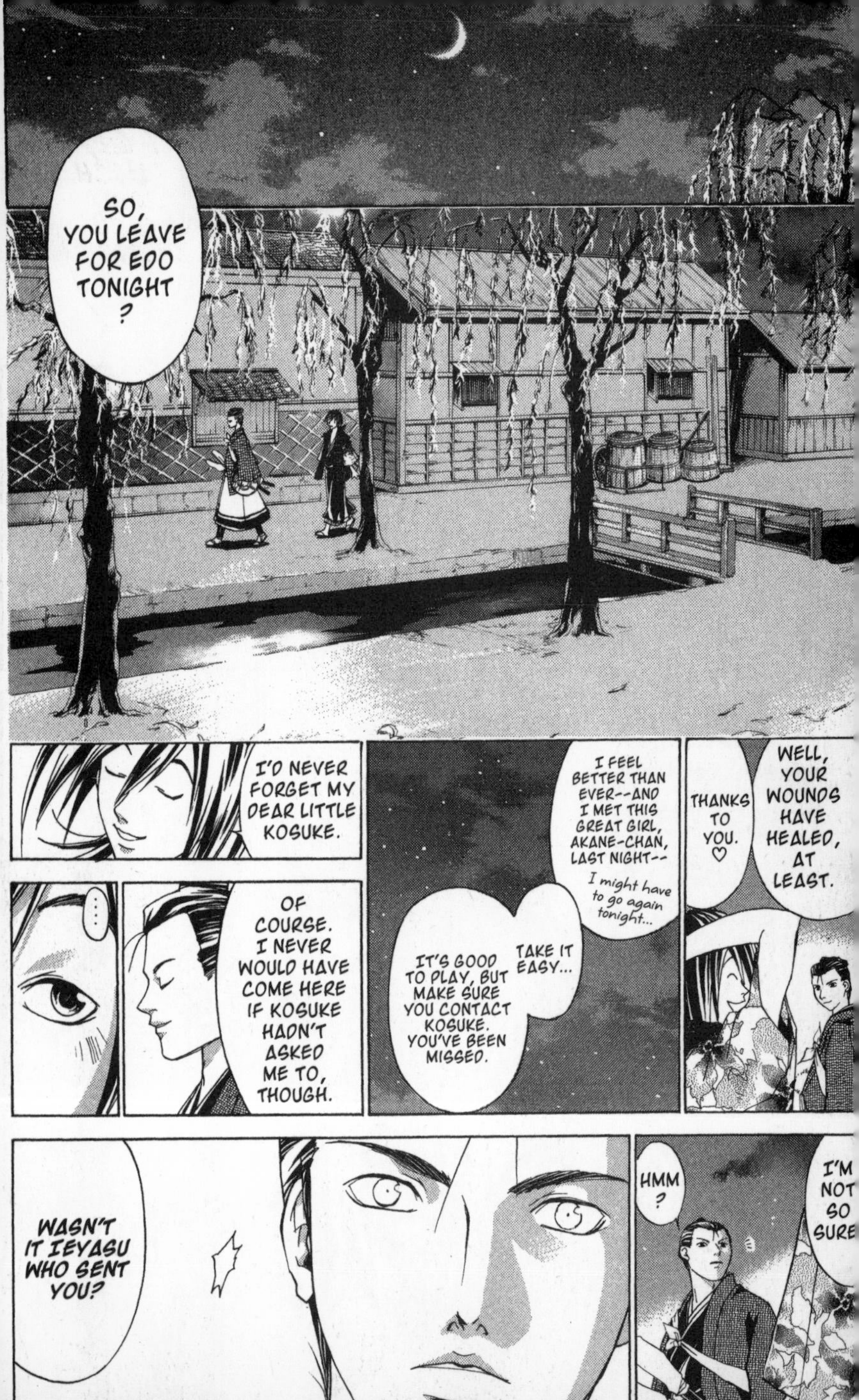
SO, YOU LEAVE FOR EDO TONIGHT?
WELL, YOUR WOUNDS HAVE HEALED, AT LEAST.
THANKS TO YOU. ♡
I FEEL BETTER THAN EVER--AND I MET THIS GREAT GIRL, AKANE-CHAN, LAST NIGHT--
I might have to go again tonight...
TAKE IT EASY...
IT'S GOOD TO PLAY, BUT MAKE SURE YOU CONTACT KOSUKE. YOU'VE BEEN MISSED.
I'D NEVER FORGET MY DEAR LITTLE KOSUKE.
OF COURSE. I NEVER WOULD HAVE COME HERE IF KOSUKE HADN'T ASKED ME TO, THOUGH.
....
I'M NOT SO SURE
HMM?
WASN'T IT IEYASU WHO SENT YOU?

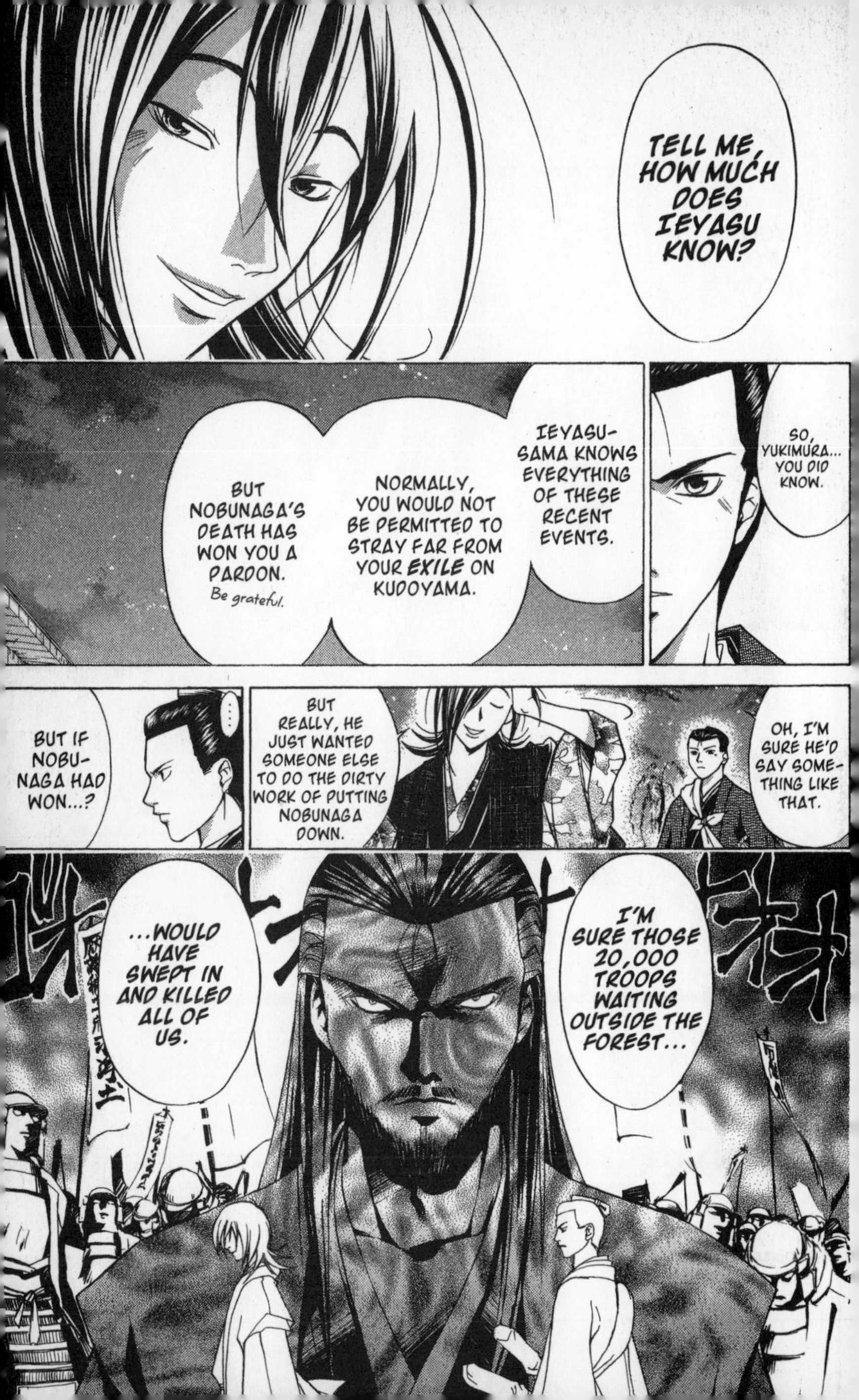
TELL ME, HOW MUCH DOES IEYASU KNOW?
SO, YUKIMURA... YOU DID KNOW.
IEYASU-SAMA KNOWS EVERYTHING OF THESE RECENT EVENTS.
NORMALLY, YOU WOULD NOT BE PERMITTED TO STRAY FAR FROM YOUR EXILE ON KUDOYAMA.
BUT NOBUNAGA'S DEATH HAS WON YOU A PARDON.
Be grateful.
OH, I'M SURE HE'D SAY SOMETHING LIKE THAT.
BUT REALLY, HE JUST WANTED SOMEONE ELSE TO DO THE DIRTY WORK OF PUTTING NOBUNAGA DOWN.
...
BUT IF NOBUNAGA HAD WON...?
I'M SURE THOSE 20,000 TROOPS WAITING OUTSIDE THE FOREST...
...WOULD HAVE SWEPT IN AND KILLED ALL OF US.

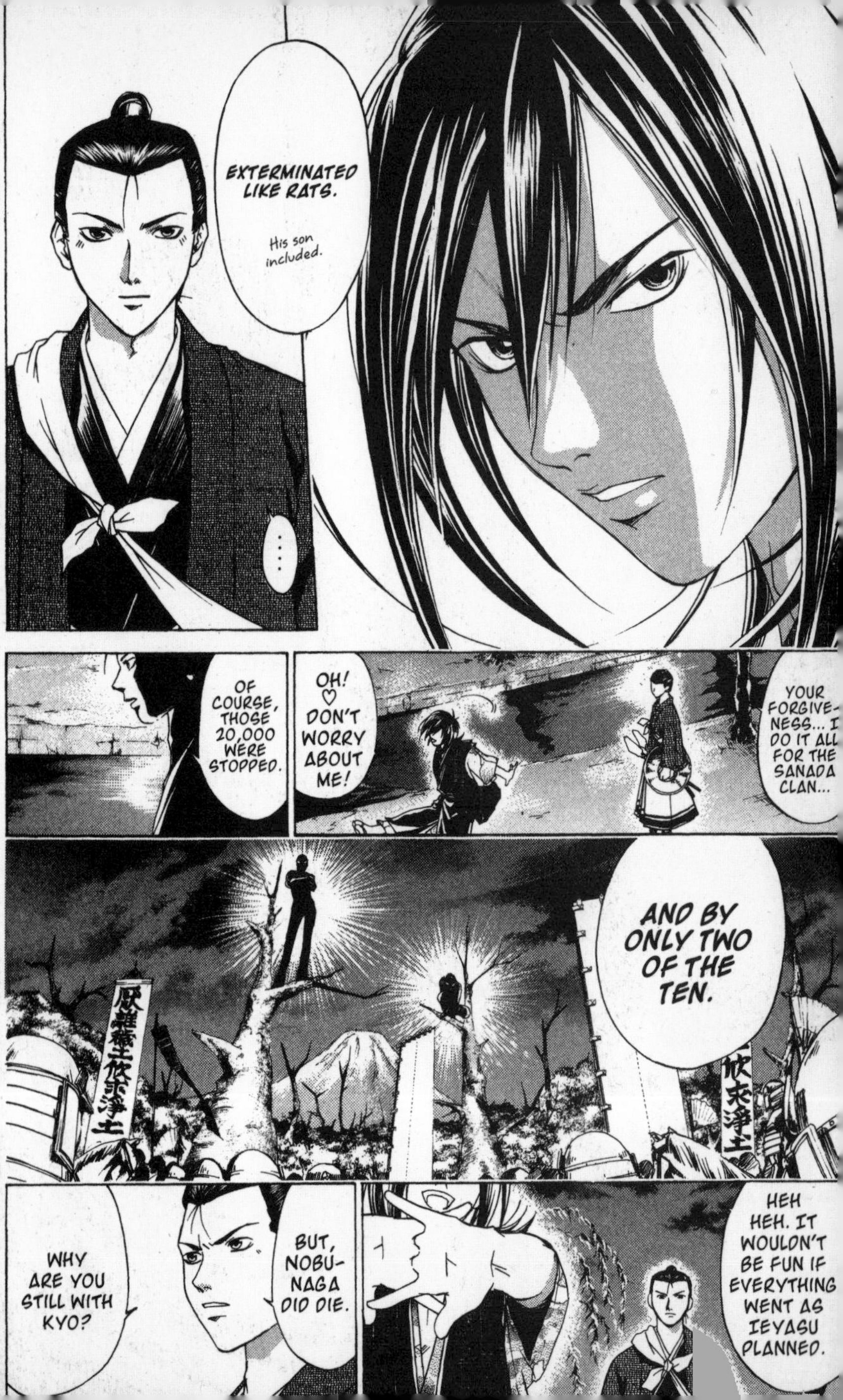
EXTERMINATED LIKE RATS.
His son included.
....
YOUR FORGIVENESS... I DO IT ALL FOR THE SANADA CLAN...
OH! ♡ DON'T WORRY ABOUT ME!
OF COURSE, THOSE 20,000 WERE STOPPED.
AND BY ONLY TWO OF THE TEN.
厭離穢土欣求浄土
欣求浄土
HEH HEH. IT WOULDN'T BE FUN IF EVERYTHING WENT AS IEYASU PLANNED.
BUT, NOBUNAGA DID DIE.
WHY ARE YOU STILL WITH KYO?

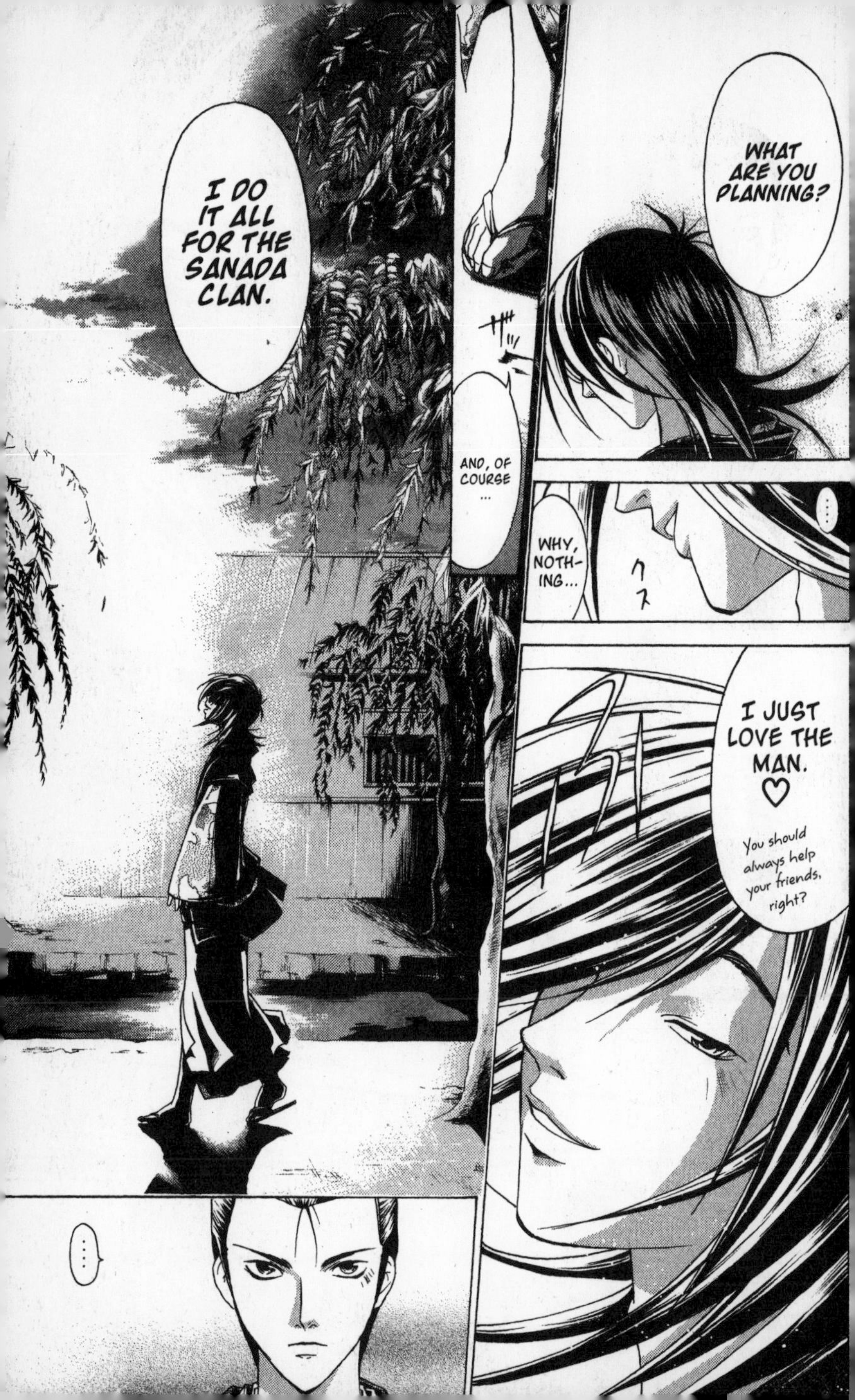
WHAT ARE YOU PLANNING?
...
WHY, NOTHING...
クス
I DO IT ALL FOR THE SANADA CLAN.
AND, OF COURSE...
I JUST LOVE THE MAN. ♡
You should always help your friends, right?
...

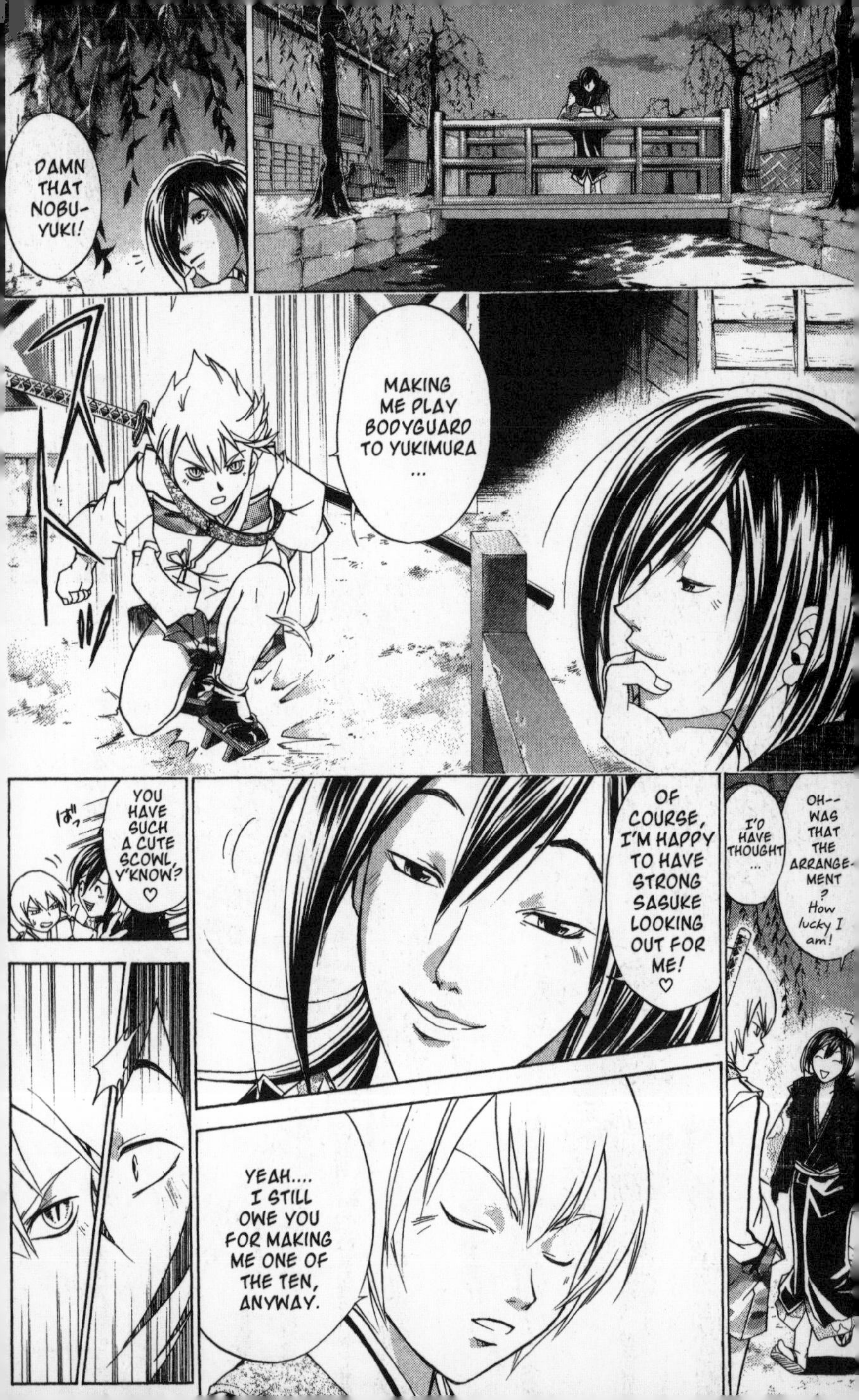
DAMN THAT NOBU-YUKI!
MAKING ME PLAY BODYGUARD TO YUKIMURA ...
OH--WAS THAT THE ARRANGEMENT? How lucky I am!
I'D HAVE THOUGHT...
OF COURSE, I'M HAPPY TO HAVE STRONG SASUKE LOOKING OUT FOR ME! ♡
ばっ
YOU HAVE SUCH A CUTE SCOWL, Y'KNOW? ♡
YEAH.... I STILL OWE YOU FOR MAKING ME ONE OF THE TEN, ANYWAY.

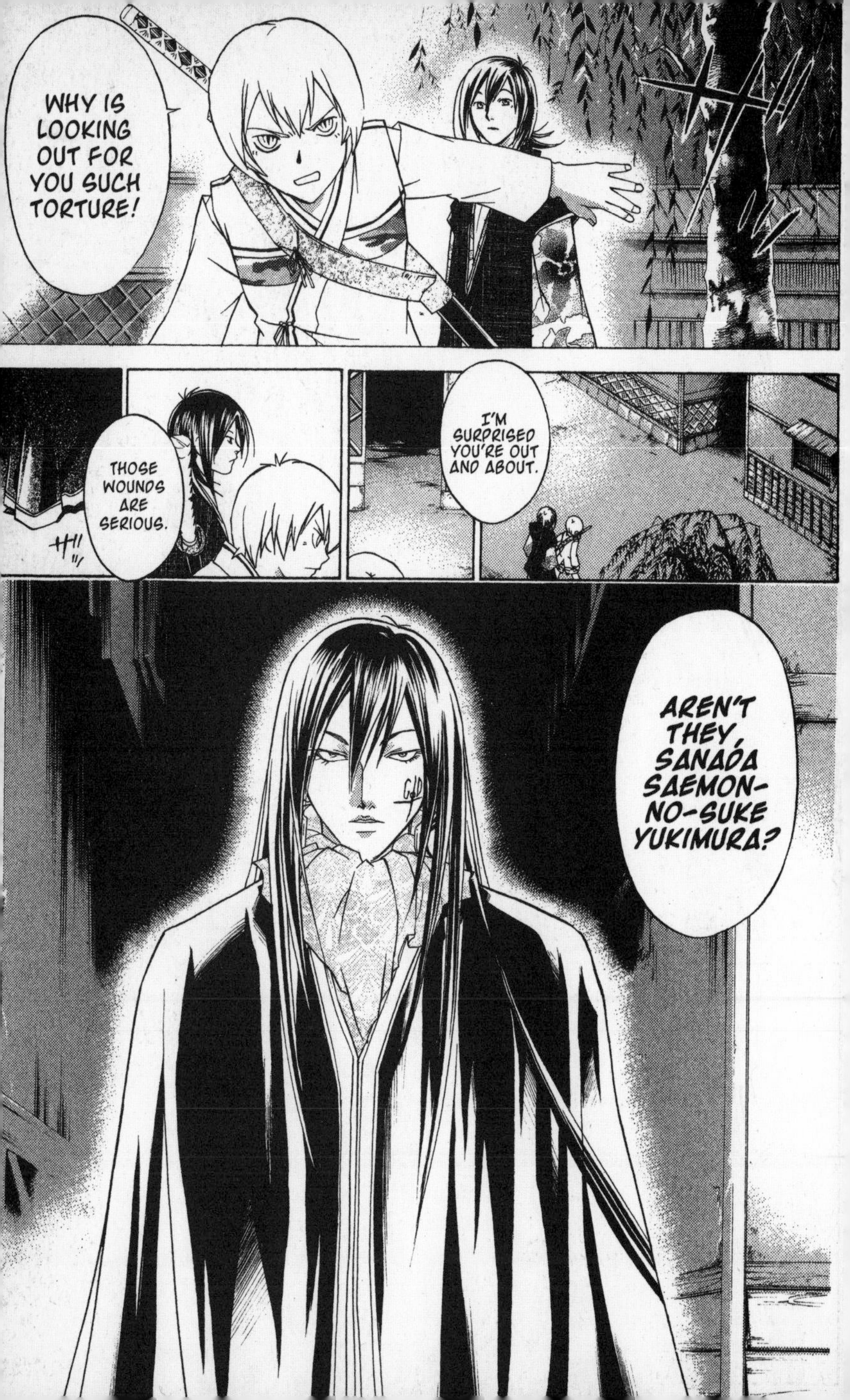
WHY IS LOOKING OUT FOR YOU SUCH TORTURE!
I'M SURPRISED YOU'RE OUT AND ABOUT.
THOSE WOUNDS ARE SERIOUS.
AREN'T THEY, SANADA SAEMON-NO-SUKE YUKIMURA?

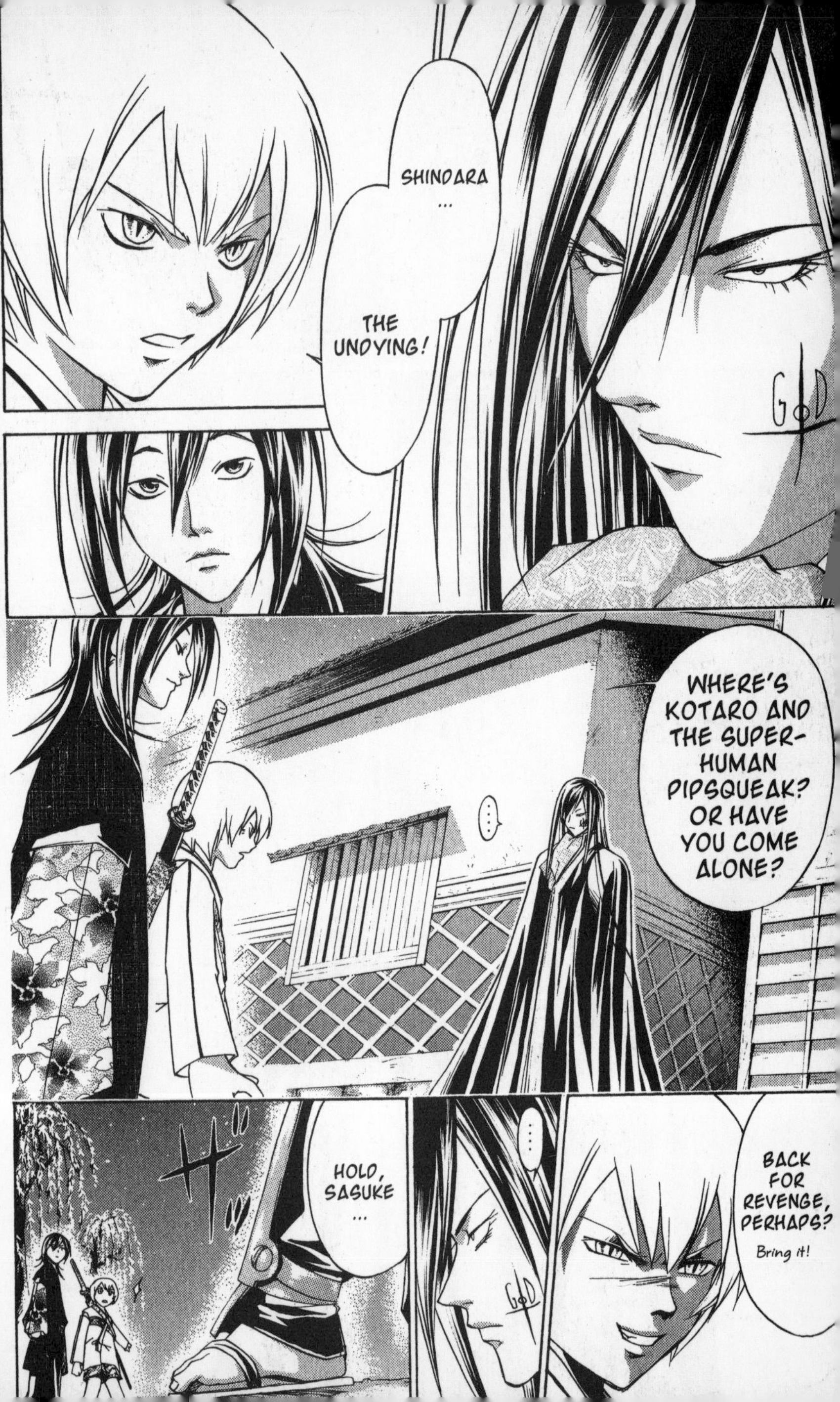
SHINDARA ...
THE UNDYING!
WHERE'S KOTARO AND THE SUPER-HUMAN PIPSQUEAK? OR HAVE YOU COME ALONE?
...
BACK FOR REVENGE, PERHAPS?
Bring it!
...
HOLD, SASUKE ...

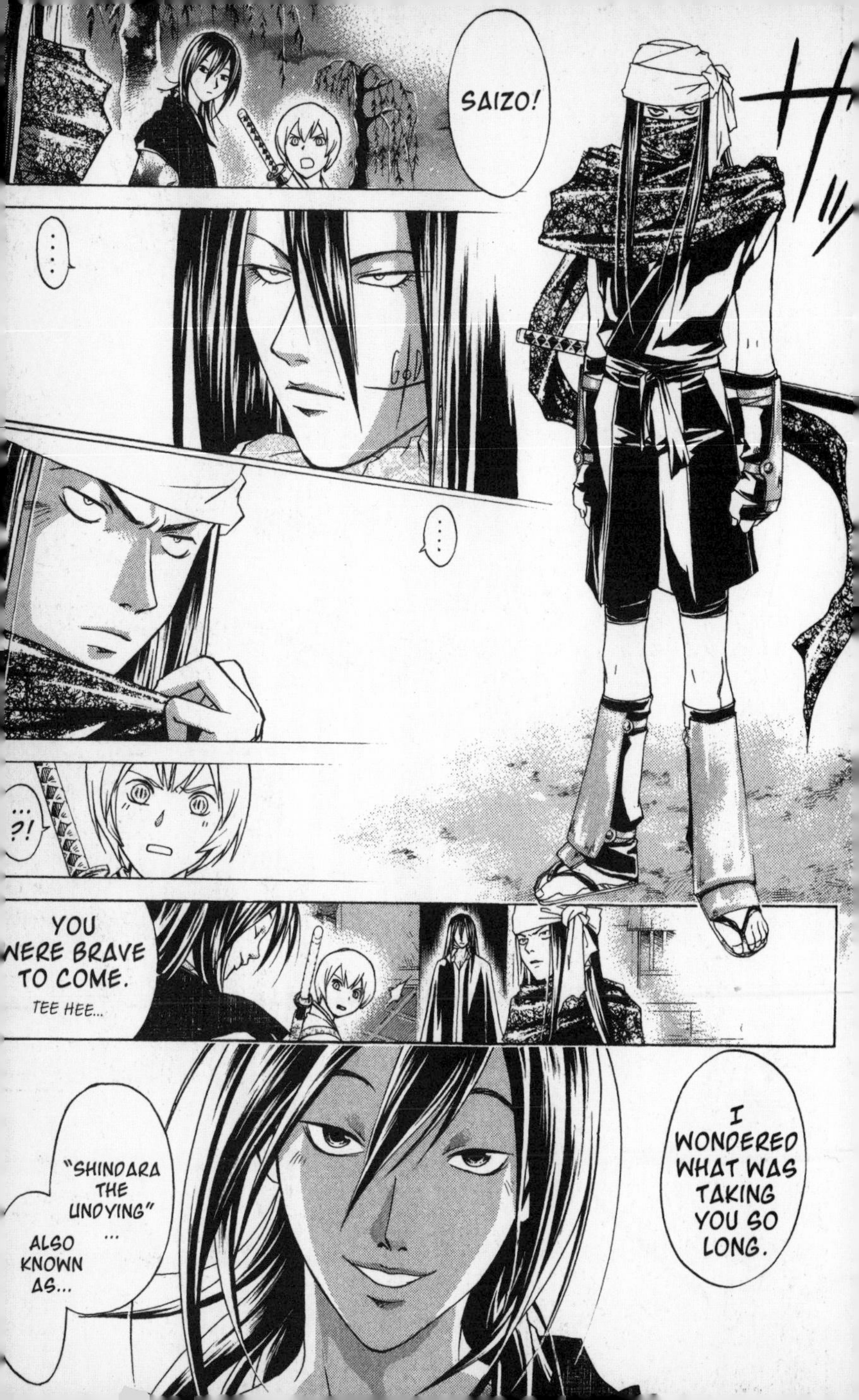
SAIZO!
...
...
...?!
YOU WERE BRAVE TO COME.
TEE HEE...
I WONDERED WHAT WAS TAKING YOU SO LONG.
"SHINDARA THE UNDYING" ... ALSO KNOWN AS...

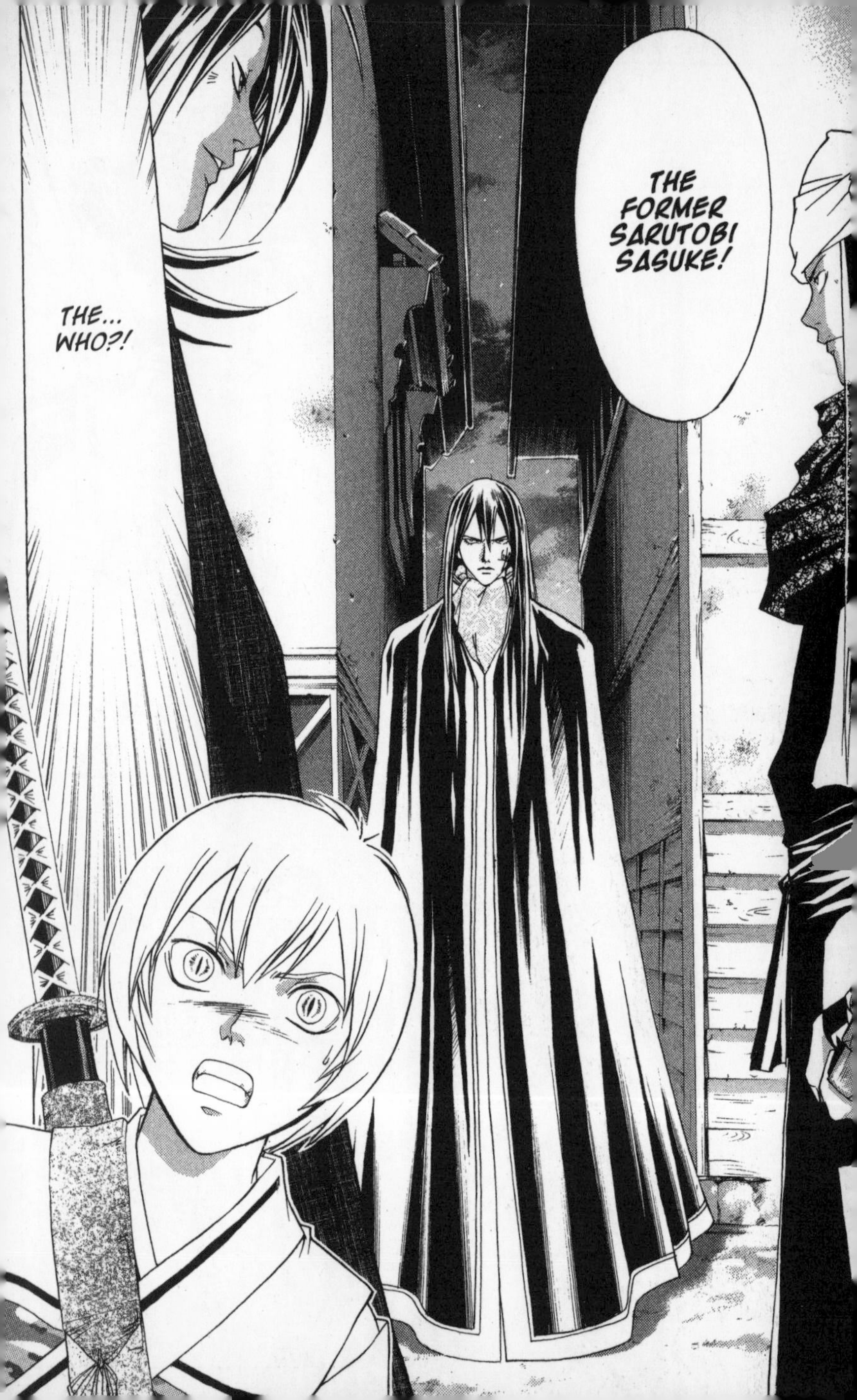
THE FORMER SARUTOBI SASUKE!
THE... WHO?!

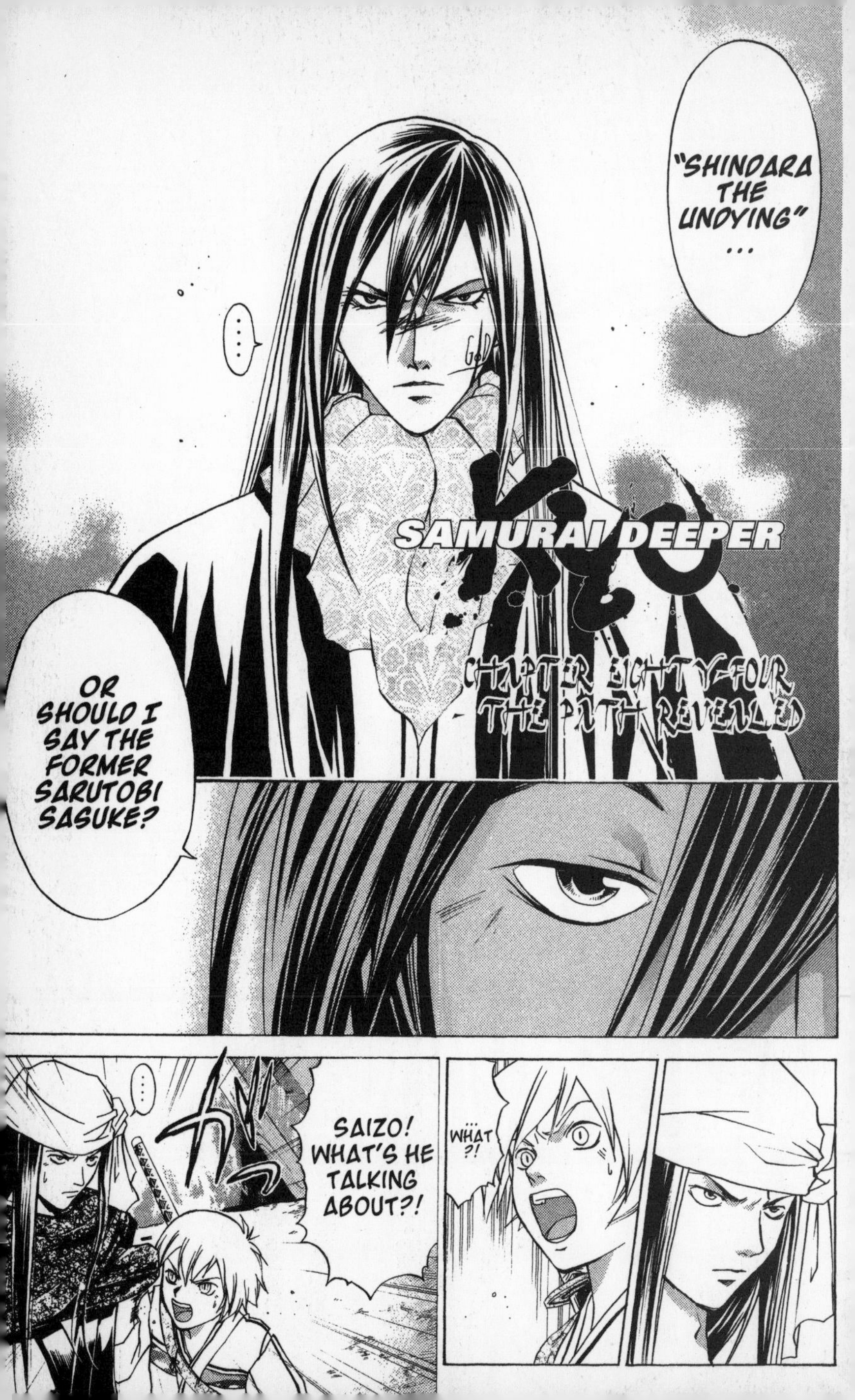

"SHINDARA THE UNDYING" ...
....
SAMURAI DEEPER KYO
CHAPTER EIGHTY-FOUR THE PATH REVEALED
OR SHOULD I SAY THE FORMER SARUTOBI SASUKE?
WHAT ?!
SAIZO! WHAT'S HE TALKING ABOUT?!
....

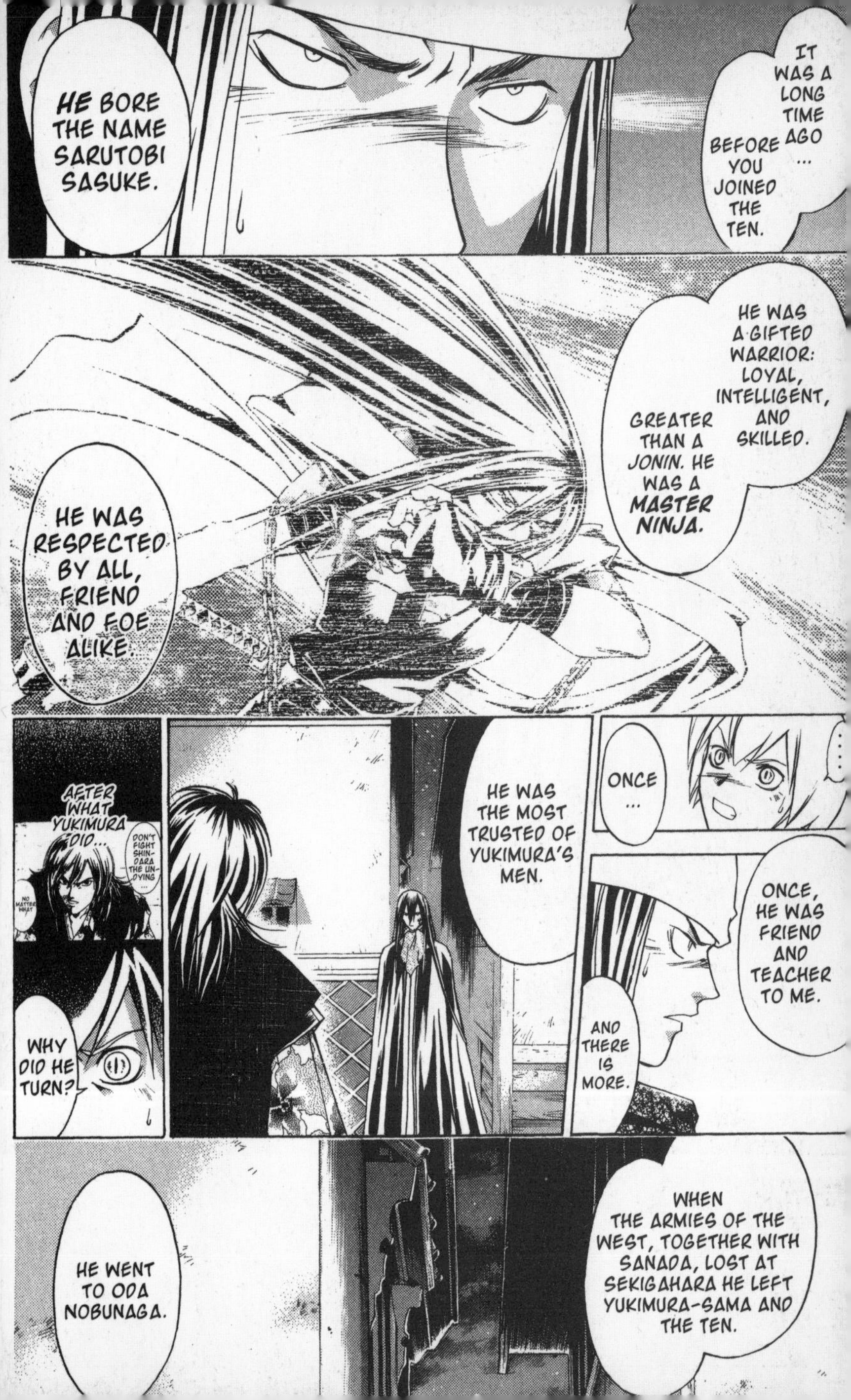
IT WAS A LONG TIME AGO ... BEFORE YOU JOINED THE TEN.
HE BORE THE NAME SARUTOBI SASUKE.
HE WAS A GIFTED WARRIOR: LOYAL, INTELLIGENT, AND SKILLED.
GREATER THAN A JONIN. HE WAS A MASTER NINJA.
HE WAS RESPECTED BY ALL, FRIEND AND FOE ALIKE.
ONCE ...
ONCE, HE WAS FRIEND AND TEACHER TO ME.
AND THERE IS MORE.
HE WAS THE MOST TRUSTED OF YUKIMURA'S MEN.
AFTER WHAT YUKIMURA DID...
DON'T FIGHT SHIN-DARA THE UN-DYING ...
NO MATTER WHAT
WHY DID HE TURN?
WHEN THE ARMIES OF THE WEST, TOGETHER WITH SANADA, LOST AT SEKIGAHARA HE LEFT YUKIMURA-SAMA AND THE TEN.
HE WENT TO ODA NOBUNAGA.

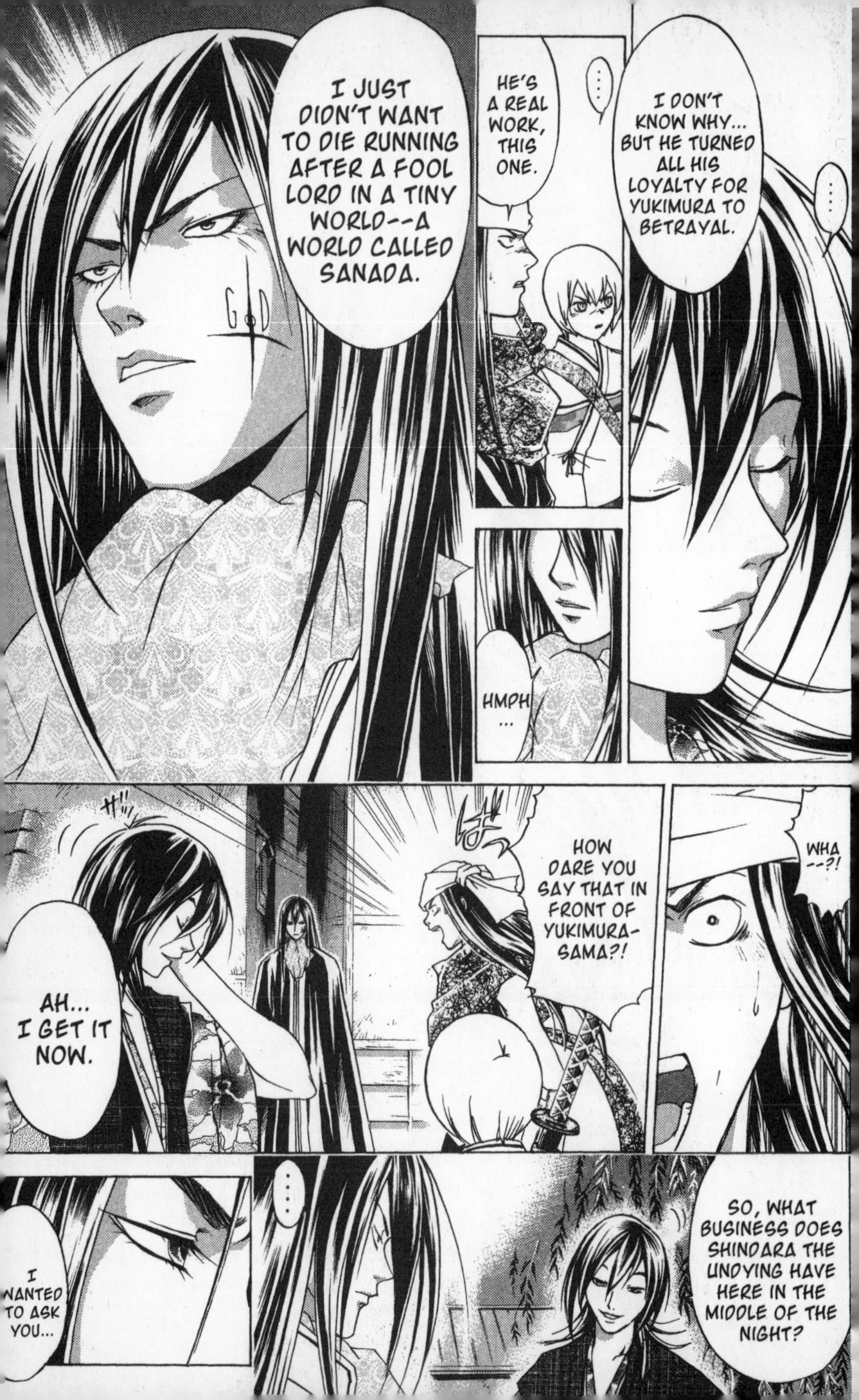
I DON'T KNOW WHY... BUT HE TURNED ALL HIS LOYALTY FOR YUKIMURA TO BETRAYAL.
....
....
HE'S A REAL WORK, THIS ONE.
HMPH...
I JUST DIDN'T WANT TO DIE RUNNING AFTER A FOOL LORD IN A TINY WORLD--A WORLD CALLED SANADA.
WHA--?!
HOW DARE YOU SAY THAT IN FRONT OF YUKIMURA-SAMA?!
AH... I GET IT NOW.
SO, WHAT BUSINESS DOES SHINDARA THE UNDYING HAVE HERE IN THE MIDDLE OF THE NIGHT?
....
I WANTED TO ASK YOU...

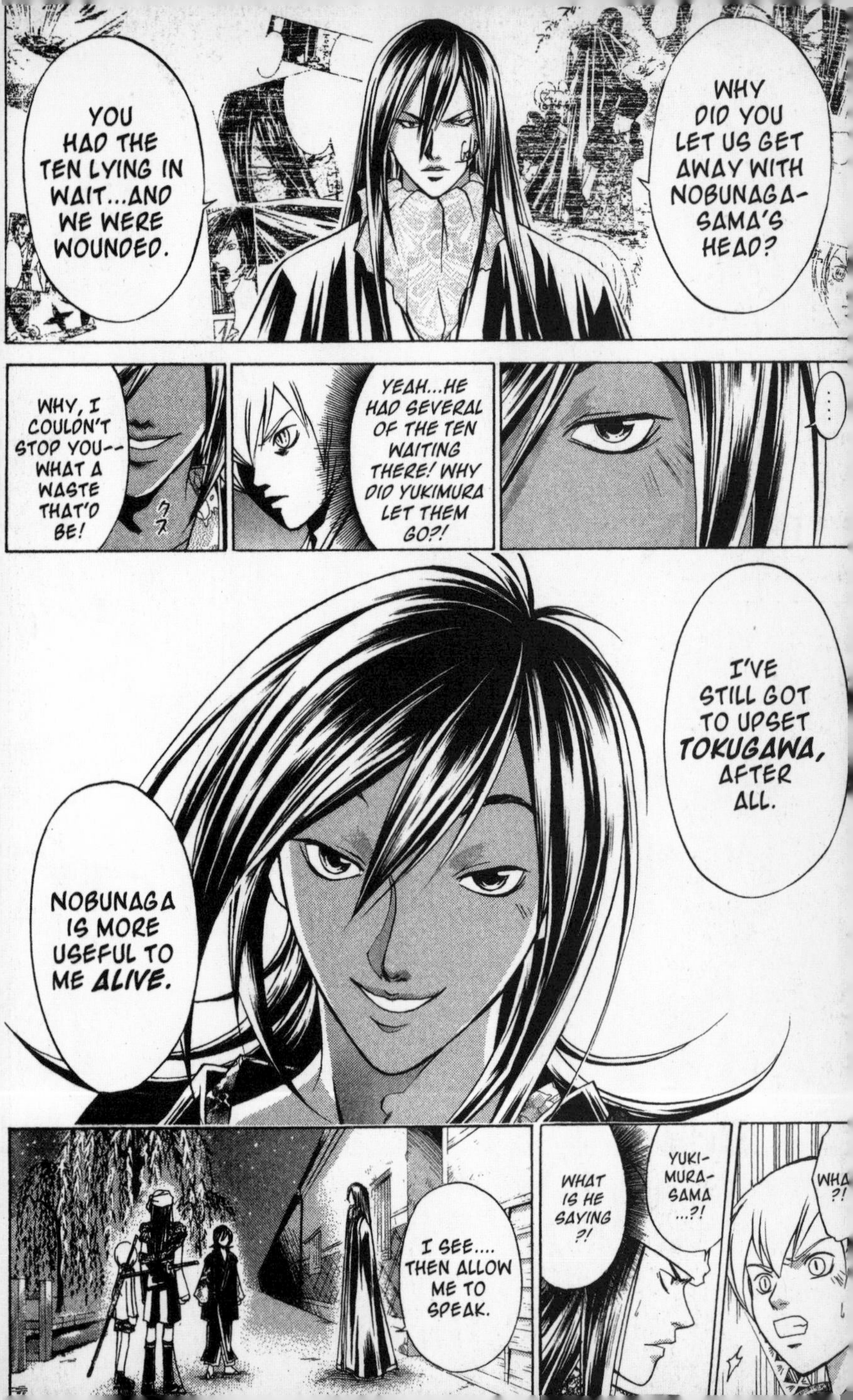
WHY DID YOU LET US GET AWAY WITH NOBUNAGA-SAMA'S HEAD?
YOU HAD THE TEN LYING IN WAIT...AND WE WERE WOUNDED.
....
YEAH...HE HAD SEVERAL OF THE TEN WAITING THERE! WHY DID YUKIMURA LET THEM GO?!
WHY, I COULDN'T STOP YOU--WHAT A WASTE THAT'D BE!
クス
I'VE STILL GOT TO UPSET TOKUGAWA, AFTER ALL.
NOBUNAGA IS MORE USEFUL TO ME ALIVE.
WHA?!
YUKI-MURA-SAMA...?!
WHAT IS HE SAYING?!
I SEE.... THEN ALLOW ME TO SPEAK.

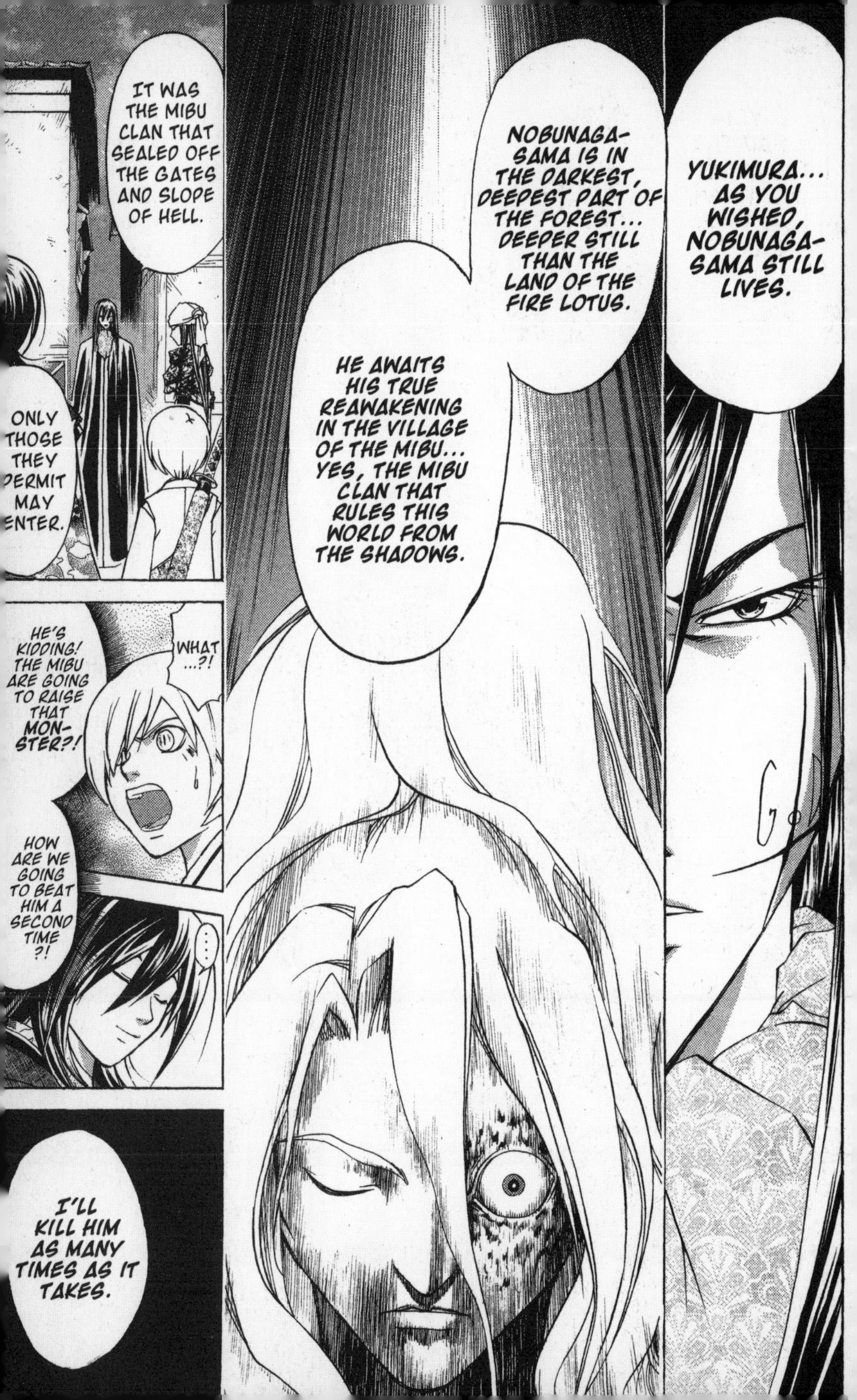
YUKIMURA... AS YOU WISHED, NOBUNAGA-SAMA STILL LIVES.
NOBUNAGA-SAMA IS IN THE DARKEST, DEEPEST PART OF THE FOREST... DEEPER STILL THAN THE LAND OF THE FIRE LOTUS.
HE AWAITS HIS TRUE REAWAKENING IN THE VILLAGE OF THE MIBU... YES, THE MIBU CLAN THAT RULES THIS WORLD FROM THE SHADOWS.
IT WAS THE MIBU CLAN THAT SEALED OFF THE GATES AND SLOPE OF HELL.
ONLY THOSE THEY PERMIT MAY ENTER.
WHAT ...?!
HE'S KIDDING! THE MIBU ARE GOING TO RAISE THAT MON-STER?!
HOW ARE WE GOING TO BEAT HIM A SECOND TIME ?!
...
I'LL KILL HIM AS MANY TIMES AS IT TAKES.

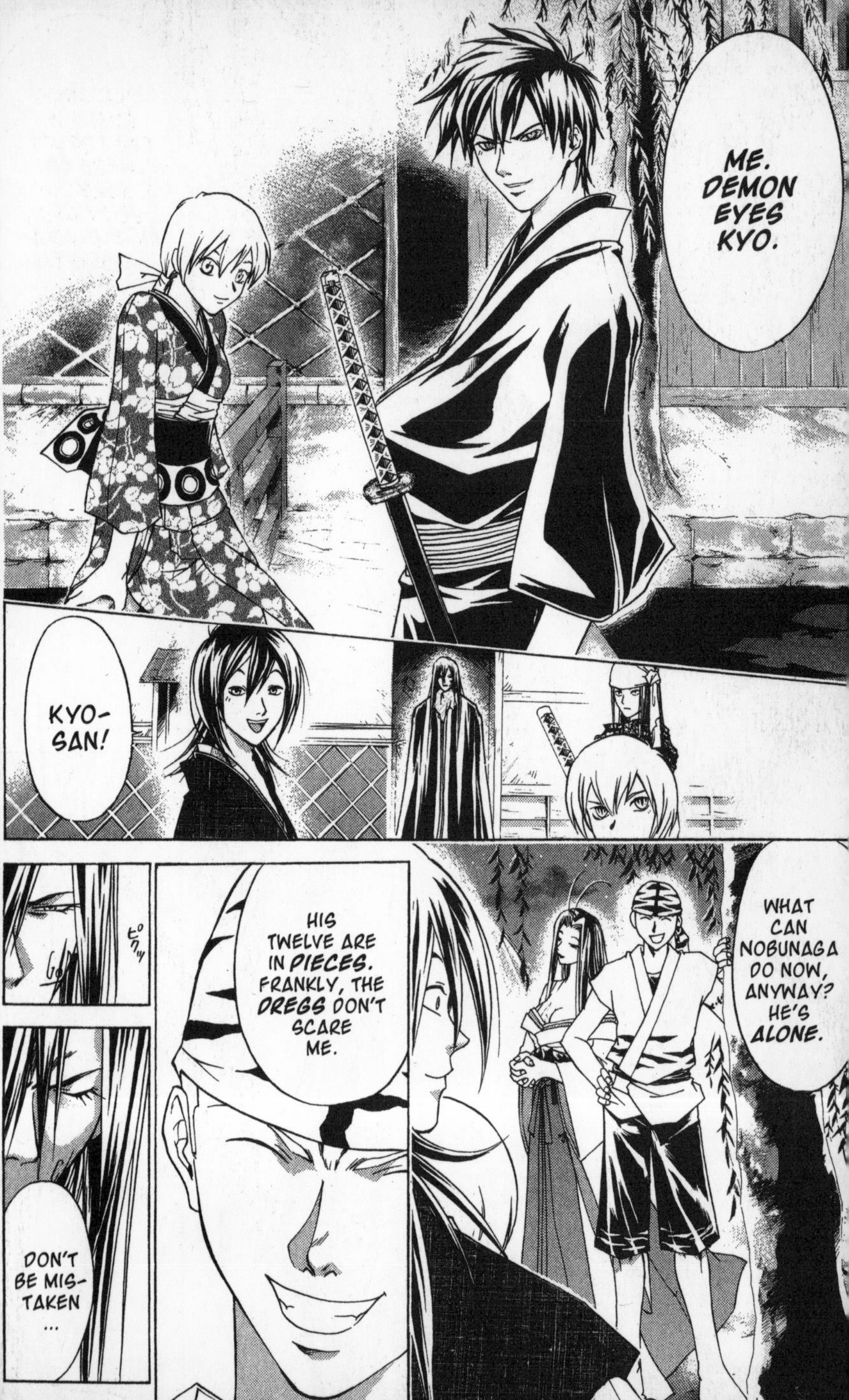
ME. DEMON EYES KYO.
KYO-SAN!
WHAT CAN NOBUNAGA DO NOW, ANYWAY? HE'S ALONE.
HIS TWELVE ARE IN PIECES. FRANKLY, THE DREGS DON'T SCARE ME.
DON'T BE MIS-TAKEN ...

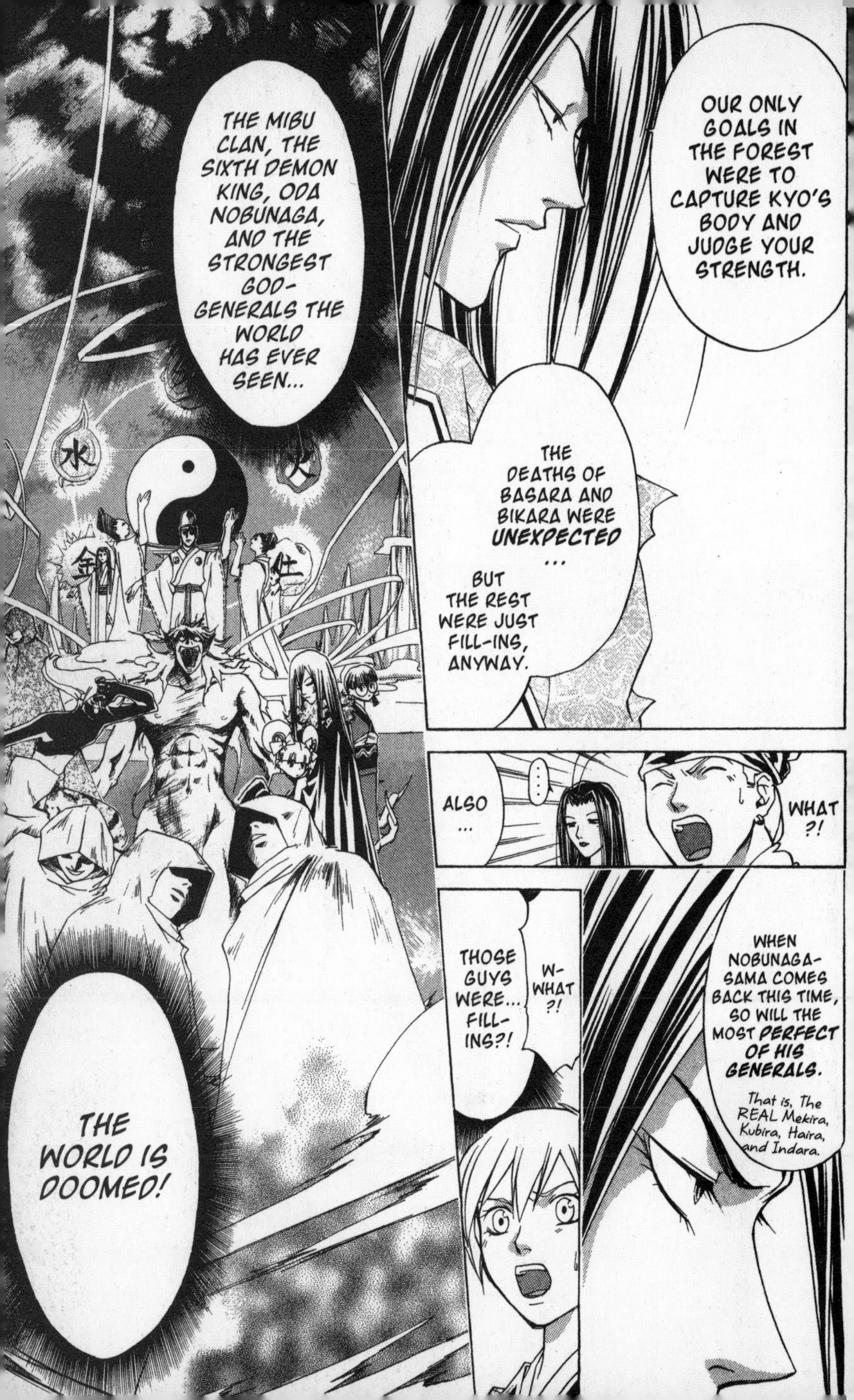
OUR ONLY GOALS IN THE FOREST WERE TO CAPTURE KYO'S BODY AND JUDGE YOUR STRENGTH.
THE DEATHS OF BASARA AND BIKARA WERE **UNEXPECTED**...
BUT THE REST WERE JUST FILL-INS, ANYWAY.
WHAT?!
...
ALSO...
WHEN NOBUNAGA-SAMA COMES BACK THIS TIME, SO WILL THE MOST **PERFECT OF HIS GENERALS.**
That is, The REAL Mekira, Kubira, Haira, and Indara.
W-WHAT?!
THOSE GUYS WERE... FILL-INS?!
THE MIBU CLAN, THE SIXTH DEMON KING, ODA NOBUNAGA, AND THE STRONGEST GOD-GENERALS THE WORLD HAS EVER SEEN...
THE WORLD IS DOOMED!

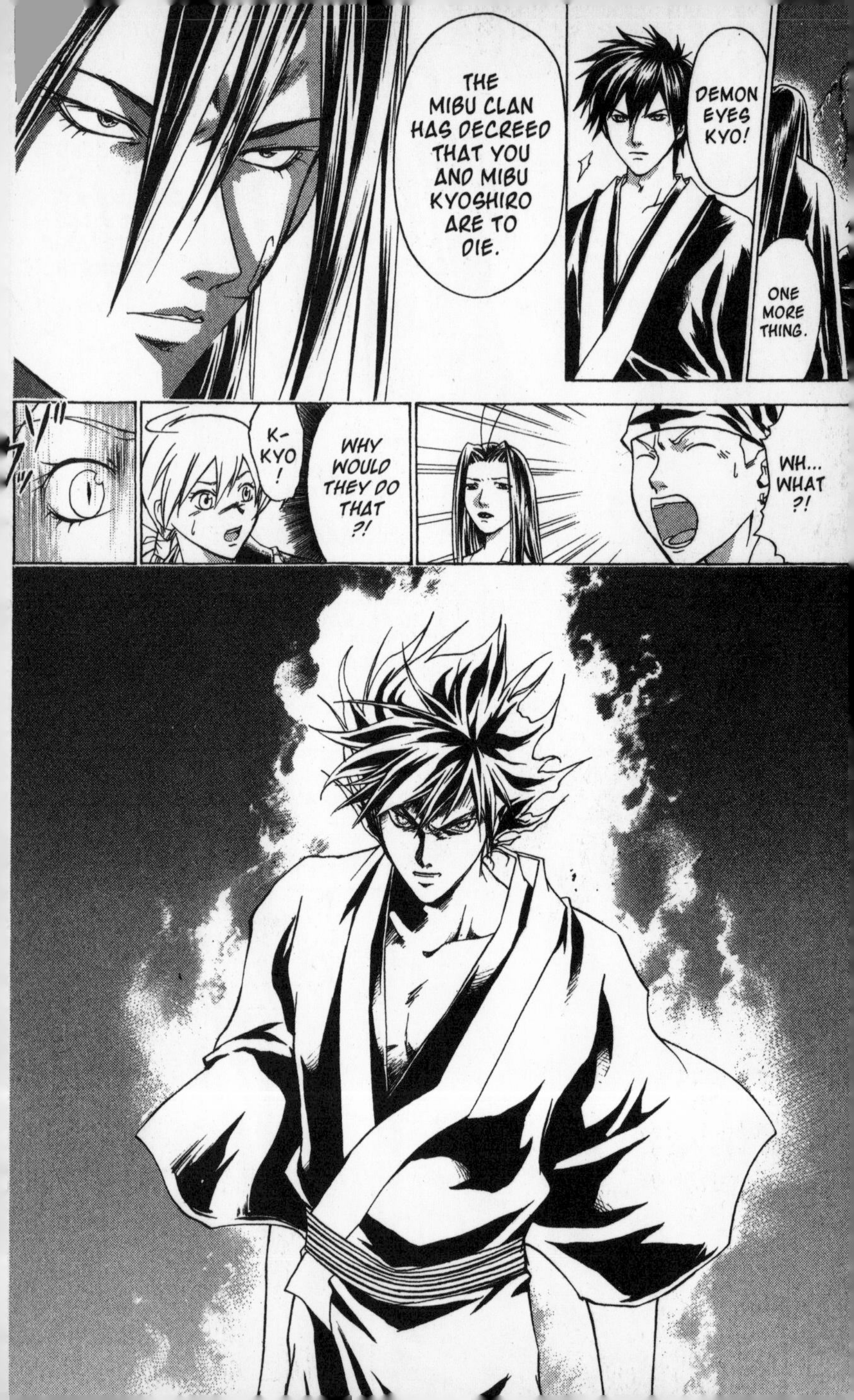

DEMON EYES KYO!
ONE MORE THING.
THE MIBU CLAN HAS DECREED THAT YOU AND MIBU KYOSHIRO ARE TO DIE.
WH... WHAT?!
WHY WOULD THEY DO THAT?!
K-KYO!

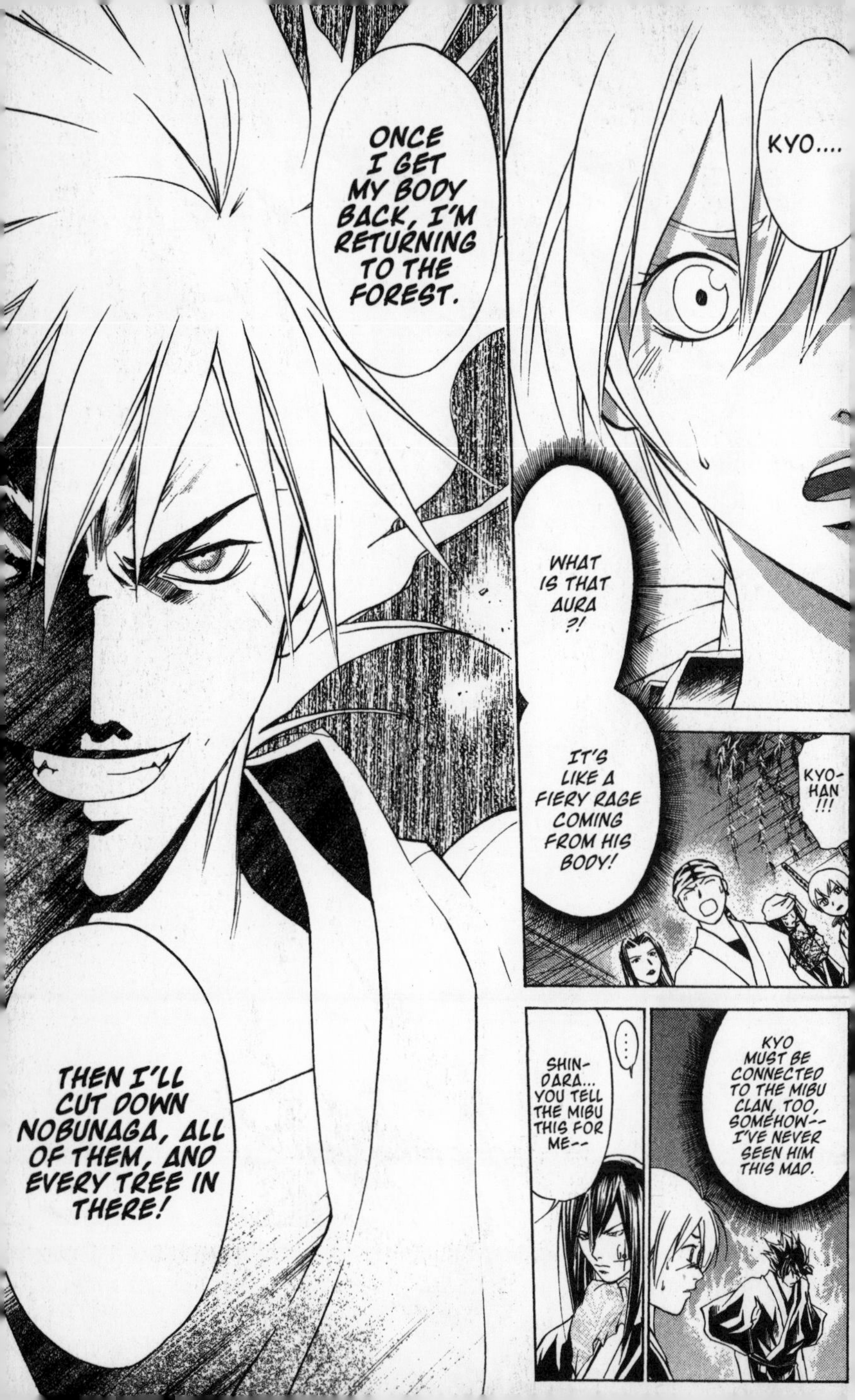
KYO....
WHAT IS THAT AURA ?!
IT'S LIKE A FIERY RAGE COMING FROM HIS BODY!
KYO-HAN !!!
KYO MUST BE CONNECTED TO THE MIBU CLAN, TOO, SOMEHOW-- I'VE NEVER SEEN HIM THIS MAD.
....
SHIN-DARA... YOU TELL THE MIBU THIS FOR ME--
ONCE I GET MY BODY BACK, I'M RETURNING TO THE FOREST.
THEN I'LL CUT DOWN NOBUNAGA, ALL OF THEM, AND EVERY TREE IN THERE!

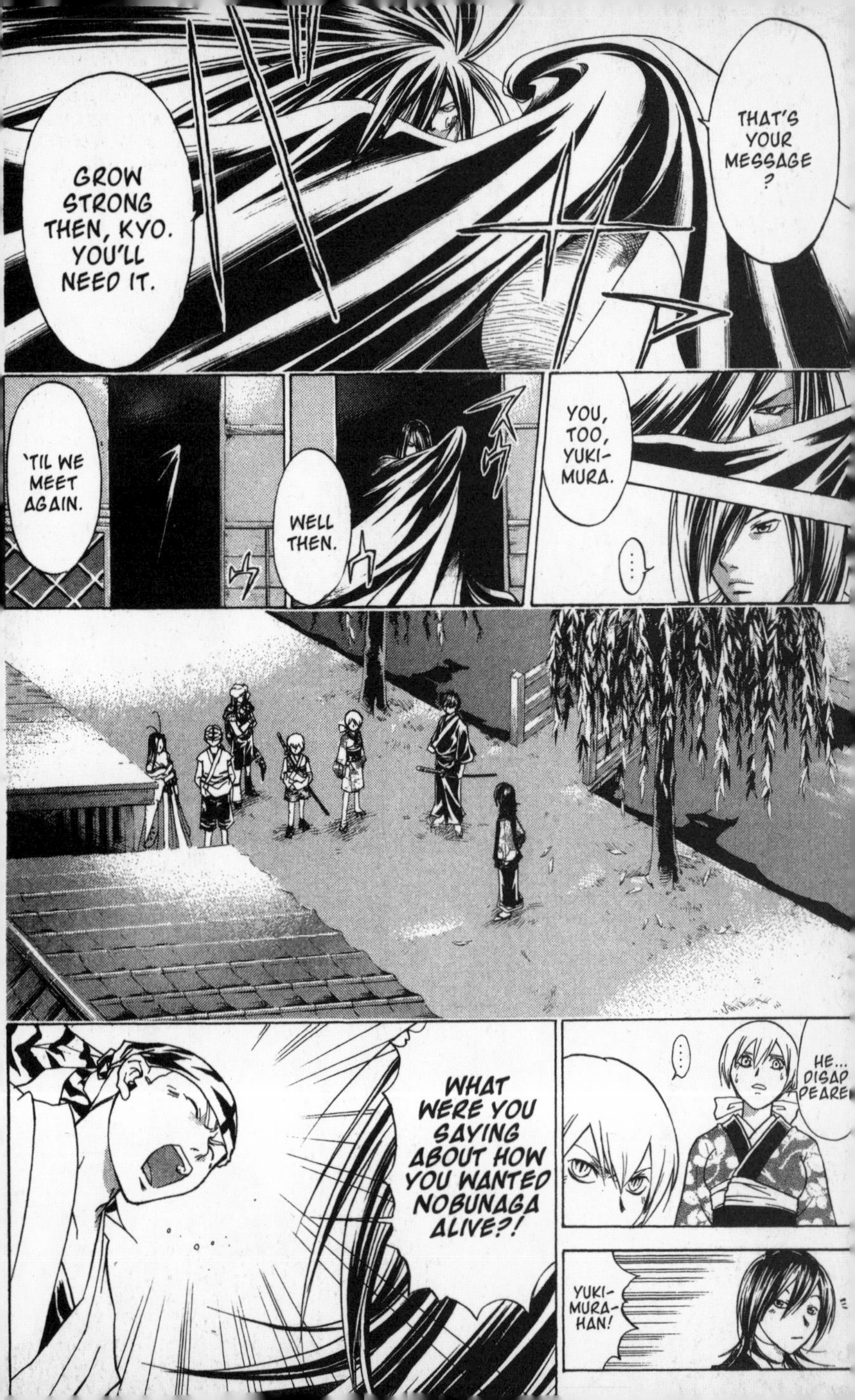
THAT'S YOUR MESSAGE?
GROW STRONG THEN, KYO. YOU'LL NEED IT.
YOU, TOO, YUKI-MURA.
...
WELL THEN.
'TIL WE MEET AGAIN.
HE... DISAP PEARE
...
YUKI-MURA-HAN!
WHAT WERE YOU SAYING ABOUT HOW YOU WANTED NOBUNAGA ALIVE?!

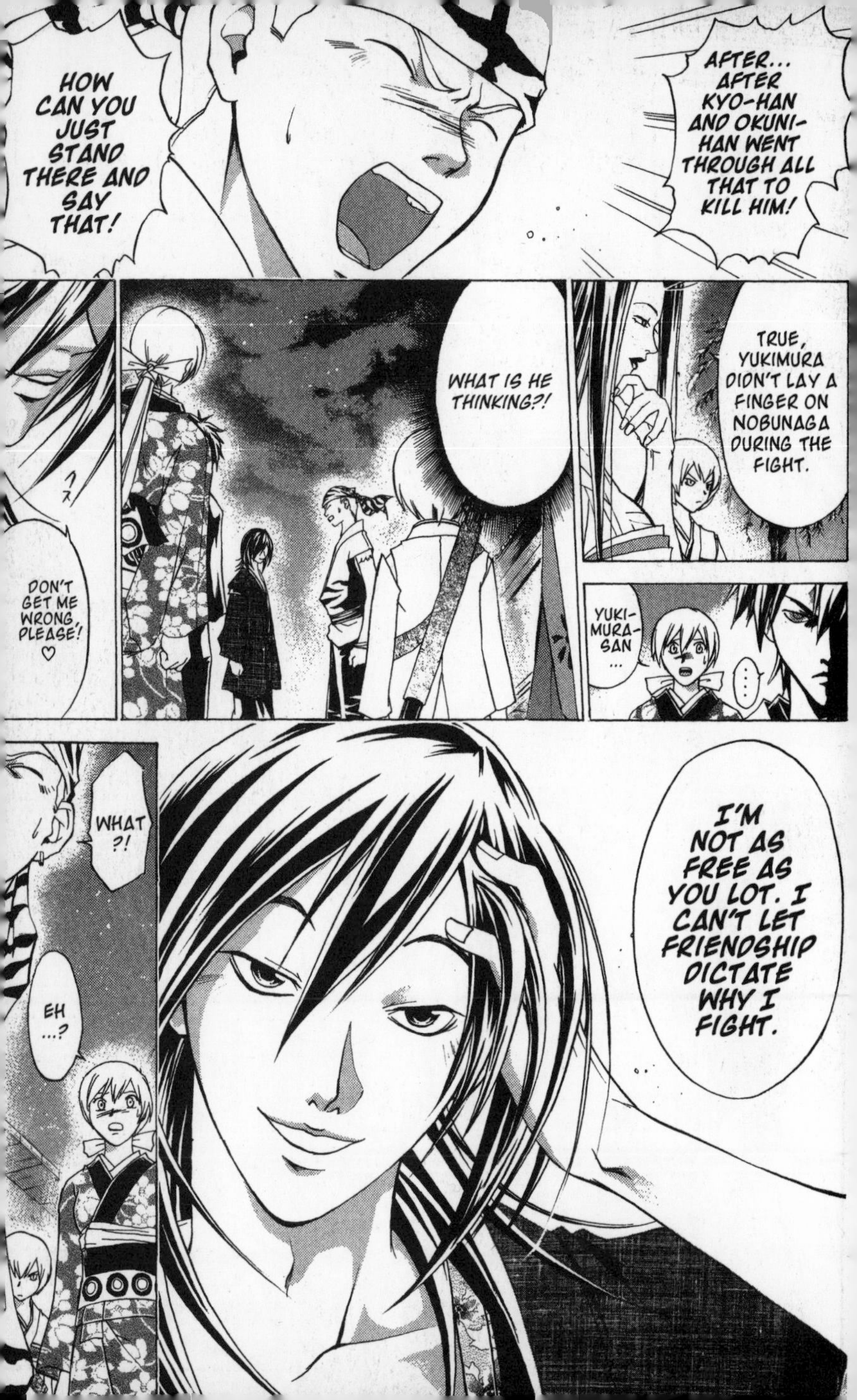
AFTER... AFTER KYO-HAN AND OKUNI-HAN WENT THROUGH ALL THAT TO KILL HIM!
HOW CAN YOU JUST STAND THERE AND SAY THAT!
TRUE, YUKIMURA DIDN'T LAY A FINGER ON NOBUNAGA DURING THE FIGHT.
...
YUKIMURA-SAN ...
WHAT IS HE THINKING?!
DON'T GET ME WRONG, PLEASE! ♡
I'M NOT AS FREE AS YOU LOT. I CAN'T LET FRIENDSHIP DICTATE WHY I FIGHT.
WHAT ?!
EH ...?

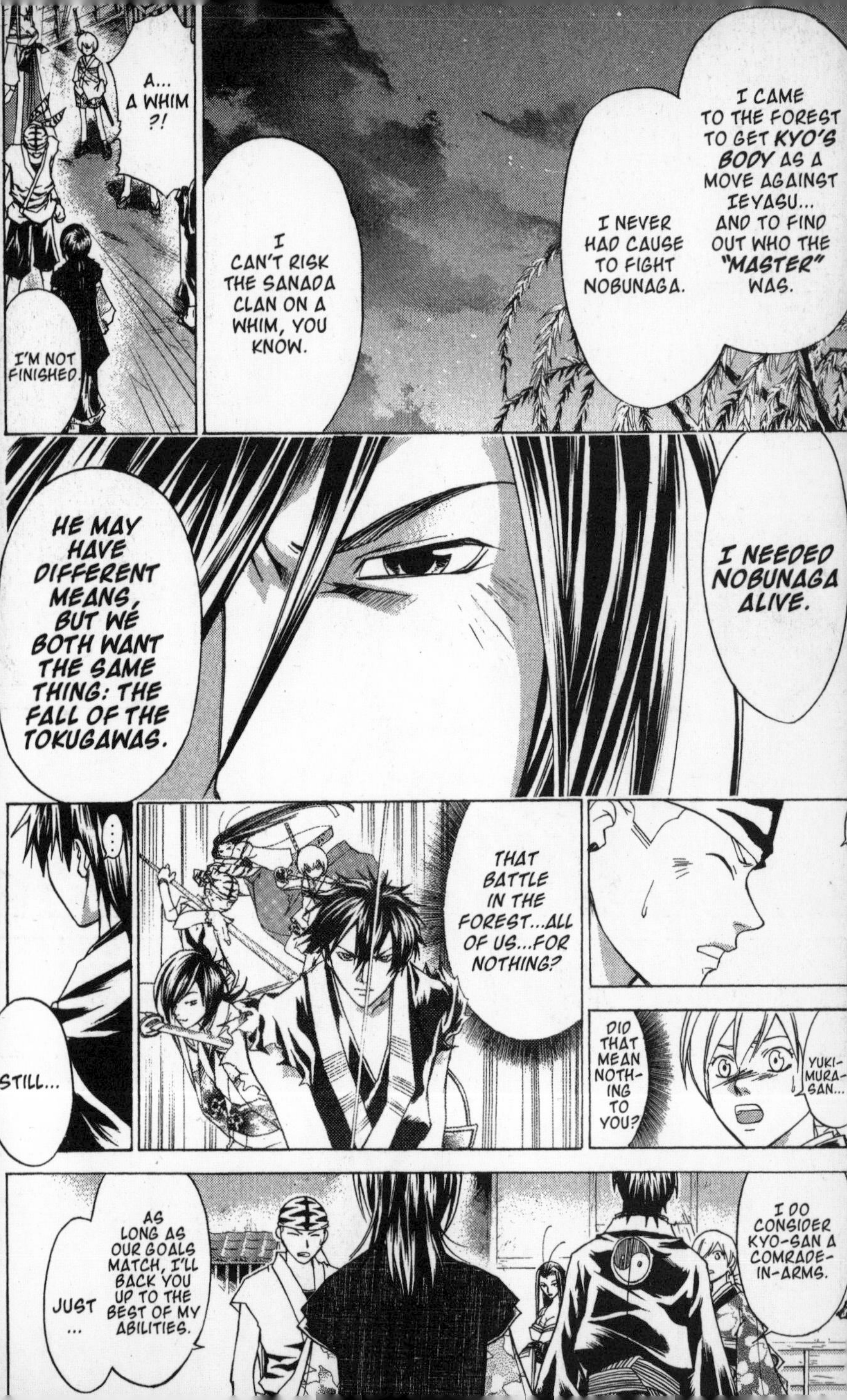
I CAME TO THE FOREST TO GET KYO'S BODY AS A MOVE AGAINST IEYASU... AND TO FIND OUT WHO THE "MASTER" WAS.
I NEVER HAD CAUSE TO FIGHT NOBUNAGA.
I CAN'T RISK THE SANADA CLAN ON A WHIM, YOU KNOW.
A... A WHIM ?!
I'M NOT FINISHED.
I NEEDED NOBUNAGA ALIVE.
HE MAY HAVE DIFFERENT MEANS, BUT WE BOTH WANT THE SAME THING: THE FALL OF THE TOKUGAWAS.
YUKIMURA-SAN...
DID THAT MEAN NOTHING TO YOU?
THAT BATTLE IN THE FOREST...ALL OF US...FOR NOTHING?
...
STILL...
I DO CONSIDER KYO-SAN A COMRADE-IN-ARMS.
AS LONG AS OUR GOALS MATCH, I'LL BACK YOU UP TO THE BEST OF MY ABILITIES.
JUST ...

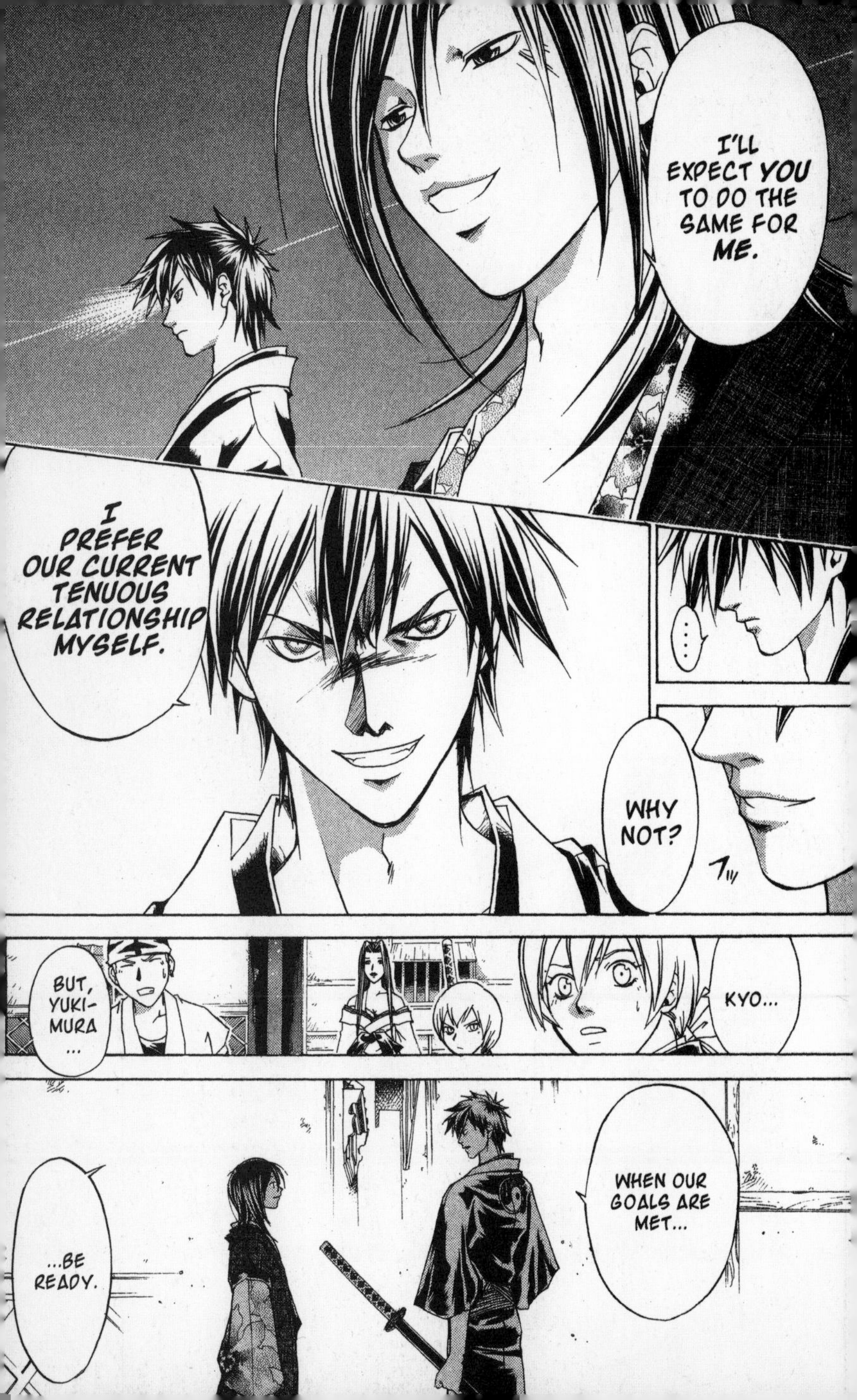

I'LL EXPECT YOU TO DO THE SAME FOR ME.
....
WHY NOT?
I PREFER OUR CURRENT TENUOUS RELATIONSHIP MYSELF.
KYO...
BUT, YUKI-MURA ...
WHEN OUR GOALS ARE MET...
...BE READY.

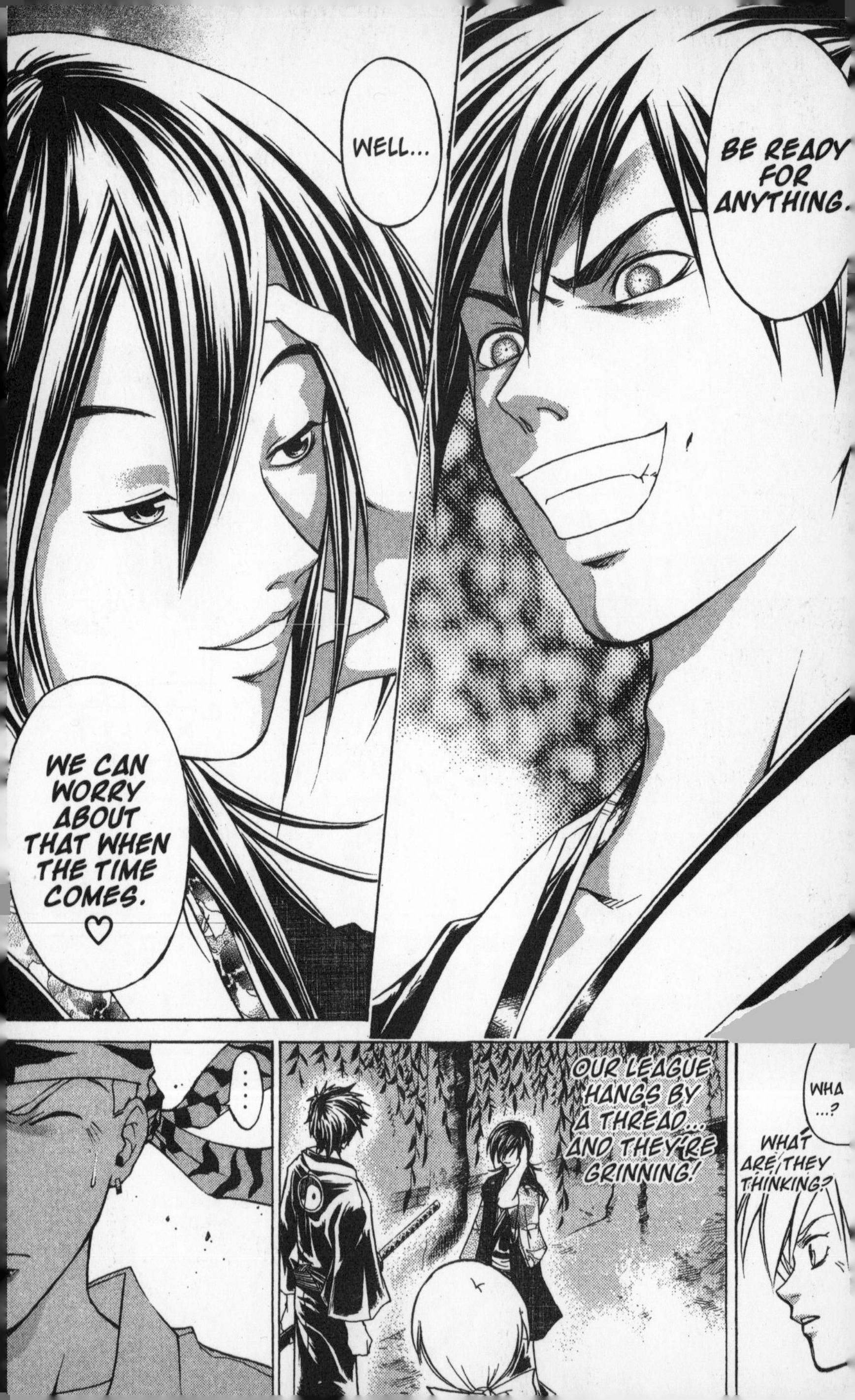
BE READY FOR ANYTHING.
WELL...
WE CAN WORRY ABOUT THAT WHEN THE TIME COMES. ♡
WHA ...?
WHAT ARE THEY THINKING?
OUR LEAGUE HANGS BY A THREAD... AND THEY'RE GRINNING!
.....

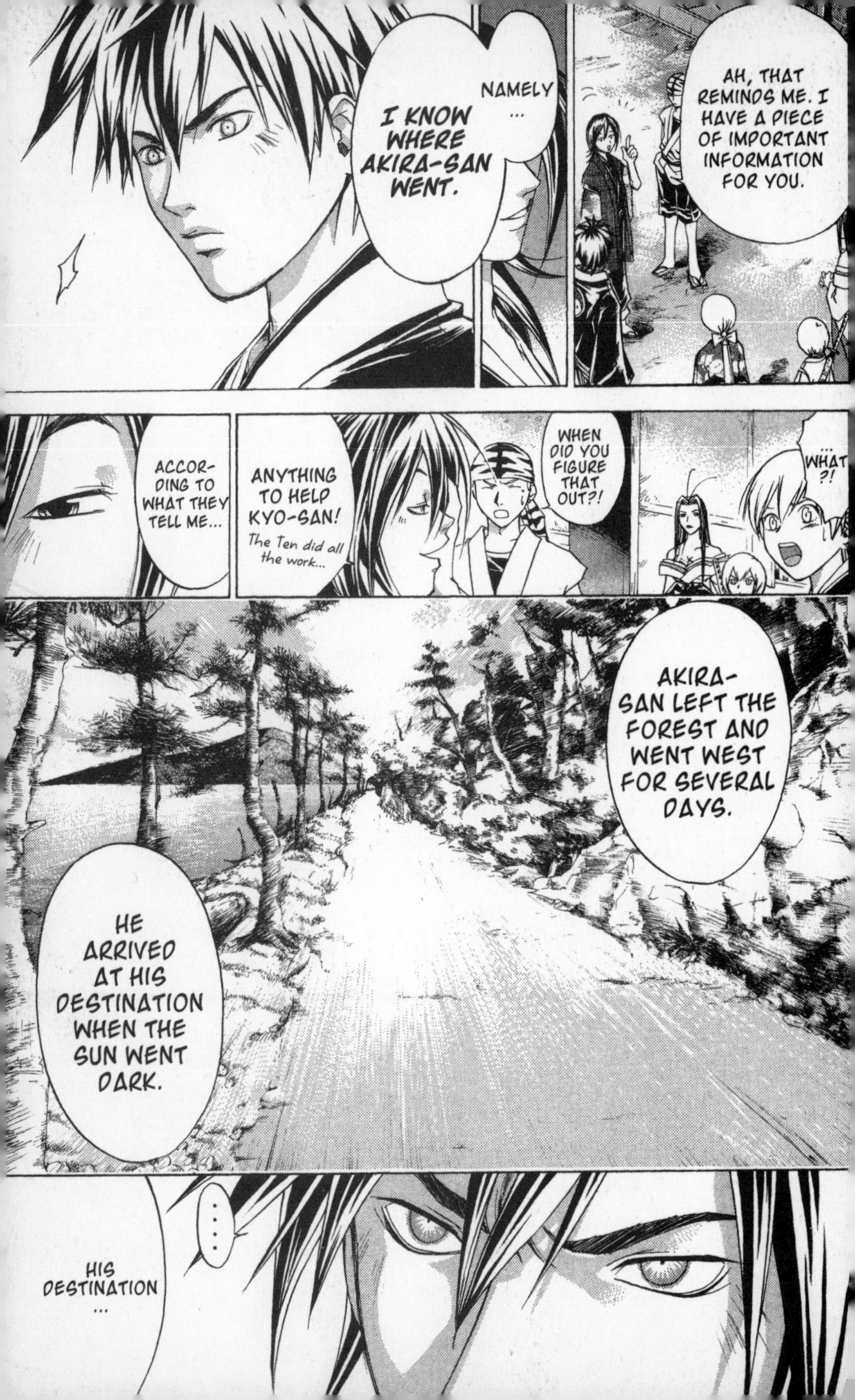
AH, THAT REMINDS ME. I HAVE A PIECE OF IMPORTANT INFORMATION FOR YOU.
NAMELY ...
I KNOW WHERE AKIRA-SAN WENT.
... WHAT ?!
WHEN DID YOU FIGURE THAT OUT?!
ANYTHING TO HELP KYO-SAN!
The Ten did all the work...
ACCOR-DING TO WHAT THEY TELL ME...
AKIRA-SAN LEFT THE FOREST AND WENT WEST FOR SEVERAL DAYS.
HE ARRIVED AT HIS DESTINATION WHEN THE SUN WENT DARK.
....
HIS DESTINATION ...

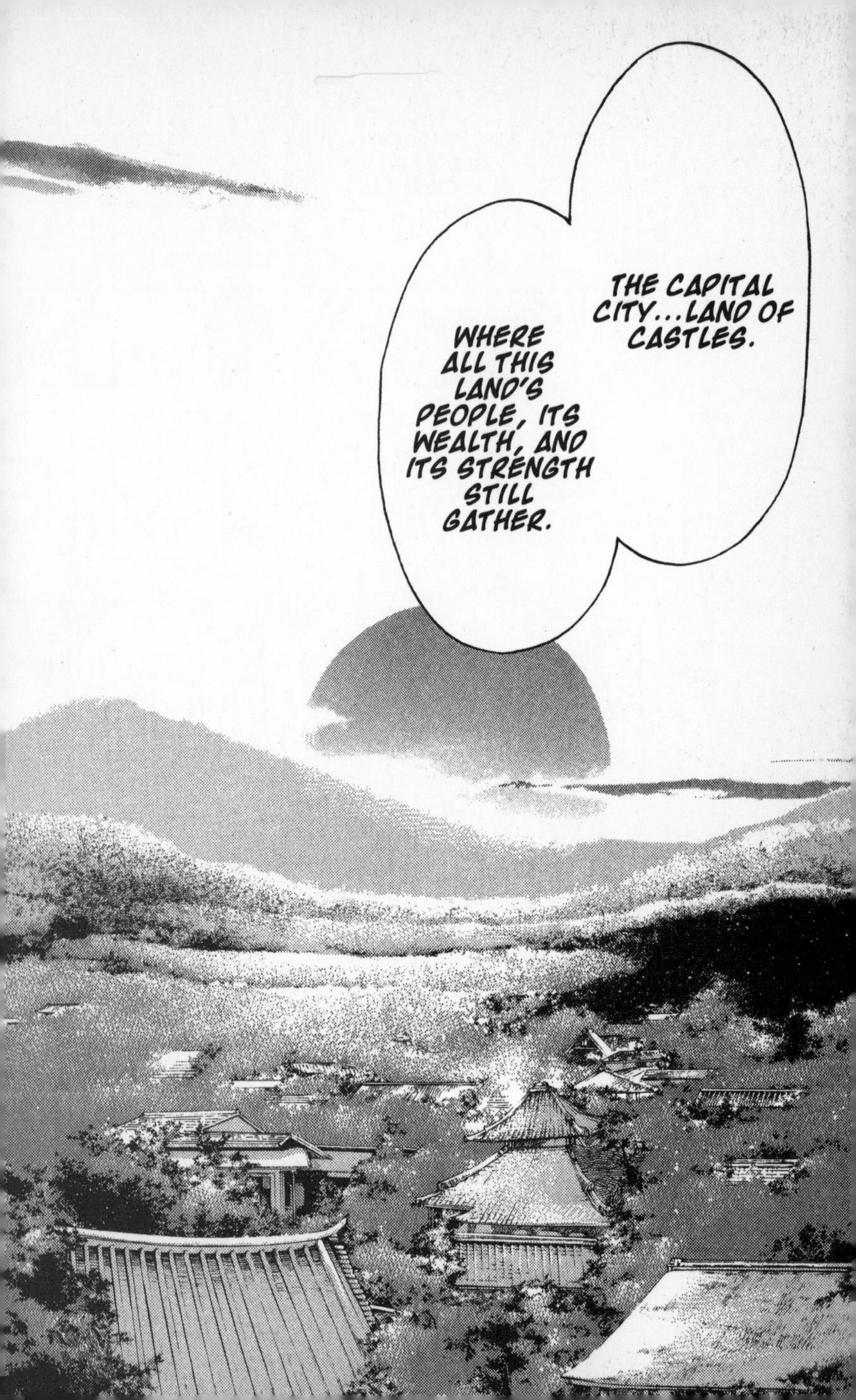
THE CAPITAL CITY...LAND OF CASTLES.
WHERE ALL THIS LAND'S PEOPLE, ITS WEALTH, AND ITS STRENGTH STILL GATHER.

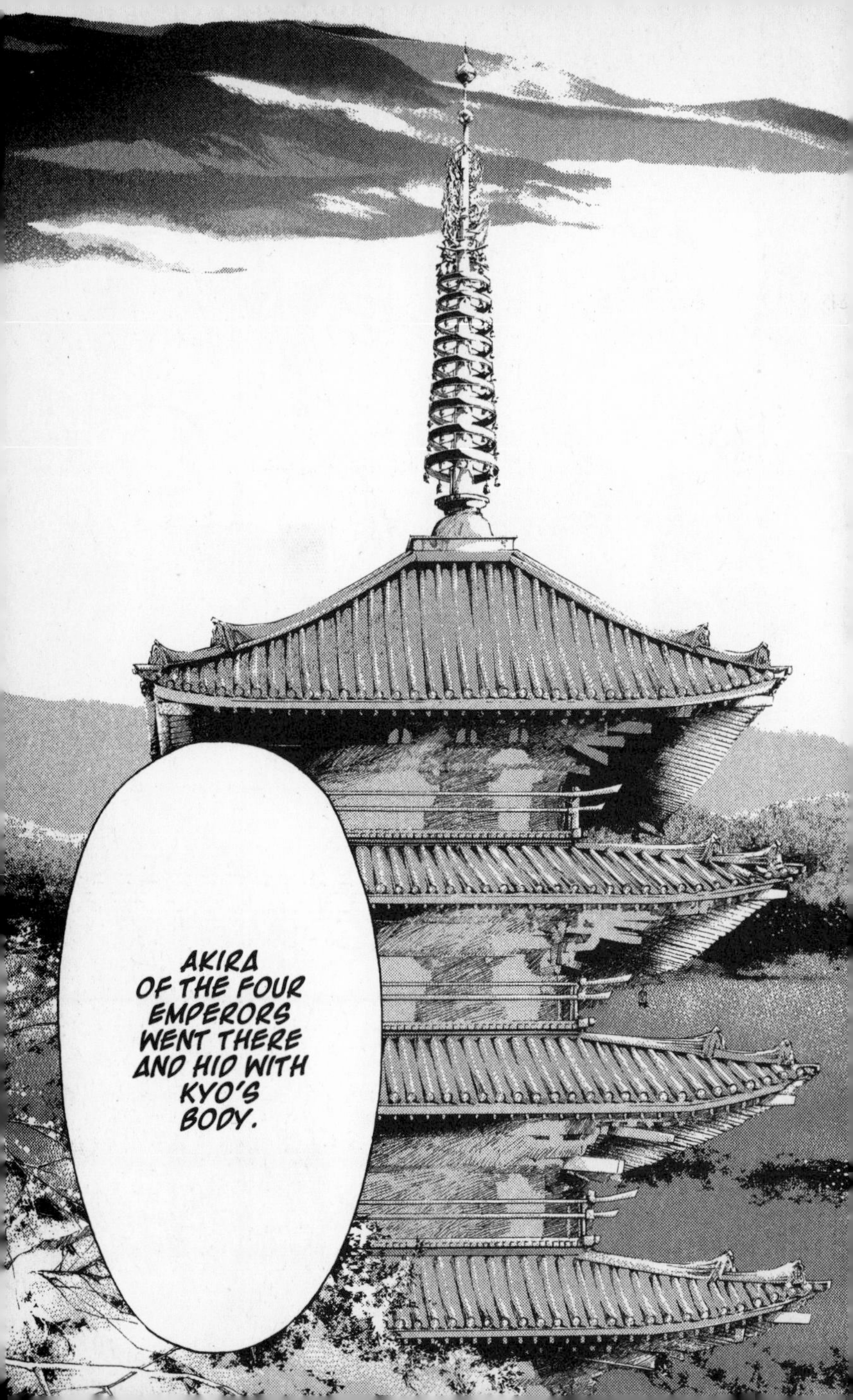
AKIRA OF THE FOUR EMPERORS WENT THERE AND HID WITH KYO'S BODY.

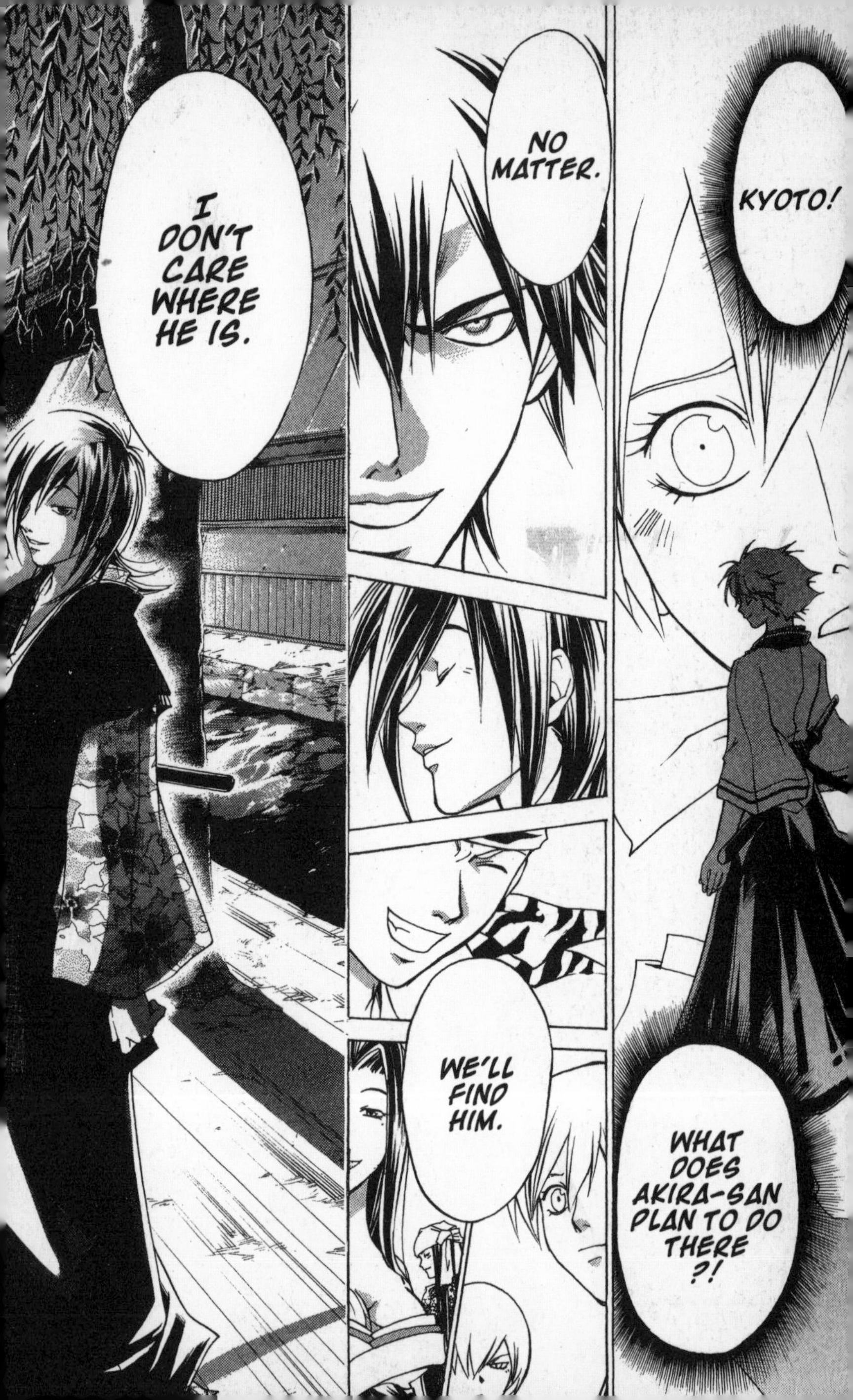
KYOTO!
WHAT DOES AKIRA-SAN PLAN TO DO THERE?!
NO MATTER.
WE'LL FIND HIM.
I DON'T CARE WHERE HE IS.

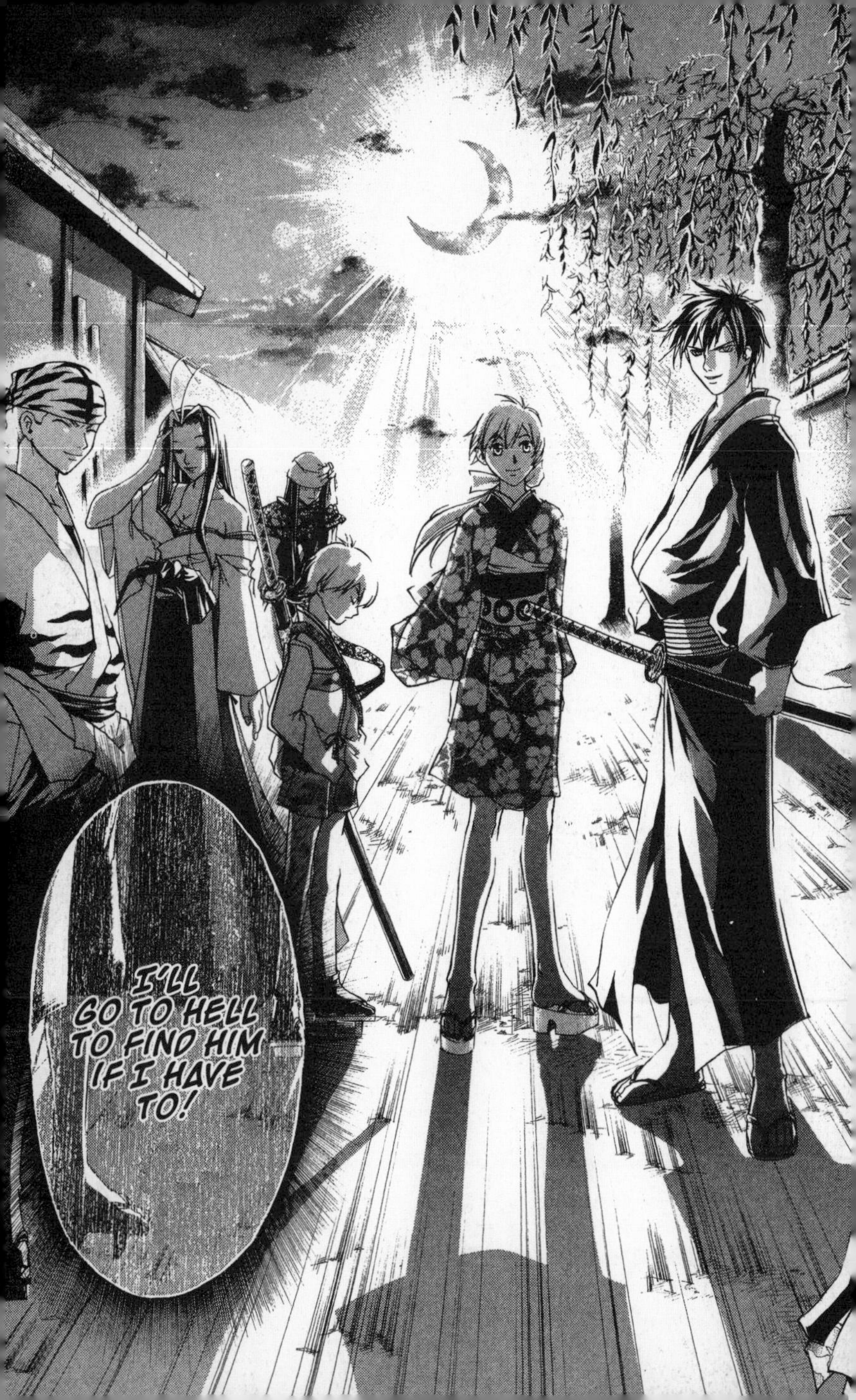
I'LL GO TO HELL TO FIND HIM IF I HAVE TO!

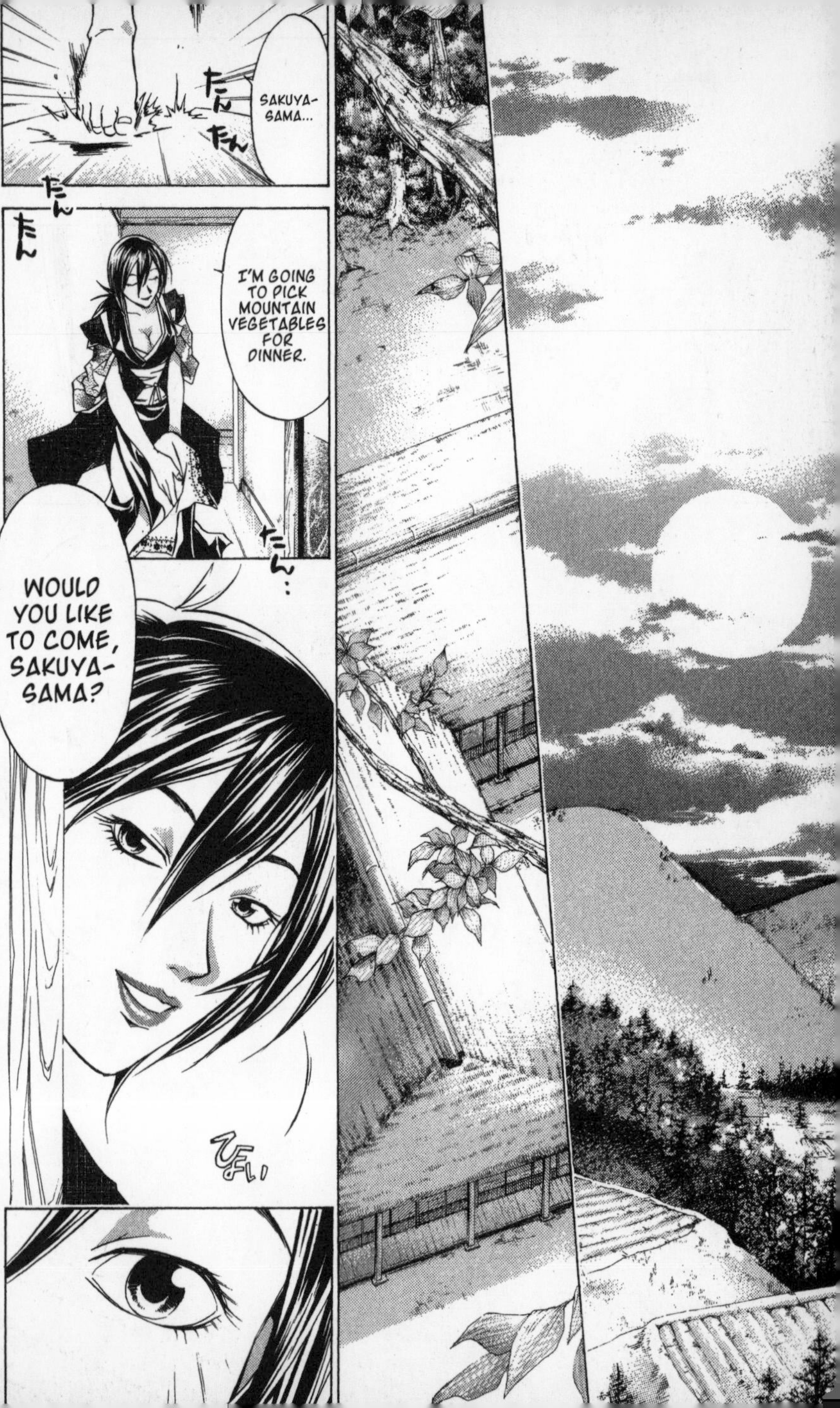
たん
たん
SAKUYA-SAMA...
たん
たん
I'M GOING TO PICK MOUNTAIN VEGETABLES FOR DINNER.
たん…
WOULD YOU LIKE TO COME, SAKUYA-SAMA?

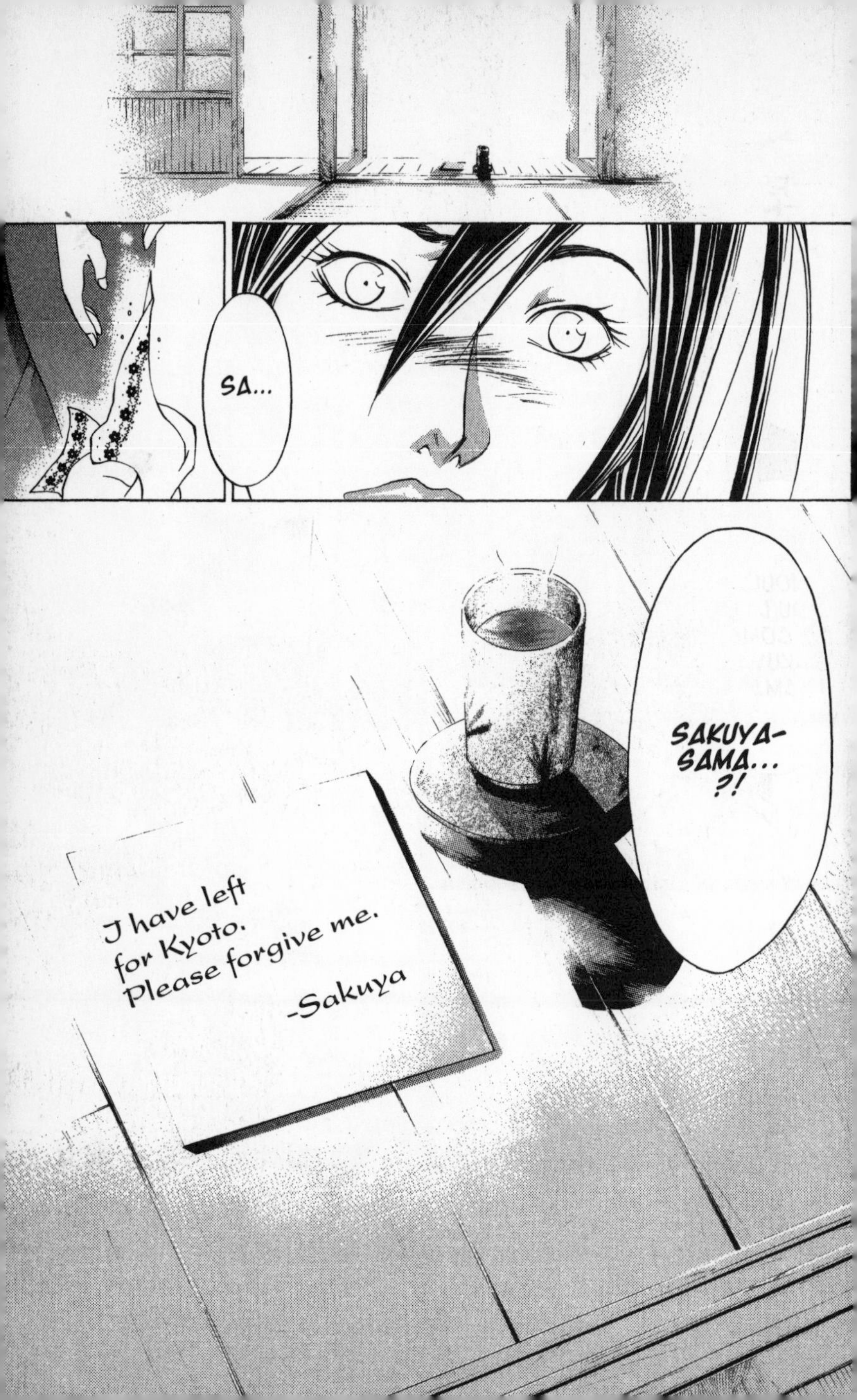
SA...
SAKUYA-SAMA... ?!
I have left for Kyoto. Please forgive me. -Sakuya

STAFF

Yuzu Haruno (The Chief)
Hazuki Asami
Ken'ichi Suetake
Takaya Nagao
Souma Akatsuki
The Gentleman Pumpkin (Chapter Eighty-Five)
Shiba Tateoka (Chapter Eighty-Six...in the next volume)

*in order of appearance

Yuzu Haruno (The Chief)

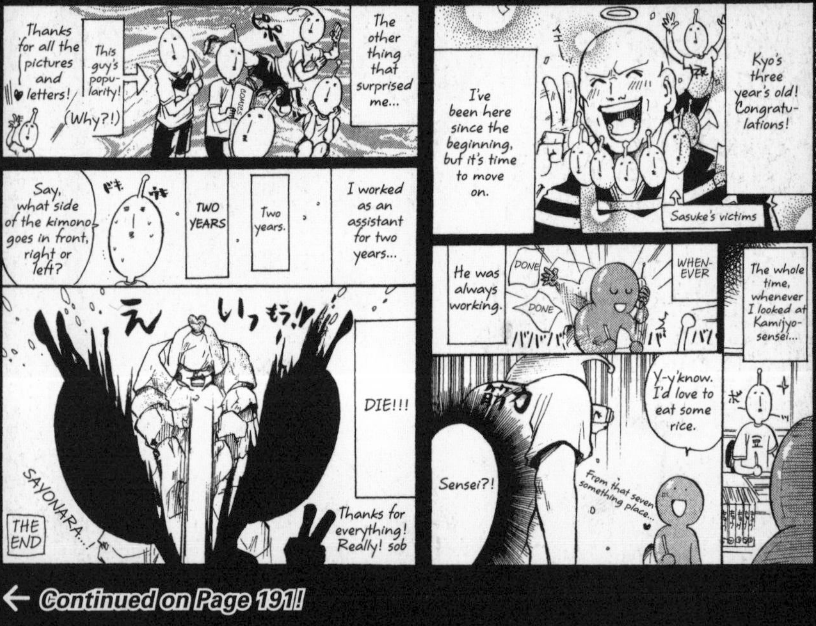
Kyo's three year's old! Congratulations!
I've been here since the beginning, but it's time to move on.
Sasuke's victims
The whole time, whenever I looked at Kamijyo-sensei...
WHEN-EVER
DONE
DONE
He was always working.
Y-y'know. I'd love to eat some rice.
From that seven something place...
Sensei?!
The other thing that surprised me...
This guy's popularity!
Thanks for all the pictures and letters!
(Why?!)
I worked as an assistant for two years...
Two years.
TWO YEARS
Say, what side of the kimono goes in front, right or left?
DIE!!!
Thanks for everything! Really! sob
SAYONARA...!
THE END

KAMIJYO: CHIEF HARUNO'S BEEN WRITING UNDER THE PEN NAME "HAYATO AYASE"--BUY HIS BOOKS!

Continued on Page 191!

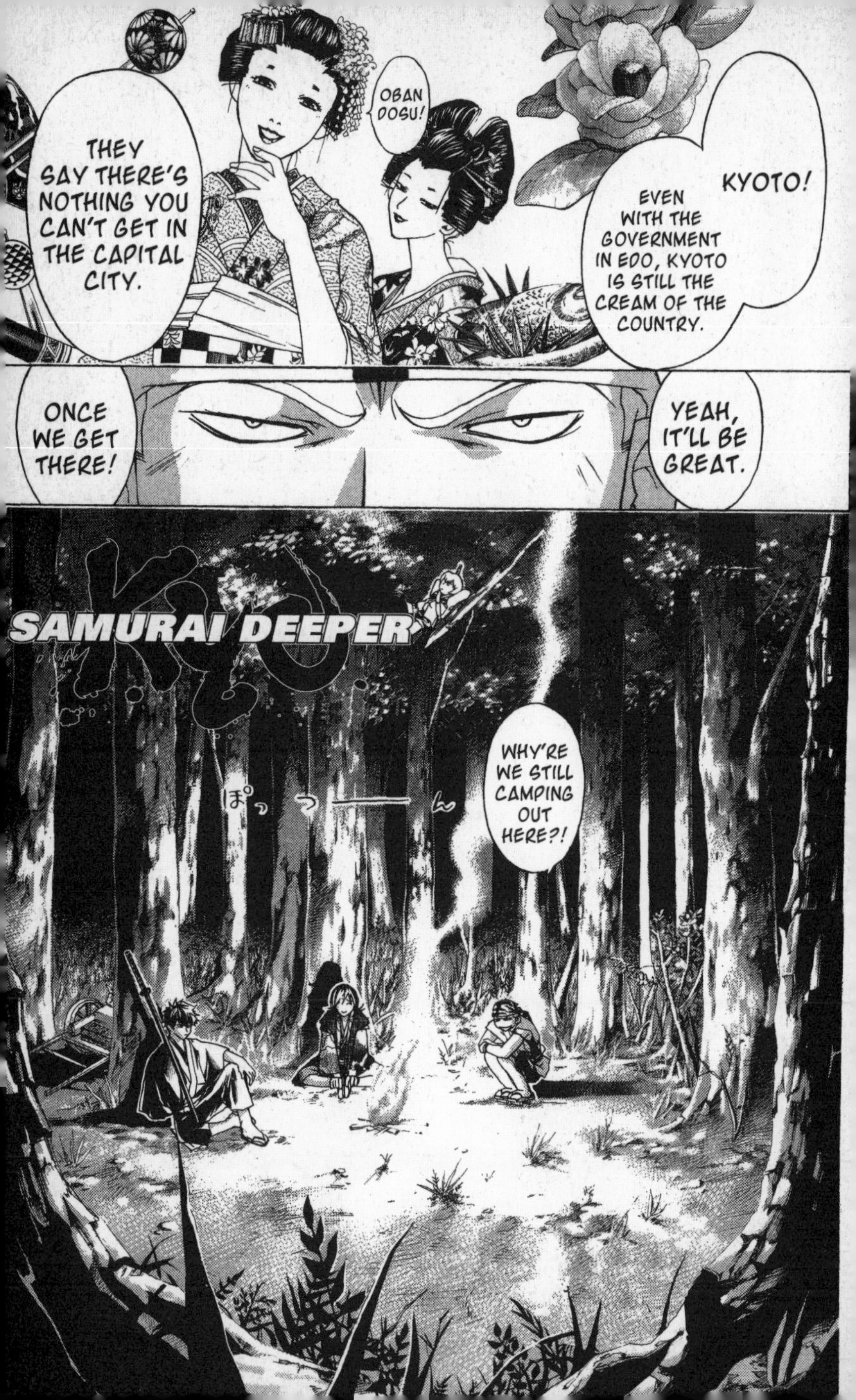
KYOTO!
EVEN WITH THE GOVERNMENT IN EDO, KYOTO IS STILL THE CREAM OF THE COUNTRY.
OBAN DOSU!
THEY SAY THERE'S NOTHING YOU CAN'T GET IN THE CAPITAL CITY.
YEAH, IT'LL BE GREAT.
ONCE WE GET THERE!
SAMURAI DEEPER
WHY'RE WE STILL CAMPING OUT HERE?!
ぽっつーーん

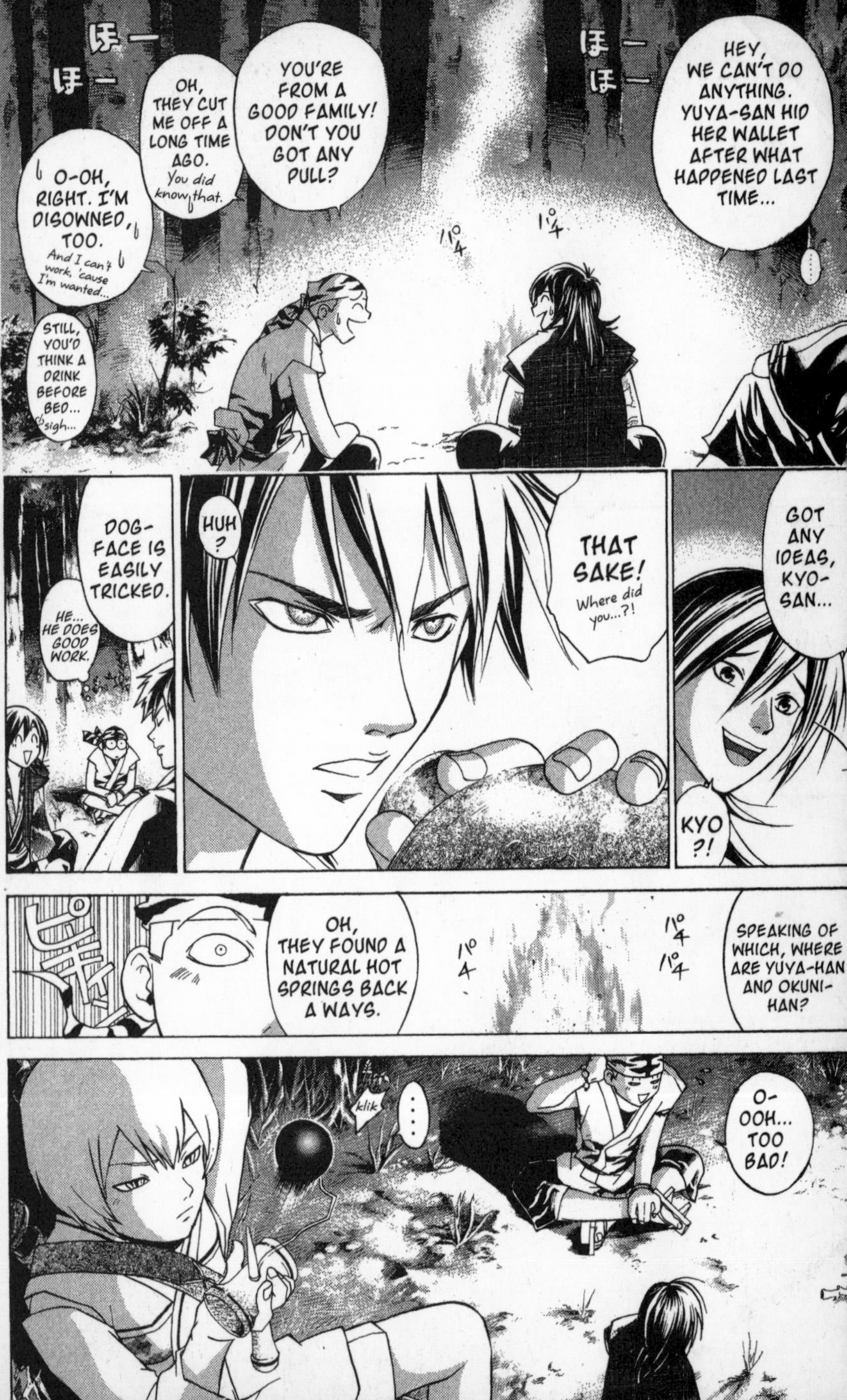
ほー ほー
HEY, WE CAN'T DO ANYTHING. YUYA-SAN HID HER WALLET AFTER WHAT HAPPENED LAST TIME...
...
YOU'RE FROM A GOOD FAMILY! DON'T YOU GOT ANY PULL?
ほー ほー
OH, THEY CUT ME OFF A LONG TIME AGO. You did know that.
O-OH, RIGHT. I'M DISOWNED, TOO. And I can't work, 'cause I'm wanted...
STILL, YOU'D THINK A DRINK BEFORE BED... sigh...
GOT ANY IDEAS, KYO-SAN...
KYO?!
THAT SAKE! Where did you...?!
HUH?
DOG-FACE IS EASILY TRICKED.
HE... HE DOES GOOD WORK.
SPEAKING OF WHICH, WHERE ARE YUYA-HAN AND OKUNI-HAN?
OH, THEY FOUND A NATURAL HOT SPRINGS BACK A WAYS.
O-OOH... TOO BAD!
...
klik

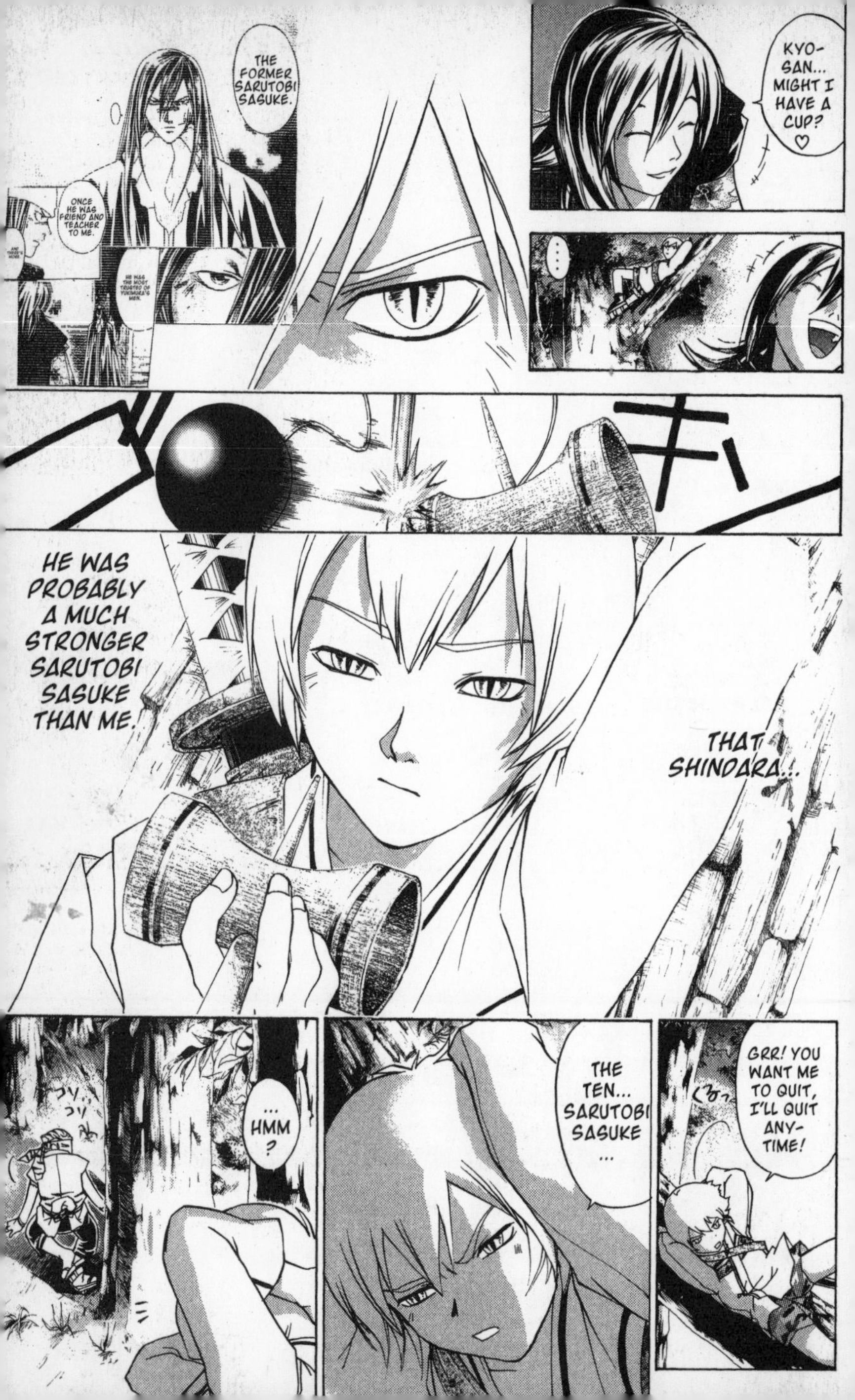
KYO-SAN... MIGHT I HAVE A CUP? ♡
...
THE FORMER SARUTOBI SASUKE.
ONCE HE WAS FRIEND AND TEACHER TO ME.
HE WAS THE MOST TRUSTED OF YUKIMURA'S MEN.
AND THERE'S MORE.
THAT SHINDARA...
HE WAS PROBABLY A MUCH STRONGER SARUTOBI SASUKE THAN ME.
GRR! YOU WANT ME TO QUIT, I'LL QUIT ANY-TIME!
THE TEN... SARUTOBI SASUKE ...
... HMM ?

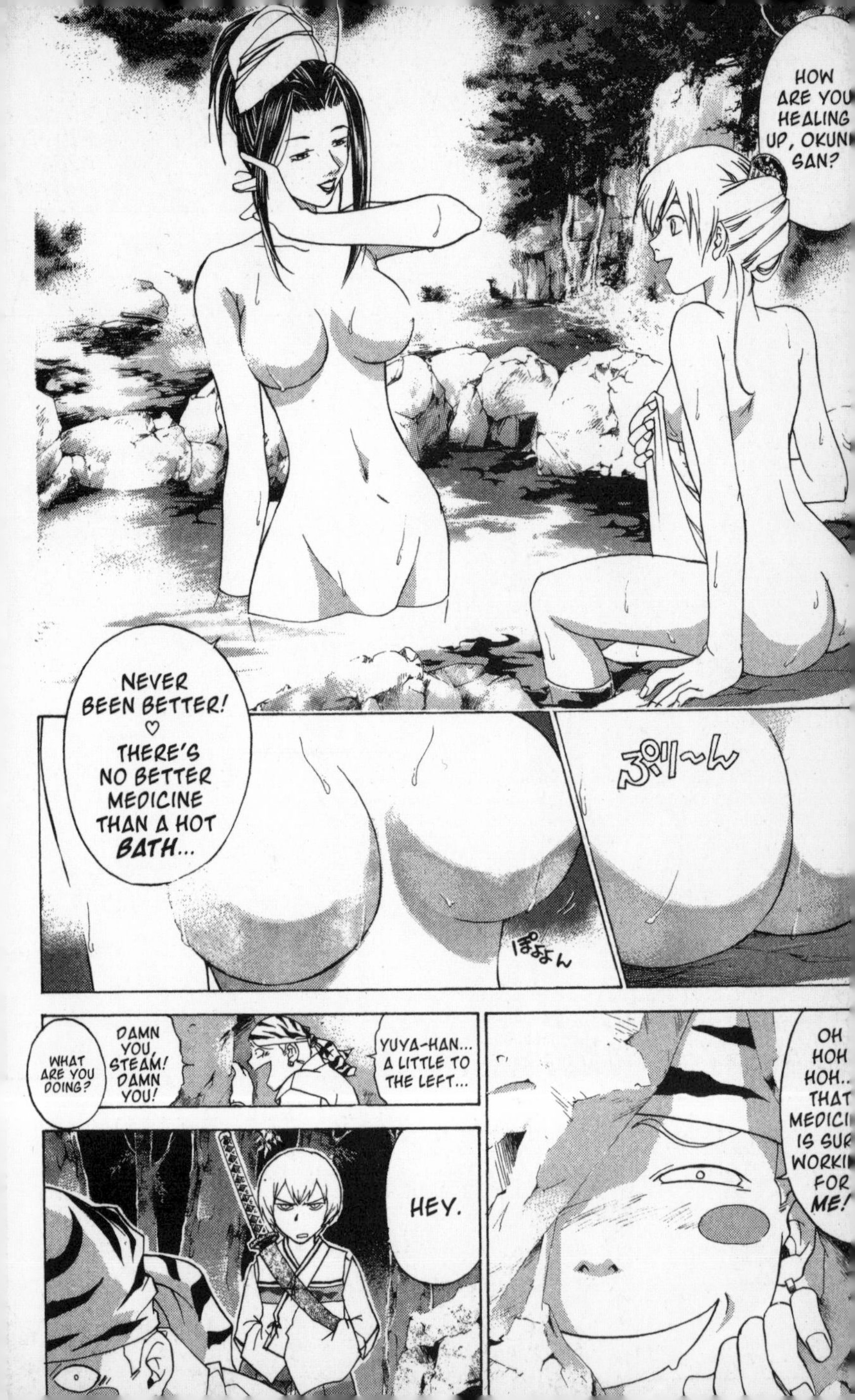
HOW ARE YOU HEALING UP, OKUN SAN?
NEVER BEEN BETTER! ♡ THERE'S NO BETTER MEDICINE THAN A HOT BATH...
ぷり〜ん
ぽよよん
OH HOH HOH... THAT MEDICI IS SUR WORKI FOR ME!
YUYA-HAN... A LITTLE TO THE LEFT...
DAMN YOU, STEAM! DAMN YOU!
WHAT ARE YOU DOING?
HEY.

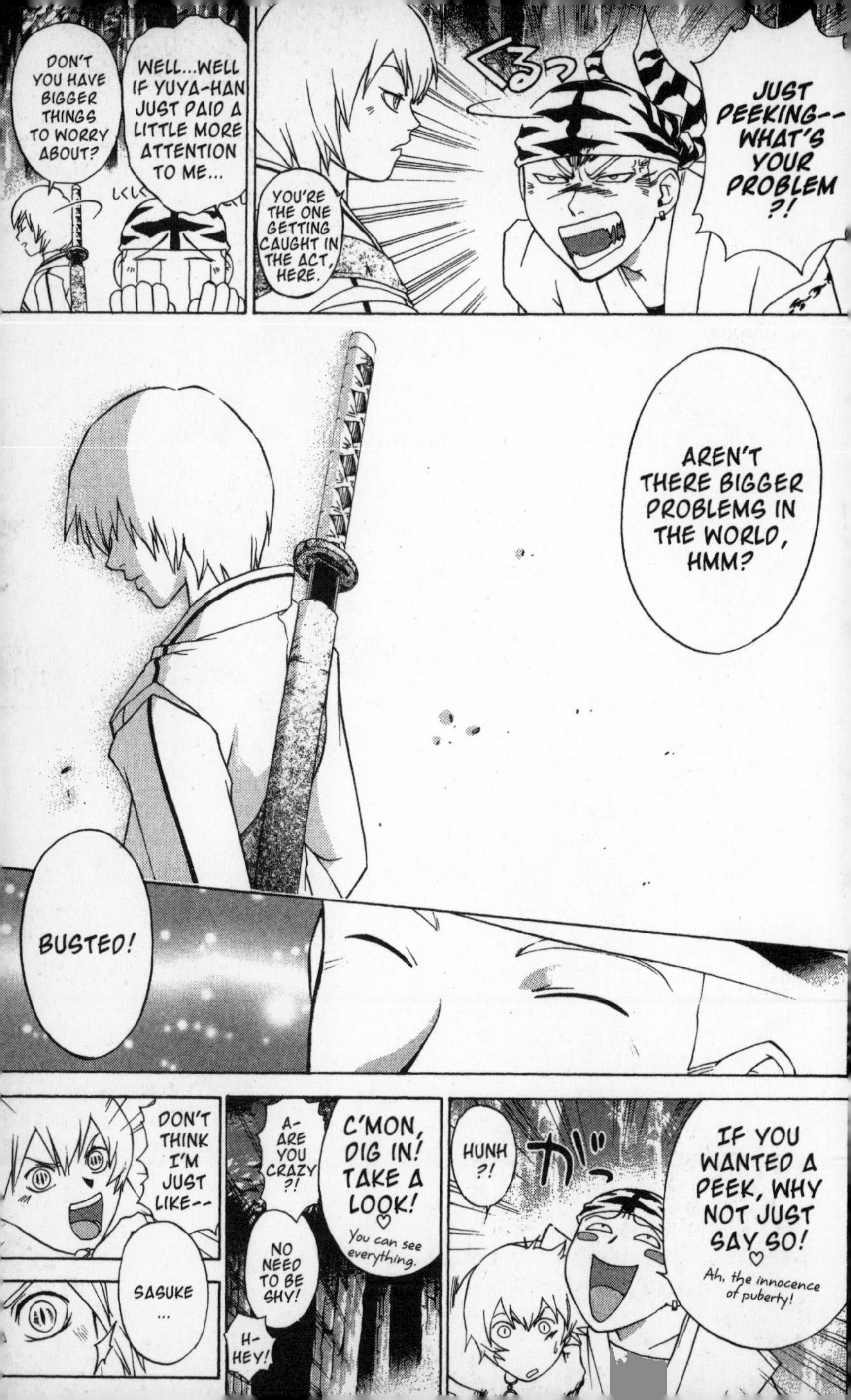
くるっ
JUST PEEKING--WHAT'S YOUR PROBLEM?!
YOU'RE THE ONE GETTING CAUGHT IN THE ACT, HERE.
WELL...WELL IF YUYA-HAN JUST PAID A LITTLE MORE ATTENTION TO ME...
DON'T YOU HAVE BIGGER THINGS TO WORRY ABOUT?
AREN'T THERE BIGGER PROBLEMS IN THE WORLD, HMM?
BUSTED!
IF YOU WANTED A PEEK, WHY NOT JUST SAY SO! ♡
Ah, the innocence of puberty!
HUNH?!
C'MON, DIG IN! TAKE A LOOK! ♡
You can see everything.
A-ARE YOU CRAZY?!
NO NEED TO BE SHY!
H-HEY!
DON'T THINK I'M JUST LIKE--
SASUKE...

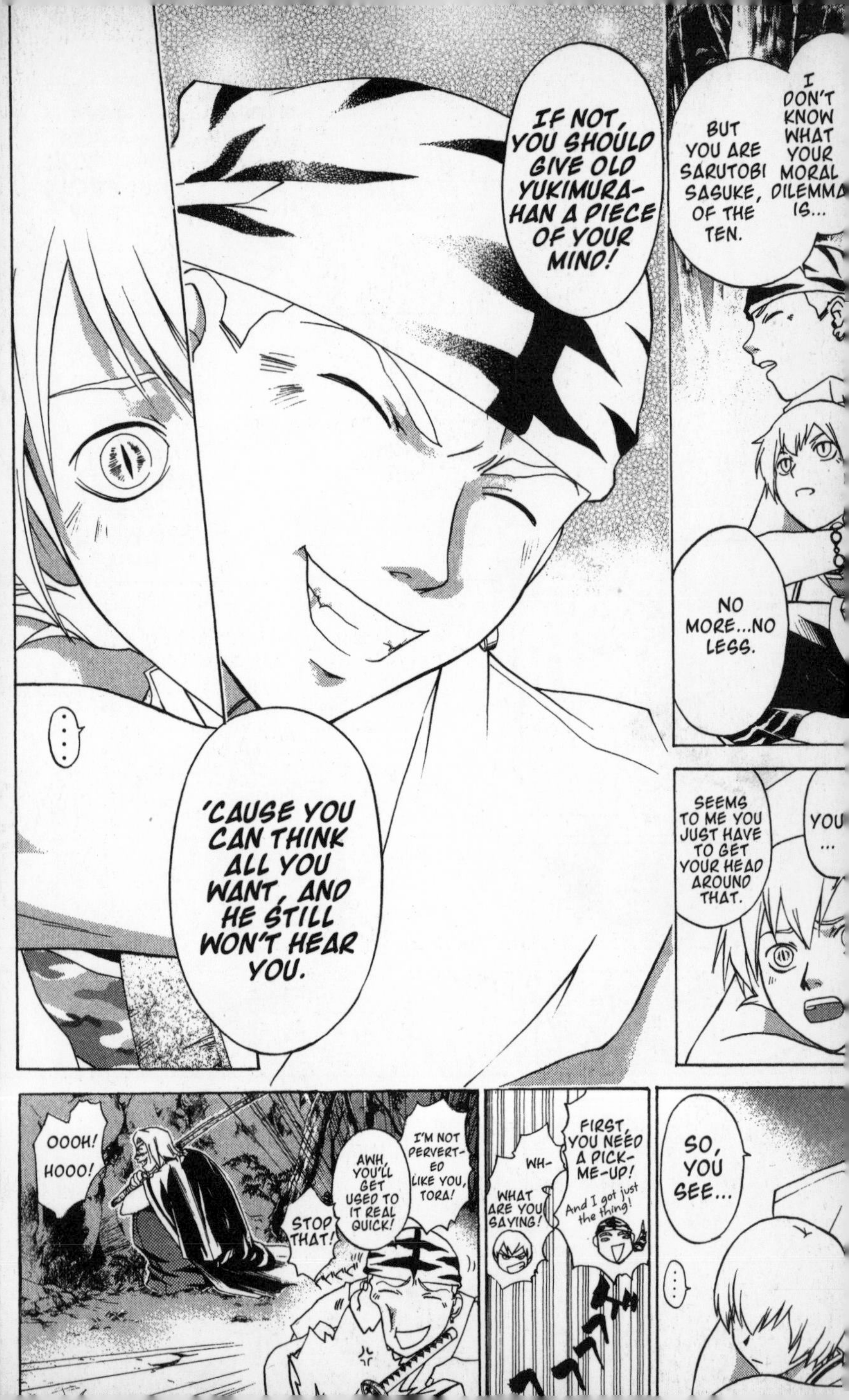
I DON'T KNOW WHAT YOUR MORAL DILEMMA IS...
BUT YOU ARE SARUTOBI SASUKE, OF THE TEN.
NO MORE...NO LESS.
YOU...
SEEMS TO ME YOU JUST HAVE TO GET YOUR HEAD AROUND THAT.
IF NOT, YOU SHOULD GIVE OLD YUKIMURA-HAN A PIECE OF YOUR MIND!
'CAUSE YOU CAN THINK ALL YOU WANT, AND HE STILL WON'T HEAR YOU.
...
SO, YOU SEE...
...
FIRST, YOU NEED A PICK-ME-UP!
WH-
WHAT ARE YOU SAYING!
And I got just the thing!
I'M NOT PERVERT-ED LIKE YOU, TORA!
AWH, YOU'LL GET USED TO IT REAL QUICK!
STOP THAT!
OOOH!
HOOO!

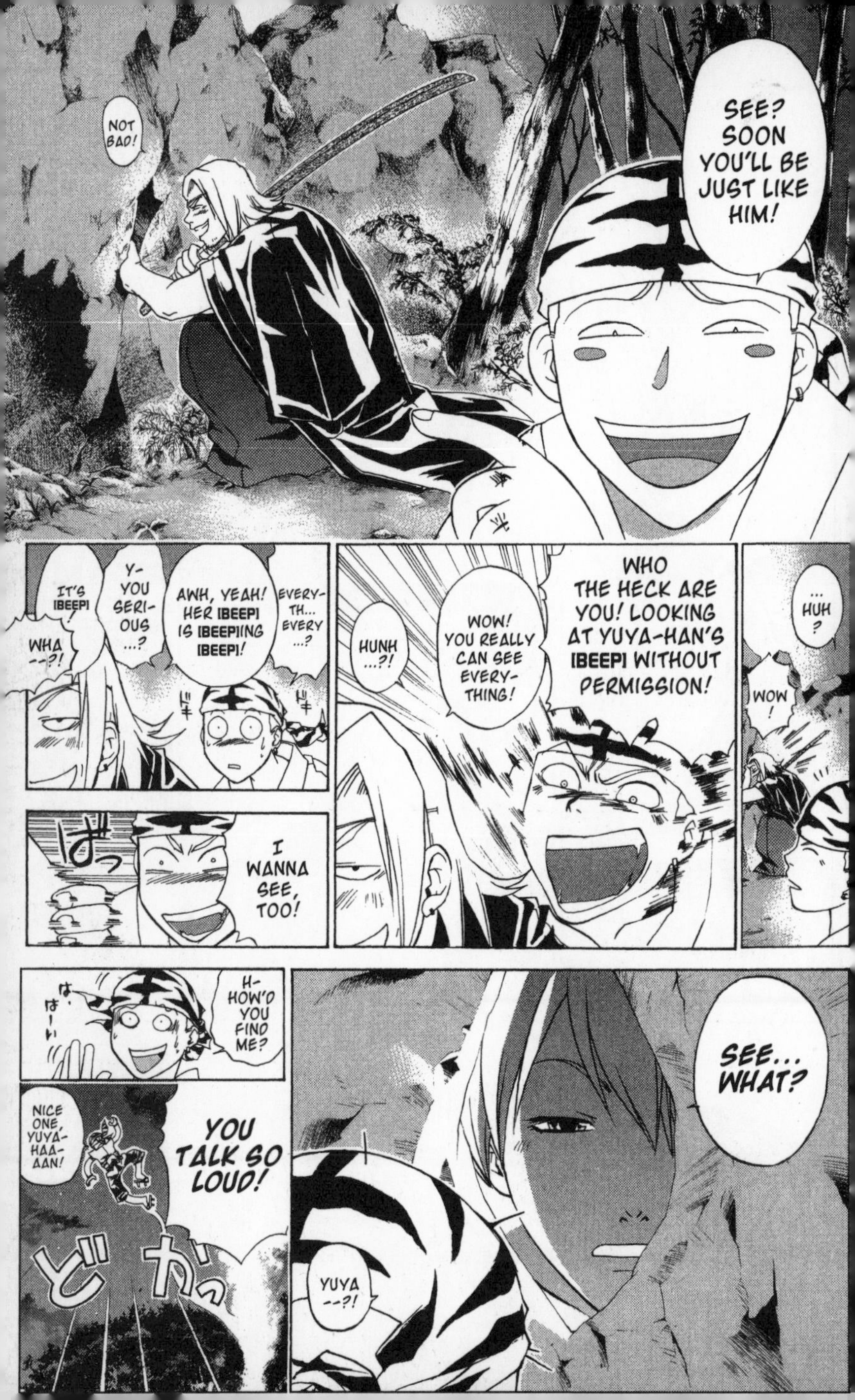
SEE? SOON YOU'LL BE JUST LIKE HIM!
NOT BAD!
... HUH?
WOW!
WHO THE HECK ARE YOU! LOOKING AT YUYA-HAN'S [BEEP] WITHOUT PERMISSION!
WOW! YOU REALLY CAN SEE EVERYTHING!
HUNH ...?!
EVERY-TH... EVERY ...?
AWH, YEAH! HER [BEEP] IS [BEEP]ING [BEEP]!
Y-YOU SERI-OUS ...?
IT'S [BEEP]!
WHA--?!
ドキ
I WANNA SEE, TOO!
ばっ
SEE... WHAT?
YUYA--?!
H-HOW'D YOU FIND ME?
は・はーい
YOU TALK SO LOUD!
NICE ONE, YUYA-HAA-AAN!
どかっ

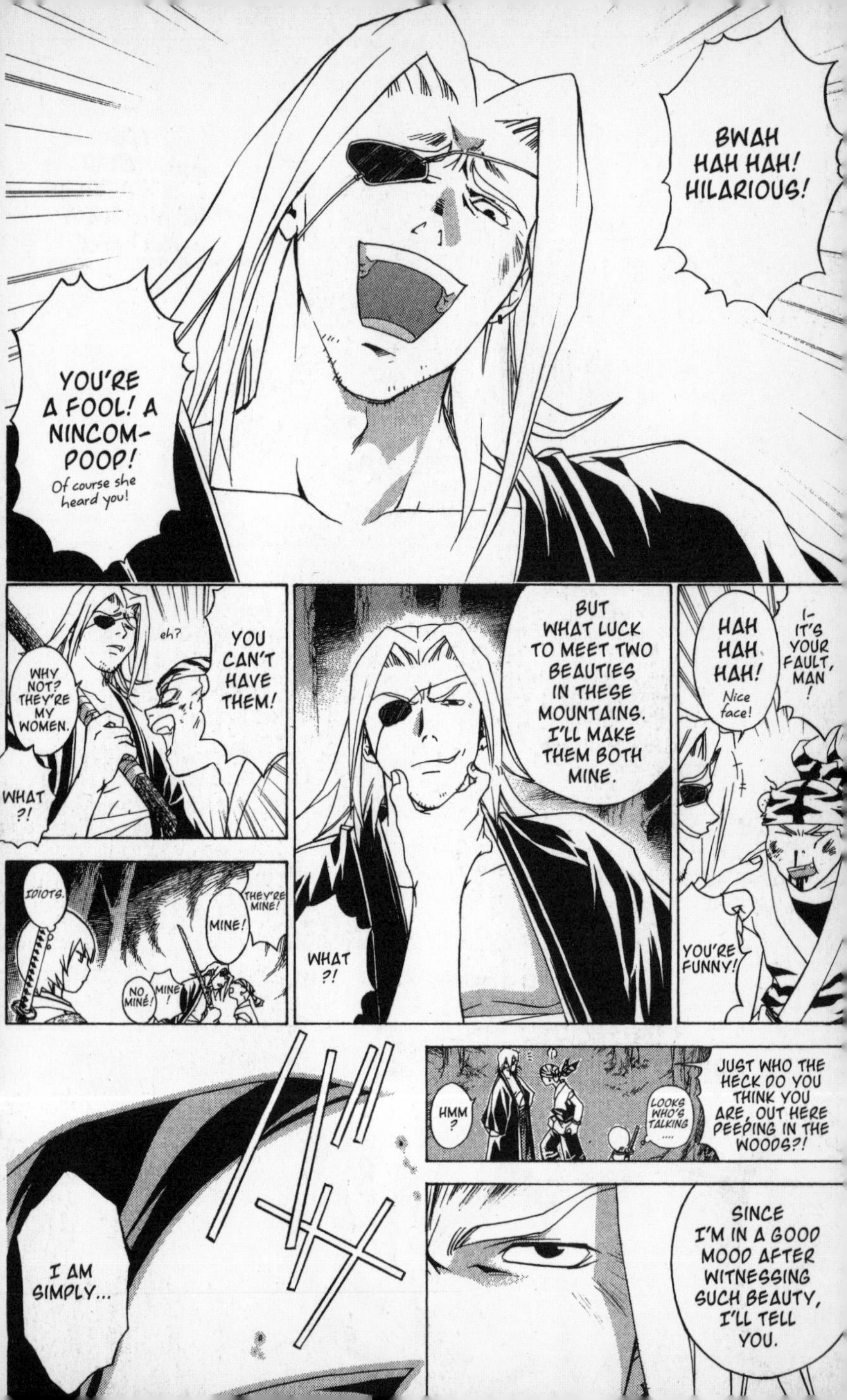
BWAH HAH HAH! HILARIOUS!
YOU'RE A FOOL! A NINCOM-POOP!
Of course she heard you!
I-IT'S YOUR FAULT, MAN!
HAH HAH HAH!
Nice face!
YOU'RE FUNNY!
BUT WHAT LUCK TO MEET TWO BEAUTIES IN THESE MOUNTAINS. I'LL MAKE THEM BOTH MINE.
WHAT?!
YOU CAN'T HAVE THEM!
eh?
WHY NOT? THEY'RE MY WOMEN.
WHAT?!
THEY'RE MINE!
MINE!
IDIOTS.
MINE!
NO MINE!
JUST WHO THE HECK DO YOU THINK YOU ARE, OUT HERE PEEPING IN THE WOODS?!
LOOKS WHO'S TALKING ....
HMM?
SINCE I'M IN A GOOD MOOD AFTER WITNESSING SUCH BEAUTY, I'LL TELL YOU.
I AM SIMPLY...

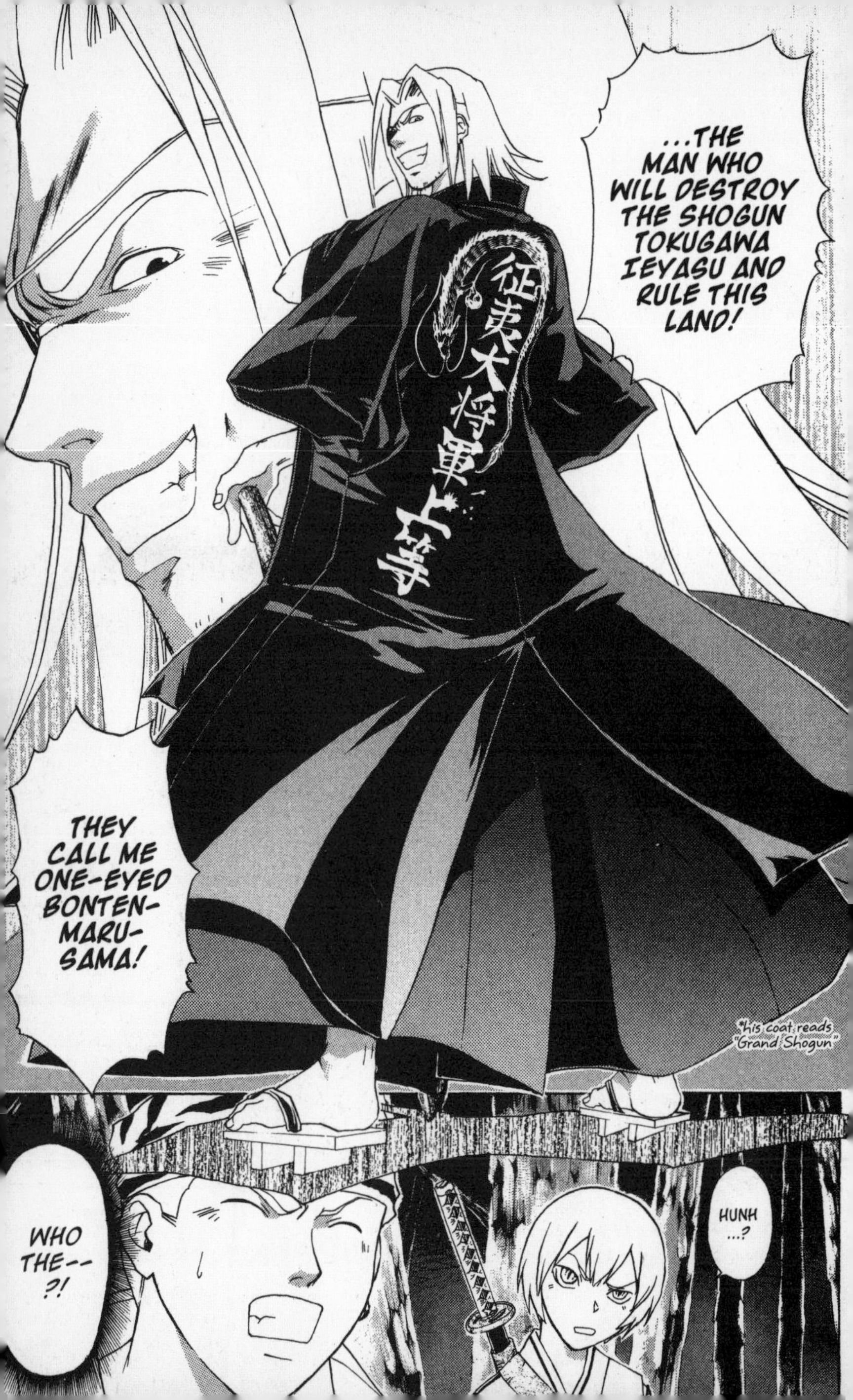
...THE MAN WHO WILL DESTROY THE SHOGUN TOKUGAWA IEYASU AND RULE THIS LAND!
征夷大将軍上等
THEY CALL ME ONE-EYED BONTEN-MARU-SAMA!
*his coat reads "Grand Shogun"
HUNH ...?
WHO THE-- ?!

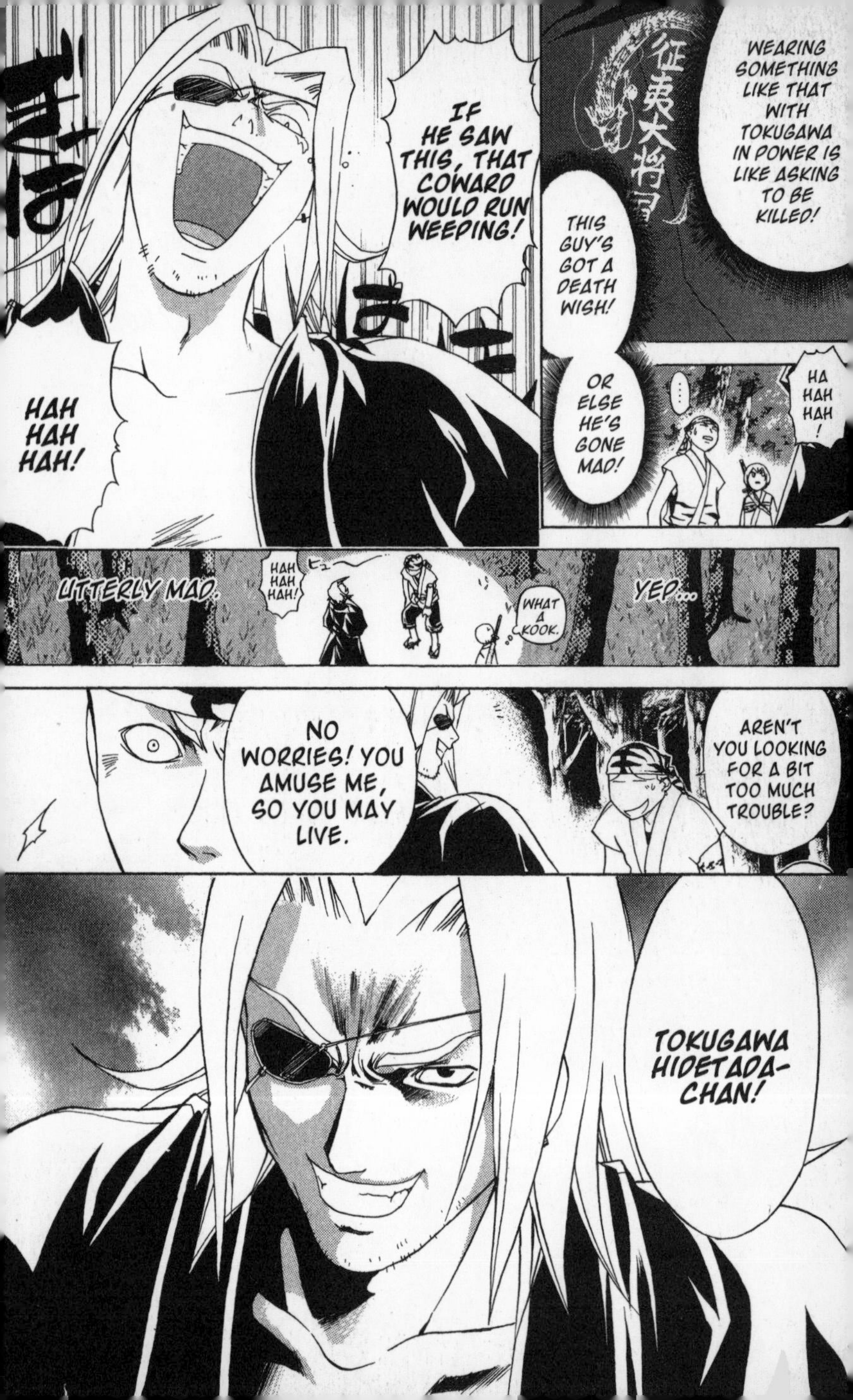
征夷大将軍
WEARING SOMETHING LIKE THAT WITH TOKUGAWA IN POWER IS LIKE ASKING TO BE KILLED!
THIS GUY'S GOT A DEATH WISH!
HA HAH HAH!
...
OR ELSE HE'S GONE MAD!
IF HE SAW THIS, THAT COWARD WOULD RUN WEEPING!
HAH HAH HAH!
YEP...
WHAT A KOOK.
HAH HAH HAH!
UTTERLY MAD.
AREN'T YOU LOOKING FOR A BIT TOO MUCH TROUBLE?
NO WORRIES! YOU AMUSE ME, SO YOU MAY LIVE.
TOKUGAWA HIDETADA-CHAN!

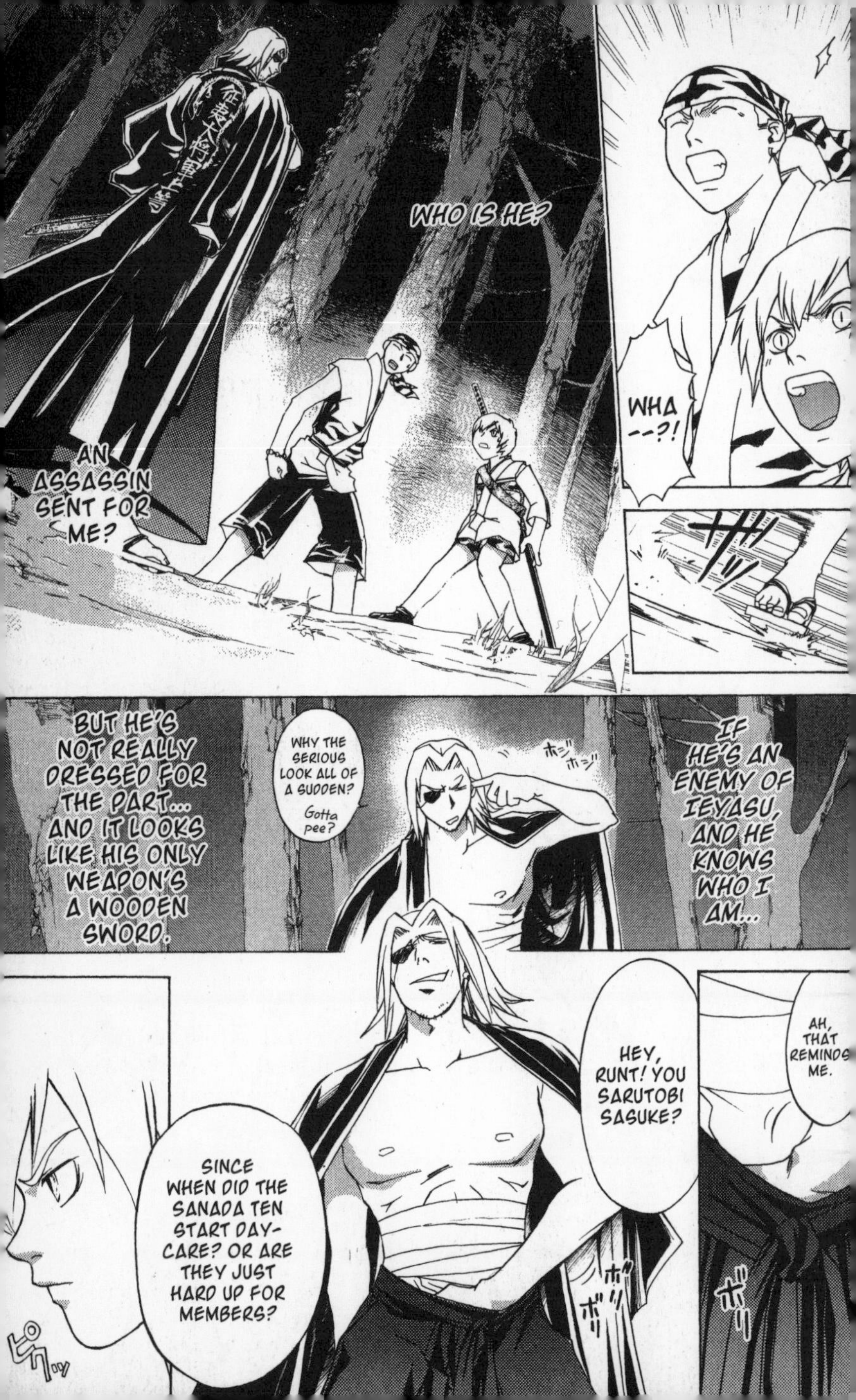
WHA--?!
ザッ
WHO IS HE?
AN ASSASSIN SENT FOR ME?
IF HE'S AN ENEMY OF IEYASU, AND HE KNOWS WHO I AM...
ホジ ホジ
WHY THE SERIOUS LOOK ALL OF A SUDDEN?
Gotta pee?
BUT HE'S NOT REALLY DRESSED FOR THE PART... AND IT LOOKS LIKE HIS ONLY WEAPON'S A WOODEN SWORD.
AH, THAT REMINDS ME.
ボリ
HEY, RUNT! YOU SARUTOBI SASUKE?
ボリ ボリ
SINCE WHEN DID THE SANADA TEN START DAY-CARE? OR ARE THEY JUST HARD UP FOR MEMBERS?
ピクッ

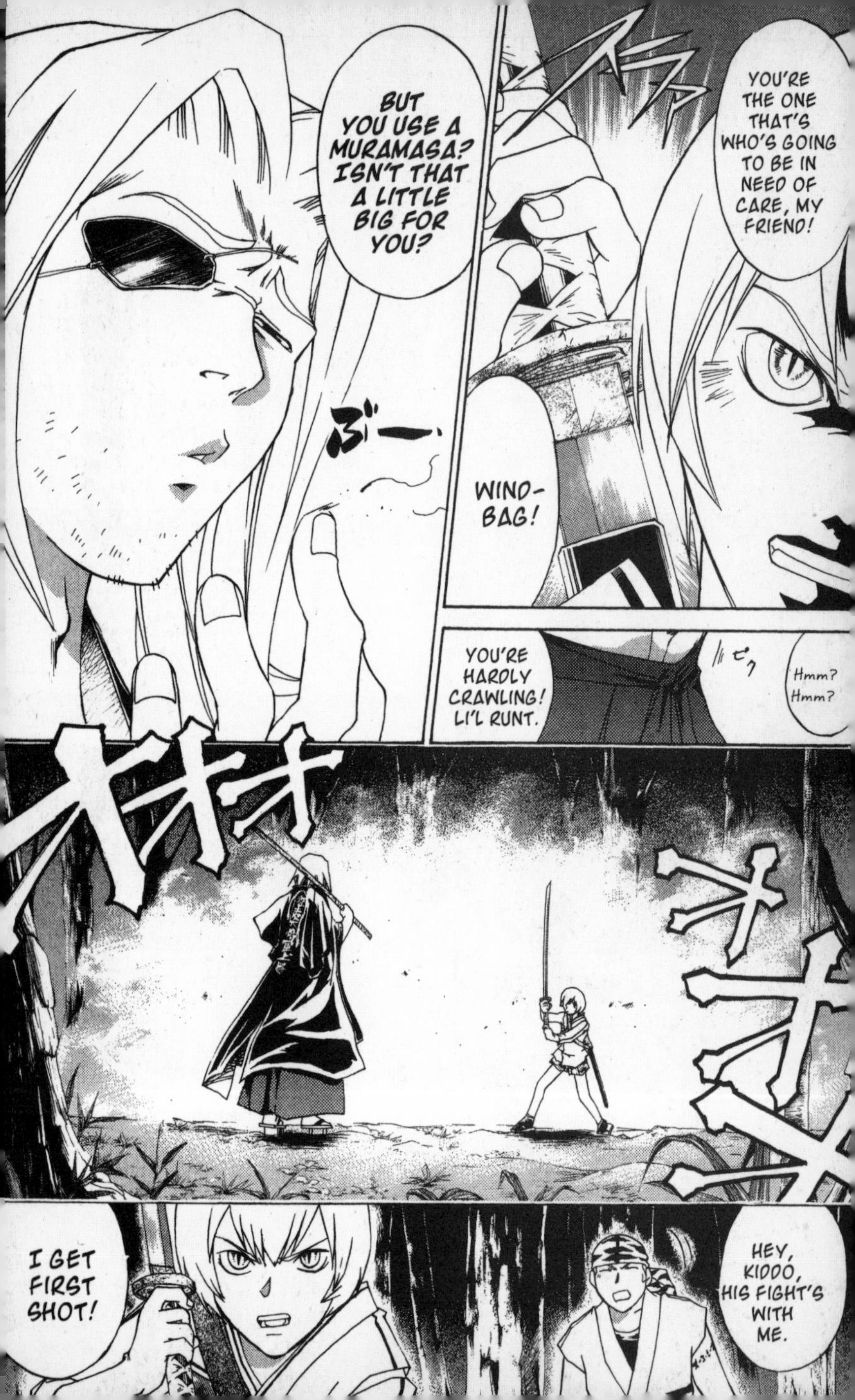
YOU'RE THE ONE THAT'S WHO'S GOING TO BE IN NEED OF CARE, MY FRIEND!
WIND-BAG!
Hmm? Hmm?
YOU'RE HARDLY CRAWLING! LI'L RUNT.
BUT YOU USE A MURAMASA? ISN'T THAT A LITTLE BIG FOR YOU?
ぶー
オオオ
オオ
HEY, KIDDO, HIS FIGHT'S WITH ME.
I GET FIRST SHOT!

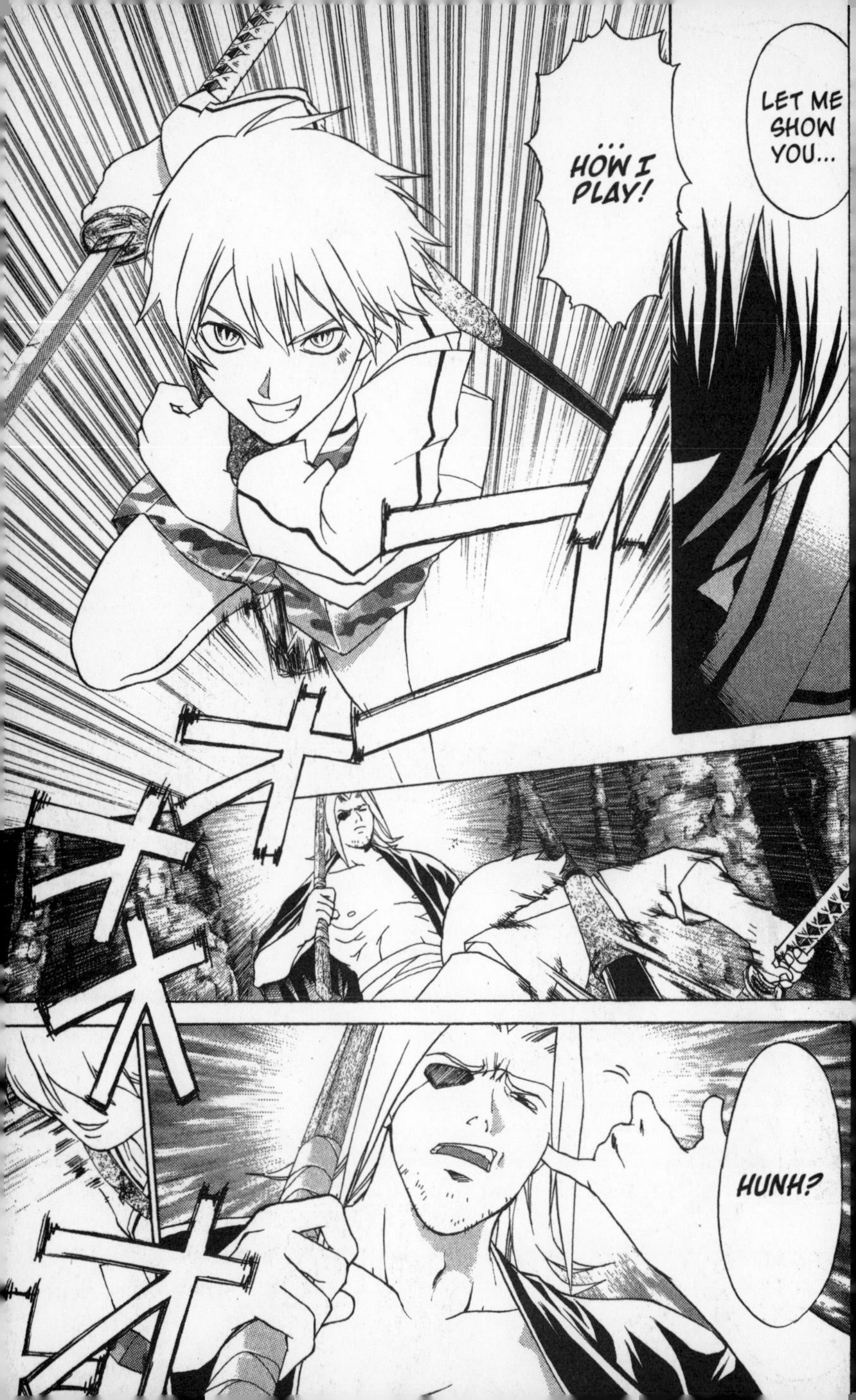
LET ME SHOW YOU...
...HOW I PLAY!
HUNH?

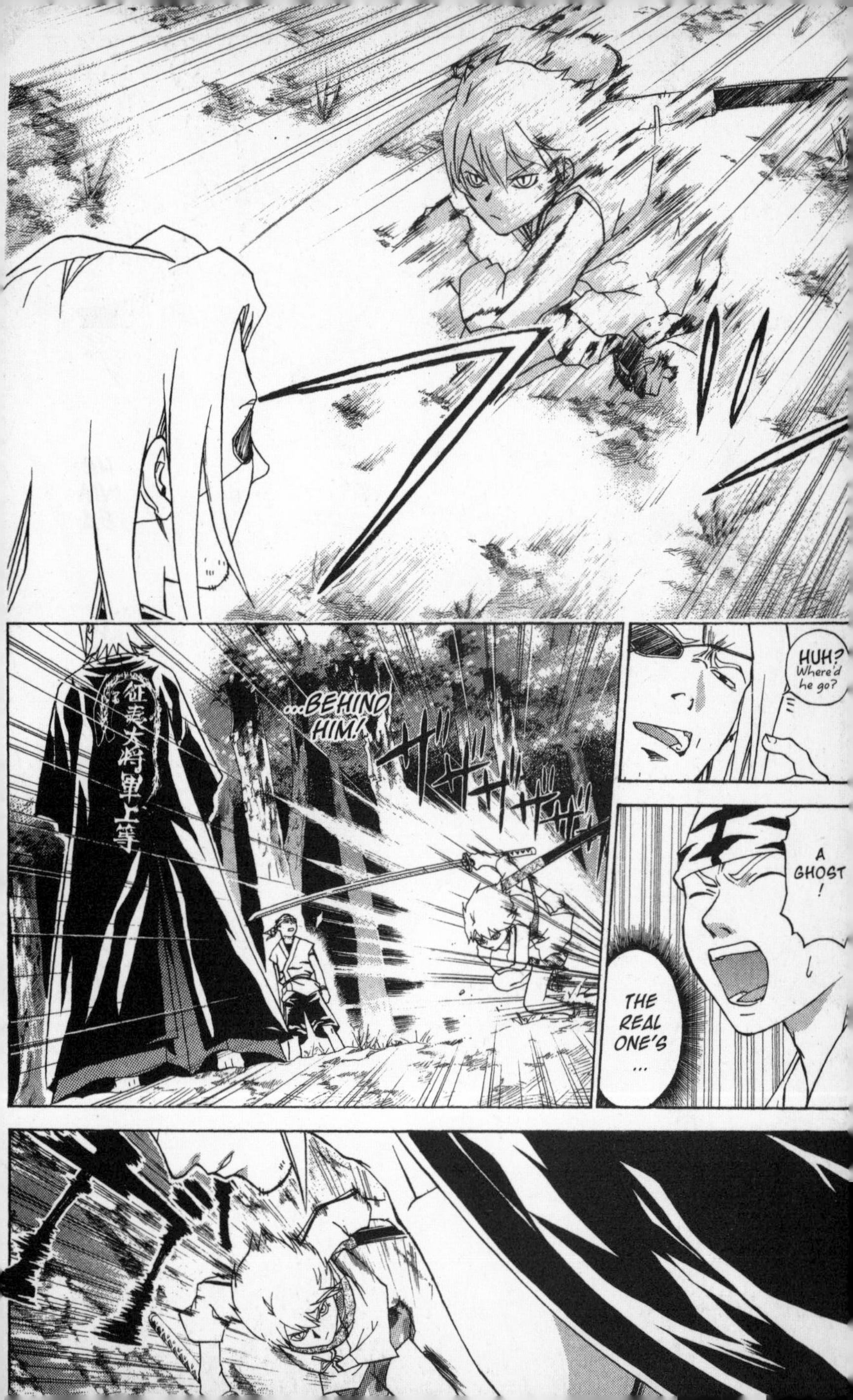
HUH? Where'd he go?
A GHOST!
THE REAL ONE'S ...
...BEHIND HIM!
征夷大将軍上等

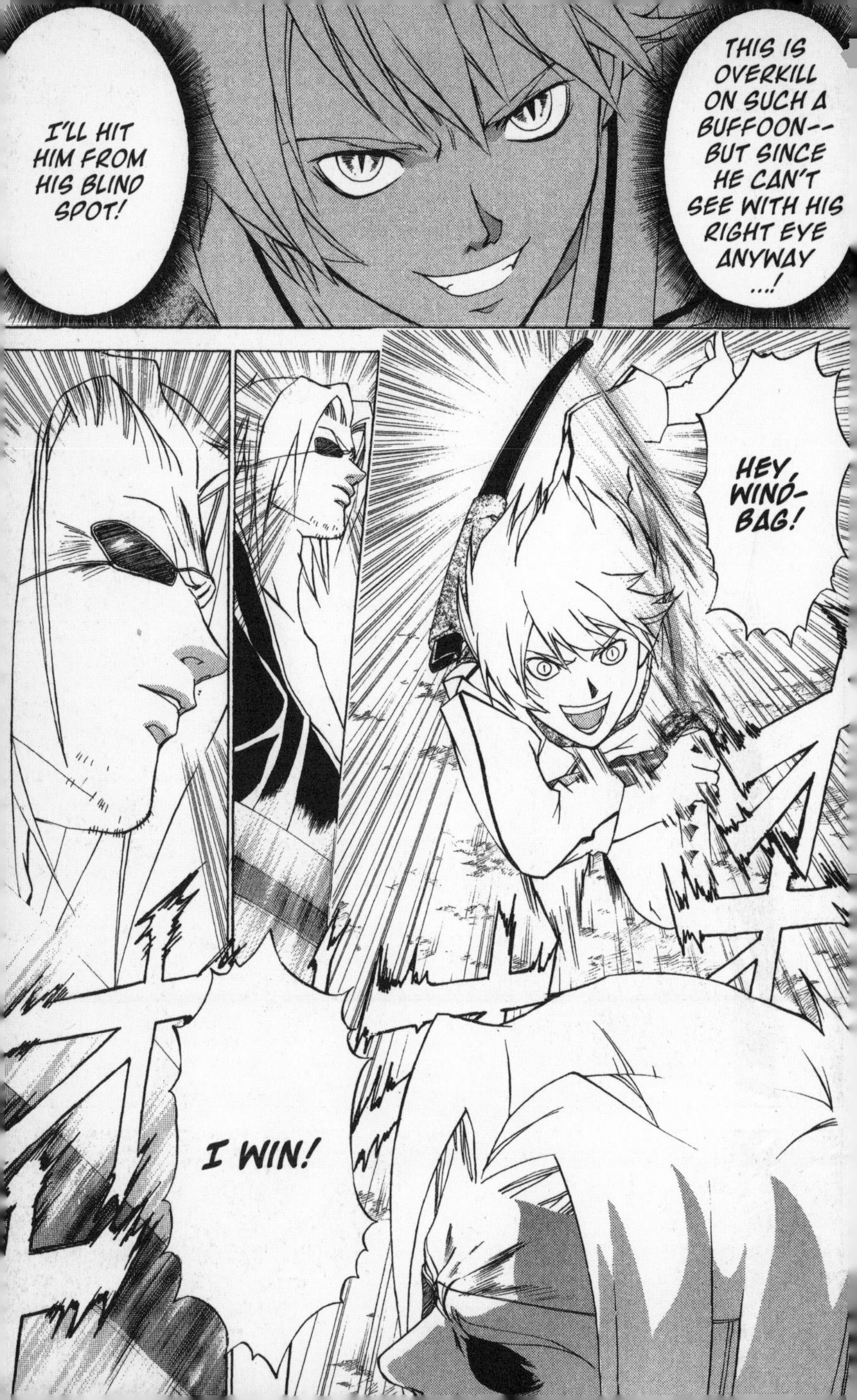
THIS IS OVERKILL ON SUCH A BUFFOON-- BUT SINCE HE CAN'T SEE WITH HIS RIGHT EYE ANYWAY ...!
I'LL HIT HIM FROM HIS BLIND SPOT!
HEY, WIND-BAG!
I WIN!

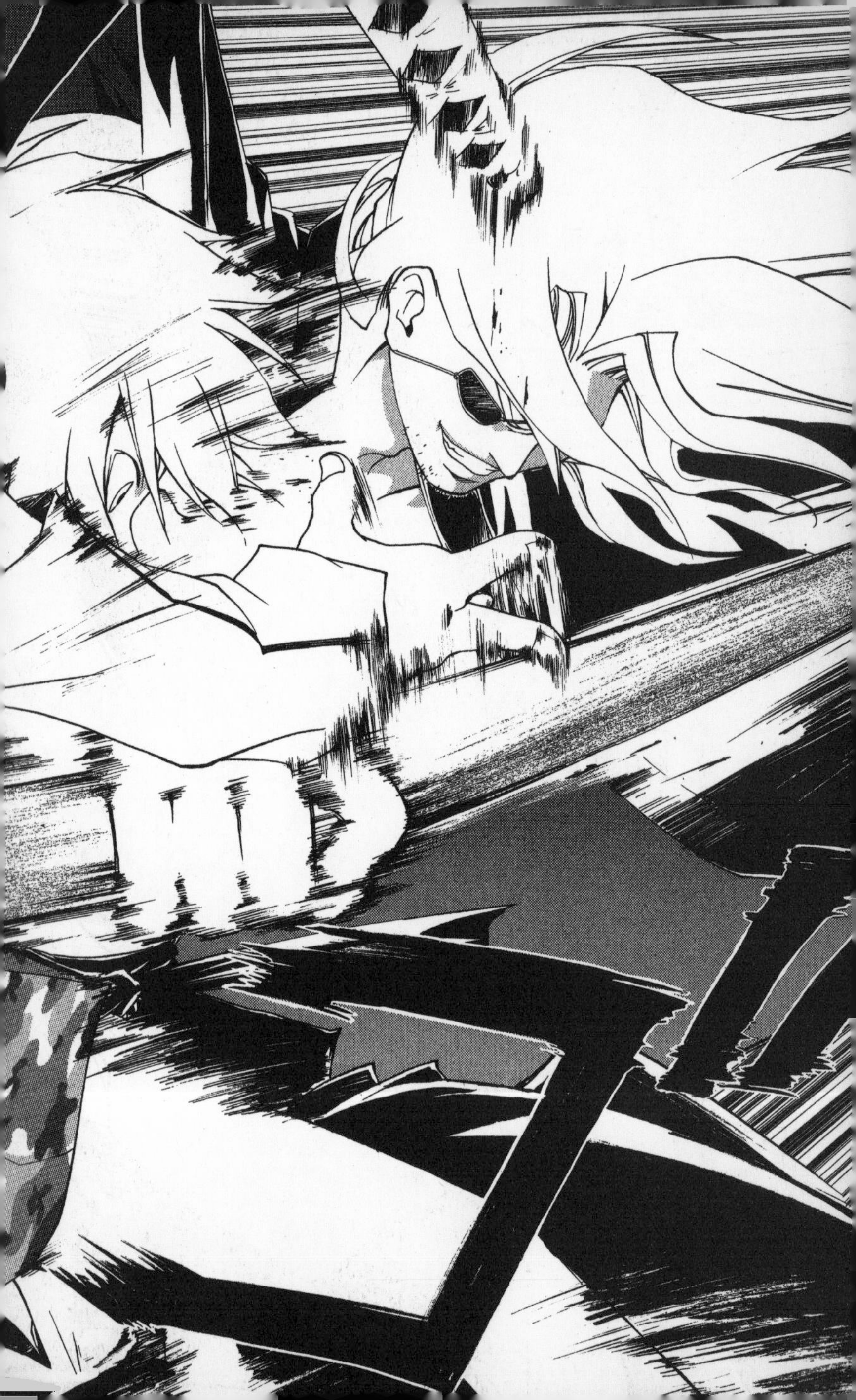

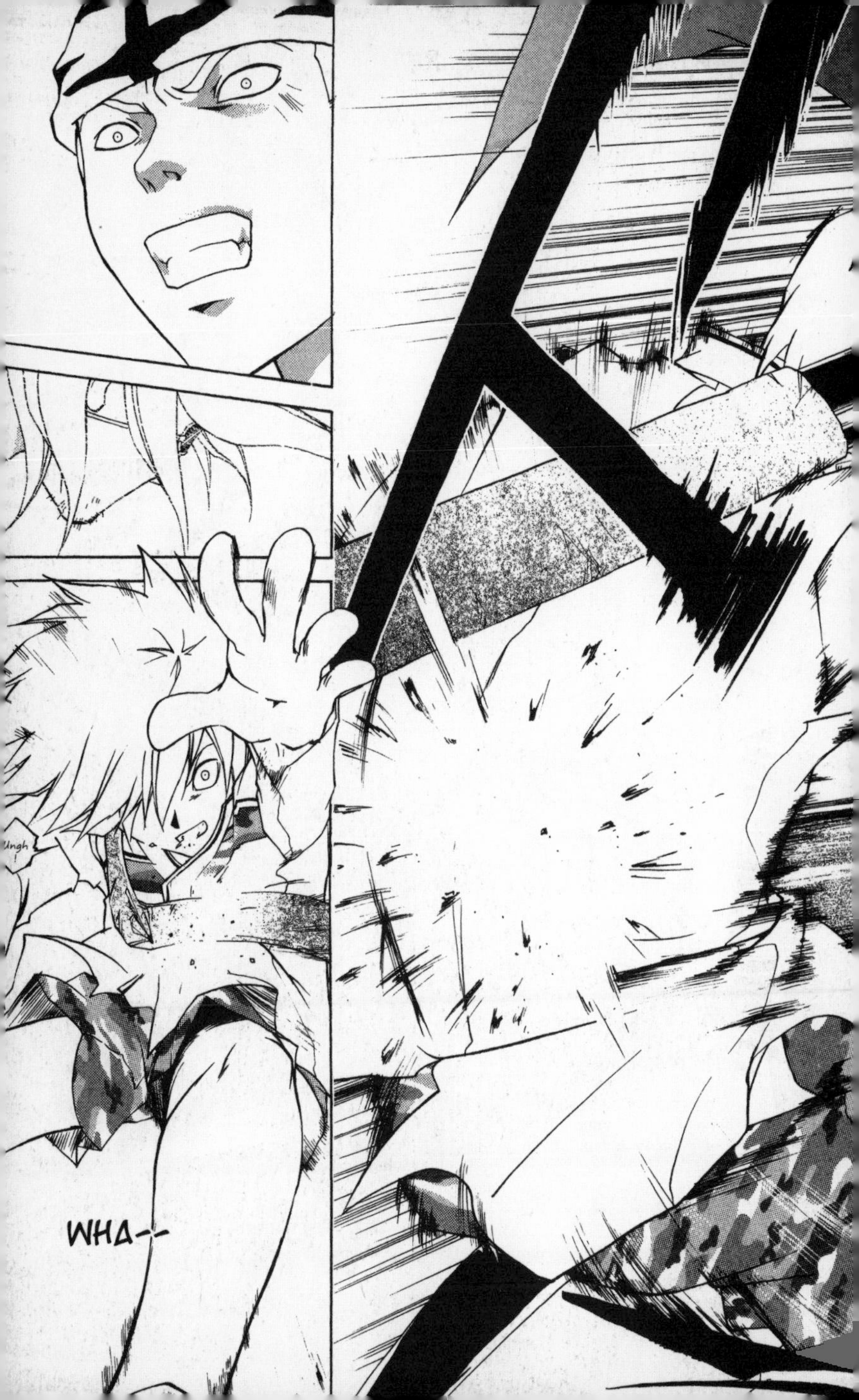
Ungh!
WHA--

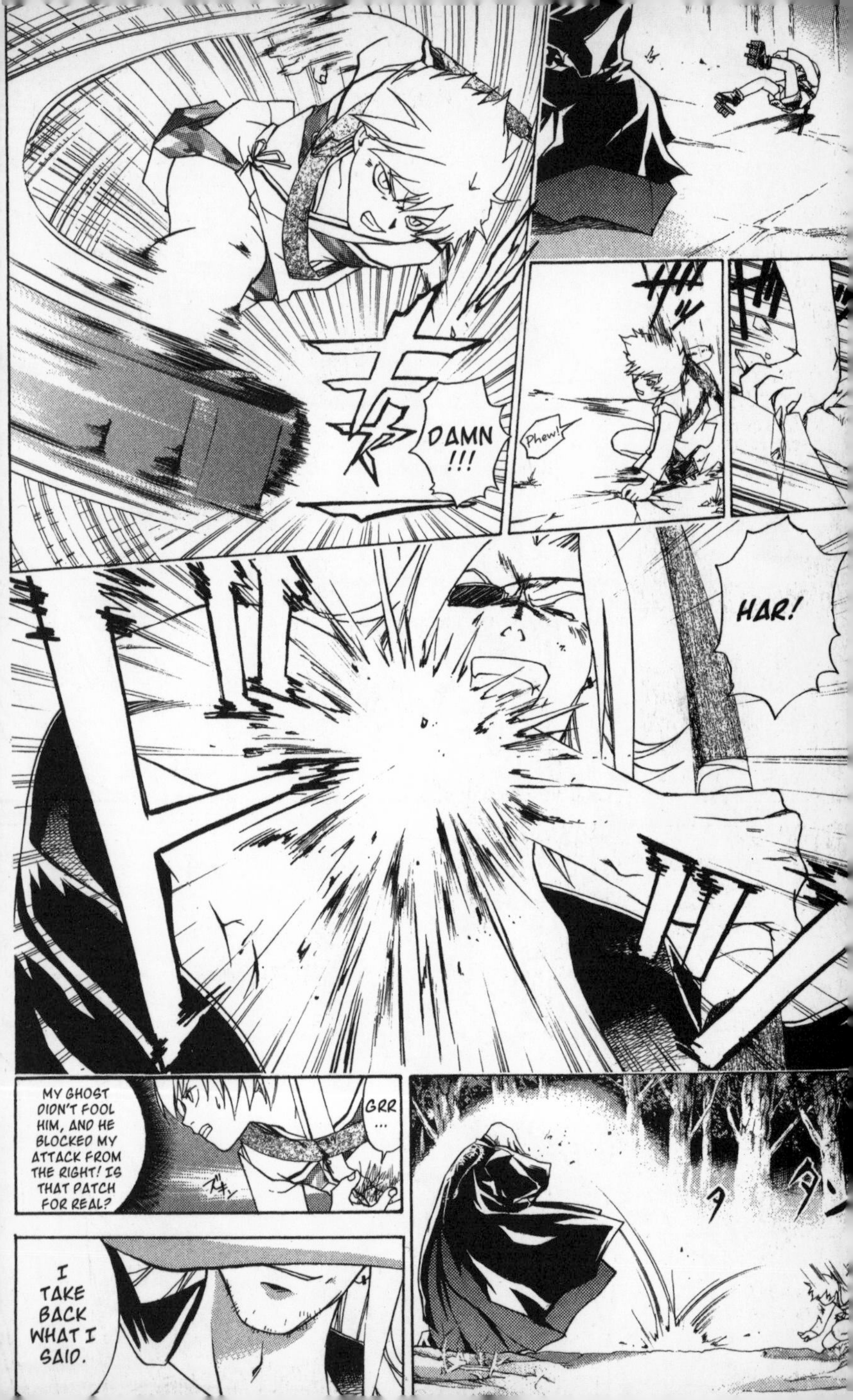
Phew!
DAMN!!!
HAR!
GRR...
MY GHOST DIDN'T FOOL HIM, AND HE BLOCKED MY ATTACK FROM THE RIGHT! IS THAT PATCH FOR REAL?
I TAKE BACK WHAT I SAID.

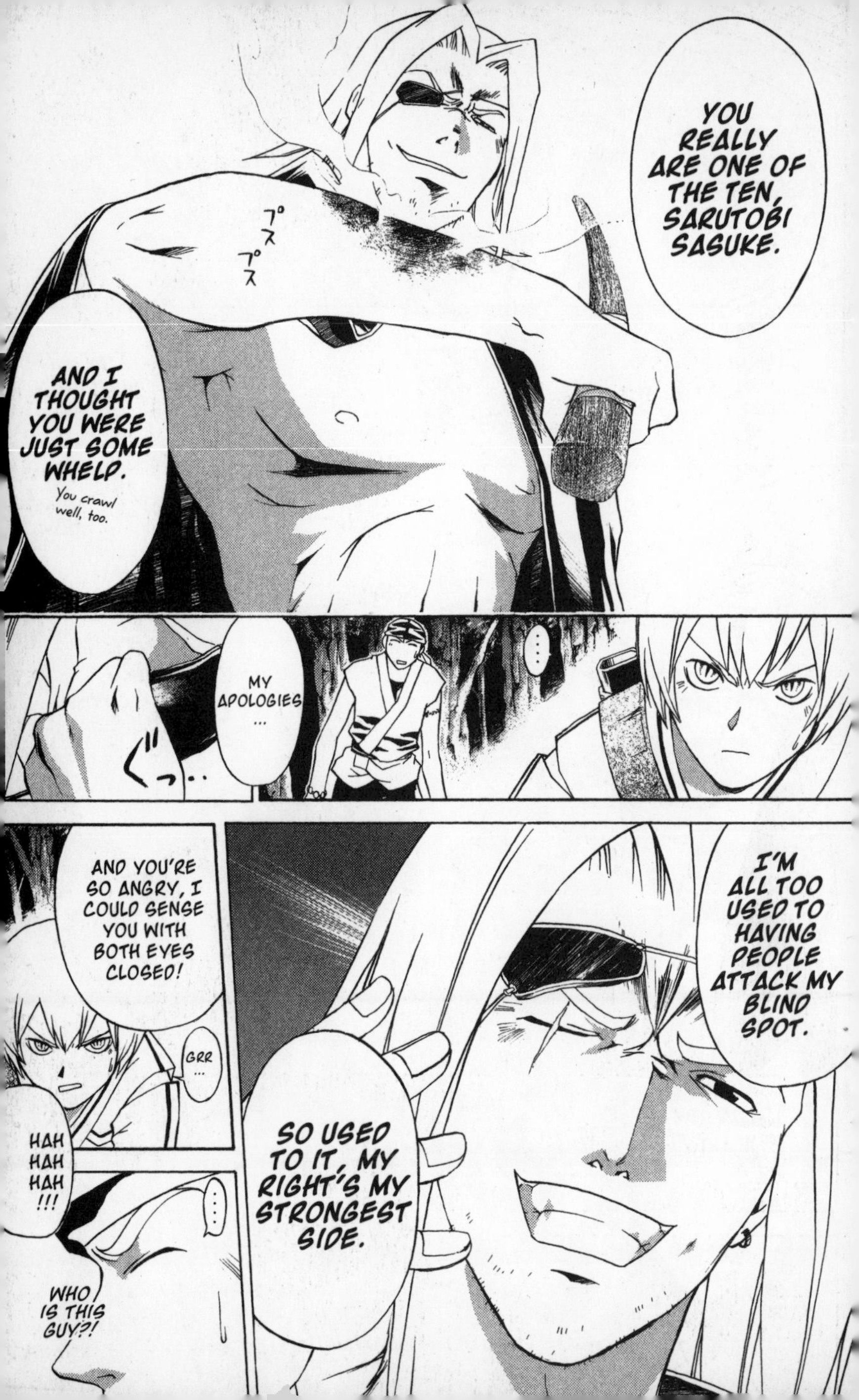
YOU REALLY ARE ONE OF THE TEN, SARUTOBI SASUKE.
プスプス
AND I THOUGHT YOU WERE JUST SOME WHELP.
You crawl well, too.
...
MY APOLOGIES...
ぐっ..
I'M ALL TOO USED TO HAVING PEOPLE ATTACK MY BLIND SPOT.
SO USED TO IT, MY RIGHT'S MY STRONGEST SIDE.
AND YOU'RE SO ANGRY, I COULD SENSE YOU WITH BOTH EYES CLOSED!
GRR...
HAH HAH HAH!!!
...
WHO IS THIS GUY?!

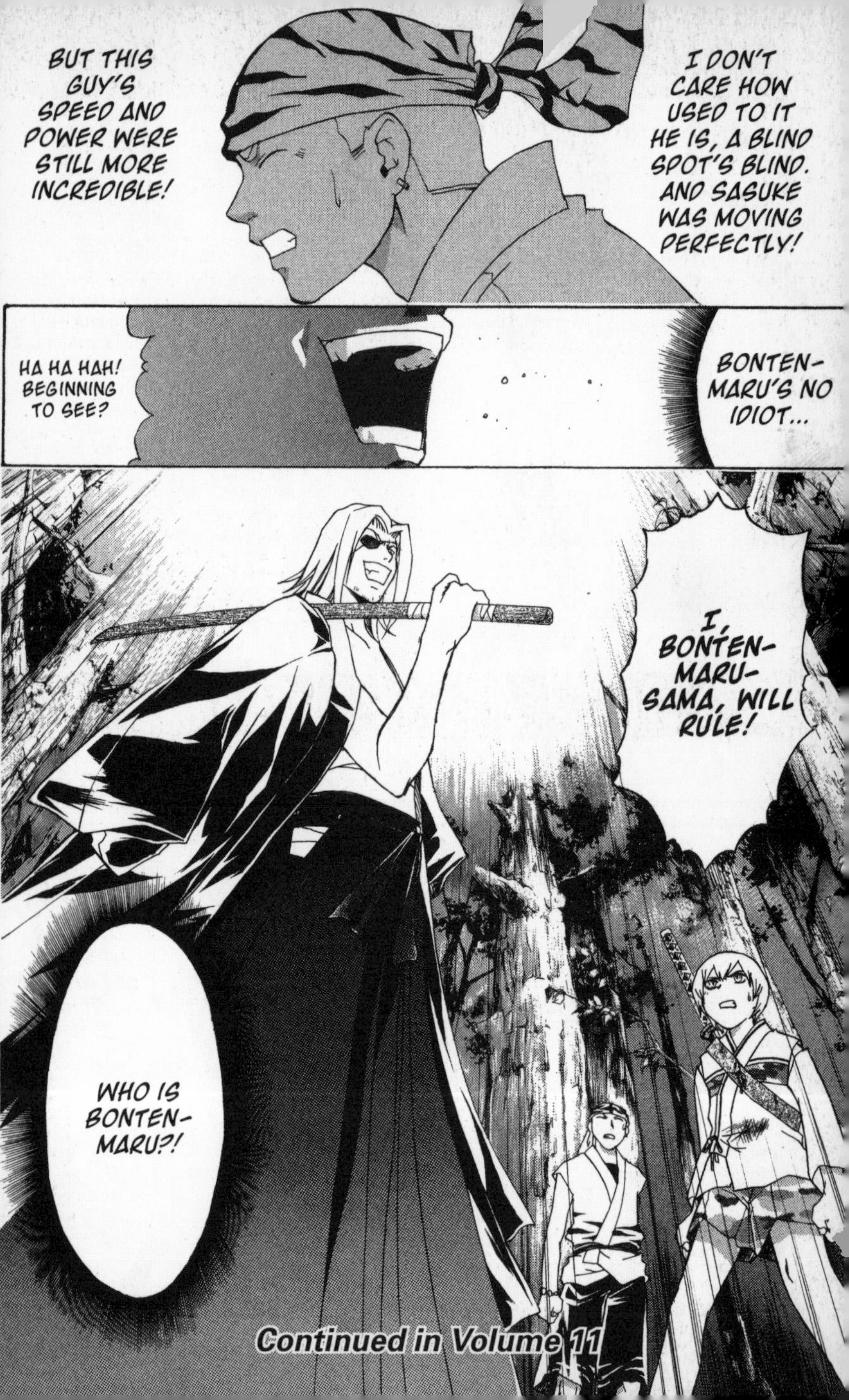
I DON'T CARE HOW USED TO IT HE IS, A BLIND SPOT'S BLIND. AND SASUKE WAS MOVING PERFECTLY!
BUT THIS GUY'S SPEED AND POWER WERE STILL MORE INCREDIBLE!
BONTEN-MARU'S NO IDIOT...
...
HA HA HAH! BEGINNING TO SEE?
I, BONTEN-MARU-SAMA, WILL RULE!
WHO IS BONTEN-MARU?!

Continued in Volume 11

← Continued from Page 170.

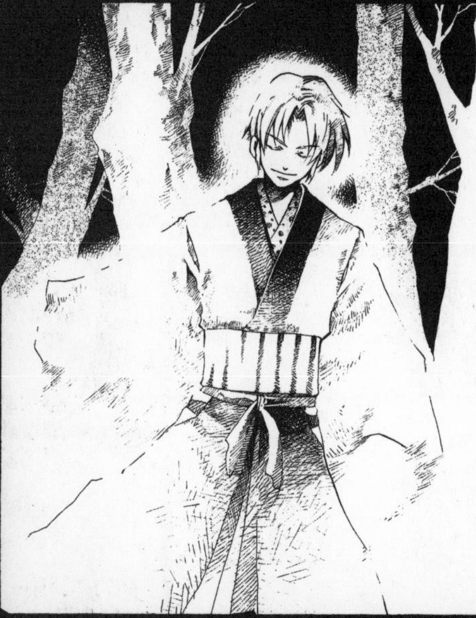

CONGRATULATIONS ON TEN VOLUMES!

I've been on the SDK project for two years now... I have nothing but thanks and more thanks for K-sensei, who still gives me work even though I show absolutely no signs of improvement. And now, Yuzu Haruno-dono is leaving us! It was fun working with you! Let's hang out! H-san, and all the part-timers, and Souma-dono, you've all helped me out since March. Thanks to M-san and the letter-writers, too! I just wanted to say thanks to everyone for making this possible.

↑**Hazuki Asami**

↓**Ken'ichi Suetake**

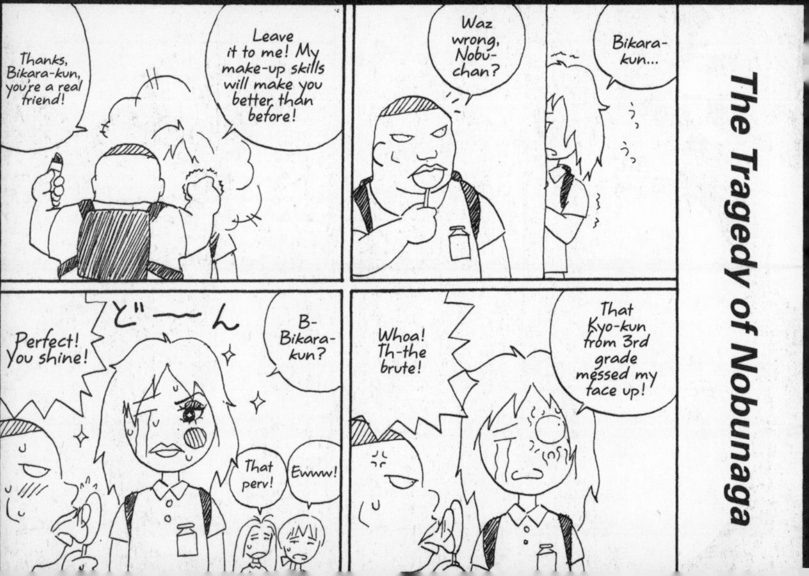
The Tragedy of Nobunaga
Bikara-kun...
Waz wrong, Nobu-chan?
That Kyo-kun from 3rd grade messed my face up!
Whoa! Th-the brute!
Leave it to me! My make-up skills will make you better than before!
Thanks, Bikara-kun, you're a real friend!
B-Bikara-kun?
どーん
Perfect! You shine!
Ewww!
That perv!

ASSISTANT NAGAO'S WORLD

(or: Invading Your Brain Cells) ♨

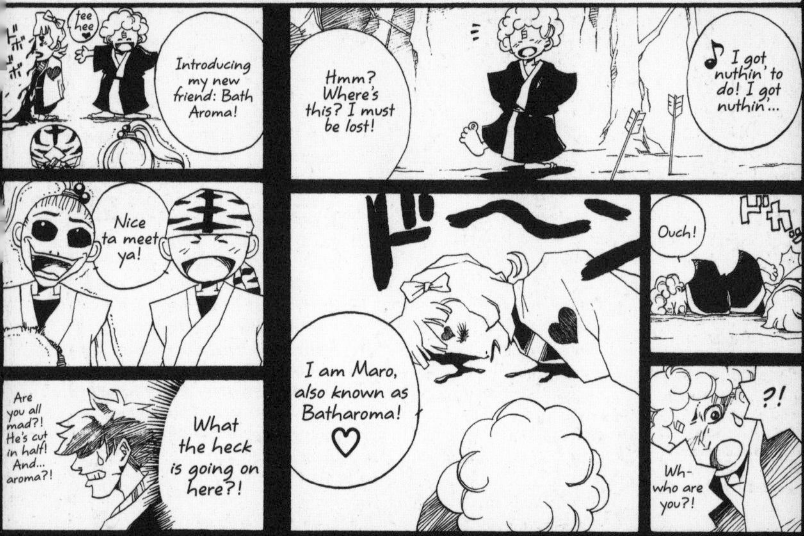

♪ I got nuthin' to do! I got nuthin'...
Hmm? Where's this? I must be lost!
tee hee ♥
Introducing my new friend: Bath Aroma!
Ouch!
?!
Wh-who are you?!
I am Maro, also known as Batharoma! ♡
Nice ta meet ya!
What the heck is going on here?!
Are you all mad?! He's cut in half! And... aroma?!

KAMIJYO: WHAT...WHAT'S WITH THE HEARTS?!

⬆ Takaya Nagao

⬇ Souma Akatsuki

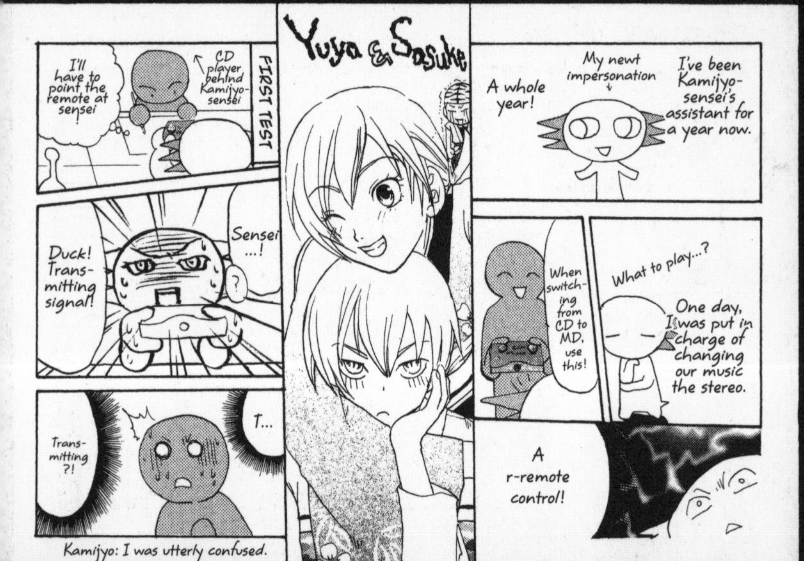

I've been Kamijyo-sensei's assistant for a year now.
My newt impersonation
A whole year!
One day, I was put in charge of changing our music the stereo.
What to play...?
When switching from CD to MD, use this!
A r-remote control!
Yuya & Sasuke
FIRST TEST
CD player behind Kamijyo-sensei
I'll have to point the remote at sensei
Sensei ...!
Duck! Trans-mitting signal!
T...
Trans-mitting ?!
Kamijyo: I was utterly confused.

KAMIJYO: "DUCK"? HEH! AKATSUKI-SAN IS OUR TOKEN UPRIGHT CITIZEN.

PUMPKIN JOINED, SORRY FOR ALL MY SLIP-UPS!

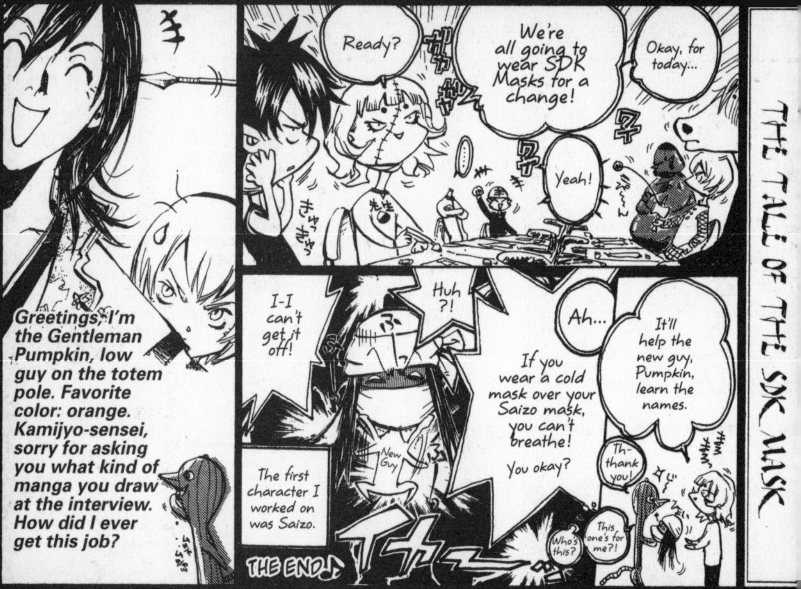
THE TALE OF THE SDK MASK
Okay, for today...
We're all going to wear SDK Masks for a change!
Ready?
Yeah!
Ah...
It'll help the new guy, Pumpkin, learn the names.
If you wear a cold mask over your Saizo mask, you can't breathe!
You okay?
Th-thank you!
This one's for me?!
Who's this?
Huh?!
I-I can't get it off!
New Guy
The first character I worked on was Saizo.
THE END♪
Greetings, I'm the Gentleman Pumpkin, low guy on the totem pole. Favorite color: orange. Kamijyo-sensei, sorry for asking you what kind of manga you draw at the interview. How did I ever get this job?

⬆ The Gentleman Pumpkin ⬇ Shiba Tateoka

HAIRY LEGS, TOO. HE EVEN CRAPS. I THINK.

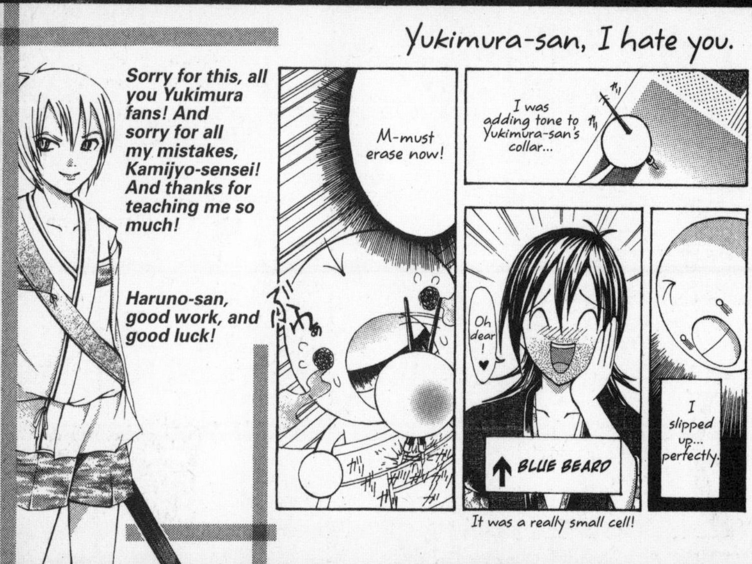
Yukimura-san, I hate you.
I was adding tone to Yukimura-san's collar...
M-must erase now!
I slipped up... perfectly.
Oh dear!
⬆ BLUE BEARD
It was a really small cell!
Sorry for this, all you Yukimura fans! And sorry for all my mistakes, Kamijyo-sensei! And thanks for teaching me so much!
Haruno-san, good work, and good luck!

TRY TO DRAW LIKE AKIMINE KAMIJYO!

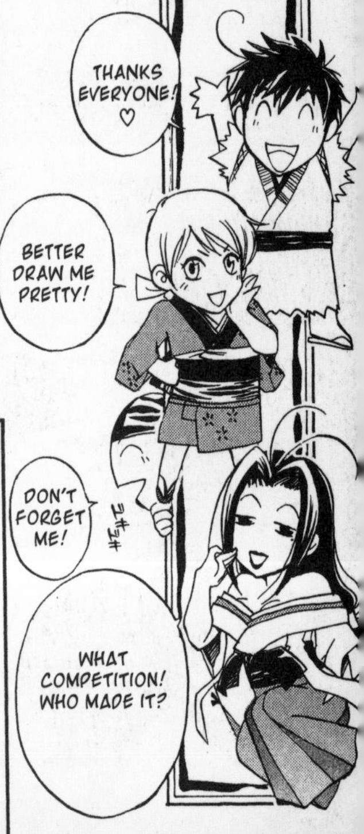
THANKS EVERYONE! ♡
BETTER DRAW ME PRETTY!
DON'T FORGET ME!
WHAT COMPETITION! WHO MADE IT?

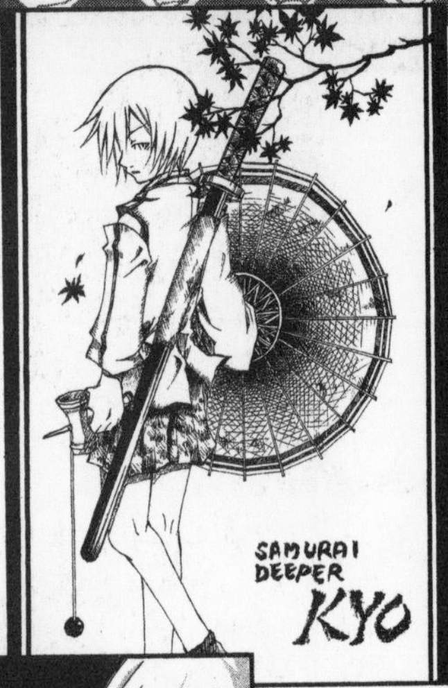
SAMURAI DEEPER KYO

[Mitsuki/Fukuoka] Great! No complaints here!

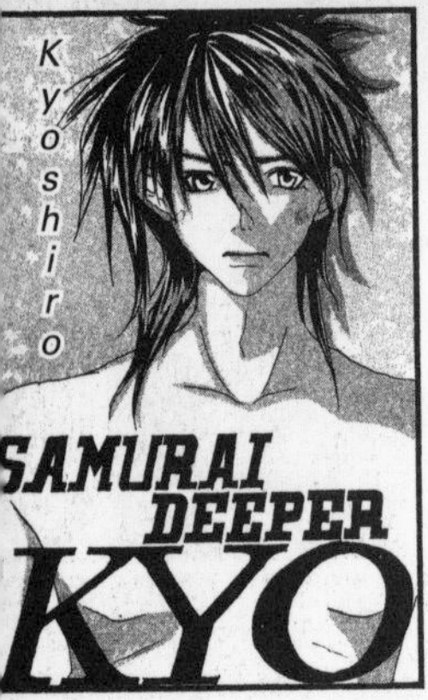
Kyoshiro
SAMURAI DEEPER KYO

Lord of the Kitchen/Osaka]
He seems gentle...and sad.

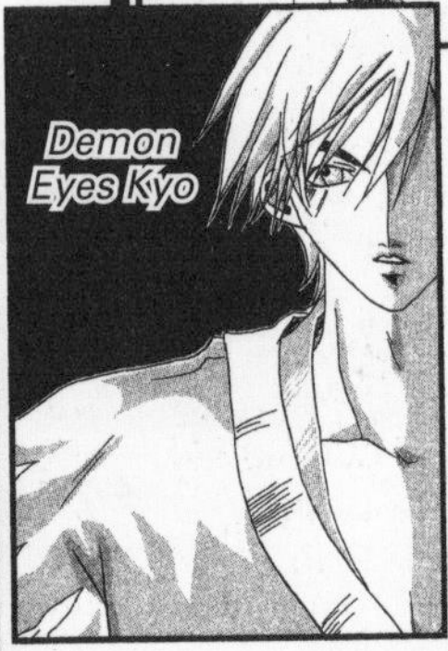
Demon Eyes Kyo

[Purple Potato/Nagano]
I like the slender feel.

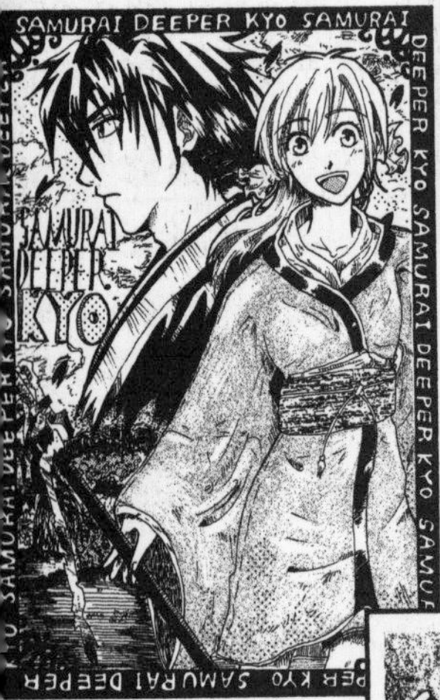
SAMURAI DEEPER KYO SAMURAI DEEPER KYO SAMURAI DEEPER KYO SAMURAI DEEPER KYO SAMURAI DEEPER
SAMURAI DEEPER KYO

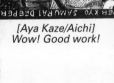

[Aya Kaze/Aichi]
Wow! Good work!

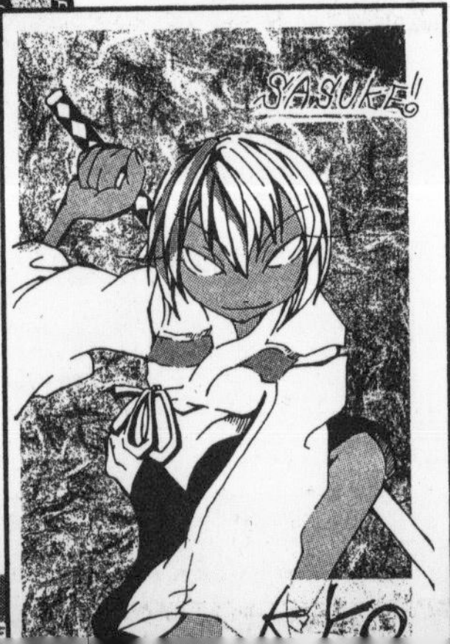
SASUKE!!

[Himekami/Okinawa]
He looks...evil! Yeah!

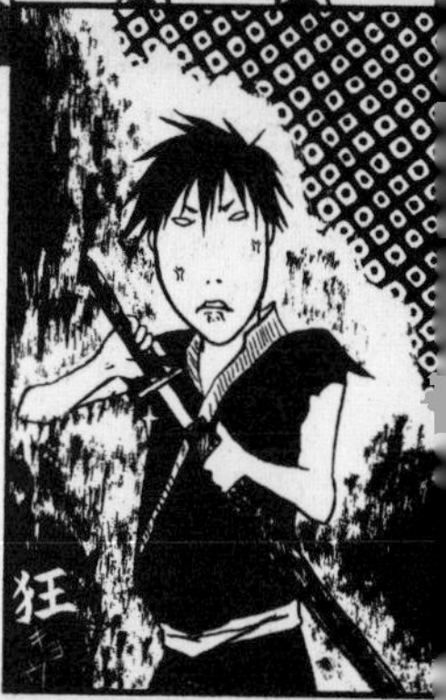
狂

[Hironko/ Yamaguchi] He's mad, oh he's mad!

Message from Kamijyo Sensei:

WE'RE GOING TO BE DOING CHARACTER GALLERIES. NEXT ISSUE: KYOSHIRO!

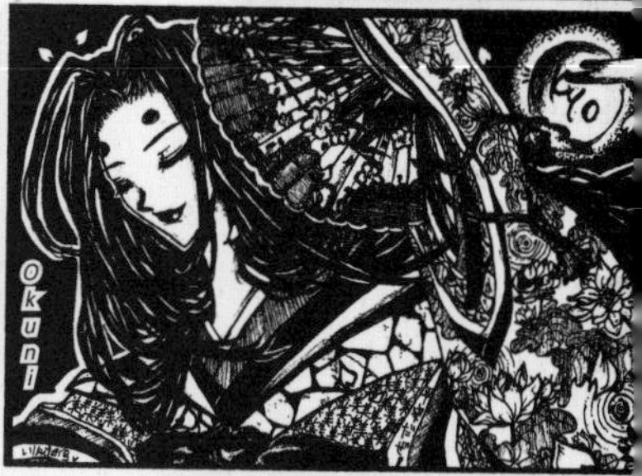
KYO
Okuni

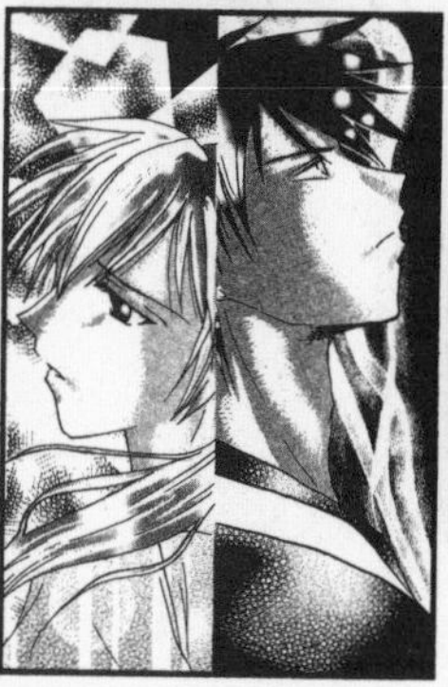

[Denny's Employee/ Chiba Prefecture] Her eyes look like bullets.

[Hiromi Funahashi/Aichi] Notice the pattern is the character "bi" for beauty?

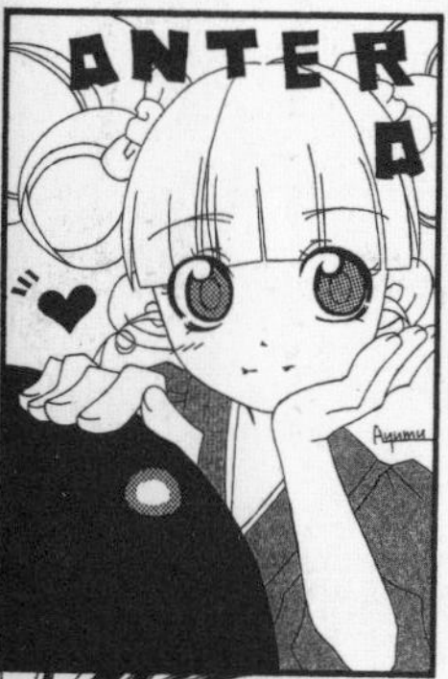
ONTER
O
Ayumu

[Kazuki Muneda/ Aichi Prefecture] Thoughtful...

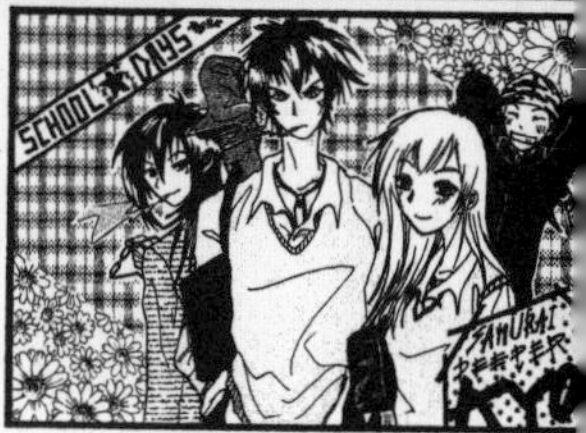
SCHOOL DAYS
SAMURAI

[Okome/Akita] Tora definitely went to an all-boys school!

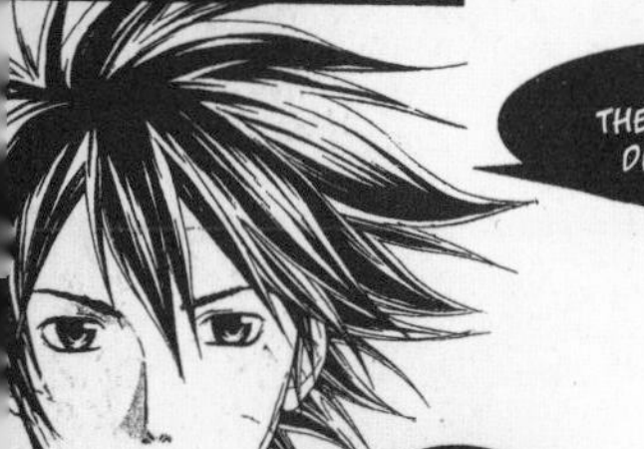
IT SEEMS THE LADIES LIKE TO DRAW ME BEST!

New guidelines! Please read carefully.

How to submit:

1) Send your work via regular mail (NOT e-mail) to:

SAMURAI DEEPER KYO FAN MAIL
C/O TOKYOPOP
5900 WILSHIRE BLVD., SUITE 2000
LOS ANGELES, CA 90036

2) All work should be in black-and-white and no larger than 8.5" x 11". (And try not to fold it too many times!) 3) Anything you send will not be returned. If you want to keep your original, it's fine to send us a copy. 4) Please include your full name, age, city and state for us to print with your work. If you'd rather us use a pen name, please include that too. 5) IMPORTANT: If you're under the age of 18, you must have your parent's permission in order for us to print your work. Any submissions without a signed note of parental consent will not be used. 6) For full details, please check out *http://www.tokyopop.com/aboutus/fanart.php*

Disclaimer: Anything you send to us becomes the property of TOKYOPOP Inc. and will not be returned to you. We will have the right to print, reproduce, distribute or modify the artwork for use in future volumes of Samurai Deeper Kyo or on the Web without payment to you.

Vanessa J.
Age 16
Planation, FL

The softer side of Kamijyo's epic. Yuya would be a lot better off if she just went with Benitora. Then she could be the future shogun's wife and wouldn't have to deal with schizophrenic psychos!

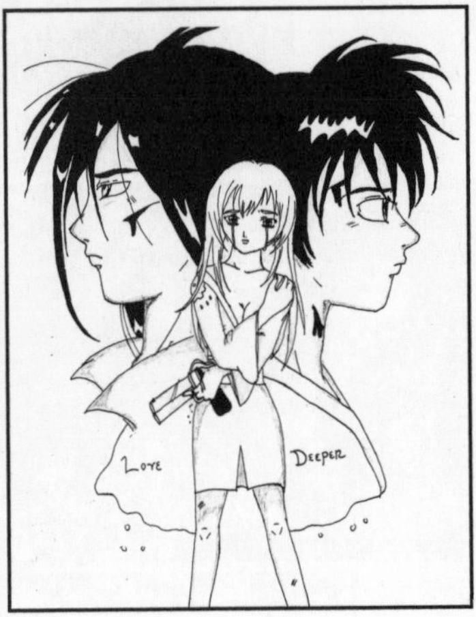
LOVE
DEEPER

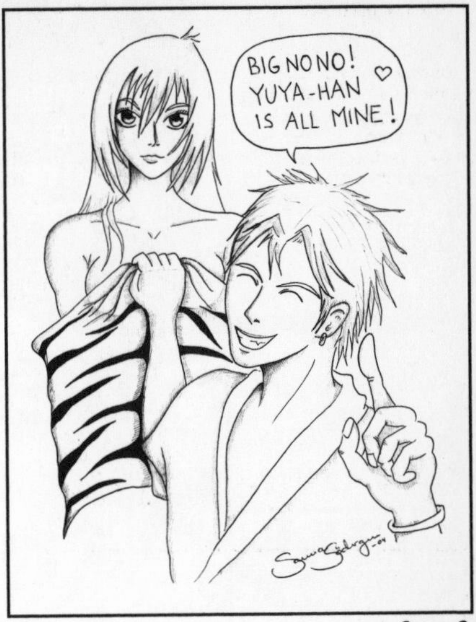
BIG NONO! YUYA-HAN IS ALL MINE!

Sanna S.
Age 24
Nogersund, Sweden

Oh my God!! Benitora took off his bandana! Is that allowed?! It's always great to hear from fans across the ocean. Thanks so much for the pic, Sanna.

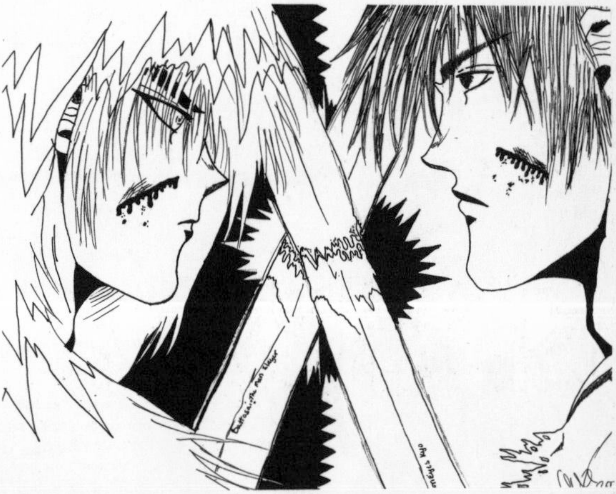

Aya T.
Age 15
Lawrenceville, GA

The eternal question brought to life! Who would win in a fight, Kyo or Kenshin? My money's on Kyo. If you ask me, that Kenshin guy is kind of a pansy. Kick his ass, Demon Eyes!

Vicky L.
East Windsor, NJ

The angel and the devil on Kyoshiro's shoulders. I like the way you captured the relationships so well with just one picture—it really tells a story!

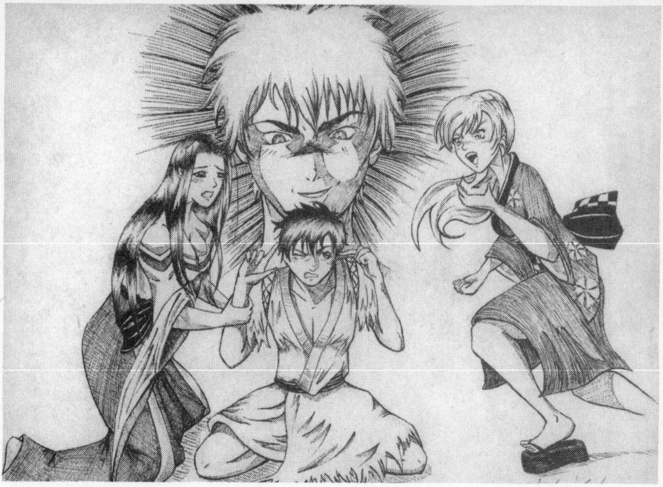

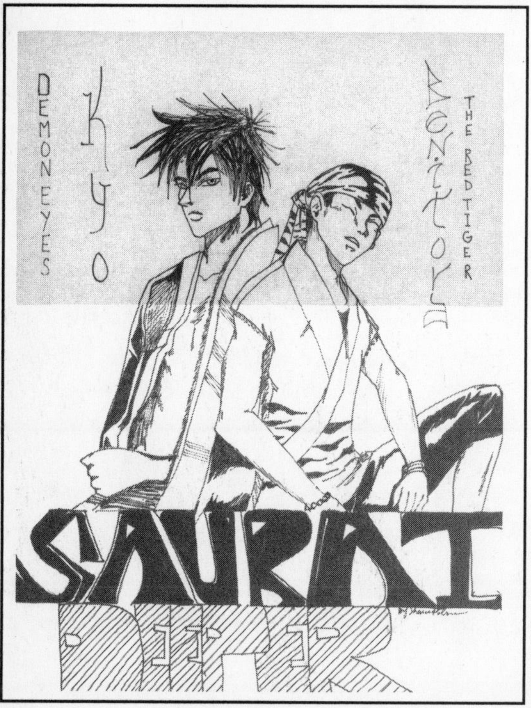
DEMON EYES
KYO
BENITORA
THE RED TIGER

Shauna P.
Age 22
Pocatello, ID

Kyo and Tora—Nobunaga's greatest enemies, and two men with deep secrets. Here's hoping that they'll stay friends!

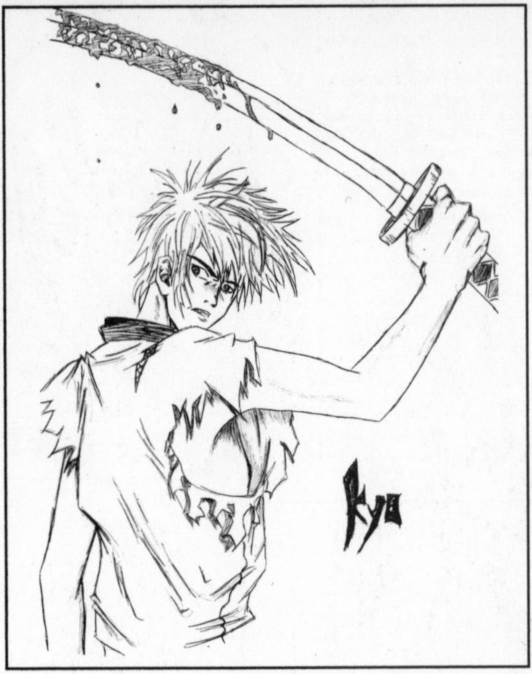
Kyo

Charlie V.
Age 13
Tampa, FL

Kyo is taking names and kicking butt! So much blood on his sword—I hope he doesn't stain his robes! Well, they are pretty torn. I guess he can replace them soon enough.

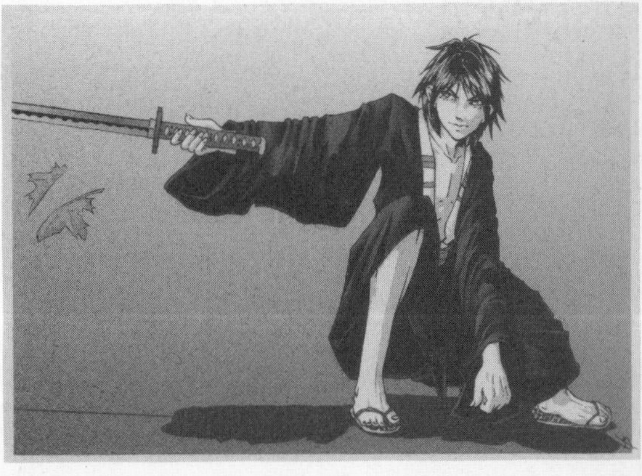

Heidi B.
Age 18
Beavercreek, OH

Beautiful picture, Heidi! Kyo at his most graceful. Truly a samurai in control of his power.

Charlie M.
Age 16
Sherman, TX

Sasuke! When it comes to ninjas, no one's cooler than this little punk! But now we find out there was another Sasuke before him? I sense a grudge match coming up!!

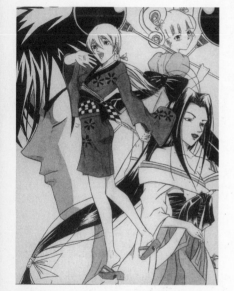

Vicky S.
Age 22
Phoenix, AZ

Te girls of Kyo. Yuya and Okuni definitely have a thing for ol' Demon Eyes, but little Antera? I hope Kyo doesn't have a lolicom. Your work is amazing, Vicky. Thanks so much.

Sara H.
Thousand Oaks, CA

Kyo and Kyoshiro… Who's the Yin and who's the Yang? Very nice pic, Sara!

GLOSSARY

Aokigahara–"The Sea of Trees." The forest at the base of Mt. Fuji. Its reputation for being haunted endures to this day.

-chan—An honorific generally used towards girls and kids. For a man like Hidetada (Benitora) to be addressed as "chan" is quite insulting.

-dono—An honorific of the highest respect. Equivalent to "Lord."

Edo Era–(1603-1868) Japan's "Golden Era" of political and economic stability after the civil wars of the Sengoku Era. During the Edo Era, all of Japan would be ruled by one Shogun from the capital at Edo (modern day Tokyo). Samurai Deeper Kyo tales place at the start of the Edo Era.

-han—The "-san" suffix as said with Benitora's Kansai accent.

Jonin—"High Ninja."

Kagemusha—Literally "Shadow Warrior." A kagemusha is a body double for a political or military leader, intended to protect him or her from potential assassins. Sanada Yukimura's kagemusha is currently in Kudoyama with Sakuya.

Kansai-ben—Regional dialect of the Kansai area (incl. Osaka, Kyoto, Kobe). Benitora speaks in this dialect, know for its fast-paced diction and unique slang.

Kensei—Great swordsman; swordsman of legend.

Mizuchi—An imaginary, four-legged snakelike creature that breathes poison–kind of like a basilisk. Here used as Kyo's signature attack name.

Nee-chan—"Big Sis." Can be used literally, or towards any older female sister figure.

Nii-san—"Older Brother." As with "nee," it can be used literally or towards brother figures.

Oban dosu—"good evening" in the Kyoto dialect.

Oda Nobunaga—(1534-1582) One of Japan's most famous and controversial historical figures. During the Sengoku Era, he attempted to unite all of Japan under his rule, mercilessly killing all who opposed him—including countless Buddhist monks. He was also the first

Japanese leader to embrace Western culture, including modern warfare (firearms and ironclad ships) and Christianity. For all his brutality, Nobunaga was also a patron of the arts and culture.

-sama—An honorific denoting great respect. Equivalent to "Sir/Madame."

-san—The Most common honorific. Equivalent to "Mr./Mrs."

Sanada Juu-yuushi—The Sanada Ten. Ten legendary elite warriors who served Sanada Yukimura.

Sanada Nobuyuki—Yukimura's brother. The historical figure sided with Tokugawa following Sekigahara, using his influence to save his brother and father's lives.

Sanada Yukimura—The son of Sanada Masayuki, who fought against Tokugawa at Sekigahara. Yukimura continued his father's fight against the Tokugawa, even after his father's defeat.

Sanzu—The Japanese equivalent of the River Styx.

Sarutobi Sasuke—A historical member of the Sanada Ten and a legendary ninja.

Sekigahara—The greatest battle in Japanese history, the Battle of Sekigahara took place in the fall of 1600 and ended years of Civil War. Tokugawa's victory paved the way for his becoming Shogun.

Shochu—A distilled liquor, made from potatoes, rice or other bases. More potent than sake.

Tenma Mukurode—"Demon Hand of Bone." The fictionalized Nobunaga's fighting technique.

Tokugawa's war banners: "Enriedo Gongujudo" = A buddhist mantra stating that "This world is polluted and must be left behind, be joyful in your heart and seek the Pure Land (heaven)" In other words, die and be happy.

Tokugawa Hidetada—(1579-1632) Tokugawa Ieyasu's son and heir, here fictionalized as Benitora. Some…liberties were taken with this historical figure.

Tokugawa Ieyasu—(1543-1616) The first shogun of the Edo Era who united all of Japan under one ruler following the Battle of Sekigahara. The historical Ieyasu merely commanded the Iga Ninjas; in SDK, Ieyasu is one-and-the-same with legendary ninja Hattori Hanzo, leader of the Iga Ninjas.

*errata: In SDK vol. 7, the descriptions for Tokugawa Hidetada and Tokugawa Ieyasu were inadvertently switched. They are correctly described here. We apologize for any confusion.

SAMURAI DEEPER KYO NEXT!!

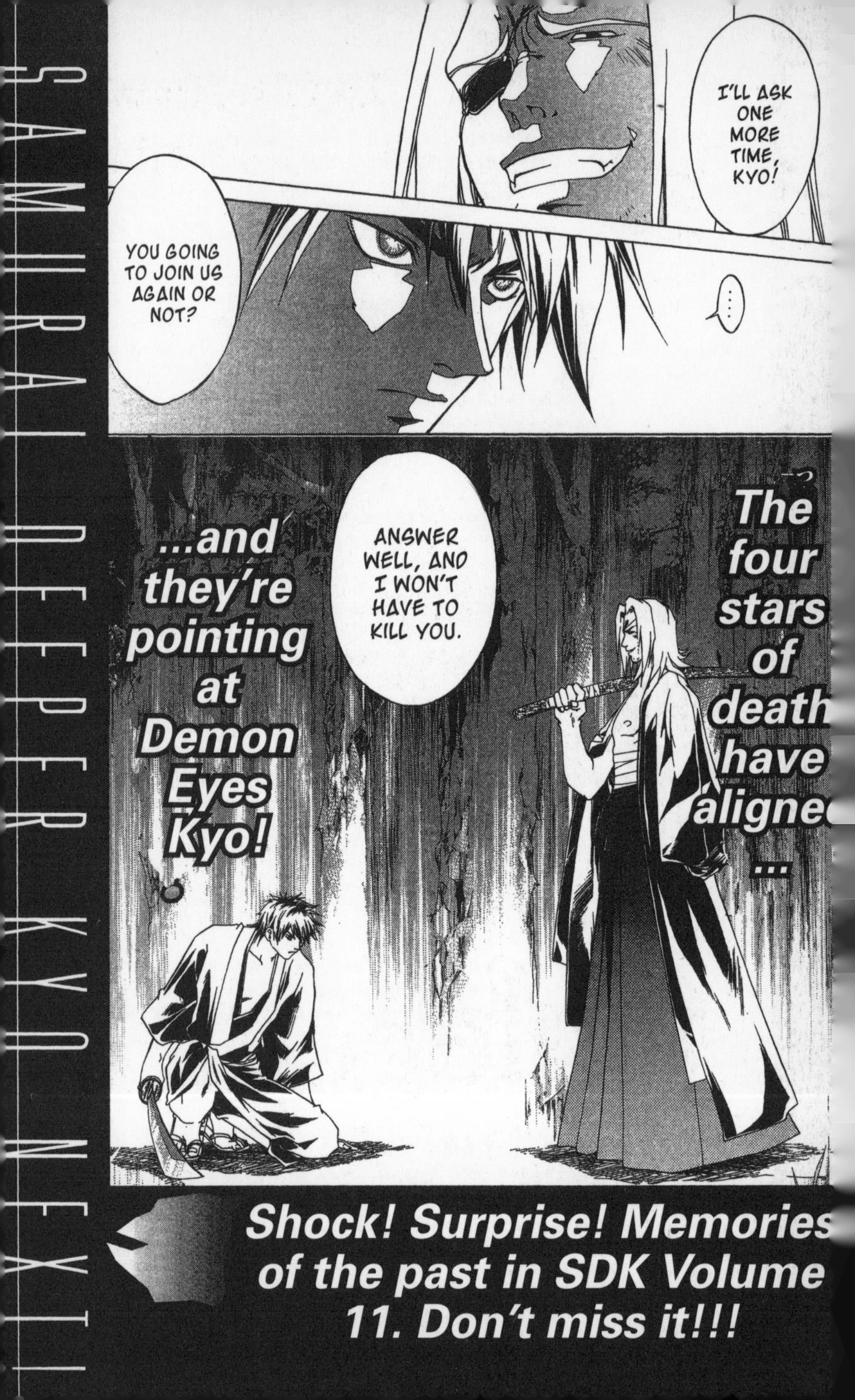
I'LL ASK ONE MORE TIME, KYO!
...
YOU GOING TO JOIN US AGAIN OR NOT?
The four stars of death have aligne ...
ANSWER WELL, AND I WON'T HAVE TO KILL YOU.
...and they're pointing at Demon Eyes Kyo!

Shock! Surprise! Memories of the past in SDK Volume 11. Don't miss it!!!

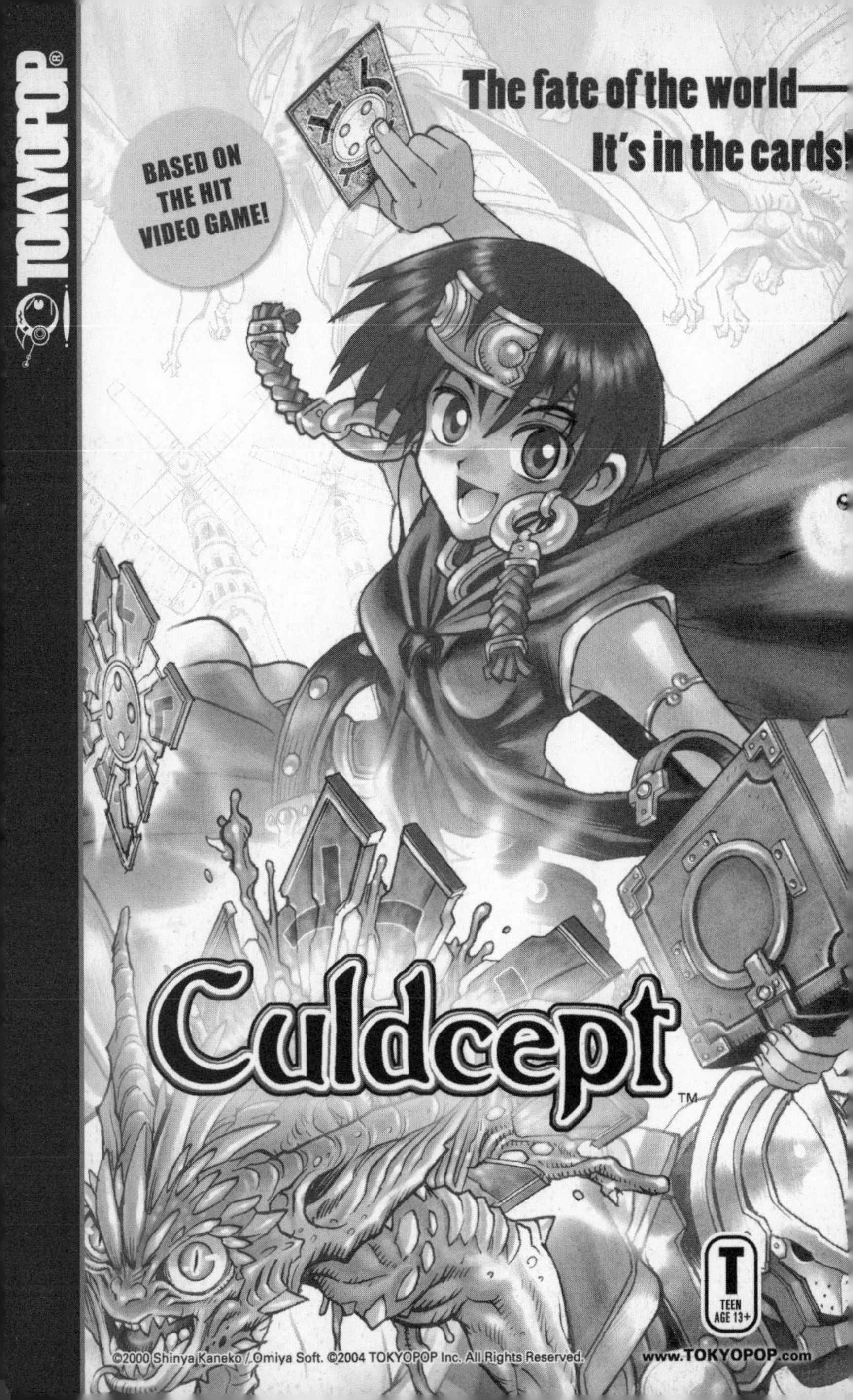

TOKYOPOP
The fate of the world—
It's in the cards!
BASED ON THE HIT VIDEO GAME!
Culdcept™
T TEEN AGE 13+

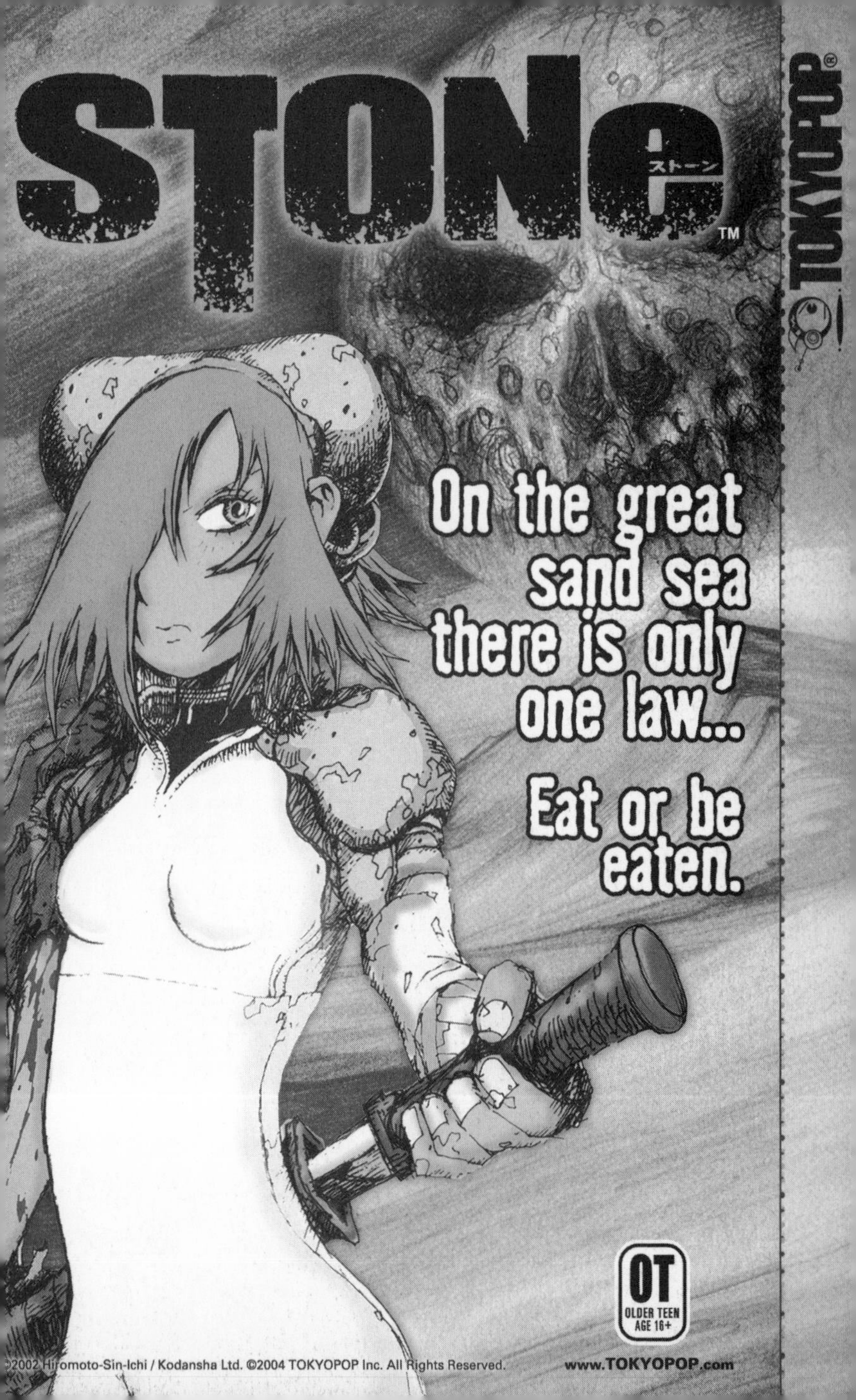
STONe
ストーン
TM
TOKYOPOP®
On the great sand sea there is only one law...
Eat or be eaten.
OT
OLDER TEEN AGE 16+
©2002 Hiromoto-Sin-Ichi / Kodansha Ltd. ©2004 TOKYOPOP Inc. All Rights Reserved.
www.TOKYOPOP.com

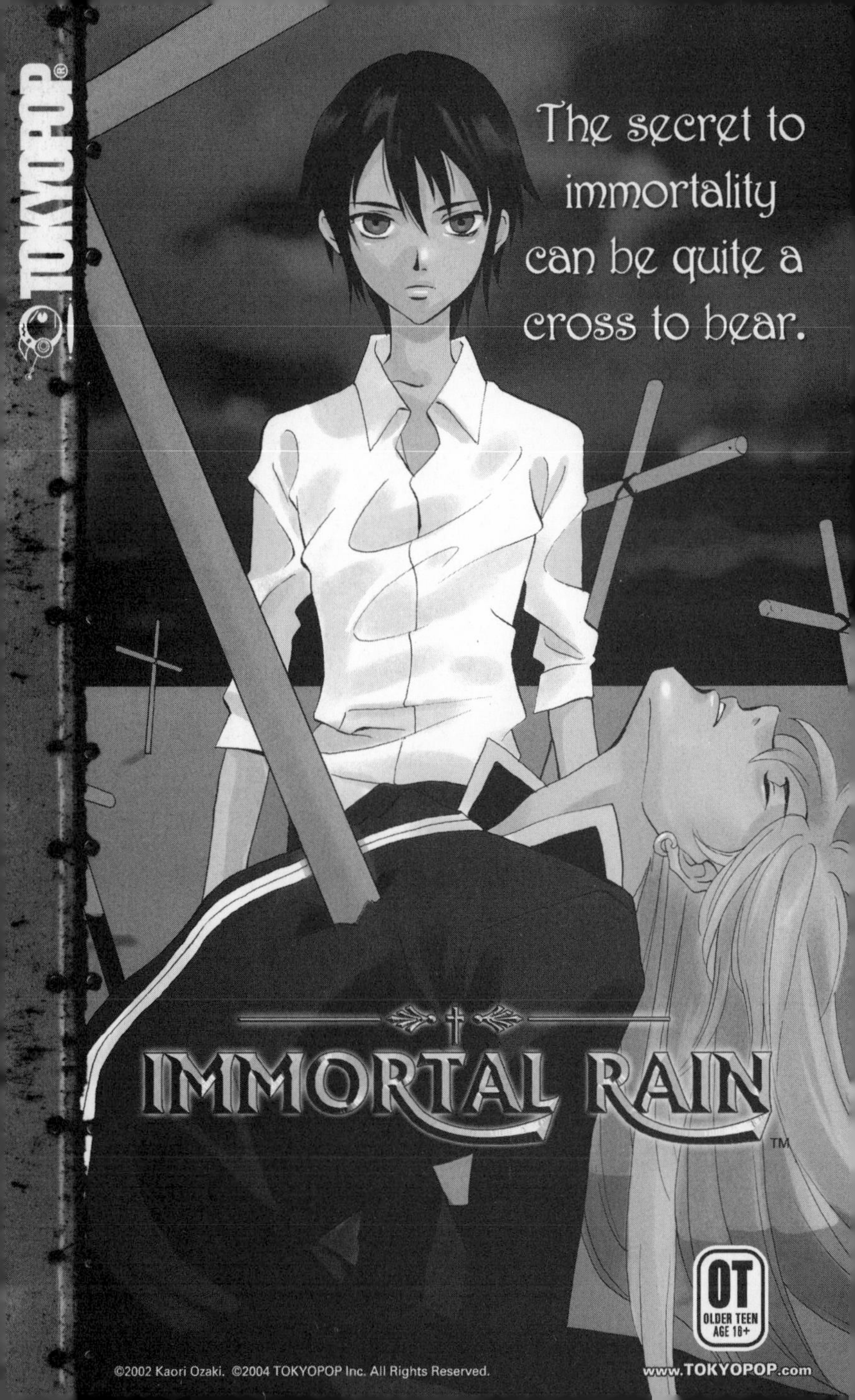
TOKYOPOP®
The secret to immortality can be quite a cross to bear.
IMMORTAL RAIN™
OT
OLDER TEEN
AGE 16+
©2002 Kaori Ozaki. ©2004 TOKYOPOP Inc. All Rights Reserved.
www.TOKYOPOP.com

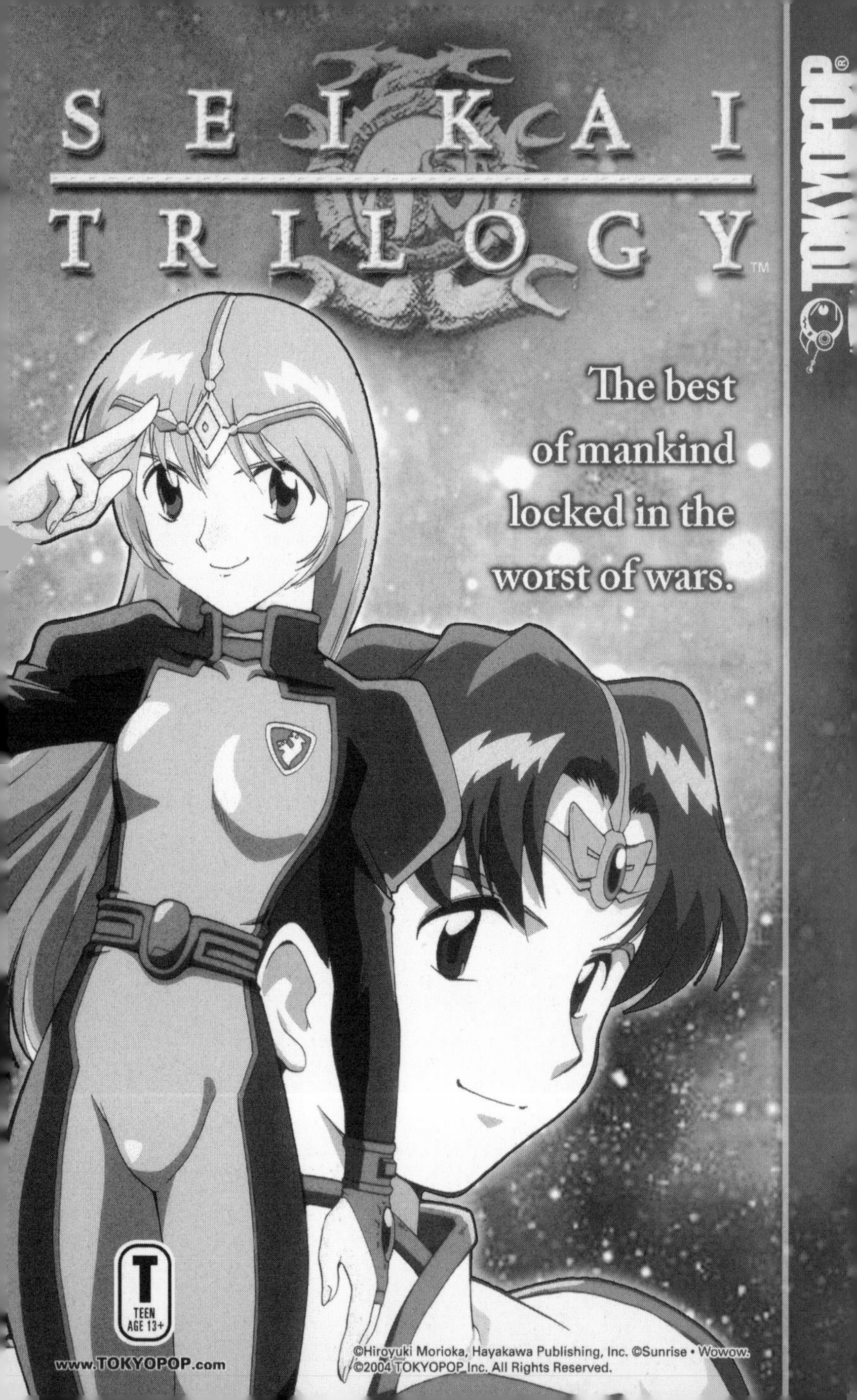
SEIKAI TRILOGY™
The best of mankind locked in the worst of wars.
TOKYOPOP®
T
TEEN AGE 13+
www.TOKYOPOP.com
©Hiroyuki Morioka, Hayakawa Publishing, Inc. ©Sunrise • Wowow.
©2004 TOKYOPOP Inc. All Rights Reserved.

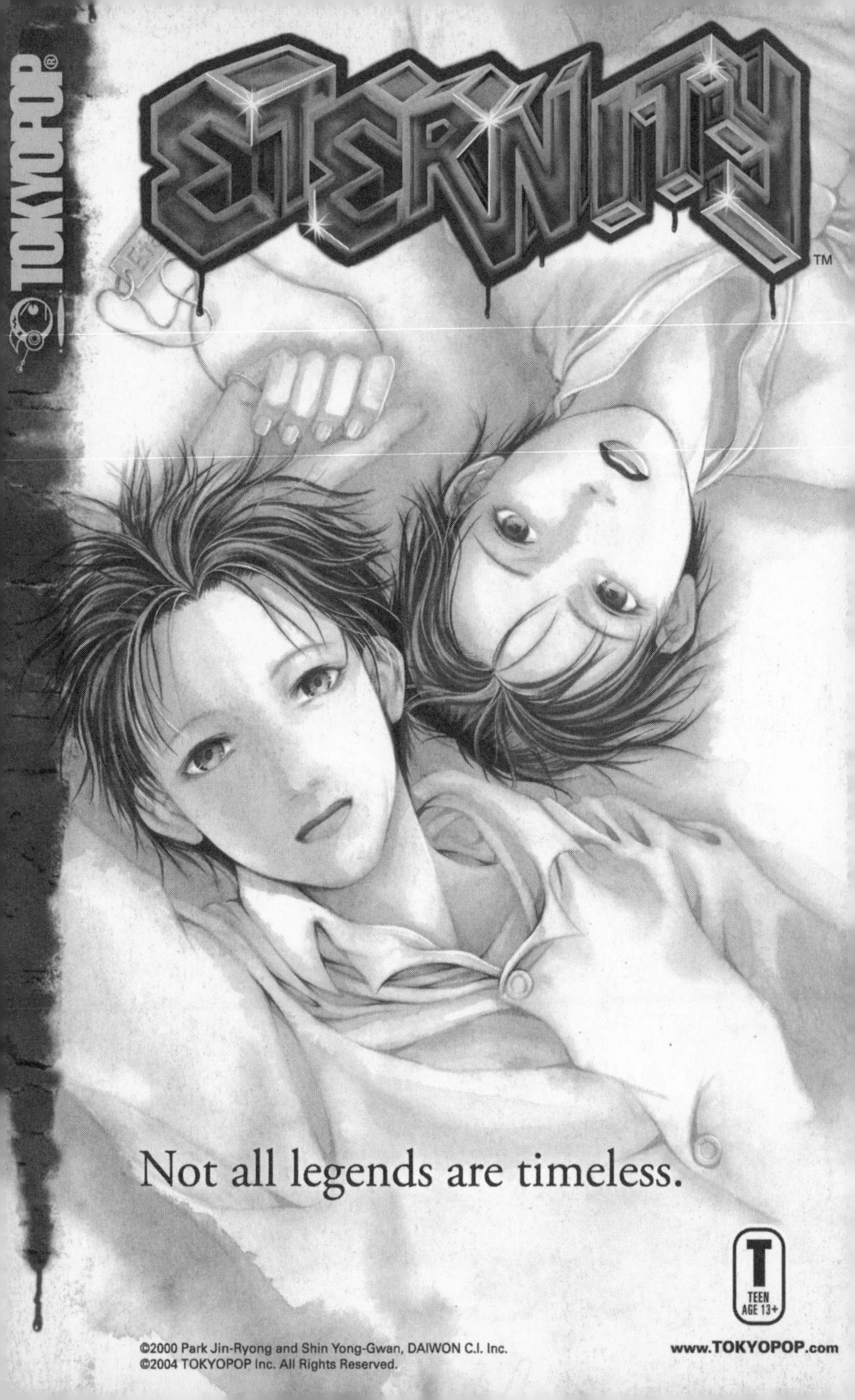
TOKYOPOP®
ETERNITY™
Not all legends are timeless.
T
TEEN
AGE 13+
©2000 Park Jin-Ryong and Shin Yong-Gwan, DAIWON C.I. Inc.
©2004 TOKYOPOP Inc. All Rights Reserved.
www.TOKYOPOP.com

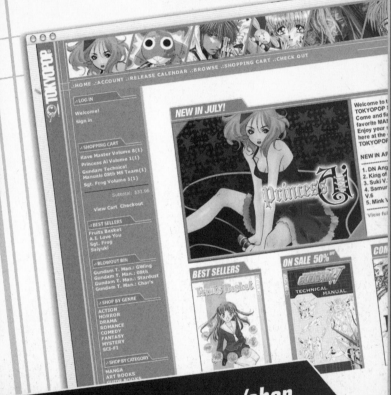

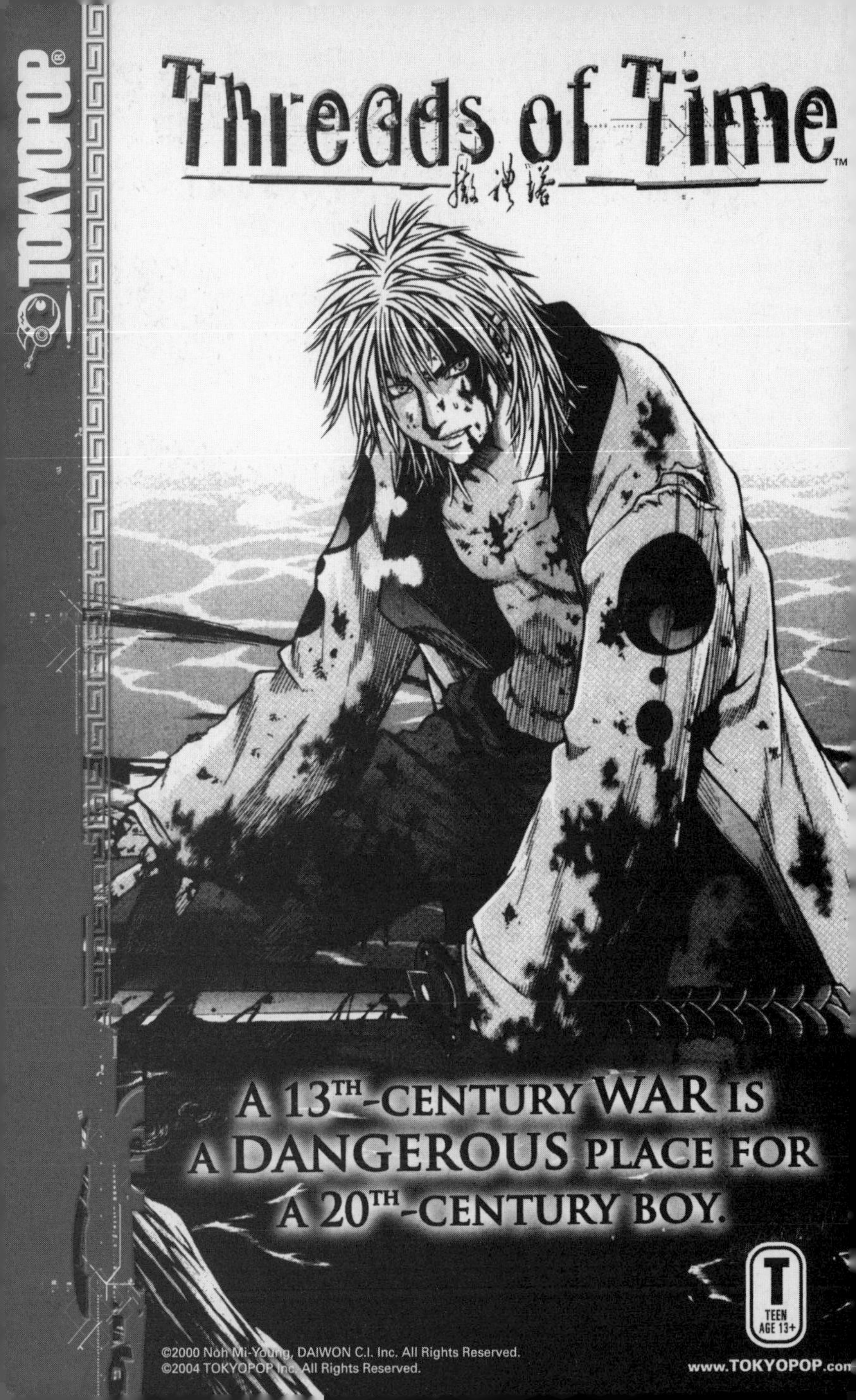

TOKYOPOP®
Threads of Time™
A 13TH-CENTURY WAR IS
A DANGEROUS PLACE FOR
A 20TH-CENTURY BOY.
T
TEEN
AGE 13+
©2000 Noh Mi-Young, DAIWON C.I. Inc. All Rights Reserved.
©2004 TOKYOPOP Inc. All Rights Reserved.
www.TOKYOPOP.com

ALSO AVAILABLE FROM  TOKYOPOP®

**You want it? We got it!
A full range of TOKYOPOP
products are available now at:
www.TOKYOPOP.com/shop**

06.21.04T

ALSO AVAILABLE FROM ⊛TOKYOPOP®

MANGA

.HACK//LEGEND OF THE TWILIGHT
@LARGE
ABENOBASHI: MAGICAL SHOPPING ARCADE
A.I. LOVE YOU
AI YORI AOSHI
ANGELIC LAYER
ARM OF KANNON
BABY BIRTH
BATTLE ROYALE
BATTLE VIXENS
BOYS BE...
BRAIN POWERED
BRIGADOON
B'TX
CANDIDATE FOR GODDESS, THE
CARDCAPTOR SAKURA
CARDCAPTOR SAKURA - MASTER OF THE CLOW
CHOBITS
CHRONICLES OF THE CURSED SWORD
CLAMP SCHOOL DETECTIVES
CLOVER
COMIC PARTY
CONFIDENTIAL CONFESSIONS
CORRECTOR YUI
COWBOY BEBOP
COWBOY BEBOP: SHOOTING STAR
CRAZY LOVE STORY
CRESCENT MOON
CROSS
CULDCEPT
CYBORG 009
D•N•ANGEL
DEMON DIARY
DEMON ORORON, THE
DEUS VITAE
DIABOLO
DIGIMON
DIGIMON TAMERS
DIGIMON ZERO TWO
DOLL
DRAGON HUNTER
DRAGON KNIGHTS
DRAGON VOICE
DREAM SAGA
DUKLYON: CLAMP SCHOOL DEFENDERS
EERIE QUEERIE!
ERICA SAKURAZAWA: COLLECTED WORKS
ET CETERA
ETERNITY
EVIL'S RETURN
FAERIES' LANDING
FAKE
FLCL
FLOWER OF THE DEEP SLEEP
FORBIDDEN DANCE
FRUITS BASKET

G GUNDAM
GATEKEEPERS
GETBACKERS
GIRL GOT GAME
GIRLS EDUCATIONAL CHARTER
GRAVITATION
GTO
GUNDAM BLUE DESTINY
GUNDAM SEED ASTRAY
GUNDAM WING
GUNDAM WING: BATTLEFIELD OF PACIFISTS
GUNDAM WING: ENDLESS WALTZ
GUNDAM WING: THE LAST OUTPOST (G-UNIT)
HANDS OFF!
HAPPY MANIA
HARLEM BEAT
HYPER RUNE
I.N.V.U.
IMMORTAL RAIN
INITIAL D
INSTANT TEEN: JUST ADD NUTS
ISLAND
JING: KING OF BANDITS
JING: KING OF BANDITS - TWILIGHT TALES
JULINE
KARE KANO
KILL ME, KISS ME
KINDAICHI CASE FILES, THE
KING OF HELL
KODOCHA: SANA'S STAGE
LAMENT OF THE LAMB
LEGAL DRUG
LEGEND OF CHUN HYANG, THE
LES BIJOUX
LOVE HINA
LUPIN III
LUPIN III: WORLD'S MOST WANTED
MAGIC KNIGHT RAYEARTH I
MAGIC KNIGHT RAYEARTH II
MAHOROMATIC: AUTOMATIC MAIDEN
MAN OF MANY FACES
MARMALADE BOY
MARS
MARS: HORSE WITH NO NAME
MINK
MIRACLE GIRLS
MIYUKI-CHAN IN WONDERLAND
MODEL
MOURYOU KIDEN
MY LOVE
NECK AND NECK
ONE
ONE I LOVE, THE
PARADISE KISS
PARASYTE
PASSION FRUIT
PEACH GIRL
PEACH GIRL: CHANGE OF HEART

06.21.04T

STOP!

This is the back of the book.
You wouldn't want to spoil a great ending!

This book is printed "manga-style," in the authentic Japanese right-to-left format. Since none of the artwork has been flipped or altered, readers get to experience the story just as the creator intended. You've been asking for it, so TOKYOPOP® delivered: authentic, hot-off-the-press, and far more fun!

DIRECTIONS

If this is your first time reading manga-style, here's a quick guide to help you understand how it works.

It's easy... just start in the top right panel and follow the numbers. Have fun, and look for more 100% authentic manga from TOKYOPOP®!